Grandmaster Preparation

LEV POLUGAEVSKY
International Grandmaster

Translated by Kenneth P. Neat

ISHI PRESS
INTERNATIONAL

Grandmaster Preparation

by Lev Polugaevsky

Introduction by Mikhail Tal

First Published in 1977 in Russian in the Soviet Union as
Рождение Варианта or "The Birth of a Variation"
by Fizkultura i Sport

Translated into English and Updated in 1980 by Kenneth P. Neat

Copyright © 1977 by Lev Polugaevsky
Copyright of Translation © 1980 by Kenneth P. Neat

This Printing in October, 2011
by Ishi Press in New York and Tokyo

with a new foreword by Sam Sloan

Copyright © 2011 by Sam Sloan

All rights reserved according to International Law. No part of this book may be reproduced by any means for public or private use without the written permission of the publisher.

ISBN 4-87187-451-6
978-4-87187-451-9

Ishi Press International
1664 Davidson Avenue, Suite 1B
Bronx NY 10453-7877
USA

1-917-507-7226

Printed in the United States of America

Foreword by Sam Sloan

Grandmaster Preparation by Lev Polugaevsky

Foreword by Sam Sloan

Andy Soltis wrote a column in **Chess Life**, or perhaps it was in the **New York Post** where Grandmaster Soltis is the chess columnist, pointing out the remarkable fact that Lev Polugaevsky was the ninth rated player in the world, yet nobody had ever heard of him.

Everybody interested in chess has heard the names of Geller, Keres, Petrosian, Tal, Korchnoi and Smyslov, yet if you mention the name of Polugaevsky they will say "Who Dat?", even though Polugaevsky was about equal in rating to those other players.

Polugaevsky defeated Tal and Mecking in matches. He qualified to the candidates matches for the World Championship five times, a record few had equaled, but he lost twice in matches against Korchnoi in the semi-finals for the World Championship. He won two major international grandmaster tournaments. He won two USSR Championships, in 1967 and 1968. Quite good for somebody whom nobody ever heard of.

It happened that I sat with Bobby Fischer as he analyzed one of Polugaevsky's games. It was in Fischer's Hotel room in the Empire Hotel in New York City. Fran Goldfarb arrived after I did, as I was looking at chess games with Bobby. I think Fran was slightly perturbed to find me there. She had hoped to see Fischer alone. Like many other female chess players, she was hoping for a private meeting with Bobby for a private lesson, if you catch my drift. Many top female chess players would have loved to get knocked up by Fischer if only they could get the chance, but he never let his guard down.

When Fischer started to play over the game by Polugaevsky, Fran Goldfarb said that she would like to see another game. To this, Fischer replied:

"I want to learn something too. This is a very important game because it is by Polugaevsky playing the Polugaevsky Variation, his own variation!"

As Fischer played through the game, Fran Goldfarb had the temerity to suggest a couple of moves. The moves she suggested were ridiculous. I was actually embarrassed by the weak moves Fran suggested. Of course, she was only a Class B player, so more could not be expected. I was careful when I was in the presence of the Great Fischer. I would only suggest a move after checking it over and over again in my mind to make sure it was at least not a major blunder and was somewhat reasonable. I was not going to disgrace myself by suggesting a ridiculous move to the Great Fischer, if I could avoid it.

Foreword by Sam Sloan

Fischer would often ask me what move I would play in such-and-such position. My objective when asked such a question was to suggest the natural move, to play it safe. I would not suggest to the Great Fischer one of those crazy moves that I actually play in tournament games.

The main reason I am recounting this incident here is to point out that Fischer held Polugaevsky in the highest regard. Even if nobody else had heard of Polugaevsky, Fischer had certainly heard of him and was deeply studying his games, and this was well before Polugaevsky had come to be regarded as one of the strongest players in the world.

The curious question remains: Why is it that nobody ever heard of Polugaevsky, even though he was rated in the top ten players in the world for nearly two decades? Was it because he did not play wild and crazy sacrificial attacks like Tal did? No, that could not be the reason, because it is difficult to imagine a more wild and crazy "defense" than his Polugaevsky Variation.

Perhaps it was because he did not play in the deadly dull positional style like Petrosian and Karpov. No, that could not be the reason either.

Perhaps it was because he never became World Champion. But Geller and Keres never became world champion and every chess player has heard of them.

I met Polugaevsky one time. That was when he gave a brief speech in English at the FIDE Delegates meeting in Thessaloniki Greece in 1988. He spoke about his idea for a world championship cycle, a subject of interest to him as he was constantly one of the players in that cycle.

The Polugaevsky Variation goes like this:

1.e4 c5 2.Nf3 d6 3.d4 cxd4 4.Nxd4 Nf6 5.Nc3 a6 6.Bg5 e6 7.f4 b5

This last move leaves the Black king nearly naked. It is an attempt to seize the initiative. If White does not react strongly to it, Black gains the advantage. However, it is a violation of principles, as it neglects development. Most grandmasters played instead the simple developing move, 7. . . . Be7 or else played 7. . . . Nbd7 or else went for the poisoned pawn with 7. . . . Qb6.

Foreword by Sam Sloan

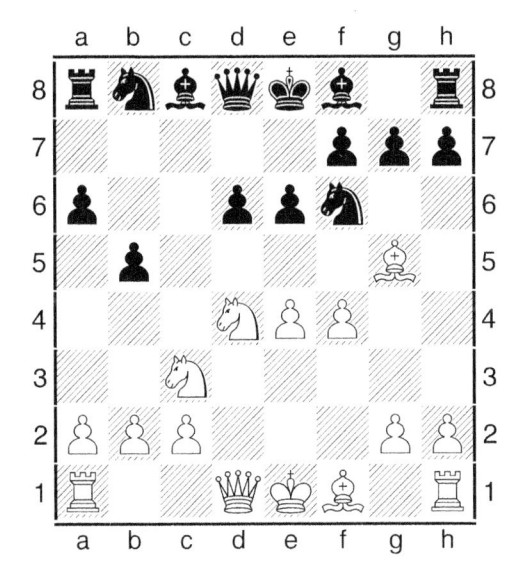

Now, in this position, the most common moves are 8.e5 dxe5 9.fxe5 Qc7 10.exf6 Qe5+ 11.Be2 Qxg5, bringing us to this position:

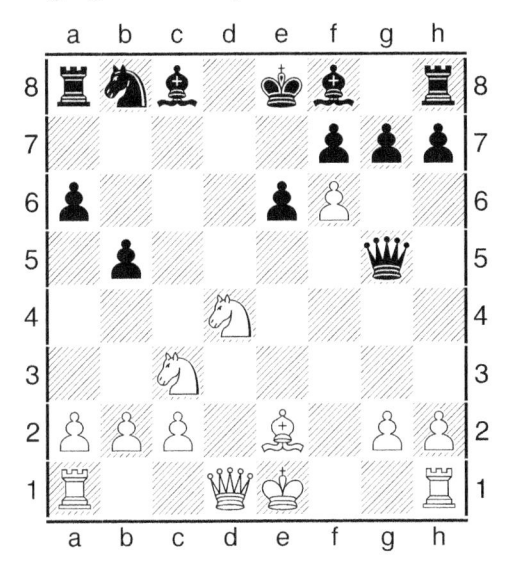

Here Black is attempting to grab a pawn but he has only one piece developed, his queen! Clearly a risky choice. Fischer did play the Polugaevsky Variation one time and he won with it. Reshevsky played it too, a strange choice for Reshevsky, a positional player.

Here is a typical game with the Polugaevsky Variation. As you will see White threatens checkmate several times. Polugaevsky leaves his king wide open to attack. It seems impossible for Black to survive, yet he does survive and goes on

Foreword by Sam Sloan

to win the game.

Rodriguez Cespedes, Amador (2505) – Polugaevsky, Lev (2600) [B96]
Biel Interzonal Biel (17), 1985
1.e4 c5 2.Nf3 d6 3.d4 cxd4 4.Nxd4 Nf6 5.Nc3 a6 6.Bg5 e6 7.f4 b5 8.e5 dxe5 9.fxe5 Qc7 10.exf6 Qe5+ 11.Be2 Qxg5 12.Qd3 Qxf6 13.Rf1 Qe5 14.Rd1 Ra7 15.Nf3 Qc7 16.Ng5 f5 17.Qd4 Qe7 18.Nge4 h5 19.Nd6+ Qxd6 20.Qxa7 Qe5 21.Qd4 Nd7 22.Qxe5 Nxe5 23.Kd2 Bd6 24.Kc1 Ke7 25.Rfe1 Bd7 26.Bf1 Rc8 27.Kb1 g5 28.h3 h4 29.Ne2 Bc6 30.Nd4 Bb7 31.Bd3 Kf6 32.Bf1 Bc5 33.c3 Bd5 34.a3 Ng6 35.Rd2 Nf4 36.Ka1 Rg8 37.Nc2 g4 38.b4 Ba7 39.Ne3 Bxe3 40.Rxe3 gxh3 41.gxh3 Rg3 0–1

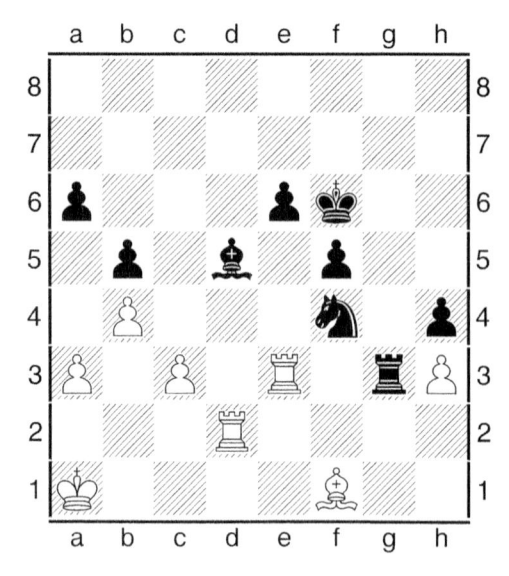

This book was first published in Russian in 1977 as ***Рождение Варианта*** or "The Birth of a Variation" The first thing about this book is that we change his name back. The original English Language edition spelled his name Polugayevsky. Other spellings have been Polugayevskii. It is difficult to understand why they keep changing the spelling of his name. His name in Russian is **Лев Абрамович Полугаевский**. This obviously transliterates to Lev Polugaevsky. It is difficult to imagine what reason they might have had to add an extra Y to his name. It also makes this book harder to find.

Lev Polugaevsky was born on 20 November 1934 in Mogilev in what is now Belarus (White Russia). He died in Paris, France on 30 August 1995 at age 60.

Sam Sloan
San Rafael California
USA
October 5, 2011

Contents

Translator's preface	vii
Introduction to the Russian Edition by Mikhail Tal	ix
1. On How This Book Found its Author	1
2.* The Birth of a Variation (1 e4 c5 2 Nf3 d6 3 d4 c×d4 4 N×d4 Nf6 5 Nc3 a6 6 Bg5 e6 7 f4 b5)	21
An Optimistic Beginning (8 Qf3)	23
Almost at a Run (8 a3)	27
One and a Half Points out of two (8 Bd3)	28
A Year-long Duel (8 Be2)	32
In the Main Direction (8 e5 d×e5 9 f×e5 Qc7 10 e×f6 Qe5+)	38
At the Source (11 Be2 Q×g5 12 0-0 Ra7)	44
Reconnaissance in Force	47
A Glance from the Side (12 ... Qe5)	54
A Trap (12 Qd3 Qh4+)	58
Memorandum from Moscow	61
The Return (12 ... Q×f6)	63
On the Rack (10 Qe2 Nfd7 11 0-0-0 Bb7)	71
The Variation Lives! (12 Qg4)	86
A New Idea (12 N×e6 f×e6 13 Qh5+)	98
3. In the Interval (The Analysis of Adjourned Games)	103
By the Method of Trial and Error	104
On What Remains Unseen	115
From a Position of Strength	122
Zig-zag of Fortune	127
Sleepless Nights in Spain	131
Without any Promptings by Theory	140
Rook Endings Can After all be Won!	150
Almost a Spy Story	159

* For the convenience of the reader, the main continuation covered in each section of chapter 2 is indicated

4. On The Eve (How to Prepare for Decisive Games)   165

A Stimulus is Provided by ... the Controllers   165
When it is One ... for All   169
Overcoming Oneself   171
Non-indifferent Indifference   175
Will the Wind be Favourable?   183
The Challenge had to be Accepted...   187
In the Name of Revenge   190
The Dream Comes True   192
When Experience Helps   200
Turning the Wheel of Fortune...   204
Who Will Make a Step Forward?   207
Meetings With World Champions   211
Don't Create an Idol for Yourself   211
It is Better Playing White   214
A Present to Ourselves   219
Shell Versus Armour   223
Don't Believe your Opponent...   225
With the Opponent's Favourite Weapon...   229
I Refute... Myself!   232

Postscript   237

Index of Opponents   239

Index of Openings   240

Translator's preface

THIS English translation of the first book written by Soviet grandmaster Lyev Polugayevsky is a considerably updated version of the Soviet edition, entitled *Rozhdeniye Varianta*, which appeared in 1977. Here is a summary of the additional material:

In his highly personal history of the Polugayevsky Variation given in Chapter Two, the author has added several pages on the most significant developments to occur up to early 1979. This includes his 'defence', hitherto unpublished, to a serious theoretical attempt by Lepeshkin to 'bury' The Variation (*Shakhmatny Bulletin*, 1979 No. 3). In order to complete the picture, at the proof stage I have added a summary of four recent and highly important games played by Polugayevsky with his Variation, including the two from his crushing victory over Tal in the 1980 Candidates' Quarter-Final Match.

Chapter Three, on the analysis of adjourned games, has been expanded slightly by the inclusion of some analyses recorded on tape by Polugayevsky's friend, chess commentator Iakov Damsky.

The fourth Chapter, in which the author describes a number of the decisive games from his career, has been expanded considerably. Of particular interest here are Polugayevsky's accounts of his 1977 Candidates' Match with Mecking, and of his most significant meetings with each of the seven post-war World Champions.

I can honestly state that this is the finest and most original work on chess that it has been my privilege to translate.

Durham, June 1980.   KENNETH P. NEAT

Introduction to the Russian Edition

All of us chess players who compete in tournaments are frequently asked in lectures, either in written form or verbally, the questions: how do you play, what is the secret of your creativity?

To answer this is not easy. It is no accident that in chess literature—incidentally, the number of monographs and games collections which has appeared in recent years has been considerable, but the dearth of chess books has grown even worse—there are many reminiscences of the great masters of the past, and many biographies by players of the older generation, but practically no accounts of the very essence of creativity.

The book which you, dear reader, are about to open is rather different from a biography. It is not a ceremonial speech by a grandmaster, but an invitation to enter into the private study of one of the strongest players in the world. Exemplary order is not always to be found there. Laid out on the table are a card-index and sheets covered in notes, and preparation is in progress for the most ordinary, every-day game. The author, to whom the study belongs, invites you to sit down alongside him during his preparations. If you wish, you may ask questions; if you consider it inconvenient, wait a little: questions can be asked later....

A game begins with the opening. And grandmaster Lyev Polugayevsky, who has frequently, and on the whole successfully, appeared in the most diverse of events, relates in the first part of this book about his work on one single opening. Should this part of the book be called a monograph? It can, of course. But a monograph contains a large collection of information, and information that is objective, whereas here there is a mass of information that is highly subjective, since what is described is the creation of a variation, which in chess theory bears the name of the author—the Polugayevsky Variation. Perhaps the variation has not gained the popularity it deserves—but we will not go into the vagaries of chess fashion. But from time to time it occurs in the games of players of very high class. From my own experience I know how much one wants to refute this variation, in which Black, contrary to the ancient laws of chess 'chivalry' (Black must defend!), immediately throws down the gauntlet to his opponent, and demands: attack, or else in the near future I will become White, and will turn to the offensive! But, while you are attacking, don't forget to burn your boats behind you...

In his material on this variation, the author does not give us the information that in such-and-such a game such-and-such was played, but instead creates something of a monograph-cum-biography. In it there is no mention of results in tournaments, but of searchings and disappointments, and of the paths to this or that idea. The author invites you to go with him into a rest home on the outskirts of Moscow, where the Russian Federation team is preparing, or to the USSR Championship in Baku, where you can become absorbed in that environment which both stimulates analysis, by creating a special psychological mood, and also hinders analysis, by introducing a purely competitive interest, alien to creativity.

Undoubtedly, the last page on the history of the Polugayevsky Variation has yet to be written. I personally think that some day White will succeed in casting doubts on the theoretical correctness of Black's set-up. But when and by whom will this be done? And what if the fervently analytical character of the author should enable him time and again to vindicate this variation, which, despite all systematic efforts to bury it, has yet to be buried?!

The second part of the book is of a quite different nature.

... Five hours has passed. The controller hands an envelope to one of the players, and either within 2 hours, or the following morning, or 3, 5, or even 7 days later—this can happen!—the opponents again sit down at the chess board. The envelope is opened, the secret sealed move is divulged, and the adjournment session begins. There begins a competition in the art of analyzing a chess position. And the winner is the one who is more precise and more accurate, the one who has seen and found more.

Initially the conditions for the two players are approximately equal. Of course, one of them knows the sealed move, while the other does not. But which is better, no one knows. If you have sealed the move, the number of continuations to be analyzed is reduced, but on the other hand, fatigued by the struggle, you may have made a mistake. However, every player has to be prepared to deal with both situations.

On the experience of the games between us, I can confirm that Lyev Polugayevsky is one of the strongest masters of the analysis of adjourned positions. And this includes positions of the most varied type.

These may be very sharp positions, where the middlegame is in full swing, where both kings are under fire, and where everything is decided by fantasy: a most striking example of this type is the adjourned game against F. Gheorghiu given in this book. Here surprises are possible literally on the second move, and at times it is incomprehensible how grandmaster X, a strong and experienced player, after a lengthy analysis could immediately sink into thought for some 40 minutes. It means that outwardly the opponent's move must have been illogical; but in chess, logic and truth are not always synonymous.

They may be positions in which there is no, or practically no scope for calculation, which is replaced by abstractions and strategic plans, as, for instance, in the game with S. Gligoric. Here a dogged game of chess patience is placed, until the cards—sorry, pieces!—tally, and a position planned beforehand is reached on the board. And the interest of endgame theorists will be awakened by, for instance, the adjourned game with E. Geller, or the afore-mentioned one with Gligoric. What's more, in the latter of these —and I again speak from my own experience—a good 90% of grandmasters would simply have agreed a draw: after all, it is not even apparent how to set the opponent any difficult problem, never mind place him on the verge of catastrophe!

Finally, each of us can remember at least one, and most probably several 'games of

Introduction to the Russian Edition xi

one's life'—when everything is at stake: the gold medal, a competitive title, or a place in the next stage of a competition. Yet another part of this book gives you Polugayevsky's recollections of games of this type. How do you gain a win, if it is absolutely essential? And what follows is an extremely frank—as, however, is also the case in the other sections—account of the various means of achieving the necessary frame of mind, which bears with it the germ of victory. The variety of these means has been determined by specific situations, differing one from another, and each time the author, so as to achieve his goal, has had to seek something new in himself or in the circumstances. And each time, be it opening research, the analysis of an adjourned position, or finally, the preparation for a decisive game, the author has sought what is frequently the only possible variation of specific moves, which will lead him to success.

The story of these searchings and finds, these failures and discoveries, is not merely interesting—it is instructive. And in this lies the chief value and originality of the book now before the reader.

M. TAL
Ex-World Champion

1. On How This Book Found its Author

If any author is asked on which date the idea of a particular book came to mind, he will at best regard the questioner with regret. But it so happens that I can name with complete confidence both the date, and the circumstances, which forced me to sit down at the writing-table.

It all began on 17th December 1969, during an International Tournament in Belgrade. The Soviet participants were Ex-World Champion Mikhail Botvinnik, grandmaster Efim Geller, and myself. The schedule was tough, the competition fierce (it is sufficient to recall that, in the end, first place was shared by no less than four players), and it was possible to maintain one's form only by a strictly-observed alternation of exertion and rest. As a relaxation we decided to go for walks. Since the hotel in which we were staying was situated on the outskirts of the town, we didn't have to go far in search of fresh air.

However, our pedestrian trio soon turned into a duet. Geller, formerly a basketball player, clearly preferred, instead of walking, to do 'overtime' work on the secrets of chess theory, and at the appointed time Botvinnik and I would set off to stroll around the avenues of Belgrade. And it was on 17th December that Mikhail Botvinnik suddenly asked me:

"Are you writing any sort of chess book?"

I glanced at him in surprise, and mumbled in reply that I played and prepared a lot, that I was still young, and that I would start writing sometime in the future. Towards the end of this lengthy explanation I suddenly sensed its complete lack of conviction, but even so Botvinnik's retort quite overwhelmed me:

"Why don't you admit it—you're a lazy-bones! You should be ashamed of yourself! It's the duty of every grandmaster to write books", declared Mikhail Moiseevich, very severely bringing the conversation to a close.

Even during the game—which had never happened before—these words of Botvinnik sounded inside me. I sensed the justness of the reproach, and the deep meaning of what had been said, and all this taken together literally gave me no peace. Over dinner I firmly decided that Botvinnik's advice would be followed.

But what to write about? My doubts on this, fortunately, did not last long.

The routine idea of a book of selected games was immediately rejected. For this I did indeed consider myself too young. Besides, I had not yet lost hope of playing my best game, and my contemporaries too had not yet started 'summing up'.

Perhaps I should write 'something' theoretical? But even now I am sincerely convinced that my knowledge of theory is, if not poor, then certainly quite inadequate, and that I do not have the moral right to begin a journey through the debris of endless opening variations.

But what about 'The Polugayevsky Variation'?! After all, I had grown accustomed to the fact that theorists persistently associated one of the systems in the Sicilian Defence with my name. So perhaps I should talk about my highly confidential work on the creation of the theoretical variation, which in its time was my most secret weapon? Talk to a wide audience about how I conducted my searchings, and about the moments of joy and sadness associated with this variation?

Decided! That's what it'll be!

But here I immediately began to have doubts. If I was going to talk about analysis in my study, about night-time work at the chess board, it meant that I was penetrating into the so-called laboratory of one grandmaster in particular, and of chess in general. And it is well known that the research conducted there is not only on opening problems, and that it does not only function prior to games. Therefore the book should definitely include accounts of the analysis of adjourned positions, and also of the methods and means of preparation. Otherwise the picture of the laboratory would simply be incomplete.

Such are the circumstances which enable me to regard 17th December 1969 as the date of birth of the present work.

Since then much water has flowed under the bridges. My participation on several occasions in various stages of the battle for the World Championship interrupted my contact with the prepared pile of white paper, and other events too did not leave me as much free time as I would have liked. However, everything in this world has an end.... But before turning to problems of a purely chess nature, I should like to try to reveal to the reader my approach to the study, or more accurately, the mastery of opening theory, and of particular opening systems.

There are various ways of comprehending the subtleties of the opening stage of the game. For instance, a number of well-known grandmasters do not allow a single fashionable variation to escape their attention, they can and do play practically everything (which is very valuable), but do not try to introduce anything of importance into opening theory. Such tactics are perhaps questionable, but in practice they allow a player to economize a great deal on time, strength and energy. These players normally transfer the weight of the struggle to the middlegame, and they can somewhat arbitrarily be called practical players. An obvious representative of such a tendency is Ex-World Champion Mikhail Tal, as is to a certain extent Boris Spassky; such an approach to opening problems is perfectly logical, and has every right to exist.

Their antipodes—and here I must repeat that this refers only to their attitude to the opening—are those who have an excellent knowledge of theory, and at the same time strive in the most varied of schemes to create something of their own; they propose new plans, new piece set-ups, finally, new moves. In effect it is they who create, or more correctly, develop chess theory. In doing this these players spend a great deal of time both on their work on opening problems, and on the opening stage during actual play, which sometimes tells in highly dramatic fashion on the subsequent course of the game.

Efim Geller and Lajos Portisch are players who fit into this category, as did the late Isaac Boleslavsky.

Finally, there is a third group of grandmasters who have a fairly narrow opening repertoire, especially as Black. But within this narrow field they themselves experiment, create innovations, and frequently proceed from the point of view of trying to refute or at least cast doubts on what theory considers correct. I am one of those who approach the openings in this way. I must admit that it is experimental work which appeals to me, however thankless and unprofitable it has sometimes been.

Indeed, an experiment by no means always proves effective, and the search for fresh ideas requires a mass of time. On top of everything, one is sometimes grieved that chess players do not receive patents, and that sometimes an innovation operates for one game only, after which it becomes common property. And even so, I wouldn't exchange for anything those rare happy moments, when a painstakingly prepared trap operates, and you see your unsuspecting opponent advancing confidently towards his doom.

It is difficult to say with complete certainty how I acquired such an approach, such a method of handling the opening. Perhaps it was a matter of character. I would also not rule out that magnetic influence which was made on me in its time by Mikhail Botvinnik's commentary to his game with Paul Keres from the 1941 Match-Tournament for the title of Absolute USSR Champion. In this encounter, Botvinnik as Black succeeded in employing an innovation in a sharp variation of the Nimzo-Indian Defence, and refuted virtually by force the conclusion held by theory, namely that the resulting position was favourable for White. And although after the game Botvinnik did not gain any further dividends from the analysis of this particular variation, in the psychological sense his gain was considerably greater. Such a defeat had a depressing effect on Keres, and right to the end of the tournament he was unable to recover from this set-back. And yet in this event Keres was justly considered one of Botvinnik's main rivals in the battle for first place!

And much later I realized that I had been drawn along the path of experimenter in the opening, either in preparations for a game or during the course of it, by another incident, which was not especially important in the competitive sense.

A few days before my 14th birthday, I, as a first category player, met an experienced candidate master A. Ivashin in the Championship of Kuybishev, a large town on the Volga, where I then lived. Although the game lasted 48 moves, its outcome was decided much earlier.

Polugayevsky–Ivashin
Ruy Lopez

1 e4 e5 2 Nf3 Nc6 3 Bb5 a6 4 Ba4 Nf6 5 0–0 Be7 6 Re1 b5 7 Bb3 0–0 8 c3 d5 9 e×d5 e4

This move has now gone out of practice, as it has been established that White can secure a good game in various ways. But my opponent correctly judged that I was only beginning to comprehend the rudiments of opening play, and that it was unlikely that I would be acquainted with all the subtleties of this sharp variation.

10 d×c6 e×f3 11 Q×f3 Bg4 12 Qg3 Re8 13 f3 Qd3

I recall how, at the time, this move seemed to me to be like the explosion of an atomic bomb. The impression was particularly strong, for the further reason that my opponent made it almost without thinking. For a certain time White was able to find at the board the correct and only moves as recommended by theory, but then he lost an important tempo, and incurred a hopeless ending, whereas with correct play he should have maintained a marked advantage.

The game continued:

14 f×g4 Bc5+ 15 Re3 Nd5 16 Qf3?

After the approved 16 Na3! White repulses Black's swift but rather premature attack. Unfortunately, I learned of this only after the game.

16 ... N×e3 17 d×e3 Re6! 18 B×e6 f×e6

By bringing a further exchange sacrifice to the altar of the attack, Black has opened the 'f' file, and his lead in development now proves decisive.

19 Qf1 Qc2 20 Na3

Alas, this move no longer brings salvation.

20 ... B×a3 21 b×a3 Rd8 22 Bb2 Q×b2 23 Rd1 Rd2 24 h3 Q×c3 25 Qe1 R×d1 26 Q×d1 Q×c6, and on the 48th move Black won.

It was then, more than a quarter of a century ago, that I firmly decided to endeavour not to fall into variations prepared by my opponents (of course, it hasn't been possible for me, or for any other grandmaster there has ever been, to avoid this completely), but to spare no time and effort so as to be able myself to set the opponent difficult opening problems as often as possible.

Whether it was this, or something else, that played its part, the rôle of experimenter became the way for me. And it would be wrong to complain about fate: several times I have managed literally to drag my opponent into forced variations, such that even with maximum ingenuity on his part there has been only one possible outcome. My pregame preparations have enabled me to set my opponent such problems in the opening that he has had no possibility of coping with them at the board. And even if my opponents should say: 'It's not worth the trouble. You play hundreds, if not thousands of games, and your opening successes can be counted on the fingers of one hand, and besides, they are gained in a strictly limited number of openings', then against this I would merely remind them of an old truth, both in life and in chess: an exceptional moment is worth more than a year serenely-lived, or a tournament won. For the reason that, at that moment, the quintessence of creativity, or some part of it very dear to one's heart, can suddenly be concentrated....

And so, let's continue our journey into the past.

1953. As an 18-year-old candidate master, rather young by the standards of the time, I went off to the Championship of the Russian Republic in Saratov, to the first genuinely strong tournament in my life. Up till then I had never played one against one against a master, and here 12 of the 16 competitors were masters, so that, to be frank, I was nervous, and considerably afraid of my famous and experienced opponents. I was afraid of them until I was caught up in the heat of the battle, after which for additional emotions I no longer had either the strength of spirit, or the free time.

At that time I played as Black even fewer openings than I do now. In particular, against 1 d4 only the Meran Defence featured in my repertoire. True, I endeavoured to study it as thoroughly as possible, and even stored up for possible use a little idea, which was destined to receive wide publicity.

In my game with the well-known master G. Ilivitsky (White), after a slight transposition of moves the main variation of the Meran Defence arose:

Ilivitsky–Polugayevsky
Meran Defence

1 c4 e6 2 Nf3 d5 3 d4 c6 4 e3 Nf6 5 Bd3 Nbd7 6 Nc3 d×c4 7 B×c4 b5 8 Bd3 a6 9 e4 c5 10 d5

At the time this last move by White had only just come into practice, but it was already quite fashionable. And for Black it is not easy to find a satisfactory plan. Besides, at that time I played not only very energetically, but also effusively, and the prospect of a passive defence in this branch of the 'Meran' did not attract me at all. It followed that counter-play had to be sought, and during my searching I managed—not long before the Championship of the Russian Republic—to hit upon an interesting strategic idea.

10 ... e5 11 b3 Bd6 12 0–0 0–0 13 Nd2

It was probably better to do without this move, and play 13 a4 immediately. But White had no idea of his opponent's intention, and planned to play a3-a4 a little later, after first preparing a blockade on the square c4. If he had succeeded in this, Black would have been left in a hopeless position.

13 ... Rb8!

Not so much to defend b5, which is in any case not possible, but rather the final preparation for a positional pawn sacrifice.

14 a4 c4! 15 b×c4 b4 16 Ne2 Nc5 17 Bc2 a5

Black has achieved his aim. At the cost of a pawn he has seized the square c5, and gained good prospects of an attack on White's Q-side. In particular, he now intends to concentrate his forces against the weak pawn at c4. Nevertheless, a pawn is a pawn, and White's hands are by no means tied: he can initiate play on the K-side by carrying out the standard advance f2-f4. In short, the position is purely experimental in character, and incidentally, it is not surprising that later some good plans were found for White. But at the time this game provoked considerable interest, and became the theme for a theoretical discussion. And during play there proved to be more than enough problems for Ilivitsky....

The effect of the innovation in this encounter can be considered exhausted, but I should like nevertheless to give the game in full, and for this reason (if it should appear to anyone that I am deviating from the basic theme, let us consider the following lines to be something in the nature of a lyrical digression).

In chess, as in other types of sport, there are constant discussions about the young, about the changing of the old guard, and about the different generations. The young are condescendingly slapped on the back, then scolded, and then raised almost up to the heavens. In all this, the basic argument used is competitive results: the places occupied, and the points scored. But, you know, in chess there is always a highly objective criterion—the moves of a game. And it is more accurate to compare not the number of wins of players past and present, but the quality of those wins, and not the degree of knowledge, but the degree of individual creativity. I hope I will not be considered immodest, but from the point of view of these criteria, even today there is nothing for which I can reproach that young candidate master who was playing Black. Moreover, being susceptible, like everyone, to the influence of the years spent in chess, in some ways I envy him....

18 Ng3 Ba6

Somewhat direct, although consistent. 18 ... g6 was more cautious.

19 Nf5 g6 20 N×d6 Q×d6 21 Re1

White plans to transfer his rook via e3 to h3, and avoids playing f2-f4. But this is wrong! By continuing 21 g3 followed by Bb2, f2-f4 and Nf3, he could have gained more effective counter-chances.

21 ... Nfd7 22 Re3 Nb6 23 Qe2 Rbc8 24 Rh3 Rc7

While coolly carrying out his plan, Black at the same time prepares if necessary to defend his K-side.

25 Bb2 Rfc8 26 f4 N×c4!

A move which some commentators on this game considered over-hasty. World Champion Mikhail Botvinnik, in the chess column which he then wrote in the magazine *Ogonyok*, recommended 26 ... f6; Aronin in the USSR Yearbook suggested 26 ... Ncd7, with the possible variation 27 Bd3 N×c4 28 N×c4 B×c4 29 B×c4 R×c4 30 f×e5 Qc5+ 31 Qe3 R×e4 32 Q×c5 R×c5, which is clearly in Black's favour. Without wishing to contest either of these opinions, I will merely remark that Black settled on the continuation in the game, because he had worked out more or less fully all the subsequent complications.

27 N×c4 B×c4 28 f×e5!

White, too, is equal to the occasion. 28 Q×c4 Nd7 29 f×e5 R×c4 30 e×d6 R×c2 leads to a very difficult position.

28 ... Q×d5! 29 Qe3!

In reply to Black's surprise move, White finds a vulnerable spot in his opponent's position—h7.

29 ... Qe6 30 Qh6 b3

No turning back!

31 Q×h7+ Kf8 32 Bd1

It was probably stronger to include 32 Qh8+ Ke7 33 Qh4+ Ke8, and only then 34 Bd1.

32 ... Nd3

The battle has reached its height; attack and counter-attack are as though intermingled.

33 Ba3+

I considered the following variation to be in my favour: 33 Qh8+ Ke7 34 Qf6+ Q×f6 35 e×f6+ Kd6 36 Ba3+ Ke5!, despite the fact that after 37 B×b3 Ba6! White is two pawns up.

33 ... Ke8 34 R×d3

34 ... Qb6+ was threatened. White therefore prepares a combination, but a nasty surprise awaits him.

34 ... B×d3 35 Bg4

Hoping for 35 ... Q×g4 36 Qg8+ Kd7 37 Q×f7+ Kc6 (*37 ... Kd8 38 Qf8+ Kd7 39 Qd6+ Ke8 40 e6*) 38 Q×b3!!, when, despite his extra rook, Black must lose in view of the threat of 39 Rc1+.

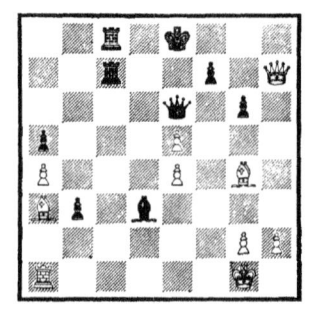

35... f5!!

Botvinnik called this 'a move of fearful strength'. White's queen comes under the attack of both black rooks, and 36 e×f6 fails to the intermediate check 36 ... Qb6+.

36 Qh8+ Kd7 37 Qh7+

The immediate retreat, 37 Qh3, offered slightly better chances of saving the game. Now, however, Black's counter-attack is irresistible.

37 ... Kc6 38 Qh3 B×e4 39 Bd1 Kb7 40 Q×b3+ Q×b3 41 B×b3 Rc3 42 Bd1 R×a3! 43 R×a3 Rc1 44 Rg3 R×d1+ White resigns.

Such a victory over one of the strongest Soviet masters of that time, several times a competitor in the USSR Championship, merely strengthened my resolve to seek and to experiment. Besides, in that Championship of the Russian Republic I was also successful in the competitive sense: I took second place, and by one and a half points surpassed the master norm....

In 1959 in the 26th USSR Championship at Tbilisi, in my game with **N. Krogius** I ended up in a variation of the Sicilian Defence which was topical at that time.

1 e4 c5 2 Nf3 d6 3 d4 c×d4 4 N×d4 Nf6 5 Nc3 a6 6 Bc4 e6 7 Bb3 Be7 8 0–0 b5 9 a3 0–0 10 f4 Bb7 11 f5 e5 12 Nde2 Nbd7 13 Ng3 Nc5

Here Krogius, who was White, carried out the basic strategical idea of the variation, the seizure of the square e4: **14 Bd5 B×d5 15 e×d5 a5 16 Bg5! Ncd7 17 B×f6 N×f6 18 Nce4,** and gained an appreciable advantage. The effect of the manoeuvre employed by White was very strong, and the whole variation immediately came under a cloud.

Can Black do anything to counter White's basic plan? Since the Sicilian Defence came into my sphere of opening interests, I got down to analysis, and discovered that the root of Black's troubles lay in the move 15 ... a5. It turned out that this was both a loss of time, and also an error in the choice of goal. After some rather painstaking work, an adequate antidote was found, and at the same time it was diagnosed that White obtains an inferior position!

In my game with **Y. Kotkov** from the 1959 Championship of the Russian Republic, Black reaped the fruits of his research, by employing the accurate move order in this position:

15 ... Rc8! 16 Bg5 Ncd7! 17 B×f6 N×f6 18 Nce4 Rc4!

Only now is Black's intention revealed. He 'dislodges' the white knight from its dominating post at e4, since 19 Qd3 fails to 19 ... Rd4, and then builds up his heavy pieces on the 'c' file, sends forward his 'e' pawn, and gains a won position.

Thus was the truth established: the variation is dubious not for Black, but for White.

In my game with **E. Gufeld** from the 1960 USSR Championship Semi-Final in Vilnius, I ran up against an interesting innovation in the Sämisch Variation of the King's Indian Defence.

1 d4 Nf6 2 c4 g6 3 Nc3 Bg7 4 e4 d6 5 f3 0–0 6 Be3 b6 7 Bd3

I knew that now the 'thematic' 7 ... c5 was refuted by 8 e5!, when Black can resign, as was shown by Bronstein's game with Lutikov in the same year: after 8 ... Ne8 9 Be4

Nc7 10 B×a8 N×a8 11 Nge2 c×d4 12 N×d4 d×e5 13 Nb3 White has a material and a positional advantage.

But my opponent introduced a significant correction into the variation, by playing 7 ... **a6?!**. In this way Black prepares the advance ... c7-c5, and, in the event of the centre being closed, the move ... a7-a6 will prove useful. During the game I was unable to find a successful response to Black's rejoinder. After **8 Nge2 c5 9 d5 e6 10 0-0 e×d5 11 e×d5 Nbd7 12 Bc2 Re8 13 Qd2 b5!** Gufeld obtained an excellent position, and won. In my game with **E. Geller** in the USSR Team Championship I attempted at the board to improve White's play by the immediate 8 d5, but even then Black, by continuing 8 ... c5 9 d×c6 N×c6 10 Nge2 Ne5, gained excellent counter-chances.

To be honest, I began to harbour a certain 'malice' against this variation, and decided to make a thorough study of it. In my preparations for the 28th USSR Championship, in which a number of 'King's Indian' players were competing, I succeeded in discovering the Achilles heel of the move 7 ... a6. And in the very first round this variation arose on the board! My opponent **L. Stein** knew all the games played previously with this line, and was not averse to following any one of the paths trodden: each of them was perfectly playable for Black. But...

8 Nge2 c5 9 e5!

It turns out that Black's seventh move has not in fact prevented the break-through in the centre. The game continued:

9 ... Nfd7 (9 ... d×e5 10 d×e5 Nfd7 11 Be4 Ra7 12 f4 is clearly favourable for White) **10 e×d6! e×d6 11 0-0 Nc6 12 Bc2 Bb7 13 Qd2 Nf6 14 Rad1**, and White had a clear advantage, which he converted into a win. This game effectively put the move 7 ... a6 out of commission. At any rate, it came to be adopted only extremely rarely in major events.

In 1965, the 33rd USSR Championship in Tallinn caused me much anxiety. I started well, scoring 8 points out of 10 in the first half of the tournament, and was not unjustified in hoping for the very highest success. But then something unaccountable occurred. In the next five rounds I didn't manage to win a single game, and misfortunes piled one on top of another. Suddenly the most promising positions 'ceased to win themselves', and however much I tried at the board, the logic in my play completely disappeared, and indecision appeared at critical moments.

It was essential that I promptly take some radical measures, but no one could suggest

1. On How This Book Found its Author

to me what they should be. Besides, in the 16th round my opponent was **Semion Furman**, who not without justification was called the World Champion in play with White. With Black against him, one could normally hope for a draw at best, and if the situation had been different I wouldn't have thought of trying for more. But on this occasion I was thinking only in terms of victory, since only this would maintain my chances of first place.

How was I to play? Surprise him? But how? To play positions known to theory against Furman was pointless: he knew them like the back of his hand. This meant that there were two courses open to me. I could either deviate immediately from the well-trodden paths, which is normally fraught with the danger of ending up in an inferior position, or else I could attempt to find something new in familiar positions.

As if by order, before the 16th round the contestants had a free day. Normally I devote such days entirely to relaxation, but here I changed my own rule, and despite my great nervous fatigue, spent the whole day working.

Furman knew that in reply to his favourite 1 d4 I normally played the Nimzo-Indian Defence. And so, picking up Taimanov's monograph on this opening, I began turning over the pages, taking note only of those variations which were considered unsatisfactory for Black. Suppose I managed to find something! My examination took in one variation, a second, a third.... Stop! Some rather lengthy reflection, and.... Had I really struck gold?! I went even deeper into the analysis, and finally breathed a sigh of relief. There could be no doubt: a second birth of the variation would take place.

This is the variation in question:

1 d4 Nf6 2 c4 e6 3 Nc3 Bb4 4 e3 c5 5 Nf3 0–0 6 Bd3 d5 7 0–0 Nbd7, and now **8 a3 Ba5**. Theory reckoned that in this position White gains a serious advantage after either 9 Qc2 a6 10 b3 Bc7 11 Bb2, or **9 Qc2 d×c4 10 B×c4 c×d4 11 e×d4**. In the second of these variations there was a reference to the game Petrosian–Moiseev from the 19th USSR Championship.

Nevertheless, it was this position which appeared to me by no means so unpromising. Meanwhile Furman, without much thought, went in for it.

Here Black made what was at first sight a totally illogical move, **11 ... B×c3!!**. Illogical, because three moves earlier he avoided this exchange. Nowadays this is all well known, but at the time, to the accompaniment of the chess clock, Furman was unable to solve all the resulting problems.

The game continued:

12 Q×c3 (practice has shown that after 12 b×c3 b6 Black again has good prospects) **12 ... b6! 13 Ne5 Bb7 14 Qe3 Qc7 15 Be2 Rfd8 16 Re1 Rac8 17 Bf1 Qd6 18 b3 Qd5 19 a4 N×e5 20 d×e5 Ne4 21 Qf4 Q×b3,** and Black was close to a win.

The innovation brought me an important point, and the variation 7 ... Nbd7 began to be widely practised. For five years this revived scheme served Black faithfully and truly, and was taken up by many leading grandmasters. And it was only in 1969 that White managed to find the key to it: 9 c×d5 e×d5 10 b4! c×b4 11 Nb5!.

I cannot avoid recalling the 'secret war' between **David Bronstein** and myself. The variation of the Sicilian Defence **1 e4 c5 2 Nf3 d6 3 d4 c×d4 4 N×d4 Nf6 5 Nc3 a6 6 Bg5 e6 7 f4 Be7 8 Qf3 Qc7** has always obsessed me. Some 10–12 years ago the variation was highly topical, just as it is now, and provoked a mass of sharp discussions, both in the press, and in practice. Many games continued 9 0-0-0 Nbd7 10 g4 b5 11 B×f6 N×f6 12 g5 Nd7 13 a3 Rb8 14 Bh3 or 14 f5, when White's attack appeared too threatening. What could Black do to oppose this? After all, he had not made, essentially, a single mistake! Perhaps he should try to change his move order, which is normally so critical in double-edged openings? And my thinking developed along the following lines: what move could Black temporarily do without, so as to economize on a tempo, and by playing... b5-b4, be the first to take active measures?

What if, instead of 7 ... Be7, Black plays 7 ... Nbd7?

Of course, there is nothing here that is particularly unexpected; this had been played before. But at the time Black avoided playing it for two reasons: White had a pleasant choice between the energetic 8 Qf3 Qc7 9 0-0-0 b5 10 e5! Bb7 11 Qh3! d×e5 12 N×e6!, and the quieter but no less dangerous 8 Bc4. And it was this that I secretly 'decided' not to agree with.

In 1967 I managed to find the time necessary for some painstaking work on my idea. But before analyzing these two continuations, the main point had to be cleared up: did Black gain any advantage if White responded to 7 ... Nbd7 just as he would against 7 ... Be7? If not, it simply wasn't worth the trouble....

And my analysis proceeded along the following lines:

7 ... Nbd7 8 Qf3 Qc7 9 0-0-0 b5 10 a3 Rb8 11 g4 b4 12 a×b4 R×b4 13 B×f6 N×f6 14 g5 Nd7 15 f5 (otherwise White is too slow in fighting for the initiative) **15 ... Ne5 16 Qh3 Qb6 17 Nb3 Be7!**

1. On How This Book Found its Author 13

In my analysis of this position, in the first instance I considered **18 g6**. The first impression is that after **18 ... f×g6 19 f×e6**, with the threat of 20 Nd5, White can feel happy with his position. But careful analysis enabled me to find a tactical stroke, which radically changed the assessment.

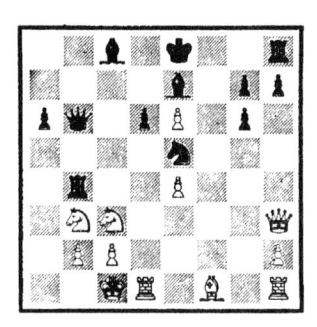

19 ... R×b3!! 20 c×b3 Q×b3 21 Qg3 (12 Nd5? Bg5+) 21 ... B×e6

Further fairly straightforward analysis quickly convinced me that the exchange sacrifice radically altered the picture, and that White's position was barely defensible.

Thus it was established that if White's play follows the normal pattern, the transposition of moves gives Black a menacing attack instead of a difficult defence.

It is probably not worth delving into that truly tropical jungle of variations, through which I had to force my way during the analysis of the two other more critical replies to 7 ... Nbd7 (8 Bc4 and 8 Qf3 Qc7 9 0-0-0 b5 10 e5): after all, this is not a reference book on the openings, nor is it a monograph on the Rauzer Attack in the Sicilian Defence. I will merely say that, on concluding my work, which lasted several weeks, somewhere in my heart I cherished the hope that my analysis of the position in the diagram would not be in vain.

And my findings came into use surprisingly quickly! In the Autumn of that year, in the Moscow Jubilee Tournament of grandmasters and masters, David Bronstein himself, one of the cleverest and most erudite players in the world, fell into this variation. All the 21(!) moves given above occurred in our game, and it was only for decency's sake that at the board I spent several minutes in thought, not wishing to shock my opponent by demonstratively rapid play.

My prepared variation decided the outcome of the game, which continued: **22 Ne2 0-0!** 23 Q×b3 B×b3 24 Rd4 Nf3 25 Rb4 Bg5+ 26 Kb1 Nd2+ 27 Ka1 Bc4 28 Nf4 N×f1 29 Nh3 Ne3 30 R×c4 N×c4, and Black realized his advantage without difficulty.

It was here that I should have realized that David Ionovich would not 'forgive' me this opening unpleasantness, and would do everything possible to try to gain his 'revenge'. I suffered the answering blow under the following circumstances.

In the 35th USSR Championship at Kharkov, **M. Taimanov** as Black adopted against me the following order of moves in the English Opening: **1 c4 c5 2 Nf3 Nf6 3 Nc3 d5 4 c×d5 N×d5 5 g3 g6.**

I continued with the standard 6 Bg2 Bg7 7 0-0 0-0, and the attempt to obtain an advantage by 8 Qb3 Nc7 9 d3 Nc6 10 Qa4 Ne6 11 Ng5 Qd4 proved unsuccessful. On arriving at my hotel after the game, I discovered that White can make an important improvement to the variation, by playing 6 Qb3 instead of 6 Bg2. It was only four years later that I managed to test this idea in an encounter with S. Furman, who had not failed to notice the move order employed in Kharkov by Taimanov. Especially since during that Championship Furman and Taimanov had been sharing a room.

My game with **Furman** occurred in the USSR Team Championship at Rostov-on-Don in 1971. I was playing for the 'Lokomotiv' team, and Furman for the Central Army Sports Club. The move 6 Qb3!? came as a surprise to my opponent, who responded with 6 ... Nb4. By continuing 7 Ne4 b6 8 Bg2 Be6 9 Qc3 f6 10 a3 Nd5 11 Qc2 Nd7 12 d4 Rc8 13 0-0, White gained a promising position, and triumphed in the subsequent battle.

Two months passed, and I again reached the position after Black's fifth move, this time playing against Bronstein. As I now remember it, before my next move, I deliberated over whether or not to make the apparently approved 6 Qb3. Common sense, and some sort of self-preservation instinct suggested, even demanded, that I should avoid trouble, and play the 'old-fashioned' 6 Bg2. But, in the first place, I am accustomed to believing my analysis, and secondly, I completely failed to take into account the possibility of a 'blood feud' on Bronstein's part. A rôle was possibly also played by simple curiosity: what could my opponent have prepared in this variation?

Be that as it may, but events developed at lightning speed:

6 Qb3 Nb4 7 Ne4

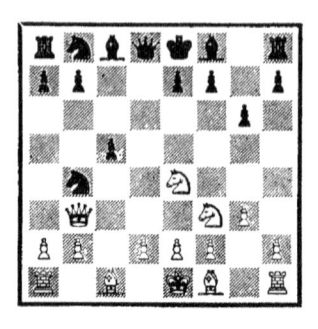

"What's this? Surely he isn't following in Furman's footsteps?" was all I had time to think, before Bronstein with his next move disclosed his intentions.

7 ... Bg7!?

This, it turns out, is the point! A typical Bronstein pawn sacrifice! Although it may seem paradoxical, at that moment I began thinking not about the position, nor about the problems facing me in this game, but about the famous Bronstein-Keres encounter at the finish of the 1950 Candidates' Tournament. A completely different opening, a different type of position, and even different colours, but how close that game was to ours in psychological content and in style of battle! Both there, and here, Bronstein was happy to sacrifice a pawn for the initiative, immediately transforming his opponent into the defending side.

I didn't consider the dilemma—whether or not to take the pawn—for long. It was essential to accept the gift, since otherwise White's opening venture would be clearly bad. But after **8 N×c5 Qa5** I had to give the matter serious thought. After all, if you simply glance at the position, you cannot help being puzzled: for what, strictly speaking, has Black voluntarily parted with material? But the more I looked into the position, the less it inspired optimism in me. Difficulties emerged, and literally piled up one on top of another. How was I to choose the correct continuation, if under the ticking of the clock it was impossible to calculate everything, and very difficult to assess the mass of resulting positions?

I quickly realized that 9 Nd3 N×d3 10 Q×d3 Na6 or 10 ... Nc6 gives Black a strong initiative, and I began examining 9 a3. But what should I do in the event of 9 ... N8c6? The threat against c2 (... Bf5) is highly disagreeable, and I felt relieved when I discovered, in reply to 9 ... N8c6, the move 10 Qc4, at the same time vacating the square b3 for the retreat of the knight. On 10 ... b5 White has the possibility of 11 Qe4 Bf5 12 a×b4!. And so, I decided on:

9 a3, driving back the annoying black knight. Somewhat to my surprise, Bronstein sank into thought, but then very calmly played **9 ... N4c6**.

(Jumping ahead, I should mention that after the game David Ionovich informed me that it was 9 ... N8c6 that he had prepared at home, but at the board, on seeing 10 Qc4, he had thought better of it.)

White again had a difficult choice to make, between 10 Ne4, 10 Qc2 and 10 Qc4. There came into my head various lines of the type 10 Qc2 Nb4 11 Qd1 (*11 Qc4!?*) 11 ... Bf5 12 Nb3 Qc7! 13 a×b4 Bc2. I similarly did not care for the more serious 10 Qc2 Bf5 11 e4 Bg4. In the end White plumped for **10 Qc4,** but here too Bronstein succeeded in setting up strong pressure, utilizing his 'b' pawn as a battering-ram.

10 ... b5 11 Qh4 b4 12 Nd3 Na6! 13 Bg2 Bd7! (13 ... 0–0? 14 Ng5) **14 0–0 Rc8 15 Nde1** (otherwise there is no way of freeing the Q-side) **15 ... Nc5 16 Nc2 Nb3 17 Rb1** (17 a×b4 Qb5!) **17 ... Qc5 18 Ne3 Ncd4**, and White literally suffocated in his own territory. After the game Bronstein smiled, content: he had landed the counter-blow, and had fully settled his old opening score with me.

When, on the conclusion of the game, we sat down to analyse it, I had not yet cooled down after the battle, and began impetuously trying to demonstrate the total incorrectness of the pawn sacrifice. I said that White had not done anything 'unlawful', such that Black should be able to give up material for nothing. I began giving various lines, trying to refute Black's venture immediately. And each time Bronstein would methodically comment on what was happening: "It's not so simple, it's not so simple. You have an extra pawn, but I have extra space!"

We even continued our discussion on the way to our hotel. And after ascending by lift to our floor, we concluded a gentlemen's agreement: to play this variation again, should the opportunity present itself, and thus continue our argument under tournament conditions, in which a move cannot be taken back.

Later, incidentally, when I had cooled down and had begun to analyse calmly, I realized that if Black's innovation was to be refuted, there was no way this could have been done during the first encounter. To solve at the board all the problems facing White was in practice a hopeless task. And with each new hour spent on analysis, it became more and more clear to me that Bronstein's clever discovery gives Black perfectly reasonable compensation in the majority of variations. At any rate, the explosive power in the innovation proved more than sufficient for one game.

I have related all this so as to convince the reader once again of the delicate role played by the experimenter. And here is some further evidence.

This occurred in the World Chess Olympiad at Lugano in 1968, during the USSR-Hungary Match. Not more than two moves had been made on any of the other boards, but in the game **Lengyel–Polugayevsky** the players had managed in one minute to make fifteen! Here they are:

1 Nf3 Nf6 2 c4 g6 3 g3 Bg7 4 Bg2 0–0 5 0–0 d6 6 d4 Nbd7 7 Nc3 e5 8 e4 c6 9 h3 Qa5 10 Be3 e×d4 11 N×d4 Nb6 12 Qd3 Qa6 13 b3 d5 14 Qc2 c5 15 e×d5

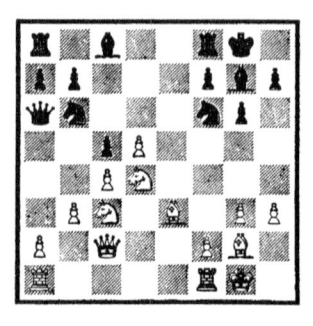

In the theory of the King's Indian Defence this position is well known, and it has also been tested in practice. Although no detailed analysis had been published of the possible piece sacrifice here—15 ... c×d4 16 B×d4, it had been successfully adopted by Gligoric in a game from the Yugoslav Championship. Somewhere in the middle of our 'blitz', I sensed that grandmaster Levente Lengyel was very well acquainted with the position resulting after the sacrifice, and that it was this that he was aiming for. The thought flashed through my mind: the trapper will himself be trapped!

The point is that once, at a training session for players from the Russian Federation, the position after White's 15th move served as a topic for discussion. At the time it became clear that if Black accepts the sacrifice, this is essentially equivalent to resigning. But it can be declined only by finding something new, or more accurately, even ultra-new, since the sacrifice itself should rightfully be considered the innovation.

I rarely play the King's Indian Defence, and for me the searching in this position was by no means a matter of vital necessity. But .... Nevertheless the analysis took place and a rejoinder which completely turned the tables was found.

For quite a long time the notebook with its recorded analysis lay untouched. Who knows how long this 'super-innovation' would have had to wait for its emergence, its 'first ball', had not Lengyel attempted to catch me in this variation. And of course, instead of the anticipated 15 ... c×d4, the unexpected **15 ... Nf×d5!!** came for him like lightning from a clear sky. Black began reaping the fruits after only three moves: **16 N×d5 N×d5 17 B×d5** (or 17 c×d5 c×d4, with a decisive advantage for Black) **17 ... c×d4 18 Bd2 B×h3**, and White found himself worse off than before—a pawn down, and without the slightest compensation for it.

It was interesting that, as soon as the move 15 ... Nf×d5 had been made on the board, and the Hungarian grandmaster had sunk into thought, participants in the Olympiad began gathering round our table. How dozens of players, who were occupied with their own games and their own problems, learned of the unusual turn of events on our board, I do not know, and I cannot explain it, other than as the genuinely magnetic attraction of everything new....

I should like to describe one further incident which I consider to be rather out of the ordinary. Early in 1969, on the outskirts of Moscow in the small town of Dubna, which is justifiably called the Physicists' Capital, I was preparing for my match with grandmaster A. Zaitsev for the title of Champion of the Soviet Union. Boris Spassky was also there, preparing for his match for the World Crown with Tigran Petrosian. Since ethics demanded of each of us that we should remain neutral with regard to each other, we decided not to touch on specific problems of pre-match preparation, but simply to work together on openings which interested us both, and which we both employed.

Among the schemes we looked at was the following variation of the Tarrasch Defence Deferred: **1 d4 Nf6 2 c4 e6 3 Nf3 d5 4 Nc3 c5 5 c×d5 N×d5 6 e4 N×c3 7 b×c3 c×d4 8 c×d4 Bb4+ 9 Bd2 B×d2+ 10 Q×d2**.

Theory states that the resulting position is level. But we managed to find a very interesting plan, and to reinforce it with specific calculations. In doing so, we proceeded on the assumption that Black should play logically, making the most sensible moves.

And so, **10 ... 0–0 11 Bc4 Nc6 12 0–0 b6 13 Rad1! Bb7 14 Rfe1 Na5** (isn't it true that this looks the most natural?) **15 Bd3 Rc8 16 d5! e×d5 17 e5!**

18   Grandmaster Preparation

It was with this unexpected pawn sacrifice that we associated the whole of our subsequent analysis, which showed that White's position is very strong. We got carried away, and advanced further and further, analysing the possible continuations move by move. Soon our advance was halted: the variation concluded, as they say, in mate to the black king....

Of course, Spassky and I agreed that either of us had the right to employ this analysis at the first convenient opportunity.

In my match with A. Zaitsev I did not require it. Later in the year, the position after White's 14th move was reached in the 5th game of the Spassky-Petrosian match. The then World Champion, who possessed a unique gift for sensing danger from afar, played 14 ... Rc8 immediately, instead of the suggested 14 ... Na5, and thus avoided the main threat, although after 15 d5 e×d5 16 B×d5 he was still unable to save the game.

I was fortunate enough to be able to 'publish' the entire variation six months later, in the second round of the 37th USSR Championship in Moscow. My opponent was Ex-World Champion Mikhail Tal.

It has to be said that I awoke that morning with very mixed feelings. A loss to S. Furman at the start had left me dispirited, and, what's more, I myself was largely to blame. One shouldn't in general play passively, but this is particularly so against Furman with Black. My disappointment was deepened by the fact that the Championship had the status of a Zonal Tournament, and that I had never yet managed to 'break through' to the Interzonal. Surely I wasn't going to fail again here?

It was this second thought which put me in the mood for a most uncompromising battle with everyone, even with Tal. Therefore, so as to 'erase' my bitter disappointment, I sat down at the board as early as possible that morning. What should I play? I remembered my analysis with Spassky, which had not been fully utilized, and decided to correct certain details, and to work over one or two small points.

It was while I was doing this that grandmaster Efim Geller called in to see me. He was surprised to see on my board a position from deep into the middlegame.

"It will very probably occur in my game this evening", I said, forestalling his question.

Efim Petrovich later related how that evening, during the round, he saw the position which had been reached in my game, and tried to remember where he had encountered it before. On glancing at me, he suddenly remembered everything, and couldn't believe his eyes....

1. On How This Book Found its Author 19

Yes, 25 entire moves, devised and 'polished up' beforehand, occurred in my encounter with Tal! The Ex-World Champion, who considered that all of Petrosian's troubles in his 5th match game with Spassky had stemmed from the fact that the white bishop had not been driven from c4 in time, played 13 ... Na5, and after 14 Bd3 Bb7 15 Rfe1 calmly played 15 ... Rc8, thus ending up in the main variation.

From the position in the previous diagram, events developed as follows:

17 ... Nc4 (if 17 ... Rc6, then 18 Nd4, with strong pressure) **18 Qf4 Nb2** (attempting to exchange off the dangerous bishop; after 18 ... h6 19 Qf5 White has a formidable attack) **19 B×h7+! K×h7 20 Ng5+ Kg6**

The first impression is that nothing comes of White's attack, but he has at his disposal a prepared move of terrible strength.

21 h4!!

This is the point of the combination. Of course, to find the whole of the subsequent lengthy variation was possible only with prepared analysis. I think that it was only here that Tal realized that he was battling under unequal conditions, but there was already no way out. Hanging over the black king is the threat of 22 h5+! K×h5 23 g4+ Kg6 24 Qf5+ Kh6 25 Qh7+ K×g5 26 Qh5+ Kf4 27 Qf5 mate. 21 ... f5 fails to save Black, on account of 22 Rd4!, with the same idea of 23 h5+ or 23 Qg3. Black's reply is therefore forced:

21 ... Rc4 22 h5+ Kh6 23 N×f7++ Kh7 24 Qf5+ Kg8 25 e6!

It was this position which Geller saw in my room that morning. And yet 25 moves have already been made!

Now on 25 ... Qe7 the piquant 26 h6! is decisive. In addition, Black was already on the threshold of severe time trouble, whereas White had spent literally only a few minutes, and most of those on the first few moves.

25 ... Qf6 26 Q×f6 g×f6 27 Rd2 (the immediate 27 Nd6 is more tempting, but the move played is perfectly sufficient to win) **27 ... Rc6 28 R×b2 Re8** (28 ... Bc8 was slightly the lesser evil) **29 Nh6+ Kh7 30 Nf5 Rc×e6 31 R×e6 R×e6 32 Rc2 Rc6 33 Re2! Bc8 34 Re7+ Kh8 35 Nh4 f5 36 Ng6+ Kg8 37 R×a7 Resigns.**

It goes without saying that an innovation lasting 25 moves is a rarity, but it once again emphasizes what a great return—both competitive and creative—a player can expect from searching, and from experimenting. It hardly has to be said that, in itself, such a success far exceeds the disappointment from other, less successful attempts, and that it is quite capable of inspiring a player, as the game with Tal inspired me in that USSR Championship. Finally, it does much to explain why I devoted so many years and so much effort to the opening variation which will be the subject of the following chapter.

2. The Birth of a Variation

The first time that the 'Polugayevsky Variation' occurred in my official tournament practice was early in 1959, in a game with A. Nikitin from the 26th USSR Championship. In April of that year the variation was employed against the Czech master J. Fabian in the International Tournament at Marianske-Lazne, and in the summer—in a training game during preparations by the Russian Republic team for the USSR Peoples' Spartakiad. Then, the number of games in which the variation was adopted began to grow in a geometric progression. But its real birth occurred much earlier, roughly at the time when, on hearing about the move 7 ... b5, I began working on it, if I remember correctly, under the following circumstances.

In the 1950s the chess-playing Ivashin family was widely known in Kuybishev. Its leader was Aleksey Ivashin, a strong and experienced candidate master, who participated in numerous events in the Russian Republic and the USSR. His sister Natalia was Lady Champion of the town and of the region on several occasions, and played in Championships of the Russian Republic. Their mother and father were also fascinated by chess, and when a tournament of chess-playing families was once held in our country, the Ivashins performed very successfully in it.

For many years the Ivashins' home was open to Kuybishev chess players. We gathered there practically every day, played a great deal, analyzed, generously exchanged ideas, and equally generously demolished any proposed innovations. One of the most authoritative analysts amongst us was considered to be the owner of the flat, Aleksey Ivashin, in effect my first trainer, to whom I am greatly indebted...

At that time (approximately 1956-57) a well-known master, Y. Shaposhnikov, moved to Kuybishev. I don't recall exactly how it happened, but during one of our analysis sessions in the Ivashins' flat, Shaposhnikov and I began talking about the move 7 ... b5 (after 1 e4 c5 2 Nf3 d6 3 d4 c×d4 4 N×d4 Nf6 5 Nc3 a6 6 Bg5 e6 7 f4). This had been played at the International Tournament in Ploesti in 1957 by N. Krogius against the Rumanian master Reicher. It is curious that the first time this move was employed was by Rumanian players in events in their own country. But both they and Krogius made this typical Sicilian move on general grounds, and did not associate it with an entire plan or system.

After our joint analysis, Shaposhnikov employed the move 7 ... b5 in what was to become a famous game with Y. Kotkov in the 1958 RSFSR Championship. In it a secondary variation occurred which, although interesting, did not, unfortunately, answer the main question: did the system have the right to exist? However, at the time it was clear to me that one game alone would be unable to give a categorical reply, and that the most deep and thorough analysis was required. And I began examining the dozens of branches of the main continuation, preparing to adopt the 7 ... b5 variation seriously, and for a long time.

And the more I analyzed, the greater the scope for reflection which opened before me. New possibilities were discovered for White, but I never failed to be astonished by Black's defensive and counter-attacking resources. Month followed month, the individual replies and tactical blows united into a system of various plans, and the commonly-occurring manoeuvres and strategy for Black in this variation became apparent. And when its original name of the 'Kuybishev Variation' gradually changed in chess literature to the 'Polugayevsky Variation', I decided at heart—and I trust I will not be considered immodest—that this was justified. Because every day for roughly six months(!) I spent hours at the board studying positions from the variation, and even went to sleep and dreamed about it. Finally, because the analysis recorded in my notebooks was so scrupulous and at the same time fantastic, much of it has not occurred in practice during the two decades of the variation's existence. To put it picturesquely, for a certain time the variation became my *alter ego*.

Incidentally, later I once thought to myself: why was it, after all, that I made a detailed study of this particular opening scheme, and not some other? And I realized that in my youth I had been attracted by an exceptionally tactical struggle, with a swift clash of pieces from the very first moves, and immediate complications. The 7 ... b5 variation fully answered all of this, as well as one further demand which was important at the time for the author. I was most unhappy, and to a certain extent annoyed, that in the Ruy Lopez, which was initially my favourite, the opponent could, without thinking, make some 17-20 'correct', 'book' moves, without risking making the slightest significant mistake. In the Sicilian, on the other hand, the value of each move was greatly enhanced, and in the 7 ... b5 variation it became positively 'worth its weight in gold': after all, at times a single inaccuracy after the seventh(!) move could lead to disaster for either side. In the resulting complications, both players had to work assiduously at the board, and this corresponded in the best way possible to the stamp of my character. In other words, the 'virgin soil' of the variation, and the complete novelty of the searching, made research work on the 7 ... b5 variation highly attractive.

Such is the pre-history of the variation.

On setting up this position on the board, in the first instance I began, of course, to analyze the continuations after 8 e5; my 'Sicilian' experience told me that if a refutation of Black's 7th move existed, it would be found in the main line of the system. It was only after 'polishing up' this main continuation that I turned to an analysis of those positions where White declines his opponent's challenge, and continues with normal moves. And I satisfied myself that in each such instance Black's early ... b7–b5 is fully justified. Black succeeds in developing his Q-side, and is the first to begin active play against White's Q-side, which is where the opposing king normally takes shelter.

From the diagram position, the moves which have occurred in practice are 8 Qf3, 8 a3, 8 Bd3 and 8 Be2. It is in this order that we will consider them.

AN OPTIMISTIC BEGINNING

8 Qf3

This is what my opponents played in the first games in which the 'Polugayevsky Variation' occurred. This 'normal' move does not set Black any particular problems.

The game **Nikitin–Polugayevsky** (26th USSR Championship, Tbilisi 1959) continued as follows:

8 ... Bb7 9 a3

If White plans to follow the familiar path (Bd3, 0-0-0 etc.), he cannot manage without this move, since Black's plan includes increasing the pressure on e4. It should in general be pointed out that, in comparison with the usual position of the Rauzer Attack, Black has made a significant gain: he has not wasted time on ...

Qc7, and can, in reply to 9 0-0-0 for instance, for the moment play 9 ... Nbd7, threatening 10 ... b4, while on 10 a3 there follows 10 ... Rc8, with the unequivocal desire, under suitable conditions, of sacrificing the exchange on c3, or of exploiting the weakening of White's Q-side in some other way. The black queen, meanwhile, can take up position at a5 or b6, according to choice. This, incidentally, is roughly the course taken by a game of mine against Spassky, which will be described later.

9 ... Nbd7 10 f5

In practice White proves unable to exploit the weakening of the square d5, and therefore he should nevertheless have continued 10 0-0-0.

10 ... e5 11 Nb3 Be7 12 0-0-0 Rc8!

A move which in this set-up is absolutely essential. Black utilizes the fact that his queen (which normally stands at c7) does not prevent his rook from taking an active part in the battle for the centre, for the square e4; the sacrifice on c3 is threatened!

13 Bd3 0-0

Already Black could have carried out the intended counter-blow: 13 ... R×c3 14 b×c3 d5, with perfectly adequate compensation for the exchange, but he decided to delay it for one move, continuing to build up threats by bringing his king's rook into action.

14 B×f6 N×f6 15 Nd5

White clarifies the situation, at the same time disclosing his plan: after the exchange on d5 he intends to seize the square e4, and after taking control of it to mount a K-side pawn storm. But Black's counterplay against White's Q-side, which has been weakened by the advance a2–a3, is so real that White never gets his hands on the square e4 ....

15 ... B×d5! 16 e×d5 Qc7!

Combining threats against the pawn at d5 (after the possible 17 Nd2 Qb7), and—indirectly—the square e4, since the c2 pawn is put under fire. Black's plans also include the positional pawn sacrifice 17 ... e4, with the follow-up 18 B×e4 N×e4 19 Q×e4 Rfe8, when both threats —... Bf6, and ... Bg5+—followed by ... Re3, are highly unpleasant. The attempt to blockade the 'e' pawn by 17 Be4 allows Black to seize the initiative completely by 17 ... a5. One is forced to the conclusion that already Black's position is the more promising.

17 Kb1

In my opinion, White should nevertheless have stuck to his guns, and played 17 Nd2, with the probable follow-up 17 ... e4 18 N×e4 N×e4 19 B×e4 Bf6.

White's extra pawn is of no significance, the black bishop is much more active than its white opponent, and the opening of further lines on the Q-side is threatened, but at the same time White's position is by no means lacking in counter-chances, associated in particular with play against the black king: g2–g4, h2–h4, Rhg1 etc.

After the move in the game, which is something of a waste of time, the initiative passes completely to Black.

17 ... Rfe8!

An important link in the implementation of the above-mentioned plan.

18 Nd2 Qb7

Once again Black could have made the break ... e5–e4, but the move played is also good. On the one hand it threatens the pawn at d5, and at the same time it exploits the departure of the white knight from the Q-side, allowing the advance of the black pawns.

19 Ne4 b4

Not, of course, 19 ... N×d5 20 f6!, when the roles are reversed: now it is White who has a deadly attack. Inciden-

2. The Birth of a Variation

tally, in reply to 19 Be4 Black would again have played 19 ... b4, with the possible continuation 20 a4 Qd7. If now 21 g4, then 21 ... Q×a4 22 b3 Qa3, and on 23 Nc4—23 ... R×c4 24 b×c4 N×e4 25 Q×e4 b3—with a decisive attack on the king, while 21 b3 is highly unpleasantly met by 21 ... Rc3 22 Qe2 Rec8 23 Rc1 Qa7, and on 24 Rhe1, either 24 ... Qd4, or even 24 ... Nd7 25 Nf3 (otherwise ... Bg5) 25 ... Nc5. Even so, it was this continuation that White should have chosen, since as the game went he was unable to organize a defence.

20 a4

After 20 a×b4 Q×b4 the lone white king is beyond saving.

20 ... b3 21 c3 Qd7

Black has achieved his aim. His threats are much more concrete than White's purely nominal possession of his e4 square, which is dangerous only in combination with a K-side pawn storm.

22 N×f6+ B×f6 23 Qe4

White openly goes onto the defensive, but his position on the Q-side is too badly compromised.

23 ... Rc5

The direct threat of ... Ra5 is extremely unpleasant, and on 24 B×a6 White gets mated: 24 ... Ra8 25 Bb5 R×b5 26 a×b5 Ra1+ 27 K×a1 Qa7+ 28 Kb1 Bg5 and ... Qa2 mate.

24 Qb4 Qa7!

The exclamation mark is deserved not so much by the move, as by the black queen itself, which in this game displays amazing mobility. Now 25 ... Rb8 is threatened, and on 26 Qe4—once again 26 ... Qd7, renewing the attack on the pawn at a4. White cannot capture the 'thorn in his flesh'—the pawn at b3: 25 Q×b3 Rb8 26 Qa3 e4, followed by the capture on c3.

25 Qe4 Ra5 26 Qb4 Qc7

The 'dance of the queens' has clearly been won by Black, and White gives in. However, in view of the threat of 27 ... Rb8, he has nothing better.

27 Q×b3 Rb8 28 Qc4

On 28 Qc2 Black would have carried out the thematic 28 ... e4, including his bishop in the attack. He now rejects 28 ... Rc5 followed by capturing on c3, in favour of something simpler.

28 ... Qb7 29 Qb4

On 29 b4, 29 ... e4 again decides, since the key point c3 falls. After the move in the game Black does not avoid the exchange of queens, since his rooks continue the attack.

29 ... Q×b4 30 c×b4 R×b4 31 Bc2 e4 32 Kc1 Rc5, and under the threat of great loss of material, **White resigned.**

The course of this game convinced me of the promising nature of Black's position after 8 Qf3, and when two months later, in a tournament at Marianske-Lazne, the Czech master **J. Fabian** employed it against me, I was secretly delighted.

The divergence from the previous game began in the following position.

Here, instead of 10 f5, White played

10 0-0-0 Rc8 11 f5 e5 12 Nde2

thus neutralizing the possible sacrifice on c3. But, in my opinion, Black's very next move refutes White's plan.

12 ... Qc7!

The threat of capturing on e4 forces White to make an awkward defence of his c2 square.

13 Rd2 Be7

Renewing the attack on e4. White plays an extravagant move, but even after the more natural 14 B×f6 his prospects would have been poor.

14 h4 Qa5! 15 Ng3

Here there were two paths leading to a great advantage for Black: either 15 ... b4 16 a×b4 Q×b4, when the threat of ... Rb8 and ... Nc5 renders White's position extremely difficult, or else the simple 15 ... h6, when White is faced with the dilemma of capturing on f6 or retreating with 16 Be3, when both 16 ... d5 and 16 ... R×c3 are good. But for some reason Black chose a third path....

15 ... 0-0

An unnecessary delay. Even without this Black was mobilized well enough to begin active play.

16 Nd5 N×d5?

A mistake, which is even more surprising, in that I had by no means forgotten the above game against Nikitin. In this type of structure, where White is unable to exploit the weakness of the square c6, it is essential to capture on d5 with the bishop, since the knight at f6 is needed by Black to control the centre. I am unable to give any sort of convincing explanation for such a strange decision—clearly it is a matter for chess psychologists. What is clear is that my defeat in this game did not blemish in any way the reputation of the opening set-up: after 16 ... B×d5 17 e×d5 b4 Black would have retained the initiative.

17 e×d5 f6 18 Be3 b4 19 Bf2

Perhaps it was this move that Black overlooked in his preliminary calculations. The pawn at a3 is now covered by the white queen, and his knight is defended. Nevertheless, for the moment Black has nothing to fear....

19 ... Nc5 20 B×c5 R×c5 21 Ne4

Frequently a mistake is not ruinous in itself, but due to the fact that a second follows in its path. Here Black should have continued 21 ... Rfc8 22 N×c5 R×c5, when he has some compensation for the exchange. After ... Kf8 the pawn at d5 will be weak, but a concrete appraisal of the position depends on the continuation 23 Qb3 b×a3 24 Q×a3 Qb6, with the threat of 25 ... Ra5.

If Black does not wish to sacrifice the exchange, he should simply retreat with 21 ... Rc7, preparing ... Rb8. The move played is undoubtedly a mistake, since Black removes the tension on the crucial section of the board, and goes into an ending which is fairly unpleasant for him.

21 ... b×a3? 22 Q×a3 Q×a3 23 b×a3 Ra5 24 Kb2 Rb8 25 Ka2 Bc8?

Yet another mistake. Correct was the immediate undermining of the white centre by 25 ... g6, and if 26 g4, then 26 ... h5! (*26 ... g×f5 27 g×f5 Bc8* is weaker in view of *28 Rf2 Rb4 29 c4*), with complications of the type *27 Rg1 h×g4 28 R×g4*, when the quiet move 28 ... Bc8! gives Black fair counter-play: *29 R×g6+ Kf7*, and if *30 Bh3*, then the preparatory *30 ... Rb4* is possible.

After failing to utilize this opportunity, Black ends up in what is evidently a lost position. The difference between the knight at e4 and the bishop at e7 is just too great!

26 Rf2 Bd8 27 Rh3 Bc7

On 27 ... Bb6, 28 Rb3 is very unpleasant.

28 c4!

White is not now distracted by the possibility of 28 Rb3, and instead shuts the black rook at a5 out of the game.

28 ... Bd7 29 g4

White's plan takes shape: utilizing his advantage in force on the K-side, he begins a pawn storm there.

29 ... Ba4

With the hope of somehow bringing this bishop into play via d1. In reply White sensibly exchanges off Black's only reasonably-placed piece.

30 Rb2 R×b2+ 31 K×b2 Kf8 32 g5 Bd7 33 Rf3 Ke7 34 g×f6+ g×f6 35 Bh3

The remainder is obvious: White is practically playing with an extra rook.

There followed **35 ... Ra4 36 Kb3 Ra5 37 h5 Ba4+ 38 Kb2**, and Black soon admitted defeat, having once again trusted in the viability of the 'Polugayevsky Variation'. Incidentally, from now on, for the sake of brevity, I shall take the liberty of calling it simply The Variation, using capital letters to distinguish the 7 ... b5 system from the countless number of chess variations.

ALMOST AT A RUN

8 a3

On a number of counts this cannot pretend to be a refutation of The Variation.

Firstly, to the active 'Sicilian' move ... b7–b5, White replies with a passive move. Secondly, it becomes dangerous for White to castle on the Q-side, since then the planned advance ... b5–b4 gains in strength. Thirdly, if he is so inclined, Black can transpose into the normal variation with ... Qc7, where the inclusion of the moves ... b7–b5 and a2–a3 is not in White's favour. Incidentally, Black is by no means obliged to develop his queen at c7, but can post it more actively at b6.

The several games played on this theme would merely appear to confirm this abstract assessment of the move 8 a3. In the game Lehmann-Tatai (Las Palmas 1972; it is amazing that even ten years later the move 8 a3 still had its adherents!), Black played very exactly, in the first instance preventing the advance e4–e5: 8 ... Nbd7 9 Qf3 Bb7 10 Bd3 Qb6! 11 Nde2 Rc8, and on the opening stage we can already ring down the curtain. It is White, rather than Black as is usual, who has problems over finding a safe spot for his king: in order to provide a shelter for it on the K-side, he had to go in for the unwieldly manoeuvre 12 Bh4 Be7 13 Bf2 Qc7, when Black had the more promising game.

The play is sharper if Black ignores the threat of e4–e5, and plays 8 ... Bb7 immediately. In a game against me in 1959, Levin embarked on an impulsive attack: 9 e5 d×e5 10 f×e5 Qc7 11 e×f6 Qe5+ 12 Qe2 Q×g5.

Tempted by the fact that Black's bishop had been diverted from the defence of e6, White now sacrificed a piece: 13 N×e6 f×e6 14 Q×e6+ Kd8 15 Rd1+ Kc7 16 B×b5 Q×f6 (it was probably possible to 'take what was being offered'—*16 ... a×b5*, when to continue his attack, White has to go in for further sacrifices such as *17 Rd5 B×d5 18 N×d5+ Kd8*, and the maximum he can hope for is perpetual check) 17 Qc4+ Kb6 18 Qb3 a×b5 19 Q×b5+ Ka7 20 Qa5+ Na6 21 Nb5+ Kb8 22 Rd8+ Bc8 23 Nd6 Ka7, and after wandering through the checks the black king feels quite safe, since on 24 N×c8+ R×c8 25 R×c8 there follows 25 ... Qe6+, and meanwhile White has simply no way of strengthening his attack.

If White keeps the e4–e5 break in reserve, and attempts, as Spassky did against Tatarintsev (Kislovodsk 1960) to increase the pressure by 9 Qe2, here too after 9 ... Be7 10 0-0-0 Nbd7 11 g4 Rc8 12 B×f6 g×f6 13 Qe1 Qb6 (*13 ... Nc5* looks even better, reserving the possibility of this queen manoeuvre) 14 h4 Nc5 Black has counter-play.

ONE AND A HALF POINTS OUT OF TWO

8 Bd3

A more solid continuation. I would not venture to state categorically who first adopted it, but it was with the game Spassky–Polugayevsky, played in the very first round of the 27th USSR Championship, Leningrad 1960, that the active life of this entire system for White first began.

Spassky made this move after some deliberation, and to this day I do not know whether he had planned this beforehand, and was merely accustoming himself during this time to the nature of the coming battle, or whether he decided on this piece set-up directly at the board.

There was no doubt that I, on the other hand, was playing at sight, so to speak. My analysis of the main continuation 8 e5 had taken too much time and effort, and having decided that The Variation would not be refuted by other moves, I studied them only when life required this.

The first thought flashed instantly through my mind: White can hardly castle short on account of the undefended state of his knight at d4. He was evidently planning to castle long, but did not wish to block in his bishop at f1, by immediately placing his queen at e2 and making ready for the break with e4-e5. If this was the case, I had to delay ... Bb7, and in the first instance prepare for this possible blow in the centre. Besides, White's e4 was already securely defended....

And I replied **8 ... Nbd7**.

There followed the immediate—and for me unexpected—**9 f5**. Normally this attempt to seize control of d5 does not bring White any benefit, and the absence of the white bishop from the a2-g8 diagonal does nothing to strengthen the pressure of the white pieces on this key square. But even so, Spassky's attempt deserves respect, if only for the reason that he instantly found a way of exploiting a completely concrete peculiarity of the position for an original manoeuvre. After **9 ... e5** he made the original advance **10 Nc6**, so as to attempt to gain a firm hold on d5, via b4. It has to be said that neither before this game, nor since it, have I encountered a similar manoeuvre by White in the Sicilian Defence.

Nevertheless, White wastes a considerable amount of time, and gives the opponent counter-play!

10 ... Qb6 11 Nb4 Bb7

Suddenly a slight, and again perfectly specific defect of the bishop's position at d3 is revealed. If in this position it were at e2, the occupation of d5 (after the preliminary *B×f6*) would assure White of a slight but fairly persistent positional advantage. But here he chooses the plan with Q-side castling. Play on opposite flanks begins, and everything depends upon who is the quicker.

12 Qe2 Be7 13 0-0-0

All is ready for the standard advance of the 'g' pawn, and if Black should give in to the natural desire to take his king into safety as quickly as possible by 13 ... 0-0, he immediately loses first the battle for the square d5 (*14 g4!*, followed by *B×f6, g4-g5 and Nd5*), and then also the game.

I should like here to mention that, in positions from the Sicilian Defence, move order is normally of decisive importance. In the Ruy Lopez, for instance, you can sometimes permit yourself to transpose, to 'confuse' one move with another in the execution of an intended plan, or even reject one plan in favour of another. Sicilian players, in contrast, are forced to judge the value of a move literally on its weight in gold—or the weight of a point in the tournament table?!—since in this opening, more than anywhere else, a transposition can radically alter the assessment of a position and the character of the struggle.

And so here, being governed not so

much by a general assessment, as by specific calculation, Black replied **13 ... Rc8!**.

Although in general this is a standard Sicilian move, it deserves an exclamation mark, for the reason that Black had another perfectly playable continuation—13 ... a5. White must reply 14 Be3, when Black can choose between the less active 14 ... Qd8 15 Nbd5 B×d5 16 N×d5 N×d5 17 e×d5 b4, and the sharp, but very promising sacrifice of his queen for only two minor pieces: 14 ... a×b4 15 B×b6 b×c3 16 B×b5 R×a2 17 b×c3 0-0.

I saw this sacrifice, and if there had not been anything better, I would have gone in for it. But in the first place, the move 13 ... Rc8 was nevertheless more soundly-based, and secondly—and I hope I will be understood correctly—I did not wish to begin an event which was so important for me, then still a master striving for the grandmaster title, with such sharp and, in many respects, risky play.

14 B×f6 N×f6 15 g4

If Spassky had sensed in time the danger threatening White, he would nevertheless have played 15 Nbd5, reconciling himself to the thought that White has not a trace of an opening advantage, since after 15 ... B×d5 16 N×d5 N×d5 17 e×d5 h5! the advance of White's K-side pawns is halted, while Black's plan—... Bf6, ... Ke7, ... Rc5, ... b5-b4, and ... a6-a5-a4-a3, gaining the square c3 for his pieces, can be carried out without hindrance.

Instead, this 'active' move in the game unexpectedly leads White to the verge of the abyss.

15 ... Qa5 16 a3 (there is no longer anything else) **16 ... R×c3 17 b×c3 d5!**

This, rather than the straightforward check 17 ... Q×a3+, which is bad on account of 18 Kd2 d5 19 Ra1, and if 19 ... d×e4, then 20 B×b5+, winning. Now, on the other hand, two more black pieces are included in the attack—the two bishops.

18 e×d5 0-0!

It may sound a rather delicate assertion, but up to a certain point Black conducts the attack in exemplary fashion, adhering completely to the principles of The Variation, and of the Sicilian Defence in general: be prepared to give up material for active play! In the resulting position it is very difficult for White to find a defence.

Apart from 19 ... Q×a3+ followed by 20 ... B×b4, Black also threatens 19 ... N×d5, which could follow, for example, on 19 Kb2. The threat of 20 ... N×c3 is then highly unpleasant, and White is forced to play for a counter-attack: *20 f6! N×f6 (not 20 ... B×f6 21 Qe4, or 20 ... N×c3 21 f×e7 N×e2 22 e×f8=Q+ K×f8 23 B×e2*, with a material advantage for White) *21 g5 c4 22 g×f6 B×f6 23 B×e4 B×c3 24+ Ka2 B×b4, or 22 Rhe1 Rc8! 23 g×f6 B×f6 24 B×e4* (bad is *24 Na2 R×c3 25 Kb1 R×a3 26 B×e4 R×a2 27 B×h7+ Kh8!*, and the game is decided) *24 ... R×c3 25 B×h7+ Kh8.*

Spassky evidently decides that there is no way of defending the white king at b2, and chooses a different plan. He brings his queen to the defence of his c3 pawn, simultaneously attacking the bishop at e7, thereby delaying the opponent's attack.

19 Q×e5 Q×a3+ 20 Kb1

The white king cannot go to d2: 20 ... B×b4 21 c×b4 Q×b4+ 22 c3 Qb2+ 23 Bc2 Rd8, and White has no defence.

But here, with Black's attack at its peak, I committed an inaccuracy, which allowed White to save the game in surprising fashion.

20 ... B×b4

Black couldn't, of course, act according to the principle 'the threat is stronger than its execution', and play 20 ... Re8, on account of 21 d6 Bf8 22 Q×e8! and 23 d7, but he could have set his opponent more difficult problems than in the game by 20 ... Bc5!. White would have had to parry both 21 ... Re8, and 21 ... N×g4, as well as to take measures against the manoeuvre of the knight from f6 to a4 via d7 and b6.

21 c×b4 N×d5?

As often happens, one inaccuracy is followed by another. Black could, and should, have tried for a win by 21 ... Q×b4+ 22 Qb2 Qc5. At the board I didn't like this, on account of 23 c4 (White has simply no other move, since *23 ... N×d5* followed by *24 ... Nc3+* is threatened), but later it was discovered that Black can then play *23 ... b×c4! 24 Q×b7 Qd6!!*, when White has to give up his queen, since he loses after 25 Ka2 Rb8 26 Qc6 Qb4. But after 25 B×c4 Rb8 26 Q×b8+ Q×b8+ the combination of black queen and knight—pieces which complement each other ideally in attack—is highly unpleasant for White. Possible, for instance, is 27 Ka2 (or *27 Kc2*) *27 ... Qb4 28 Bb3 Ne4*, when the white passed pawn is securely blockaded, and Black's opposite number will shortly begin to advance.

But in the game after **22 Qb2 Nc3+ 23 Kc1** Black forced a **draw** by **23 ... Na2+ 24 Kb1 Nc3+**, since the ending resulting after the exchange of queens and the capture of the rook at d1 is now favourable for White.

Nevertheless, this game did not deprive the move 8 Bd3 of its supporters, although on the ninth move no one now played f4-f5. Earlier than anyone else, the Kiev master **Y. Sakharov** made an attempt to vindicate 8 Bd3. Roughly three weeks later, in the 15th round of that same USSR Championship, after 8 Bd3 Nbd7 he chose against me **9 Qe2**.

Of course, during the tournament there was no time for the analysis of secondary variations—and that is how I regarded the continuation 8 Bd3—but after a couple of minutes' consideration, I decided that I should immediately 'dislodge' the now undefended knight at d4 from its centralized position. Black played **9 ... Qb6**.

The reply **10 N×e6** came so quickly that it was obvious that on this occasion I was up against a prepared variation, possibly even by a whole group of Ukrainian players who were participating in the Championship. My vigilance was trebled, but it did not prove so difficult to refute the preparation: after **10 ... f×e6 11 e5 d×e5 12 f×e5** I had to find only one move—**12 ... Qc5!**—for it to become clear that White's attack did not compensate for the sacrificed knight.

Sakharov spent a mass of time in thought, and it was obvious that his fellow-analyzers felt highly uncomfortable, since White is unable to regain his piece. There followed **13 Bf4 Nd5 14 N×d5** (White cannot play either 14 Ne4 N×f4, or 14 Qh5+ g6, when the black king safely crosses over to the Q-side) **14 ... e×d5 15 0-0-0** (if 15 Qh5+ g6 16 B×g6+, then 16 ... h×g6 17 Q×h8 Qb4+! 18 Bd2 Qe4+, and Black dominates the position) **15 ... Qc6!** (in this way Black simultaneously achieves three aims: he vacates the square c5 for his knight, and controls both e6, and, most important, g6) **16 Bf5 Be7 17 Qg4 g6 18 e6 Nc5**, and in desperation White sacrificed a second piece, **19 B×g6+ h×g6 20 Q×g6+ Kd8**, but after **21 Rhe1 B×e6 22 b4 Kd7! 23 b×c5 Rag8 24 Qd3 R×g2 25 Qf3 Rg6** he **resigned**.

It is possible that White's play in this game could at some point have been improved, but even so a piece is a piece, and in subsequent games supporters of such an expensive attack were not to be found. **And** when in a game Tolush–Hottes from the USSR–West Germany match (Hamburg 1960), White attempted to manage without the sacrifice—and in reply to 8 Bd3 Nbd7 9 Qe2 Qb6 retreated with 10 Nf3—there followed 10 ... Bb7 11 Bh4 (with the already familiar idea of allowing K-side castling after *Bf2*) 11 ... b4 (the quiet *11 ... Be7* is also perfectly possible) 12 Nb1 d5 13 e5 Ne4, and White was forced onto the defensive. The fact that he subsequently won was by no means on account of his successful handling of the opening.

A YEAR-LONG DUEL

In the series of games mentioned above, which enabled the truth regarding The Variation to be approached, my theoretical duel with A. Suetin holds a rather special position. It began with the move **8 Be2**, and caused me many anxious moments, before I was able to see my way through the resulting problems.

It has to be said that this move, for all its apparent modesty and lack of pretension, is full of venom. White intends to transfer his bishop to f3, and to make the e4-e5 break under the most favourable conditions. Just how dangerous a plan this is was first demonstrated in the game Bhend-Walther (Zurich 1959), where Black continued 8 ... Bb7 (for the moment he does not fear 9 e5, since he has in reserve a counter-attack on the knight at d4—*9 ... d×e5 10 f×e5 Bc5*) 9 Bf3 Nbd7 10 e5 B×f3 11 N×f3 d×e5 12 f×e5 h6 13 Be3 (*13 Bh4 is more accurate, provoking a further weakening of Black's K-side, e.g. 13 ... g5 14 Bf2 Ng4 15 Bd4 Bg7 16 Qe2 Qc7 17 0-0-0 Ng×e5 18 Rhe1*, with a highly formidable attacking position) 13 ... Ng4 14 Bd4 Qc7 15 0-0 Nd×e5 16 N×e5 N×e5, and instead of the erroneous 17 Kh1, after 17 Re1 Bd6 (if *17 ... Bc5, then 18 Kh1 Rd8 19 B×e5*) 18 Qh5 Bc5 19 B×c5 Q×c5+ 20 Kh1 White could have won the e6 pawn.

However, by the time of the USSR Spartakiad that same year, 1959, in Moscow, where Suetin first played the quiet 8 Be2 against me, I was not yet acquainted with the above game, and even now I do not especially blame myself for this. There was less than two months between the finish of the Zurich tournament and the start of the Spartakiad, we then had no efficient publication such as *64*, and information, especially from abroad, was received with considerable delay.

Later it was once again confirmed that Black should not develop his bishop at b7 too early, since this move hinders his best piece set-up on the Q-side. In the game Kalinkin-Gusakov (RSFRS Zonal Championship 1960) 8 ... Bb7 9 Bf3 Qb6 10 e5 d×e5 11 f×e5 Nfd7 12 B×b7 Q×b7 13 Qe2 Bb4 14 0-0-0 B×c3 15 b×c3 0-0 16 Rd3 Qd5 17 Nf5 Q×e5 18 Ne7+ Kh8 19 Qh5 Nf6 20 Qh4 Nbd7 21 Rf1 led to a strong attack for White, which ended in complete success: 21 ... h6 22 B×h6 g×h6 23 Q×h6+ Nh7 24 R×d7, and Black could find nothing better than to go into an ending, 24 ... Qg5+, which he was unable to save.

But this happened later. At that time, in the Spartakiad, I avoided the set-up with ... Bb7 intuitively, rather than as a result of specific calculation. I realized that the exchange of bishops, inevitable after Bf3 and e4-e5, was in White's favour, and that Black again had to seek counterplay in Q-side activity, i.e. in the spirit of the main idea of The Variation.

The correct idea, **8 ... b4,** was thus conceived, but after **9 Na4** I could find nothing better at the board than to try to exploit immediately the position of the white knight on the edge of the board by **9 ... Qa5.** There followed **10 B×f6 g×f6 11 b3 Bd7 12 0-0 Nc6** (the more consistent 12 ... B×a4 13 b×a4 is interesting, and now not 13 ... Q×a4 14 f5!, with an attack for White, but that which occurred in the game Timofeev-Shaposhnikov, Ulyanovsk 1960: 13 ... Qc5! 14 Kh1 Be7 15 Bg4 Nc6 16 Nb3 Qe3 17 f5 h5! 18 Bf3 Rc8 19 f×e6 f×e6 20 B×h5+ Kd7 21 Bg4 Ne5, which gave Black sufficient compensation for the pawn; however White, who has the more promising position, is by no means obliged to copy blindly and completely this order of moves) **13 Kh1 Be7 14 f5! Qe5 15 f×e6 f×e6 16 Bh5+ Kd8 17 N×c6+ B×c6 18 Nb6 Rb8 19 Nc4.** Here Black, despite the fact that he has two bishops, stands worse, since his king will remain a cause for constant concern, while his pawn phalanx in the centre is weak.

This began to tell very quickly: **19 ... Qc5 20 Qg4! Qg5.**

21 Q×e6!

White embarks on a long and correct combination, planning to sacrifice a rook. After the exchange of queens, 21 Q×g5 f×g5 22 Rad1, the drawbacks to Black's position would threaten to become advantages, while the purely concrete threat to the d6 pawn could be parried by 22 ... Bb5.

21 ... Q×h5 22 Rad1

White plays very accurately. In the variation 22 N×d6 Bd7 23 Nf7+ Ke8 24 Nd6+ Kd8 Black has a draw.

22 ... Bd7 23 R×d6 B×d6 24 Q×d6

In the event of 24 Q×f6+ Be7! 25 Q×h8+ Kc7 Black repels the attack while maintaining a material advantage, but what is he to play now? The rook at b8 is attacked, and 25 Q×f6+ is also threatened. The natural 24 ... Qb5 is met by the unexpected 25 Rf5, when Black loses by force. He therefore has to reconcile himself to a 'wandering king'.

24 ... Kc8 25 Q×a6+ Kc7 26 Qd6+ Kc8 27 Rd1

If White had been tempted to establish material equality by 27 Nb6+, Black's pieces would have come to life. The move played is much stronger. White now threatens 28 Rd5! followed by 29 Rc5+.

27 ... Rb7!

The only move which allows Black to put up any resistance. He attempts to somehow establish co-ordination between his pieces, and to allow his king to move to d8.

28 Rd5 Qh4 29 h3

Alas, White's position is so strong that even this enforced loss of time for prophylaxis does not ease Black's lot.

29 ... Rg8 30 Rc5+ Kd8 31 Ra5 Qe1+ 32 Kh2 R×g2+

I could see no other defence, since after 32 ... Ke8 33 Ra8+ Kf7 34 R×g8 K×g8 35 Qd5+ White regains his sacrificed material with considerable interest.

33 K×g2 Qe2+ 34 Kg3 Qe1+ 35 Kf3 Qf1+ 36 Ke3 Qe1+ 37 Kd3 Qf1+ 38 Kd2 Qf2+ 39 Kd3 Qf1+ 40 Kd2 Qf2+ 41 Kc1 Qe1+ 42 Kb2 Qc3+ 43 Kc1 Qe1+ 44 Qd1 Q×d1+ 45 K×d1 B×h3

In the resulting ending White has every chance of winning, since, apart from having an extra pawn, his rook and knight are excellently placed. The simplest now was 46 Ke2, but my opponent was tempted by a forcing variation, and exchanged his excellent knight for the black bishop.

46 Ne3? Re7 47 Ra8+ Bc8 48 Nd5 R×e4 49 Nb6 Kc7 50 N×c8

It was this position that White was aiming for, reckoning that after 50 ... Rd4+ 51 Ke2 Kb7 52 Ra7+ K×c8 53 R×h7 he has an easily-won rook ending, since the black king is cut off from its pawns. But this variation is by no means obligatory for Black.

50 ... h5!

For a short time White remains a piece ahead, but it becomes difficult for him to realize his material advantage.

51 Na7

51 Ra5! was probably stronger, with winning chances after 51 ... K×c8 52 R×h5, while if 51 ... h4, then 52 Rc5+!, when White retains his material advantage.

51 ... Kb7 52 Rh8 K×a7 53 R×h5 Rf4!

Otherwise White on his next move plays 54 Rf5.

54 a3 b×a3 55 Ra5+ Kb6 56 R×a3 Rf2 57 Ra8 f5 58 Kc1?

A serious inaccuracy. 58 Rd8 followed by Rd2 was preferable.

58 ... f4 59 Rc8 Rg2 60 Rf8 Rf2 61 Kb2

Only here did Black breathe a sigh of relief. Things would have been more difficult for him after 61 Rf5!.

61 ... Kc5 62 Rf5+ Kd4 63 Rf8 f3 64 Rd8+ Ke3 65 Kc3 Re2 66 b4 f2 67 Re8+ Kf3 Drawn.

The impression left by my game with Suetin was a highly painful one, especially since shortly afterwards, in the 1960 RSFSR Championship Semi-Final, the then young candidate master Kalinkin literally crushed G. Ilivitsky, a highly experienced master of defence.

After 8 Be2 b4 9 Na4 Qa5 he did not exchange on f6, but immediately played 10 b3, boldly sacrificing his central pawn. There followed 10 ... N×e4 11 Bf3 d5 12 B×e4 d×e4 13 Qe2, when the square d8 clearly began to 'creak', and the position of the black king to 'fray at the seams'. After 13 ... Bb7 14 0-0-0 Nd7 15 f5! White began a direct attack, and what's more, Black couldn't prevent the opening of lines in the centre by 15 ... e5, on account of 16 Ne6 f×e6 17 Qh5+. He was therefore forced to further expose his king—15 ... e×f5 16 Rhf1 g6 17 g4! f×g4 18 Q×g4—when all the white pieces, with the exception of the knight at a4, were directed against Black's sovereign. He tried 18 ... Ne5 19 Qf4 Bg7 20 Bf6, and, since 20 ... B×f6 21 Q×f6 0-0 22 Nf5 g×f5 23 R×f5 is totally bad, he gave up a pawn by 20 ... g5, which similarly failed to save him: 21 B×g5 0-0 22 Qf5 Rae8 23 Bf6 B×f6 24 Q×f6 Qd8 25 Qh6 Nd3+ 26 R×d3, and Black resigned.

All this prompted me to think that an improvement for Black had to be sought at a very early stage of the game, somewhere between moves 8-10, and no later.

It goes without saying that 8 Be2 was studied literally under the microscope, but for a long time I was unable to find any plan that was at all acceptable. I first of all noted that if Black doesn't play 8 ... b4, but contents himself with 8 ... Nbd7, then 9 Bf3 Bb7 10 e5 will give White the initiative: 9 ... B×f3 10 N×f3 (*10 Q×f3* and *11 Nc6* is also interesting) 10 ... d×e5 11 f×e5, as occurred (with an unimportant transposition of moves) in the Bhend–Walther game given above. Black's misfortune here is not even that he is forced to suffer, but that he suffers without any particular prospects for the future.

I attempted to include (after *8 Be2*) the intermediate move 8 ... h6, and it appeared that after 9 Bh4 b4 10 Na4 g5 Black could hope to 'go fishing in troubled waters': 11 f×g5 N×e4. But then I gave up this idea once and for all, since the elementary 9 B×f6 Q×f6 10 0-0 affords White such a lead in development, that the attempt to neutralize it would be merely a pipe-dream.

Besides, the almost obligatory 10 ... Be7 (so as to somehow at least safeguard the king) cuts off the queen from its 'lawful place' in the region of c7 to b6, and it must inevitably come under fire from the attacking white pieces. To clear my conscience, at the time I analyzed roughly the following variation: 11 f5 Qe5 12 f×e6 B×e6! 13 N×e6 f×e6 14 Bh5+ Kd7 15 Qg4 Nc6, and now neither 16 Nd5, nor 16 Rad1 Qc5+ 17 Kh1 Ne5, is particularly terrible for Black, but 16 Rf7 looks very dangerous for him. Black cannot now play 16 ... Qc5+ 17 Kh1 Ne5, on account of 18 R×e7+, and I delved further into the maze, 16 ... Raf8 17 R×g7 Rf4 18 Qg3 Rhf8 19 Bf3 Nd4 20 Rf1 b4 21 Nd1 R×f3, and Black wins.

Oh, if only this was obligatory for White! Alas, he can strike a blow on a different part of the board, weakened by the absence of the queen: 11 a4! b4 12 Na2 Bb7 13 f5! e5 14 Nb3 B×e4 15 N×b4, when White's advantage is undisputed. The move 8 ... h6 was therefore rejected, and I give it here now, merely as an illustration of the work that had to be done.

The attack on the knight with 8 ... b4 was, in the end, judged to be best, and from this starting point I began analyzing further.... I succeeded in establishing that after 8 Be2 b4 9 Na4 there was no necessity to despatch the queen to a5, which cuts it off too early from base. It was better to first complete the development of the K-side pieces, and in the event of White attacking the rook at a8 by Bf3, to move it along the route a8–a7–c7. Then Black's bishop, exploiting the undefended state of the white knight, could occupy d7 with gain of tempo....

The idea was born. But it only took shape almost a year later, in my next game with **Suetin** in the 27th USSR Championship in Leningrad.

As a matter of principle, we both chose this same variation as in the 1959 Spartakiad, but I now played 'in the light of the latest achievements of science': **9 ... Be7**, and on **10 Bf3—10 ... Ra7**. There is now no threat of e4–e5, and White cannot bring the knight at a4 into play by 11 c3:

11 ... Qa5 12 c×b4 Q×b4+ 13 Nc3 h6!, and if 14 Bh4, then 14 ... N×e4. All that remained for him was to follow the course studied by me.

11 0-0 Bd7 12 b3 B×a4 13 b×a4 0-0

Black's development problems are now decided. He plans ... Qb6, ... Nbd7, and the Q-side pawn weaknesses may become an overall weakness for White.

A'light-hearted' game Kalinkin-Sorokin (Krasnoyarsk 1960) was played 'on the theme' of 13 ... Qb6 (instead of *13 ... 0-0*), and after a swift and stormy clash it ended in a draw: 14 Kh1 h6 15 Bh4 N×c4 16 N×e6 Nc3 17 Qe1 B×h4 18 N×g7++ Kf8 19 Q×h4 K×g7 20 Qg4+.

My game with Suetin continued **14 Nb3 Nbd7 15 Qe2 Qb6+ 16 Kh1 Rc7 17 Rad1**, and Black himself made an advance in the centre—**17 ... e5**, since White can now only dream about occupying d5.

Now White cannot merely sit and wait as the opponent's initiative on the 'c' file develops, and to counter it he himself prepares to double rooks on an adjacent file.

18 a5 Qc6

Better, of course, is 18 ... Qb7, when the queen does not hinder Black's rooks in pressing—and breaking through!—on the file which is open and already controlled by him.

19 Rd2 Rfc8 20 Rfd1 Bf8 21 f5 (otherwise Black himself exchanges on f4, and then plays ... Ne5) **21 ... Qb7**

Black has to waste a tempo, since otherwise he cannot strengthen his position.

22 Re1 Rc4 23 g4

2. The Birth of a Variation   37

Here Black should have adopted energetic measures, 23 ... d5! 24 e×d5 e4! 25 Bg2 Qc7, and if 26 B×f6 N×f6 27 g5, then 27 ... e3! 28 Q×e3 Ng4 29 Qg3 Bd6 30 Rde2 Rf8 31 Qd3 B×h2, when he has numerous threats. White should evidently play 26 Nd4, but even then 26 ... N×d5 27 Q×e4 N5f6 gives Black excellent chances, in view of the weakness of virtually all the white pawns. For example 28 Qf3, is unpleasantly met by 28 ... Ne5 29 Qe2 Re8.

With his reply in the game, Black misses this favourable opportunity.

23 ... Qb5 24 Qg2 Qc6 25 B×f6 N×f6 26 g5 Ne8 27 Bd1 (if 27 Ree2, then 27 ... Nc7 28 g6 f×g6 29 f×g6 Ne6 30 Qh3 Ng5, with an unclear position) **27 ... g6** (here also 27 ... Nc7 deserved consideration) **28 Bg4 Rc7 29 f6 R×c2 30 R×c2.**

A mistake. White should have advanced his 'h' pawn, when Black would be forced to reckon with the break-through 31 h5. But now the game transposes by force into an ending, where Black has nothing to fear: **30 ... Q×c2 31 Q×c2 R×c2 32 Rc1 Rc3 33 Be2 Nc7 34 Bc4 h6 35 R×c3** (35 h4 deserved consideration, when 35 ... Rh3+ 36 Kg1 R×h4 fails to 37 Bf1, and on 37 ... Ne6—38 B×a6; after the move played the advantage is with Black) **35 ... b×c3 36 h4 h×g5 37 h×g5 d5 38 e×d5 e4,** and with little time left on the clocks, a **draw** was agreed.

It goes without saying that Black could

still have played for a win; e.g. 39 Kg2 Bd6 (*39 ... c2 40 Kf2 Ba3 does not work—41 Ke2! c1=Q 42 N×c1 B×c1 43 d6*, and it is now White who wins) 40 Nd4 Bf4 41 Nc2 c2 42 Bb3 B×g5 43 d6 Ne6 (if *43 ... Nb5, then 44 d7 B×f6 45 B×c2*, and the 'e' pawn falls, after which White merely has to exchange the knights) 44 d7 B×f6 45 B×c2 Nc5 46 Ng3 N×d7 47 N×e4 Be7! 48 Bd3 Nb8, and White still has a lot to do to gain a draw. However, it probably can be attained by the manoeuvre 49 Nc3 f5 50 Nd5 Bd6 51 a3! B×a3 52 Nc7, and if 52 ... Bb4, then 53 N×a6 N×a6 54 B×a6 B×a5, since with opposite-coloured bishops, 'f' and 'g' pawns do not win...

As a result of this opening 'slanging match' with Suetin, the truth about the move 8 Be2 was more or less established. As for myself, after moving yet again from a feeling of doubt to one of satisfaction, I got down to analyzing the main continuation of The Variation.

It is true that there is another move, which is not of independent significance, and which has hardly been tested in practice—8 Qe2, suggested by Y. Murei. I did not analyze it seriously, since it can transpose into other, already familiar, variations. Black should merely avoid playing the opening carelessly, as was done by Korzin against Murei in a 1970 event: 8 ... Qc7 9 0-0-0 Nc6??, and after 10 B×f6 g×f6 White's idea, based on the opposition of the white queen and black king, was fully realized: 11 Nd5 e×d5 12 N×c6, and Black can resign.

If 9 ... Nbd7 is played, a familiar position is reached, but no longer from The Variation: 1 e4 c5 2 Nf3 d6 3 d4 c×d4 4 N×d4 Nf6 5 Nc3 a6 6 Bg5 e6 7 f4 Nbd7 8 Qe2 Qc7 9 0-0-0 b5. Here, as is well known, the sacrifice on d5 does not work: 10 Nd5? e×d5 11 e×d5+ Be7 12 Nc6 Nb6. However, if such play is not to Black's taste, then in The Variation after 8 Qe2 he can simply play 8 ... Be7 9 0-0-0 b4!, when the early ... b7-b5 is utilized one hundred per cent.

IN THE MAIN DIRECTION

All these secondary branches were of considerable importance, but even so, they would have been of purely academic interest, had Black not been able to find sufficient defensive resources and counter-attacking chances in the main line of The Variation. In it White immediately casts doubts on the opponent's Q-side activity, and strikes a blow in the centre, exploiting the pin on the knight at f6.

8 e5 d×e5 9 f×e5 Qc7

Here there are several continuations —10 Nf3, 10 Qe2— but the most critical is clearly 10 e×f6, and it was with this that I began my analytical work in 1958. And so, **10 e×f6, Qe5+**.

The most natural reply for White is 11 Be2. It was this that I ran up against the very first time that this position occurred in one of my games (**Zagorovsky-Polugayevsky**, RSFSR Championship, Voronezh 1959).

But at a training session for Russian Federation players in the summer of that

2. The Birth of a Variation 39

same year at Solnechny, near Leningrad, in a consultation game White played here **11 Ne4**. The idea of this move belongs to the late R. Nezhmetdinov, and consists in returning to Black not the bishop at g5, but the knight. At first sight such a method of defending appears rather strange, but in fact it is not without venom.

Here is how the consultation game continued: 11 ... Q×e4+ 12 Ne2 (clearly unsatisfactory is *12 Be2 Q×g2 13 Bf3 Q×g5 14 B×a8 Qh4+*; incidentally, this rather simple variation unexpectedly occurred later, in 1967, at a tournament in Zwolle, in a game between two strong players, Ghitescu and Kavalek. White apparently overlooked the check at h4, and suffered a rapid defeat after *15 Kf1 Q×f6+ 16 Nf3 Bc5 17 Qd3 0-0 18 Kg2 Rd8 19 Qe2 Qg6+ 20 Kf1 e5 21 h3 Be6 22 b3 Nd7 23 Bc6 Bf5 24 B×d7 B×d7 25 Q×e5 Q×c2*) 12 ... Nc6 13 Qd2 Ra7 14 0-0-0 Rd7 15 Nc3!.

White's idea is clear: the ending is favourable for him in view of the weakness of Black's Q-side pawns (after a timely *a2-a4*) and—in certain variations—the square d6. Besides, the exchange of queens and one pair of rooks by no means fully relieves Black of concern over the square d8, which the bishop at g5 continues to observe by 'X-ray'. For this reason, Black stayed in the middlegame, 15 ... Qb4, and after the following great complications the game ended in a draw: 16 Bd3 Ne5 17 Kb1 Nc4 18 B×c4 R×d2 19 R×d2 g×f6 20 B×f6 Be7 21 B×b5+ a×b5 22 B×h8 Bb7 23 Bd4! Qa5 24 a3 b4 25 a×b4 B×b4 26 Re2 Qa6 27 Rc3 B×g2 28 Rg1 Bd6 29 Rd3 Qc6 30 Rd2 Bf3 31 Bf6 Kf8, and so on.

After the game, analyzing in the main the opening stage, we jointly came to a definite conclusion: in the following position

White can gain an advantage by 17 a3, since the black queen has no retreat other than to a5 (*17 ... Qc5* or *17 ... Qd6, 18 Ne4*), from where it loses control over d6. After this 18 Qe1! gives White a clear advantage, while after 17 ... N×d3+ he again does not object to an ending: 18 Q×d3.

Such a turn of events disheartened me somewhat, since virtually all Black's moves are forced, with the possible exception of 12 ... Nc6. But I considered this particular move to be obligatory, since earlier, in an analysis of the following position

R. Nezhmetdinov had refuted time after time my attempts to block the access of the white pieces to d8 by 12 ... Nd7. I could find no way to hold the position after the simple 13 f×g7 B×g7 14 Qd6. And although in the USSR Spartakiad, immediately following the training session referred to, Nezhmetdinov lost in this variation to B. Gurgenidze (that game went *14 ... Bf8 15 Qd2 h6 16 Be3 Qb4 17 c3 Qd6 18 Nd4 e5 19 Qe2 Qe7 20 Nf5 Qe6 21 g4 Bb7 22 Bg2 e4 23 0-0 Rg8 24 a4 Ne5 25 h3 h5 26 g5 Nf3+ 27 R×f3 e×f3*), it was obvious that Black's position after 12 ... Nd7 did not inspire confidence.

Jumping ahead a little, I should remark that this conclusion received a convincing demonstration in the game Kotkov-Tilevich, in a tournament of masters and candidate masters at Cheboksary, in 1960. Black decided to manage without the move 15 ... h6, against which 16 Bf4 deserves consideration (after *16 ... Qb4 17 c3* Black is denied the square d6, while on *16 ... e5* White replies *17 Bg3* followed by *0-0-0*), and played 15 ... Qb4 immediately. There followed 16 c3 Qd6 17 Nd4 f6 (*17 ... e5* nevertheless signifies loss of control over a whole complex of central squares: *18 Qe3* is possible, or even *18 Nf5*) 18 Bh4 Bg7 19 0-0-0 0-0.

It is obvious that the resulting position is in favour of White. He energetically exploited his advantage: 20 Qe3 (aiming towards e6) 20 ... Qe5 (on *20 ... Ne5, 21 Bg3* is strong, while *21 Nf5* is also pretty unpleasant) 21 Qf3! (gaining a tempo by the attack on the rook, and intending to exploit the advanced position of the black queen as a target for attack) 21 ... Nb6 22 Bd3 (the simplest: White's offensive develops unhindered) 22 ... Nd5 23 Kb1 (prophylaxis: the threat is now *24 Rhe1*) 23 ... Qf4 24 Qh5 Qh6 25 Q×h6 B×h6 26 Be4 Ra7 27 Rhe1, and White's overwhelming advantage is beyond dispute.

All this appeared perfectly convincing (we had also examined similar continuations during our training session), but one thought constantly nagged away in my mind: the moves 11 Ne4 followed by 12 Ne2 are very clumsy. Could it really be that, despite their antipathy, they were so strong that they could immediately cast the whole Variation onto the scrap-heap?

Anyone who in his work has had occasion to be an author—irrespective of what: an engineering project, a story, or a chess system—knows how important his brain-child is, and how much he wants it to be accepted and to receive recognition. And I decided to continue my searchings, by once again going through the score of the game played at the training session. My analysis commenced with the move 12 ... Nc6. Several obligatory replies for both sides followed, and on the board once again was reached the position after White's 15th move, as given on p. 39.

In it I succeeded in finding a different queen move to that in the training game: 15 ... Qe5. Calculation confirmed that this was stronger, and that at e5 the queen was much more comfortably placed than at b4. I give here in full the whole of the analysis made then, in 1959, quite deliberately, without correcting it, and with precisely nothing changed. Even if the reader should discover in it some inaccuracies or mistakes, he will realize what a maze I had to go through, so as to uphold my idea, and to retain the right to adopt The Variation in practice.

And so, 15 ... Qe5 16 Bd3 g×f6.

2. The Birth of a Variation

17 Rhe1 was threatened, and the pawn has to be taken, if only so as to know for what Black is suffering.

17 Bf4 Qd4 18 Be3 Qb4.

Incidentally, a year later at the tournament in Buenos Aires, this position occurred in the game Olafsson–Reshevsky. Black once again moved his queen to e5, 18 ... Qe5, and after 19 Bf4 Qd4 20 Be3 Qe5 21 Bf4 a draw was agreed. I do not think that White is obliged to agree to a repetition of moves. The position is extremely sharp and full of life, and White has various alternatives at his disposal: 19 Rhe1, 19 Qf2 and 19 Rhf1, although in the first case he has to reckon even with 'pawn-grabbing' such as 19 ... Q×h2, in the second—with 19 ... Ba3, and if 20 Kb1, then nevertheless 20 ... B×b2, and in the third—with 19 ... Bb4.

What forced me to analyse 18 ... Qb4 was, in the first instance, the aggressive nature of my chess character. What sickened me was the thought that, whereas Black had to go in for such complications and risks, in the event of 18 ... Qe5 White could, if he wished, force a draw without any trouble. Although I realized that, in principle, a draw should be considered a 'gain' for Black.

At first it appeared to me that after 18 ... Qb4 Black's position was nevertheless alright (despite the obvious defects in the positioning of his queen, compared with its place at e5), since after 19 a3 Qa5 20 Qf2 b4 he has counter-play (e.g. *21 Bb6 Qe5*, or even *21 ... Bc5*). But then I discovered that White can play 19 Qf2, and this is much stronger than the immediate 19 a3. Now the pawn at f6 is hanging, and Ne4 is threatened. If, for instance, 19 ... Qe7, then 20 Ne4 Bg7 21 Bc5, and it is unlikely that White's attack can be resisted. I therefore considered the main continuation for Black after 19 Qf2 to be 19 ... f5.

Now the plausible 20 B×f5 fails to 20 ... e×f5 21 R×d7 B×d7 22 Nd5 Qd6 23 Rd1 Bh6, when 24 Nb6 is met by the elegant 24 ... Qc5! (*25 Re1 Be6*). On 20 a3 the black queen retreats: 20 ... Qe7, when the move which causes Black the most difficulty is the aggressive 21 g4. Now 21 ... f×g4 is essential (on *21 ... Ne5* there follows not, of course, *22 g×f5 Ng4 23 Qf3 N×e3 24 Q×e3 Qc5 25 Rhe1 Q×e3+ 26 R×e3 Bh6*, but the simple *22 Be2*, and White retains all the advantages of the opponent's king being stuck in the centre; also bad is *21 ... Bg7 22 g×f5 B×c3 23 b×c3 Q×a3+ 24 Kb1*, and it is Black's king, rather than White's, which is nevertheless destined to come under attack) 22 Ne4 f5 (forced, otherwise there follows *23 Bg5*) 23 Bg5! (all the same!) 23 ... Qg7 24 Nf6+ Kf7.

On reaching this fantastic position, I once again felt pleased: the white bishop at g5 is hanging, and Black seems to be holding on, but then I found for White a move of terrible strength: 25 h4!!. Black has essentially only two possible replies: 25 ... g×h3 and 25 ... Rd4.

On the first of these there follows 26 Rhg1 Be7 (no better is *26 ... Rd6 27 Ne4! Rd4 28 Bf4*, when the inevitable *29 Ng5+* again gives White an irresistible attack, while *26 ... R×d3* is parried by the simple *27 R×d3 Be7 28 Ne4*. The attempt *26 ... Rd4* is also doomed to failure—*27 Nh5 Qg6 28 Bf6 Qh6+ 29 Kb1 R×d3 30 R×d3 Rg8 31 R×g8 K×g8 32 R×h3*, and White's attack is by no means finished; however, the very first move in this line, *27 Nh5*, is not obligatory for White; the quieter *27 Kb1* is also possible) 27 N×d7 B×g5+ 28 Kb1 B×d7 29 B×f5, with a very strong attack.

In the event of 25 ... Rd4 White continues simply 26 c3 Rd6 27 N×g4, retaining all the advantages of his position.

After all this anxiety and searching, Nezhmetdinov's idea underwent a new test at the 1961 USSR Championship in Baku. In our meeting the draw gave him the white pieces. An outstanding master of combination, who more than once had inflicted defeats by direct attacks on such great players as Spassky and Tal, my recent 'neighbour' on the Volga, Nezhmetdinov, almost invariably opened with the advance of his king's pawn. On this occasion we both, without prior agreement of course, firmly decided to play The Variation; Nezhmetdinov—because he always upheld his ideas as a matter of principle—and I, for the same reason. But already before the game there was an advantage on Black's side, since during my endless analysis I had succeeded in finding a move to breathe new life into the apparently dying Variation.

We made the first 13 moves instantly, and in the following position the 'mine' was detonated:

13 ... h6!

I will permit myself to digress for a moment from specific analysis, and to recall once again what it was that caused me to search for a new continuation in this particular position.

First of all, common sense. However risky The Variation was, I thought, it was just not possible that White should refute it by removing from the centre his excellent-placed knight from d4 to e2, thereby losing time and hindering the development of his own pieces. Of course, surprises, normally unpleasant ones, have frequently awaited Black in The Variation, and will continue to do so, but so-called intuition strongly suggested to me that on this occasion White was seeking a refutation of The Variation in a blank space, and that the golden truth lay elsewhere. It was a general understanding of what had long since become familiar problems, which caused me to seek a defence here, rather than by further move-by-move analysis. After all, at this particular moment White himself has withdrawn his actively-placed pieces, and for a certain time the only piece which is still available for sharp attacking possibilities is the bishop at g5. This means that Black should not bother with prophylaxis such as 13 ... Ra7, as played earlier, but should utilize this favourable opportunity to drive the bishop from its active position.

I have to admit that when I found the move 13 ... h6, for a certain time I was unable, due to excitement, to continue the analysis. It became clear to me that Nezhmetdinov's idea—11 Ne4—which appeared so menacing, would be cut off at the root by this modest pawn advance, and that the triumph of The Variation in this line would be complete. During the game I was particularly glad that the innovation was being employed against the actual inventor of this system of attack.

14 Be3 Bb7 15 Ng3

The first fruits of the innovation: at the board White fails to choose the strongest route for his knight. However, 15 Nc3 would have been met by the simple 15 ... Qh4+ and 16 ... Q×f6, while in the event of 15 f×g7 B×g7 16 0-0-0 Rd8 17 Nc3 Black has both 17 ... R×d2, with a reasonable ending, and 17 ... Qg5. His opening difficulties are behind him.

15 ... Qe5 16 f×g7 B×g7

Here we can sum up: the strategic plan of The Variation has been implemented one hundred per cent. Black is excellently developed, and the placing of his bishops is particularly good. This allows his position to be considered the more promising.

17 Bd3 Nb4!

The time lost by White on his knight manoeuvres begins to tell: in evacuating his king, he is forced to part with one of his bishops.

18 0-0 N×d3 19 Q×d3 Rd8 20 Qe2 h5!

Leaving his king in the centre, Black begins an attack.

51 Rae1?

A serious mistake, after which White's position is barely defensible. 21 Qf2 is correct, although even then 21 ... Q×e3 22 Q×e3 Bd4 23 Q×d4 R×d4 gives Black the better chances in the ending.

21 ... h4 22 Qf2 Rd7 23 Ne2 h3 24 g×h3

On 24 Bd4 Black has the very strong reply 24 ... Q×d4. But now the devastated residence of the white king creates a painful impression.

24 ... R×h3 25 Ng3 Qd5 26 Bb6 Be5

The threat of 27 ... R×g3+ forces White to part with the exchange. But his misfortunes do not end there: the second 'storm column'—the 'f' pawn—is sent forward.

27 R×e5 Q×e5 28 Re1 Qg5 29 Be3 Qg4 30 Rf1 f5 31 Bf4 Rd1 32 c3 Rh4 33 Bc7 f4 34 Q×f4 Q×f4

White resigns. After 35 B×f4 R×f1+ 36 N×f1 R×f4 he comes out a rook down.

The impression made by this game was so great, and the virtues of the move 13 ... h6 were so obvious, that the Nezhmetdinov system immediately lost its topicality, and subsequently there were essentially no more serious games played on this theme. For The Variation there was one less 'enemy' ....

AT THE SOURCE

But let us revert to chronology. The move 11 Ne4 demanded of me considerable mental effort and a mass of time, but when I was first analyzing The Variation, it simply did not enter my head. As I have already mentioned, the first time I reached this position

in practice, I had to do battle against the move 11 Be2, which was played by V. Zagorovsky. But I was also prepared for another possible continuation: **11 Qe2**.

Moreover, this was the move that was first subjected to analysis, since after it play is to a certain extent forced, and if after 11 Qe2 Black were unable to find adequate counter-play, the whole idea of The Variation would turn out to be false.

In reply to 11 Qe2 Black has no choice: 11 ... Q×g5 12 Ne4 Qe5 13 0-0-0 Ra7.

This move is essentially forced, since Black must in the first instance neutralize both his opponent's lead in development, and his threats down the 'd' file. The attempt to provoke the exchange of queens, for instance, loses quickly: 13 ... Bb7 14 N×b5 a×b5 (*14 ... B×e4 15 Q×e4*) 15 Qd2!, and White's attack is irresistible.

It is curious that in Reicher-Krogius, the first game played with The Variation to be published, this is what occurred (true, here Krogius offered a draw, and Reicher accepted, whereas after *15 ... Bd5 16 B×b5+* Black can resign). It was then that the main strategic idea of this line of The Variation came into my head: by the transfer of the rook to d7 via a7, to parry White's basic threat—his attack along the 'd' file.

14 Qe3. In my analysis it was this move that I considered strongest. In a game from a Ukrainian tournament between L. Stein and Y. Sakharov in 1960, White played differently: 14 Nf3(?) Qf4+ 15 Kb1 Rd7 16 R×d7 N×d7 17 g3 Qc7. Now White's undefended pawn at f6 is forced to help Black with his development: 18 f×g7 B×g7 19 Qd2 0-0.

Black has two bishops, and objectively speaking his position is already preferable. In order to avoid coming under an attack, White exchanged queens: 20 Qd6 Q×d6 21 N×d6 Nb6 22 N×c8 R×c8 23 c3 Na4! 24 Bd3? N×b2, and Black won within a few moves. Of course, White was not bound to blunder on his

24th move, but even after 24 Bg2 b4 the initiative is with Black.

Clearly, the attack on the black queen by 14 Nf3 is premature. The move 14 Qe3 prepares it, without allowing the black queen in at f4, but even in this case Black has perfectly adequate resources for creating counter-play: 14 ... Rd7 15 Nf3 R×d1+ 16 K×d1 Qc7 17 Bd3 Nd7. After 18 f×g7 Black can again count on obtaining the initiative, while 18 Qd4 g6 19 Ke2 e5! 20 Qe3 h5! followed by ... Bh6, ... 0-0 and ... Bb7 also enables him to face the future with confidence.

This analysis, which was carried out as long ago as 1958, convinced me that after 11 Qe2 it is White, rather than Black, who has reason to be afraid....

Then came the time for the analysis of the main and most interesting line, continuing from the position in the diagram on p. 44: **11 Be2 Q×g5 12 0-0 Ra7**. This was the course taken by my game against Zagorovsky (Voronezh 1959), which has already been mentioned, and which gave life to The Variation.

13 Qd3 Rd7 14 Ne4 Qe5 15 c3 Bb7 16 Bf3 B×e4 17 B×e4

If 17 Q×e4, then possible is either 17 ... Q×e4 18 B×e4 g×f6, or the immediate 17 ... g×f6.

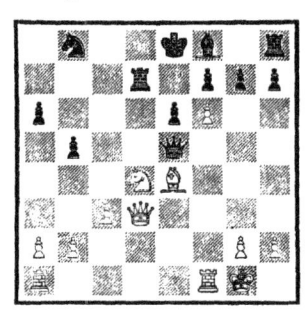

17 ... Bd6!

Of course, Black could also have managed without this move, and contented himself with the simple 17 ... g×f6, but during the game I considered it advantageous to 'lure' the white pawn to g3: it is after all an additional weakening of White's K-side!

18 g3 g×f6 19 Kh1

White forestalls an unpleasant and absolute pin on the d4 knight along the a7-g1 diagonal, but has no possibility of avoiding an almost equally unpleasant relative pin on the knight along the 'd' file. On the possible 19 Rae1 Black would again have replied 19 ... Bc5, since 20 Bc6 N×c6 21 R×e5 f×e5 22 Qf3 Rc7 is perfectly satisfactory for him.

19 ... Bc5 20 Rad1 Kf8!

Intending to castle artificially, and to bring his second rook into play along the central open file. At the same time, it should not be forgotten that Black has an extra pawn (and even two, essentially, since White's Q-side majority is insignificant, whereas on the K-side Black has four pawns against two), and he has merely to parry possible tactical threats by his opponent, when the outcome will be settled.

And in the game that is what happened.

21 Rfe1 Qg5 22 a4 Kg7 23 a×b5 B×d4 24 c×d4 Q×b5 25 Qe3 Rhd8

It is clear that White has lost not only the opening battle, but also the game as a whole. And although the realization of Black's advantage dragged out for a further thirty and more moves, his material superiority—in the absence, of course, of any blunders on his part—is in the end bound to tell.

26 d5 Nc6! 27 Rf1 e×d5

Black worked out accurately all the subsequent events, and foresaw the transition into the ending.

28 Bd3 Q×b2 29 Rf5

White has simply no time to win back even one of Black's three extra pawns: 29 B×a6 Qe5, and the threat of a check at e4 is highly unpleasant.

29 ... Qd4 30 Qc1 Ne5 31 Rh5 N×d3 32 Qh6+ Kg8 33 Q×h7+ Kf8 34 R×d3

There is nothing else, but on this occasion the 'traditionally drawn' rook ending proves to be not at all so.

34 ... Qe4+ 35 Kg1 Q×h7 36 R×h7 a5

One of Black's passed pawns will now advance 'seriously' towards the queening square, while the other will divert White's attention.

37 Rh4 d4 38 Kf2 f5 39 Ke2 Ke7 40 Kd2 Ke6 41 Ra3 Rd5 42 Kd3 Ke5 43 Ra2 Ra8 44 Rh6

Black might just play the direct 44 ... a4??, and be mated by 45 Re2.

44 ... Rb5 45 Re2+ Kd5 46 Rf2 Rb3+ 47 Kc2 Rab8

Black's pieces have become so active, and his pawns so strong, that he is prepared to allow re-establishment of material equality: 48 R×f5+ Ke4 49 R×f7 d3+ 50 Kd1 Rb1+ 51 Kd2 R8b2+ 52 Kc3 Rc2 mate.

48 Rd2 a4 49 Ra6 a3 50 Ra7 R8b7 51 Ra8 Rb2+ 52 Kd3 R7b3+ 53 Ke2 Re3+ 54 Kd1 Rb1+ 55 Kc2 Rb2+ 56 Kd1 d3 57 Rd8+ Ke4 White resigns.

A slight digression. It would appear that this game should have dotted all the 'i's as regards the assessment of the variation involving the capture of the white knight at e4. White, without making a mistake, completely lost the opening battle. But both a year later in the game Lenchiner-Gufeld from the Ukrainian Championship, and eight years later in the Steiner-Szabó encounter from the international tournament in Krems (1967), all this was repeated, although Black avoided the intermediate move 17 ... Bd6, and played 17 ... g×f6 immediately.

In the first of these a variation given by me above occurred: 18 Rae1 Bc5 19 Bc6 N×c6 20 R×e5 f×e5 21 Qf3 Rc7 22 Kh1 e×d4 23 c×d4 B×d4 24 Rc1 Kd7 25 Q×f7+ Kc8 26 Q×e6+ Kb7, and Black realized his advantage. In the second game everything was much simpler: 18 Rae1 Bc5 19 Kh1 B×d4 20 Bc6 N×c6 21 R×e5 B×e5, and it was time for White to resign.

How is such a dramatic coincidence to be explained? Clearly the players with White were simply not familiar with the Zagorovsky-Polugayevsky game.

Earlier, back in 1959, i.e. practically at the same time as us, Gligoric and Bhend played a game with The Variation at the tournament in Zurich. But the Swiss master had clearly not spent sleepless nights in analysis, and went wrong in the following position by moving his queen to a different square.

14 ... Qg6.

Black soon had cause to regret this: 15 Qe3! Bb7 16 Bf3 Qh6.

It turns out to be very difficult to find an alternative for Black, since the natural 16 ... g×f6 is met by 17 N×e6!, and wins (*17 ... f×e6 18 Bh5*), and he has no other way of completing his development.

In the game White continued 17 Q×h6 g×h6 18 Nb3, when it became clear that Black stood badly. He was forced to play 18 ... B×e4 19 B×e4 Bd6 20 Rae1 (in order to answer *20 ... Be5* with the simple *21 c3*) 20 ... Rc7 21 c3 Nd7 22 Na5 0-0 23 Rd1 Be5 24 Bc6 Nc5 (if *24 ... N×f6, then 25 Rde1*) and now again 25 Rde1. There followed 25 ... Bd6 26 Re2 Nd3 27 Be4, and White, having retained his advantage, gradually converted it into a win.

Returning to the source game, to my encounter with Zagorovsky, I can only add that, out of the many hundreds of games I have played, I was probably more anxious in this one than in any other. My tournament colleagues could not understand the reason for this intense excitement. At the time I naturally was unable to explain this, but I myself knew that a new variation was being born, or more precisely, a new scheme with a whole network of highly complex variations .... Moments can occur which, as it were, raise a man above his humdrum, everyday self. It was this that I experienced during

2. The Birth of a Variation

my game with Zagorovsky, and for it (and not only for points in the tournament table) I am grateful in the first instance to The Variation....

But let us come back to earth. The game received wide coverage in our Country's press, and became a topic for study by many theorists, and practical players too, while in international tournaments (as I have already mentioned) even several years later one could come across 'copies' of the game, where White, being unfamiliar with it, plunged in similar fashion into a lost position.

RECONNAISSANCE IN FORCE

The next landmark in my research into The Variation was my game with Bagirov, played in January 1960 in the USSR Championship in Leningrad. I recall how, after making my 15th move, I got up from the board, and Vasily Smyslov came up to me and said reproachfully: "Oh Lyev, Lyev. Why do you take such liberties? All your pieces are on the back rank! You've played this variation once in the Championship, and that's enough! You'd do better to look after your nerves!"

In reply, I made a joke in roughly the following spirit: "I realize it myself, and my head orders one thing, but my hands do another." But in fact I definitely knew that I would play The Variation until I encountered a complete refutation of it, and then... I would again get down to analysis. I would seek a refutation of the refutation....

I came up against something of a surprise literally a minute after the given dialogue with Smyslov. Bagirov, who before the game had made special preparations for The Variation, played in the diagram position.

16 Qg3. In principle, after the exchange of queens Black has nothing to fear—White can refute his opponent's apparently rather risky strategy only by an attack—and with an easy heart I replied **16 ... Q×g3** (clearly, 16 ... Q×e4 17 Q×b8+ Rd8 18 Qg3, with the threats of 19 f×g7, 19 Bf3 and 19 Rae1, is in White's favour) **17 N×g3 Nc6** (five years later in the game Matai-Nicevsky, Yugoslav Championship 1969, Black continued 17 ... g×f6, and it turned out that after 18 Nh5 Be7 19 N×f6+ B×f6 20 R×f6 Rg8 21 Bf3 Rg6 22 Rf4 B×f3 23 N×f3 Nc6 24 a4 e5 25 Re4 the position had simplified in favour of White, who retains a certain pressure).

White was practically forced to play **18 Nb3**, otherwise after 18 N×c6 B×c6 Black would play his bishop to c5 with check, and at the board I made the most natural move: **18 ... g×f6**. After **19 Ne4 Be7 20 N×f6+ B×f6 21 R×f6 Ke7 22 Rf2 Ne5** the position was still level and markedly simplified, and following **23 a4 Bc6 24 Nd4 Rb8 25 Re1 Rd5 26 a×b5 a×b5 27 N×c6+ N×c6 28 Bf3 Rc5 29 B×c6** a **draw** was agreed.

Strictly speaking, Bagirov's continuation did not shake my faith in The Variation, but the fact that White could draw without any particular trouble left me somewhat disillusioned.

However, that very same night after my game with Bagirov, I discovered, much to my annoyance, that, instead of the plausible developing move 17 ... Nc6, Black had at his disposal the rather curious manoeuvre 17 ... Rg8, when it turns out that White has to worry both about his g2 square, and, more important, about his knight at d4, since Black threatens the simple 18 ... Bc5 and then 19 ... Nc6, winning a pawn. I cursed myself for my haste during the game with Bagirov, but all that remained was to regret my omission.

In this USSR Championship, several times, and highly successfully, I upheld 'my system in practice', to borrow a term from Nimzowitsch. But after the tournament I wanted to generalize on the accumulated experience. A month later I again sat down to work. And one day, when I was examining the position which had occurred in my games with Zagorovsky and Bagirov, I unexpectedly hit upon a move which had earlier remained unnoticed, both by me, and by my opponents. It turned out that in this position

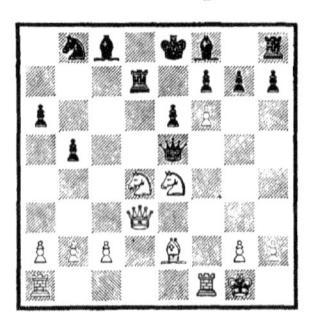

instead of 15 c3 White can play 15 Nf3, which sets Black a number of serious problems.

Now Black cannot play 15 ... R×d3 16 N×e5 Re3, when there are two equally strong alternatives: 17 f×g7 B×g7 18 Nd6+ Ke7 19 N×c8+ R×c8 20 R×f7+ Kd6 21 R×g7 R×e2 22 Nf3, and the simpler 17 Bd3, with the threat of 18 Kf2. The white knights similarly do not become

2. The Birth of a Variation

entangled if the black rook retreats to d5: 16 ... Rd5 17 f×g7 B×g7 18 N×f7 0-0 19 Nfd6, and the threat of 20 R×f8+ and 21 N×c8 allows White to gain a tempo for the move c2-c3, and thereby retain his extra pawn.

It may seem paradoxical, but already after these two 'single-branch' variations which were easy to calculate, Black's position immediately ceased to appeal to me. As often happens in chess, the most modest move in the position, 15 Nf3 (blocking the 'f' file, along which White is attacking, offering the exchange of queens etc.), proved to be the strongest. And I decided to study the position resulting from this, in which the black queen retreats to c7, although it too did not appear particularly promising. As for the move 15 ... Q×b2, at heart I immediately condemned it as suicidal, and did not bother to reinforce this feeling with variations.

Here it would seem appropriate for me to give my approximate train of thought, which caused me to reject completely 15 ... Q×b2.

The point is that, in choosing The Variation, to a certain extent Black acts contrary to the basic laws of chess, which demand rapid mobilization in the opening. Indeed, in the position after 15 Nf3 practically all of Black's pieces are still on their initial squares, the black queen has already moved four times, and a further raid into the opponent's position cannot fail to tell against him.

What's more, the basic strategic idea of The Variation is not to gain material, but, by creating threats, to develop the pieces with gain of tempi, and if possible to force White to assist this (e.g. by the capture f×g7). Black can gain tempi both by attacking the knight at e4 (by ... Bb7), and by attacking the white king (by ... Bc5+). And any deviation from this strategic idea, any material-grabbing, makes The Variation, which is already risky for Black, too reckless.

It is interesting that subsequent tournament practice (of other players, of course, since I simply could not act counter to my own logic, and did not once play 15 ... Q×b2) fully confirmed the correctness of my judgement. The overwhelming majority of games played with the capture on b2 by the queen ended in a rapid and crushing defeat for Black. It is noteworthy that, while many grandmasters could not resist the temptation to employ The Variation, if only once or twice, the move 15 ... Q×b2 was nevertheless made only by players of lower class, who had evidently not grasped the strategy of The Variation so deeply.

This once again confirmed an ancient truth: first and foremost it is essential to understand the essence, the overall idea of any fashionable variation, and only then include it in one's opening repertoire. Otherwise the tactical trees will conceal from the player the strategic picture of the wood, in which his orientation will most likely be lost.

Thus, for instance, the game Simovich-Vitolinsh, School Children's Spartakiad 1961, went 15 ... Q×b2 16 Qe3 (clearly the only move) 16 ... Bb7.

Boleslavsky recommends as strongest here—and I agree with him—17 a4.

However, 17 Rad1 has also occurred several times in practice: 17 ... B×e4 (*17 ... g×f6 is bad on account of 18 Rb1*), and now either 18 Q×e4 (it has been stated that *18 R×d7 N×d7 19 Q×e4* is stronger, with the possible continuation *19 ... Bc5+ 20 Kh1 0-0 21 Ng5 g6 22 Qh4 h5 23 Ne4, but 23 ... Qe5* enables

Black to hold on) 18 ... Q×f6! (Black includes his queen in the defence, since he cannot play *18 ... Bc5+ 19 Kh1 0-0* on account of the analogous variation *20 Ng5 g6 21 Qh4 h5*, and now the fact that his pawn at f6 is defended allows White to smash open the black king's position by *22 B×h5*), or 18 f×g7.

In the game Bakulin-Titenko, Moscow 1961, Black went wrong with 18 ... B×g7, and after 19 Q×e4 Qc3 20 Kh1 Qc6 21 Qb4 Qc3 22 Qg4 R×d1 23 R×d1 0-0 24 Ng5 h6 25 Ne4 f5 (*25 ... Q×c2 26 Nf6+ Kh8 27 Bd3 Qa4!* was better) 26 N×c3 f×g4 27 Ne4 an ending was reached, in which Black was unable to defend his weak pawns.

But then in the highly important game Van den Berg-Langeweg (Amsterdam 1961) Black played 18 ... Q×g7! 19 Q×e4 (in a game between the Russian players Kiryanov and Sorokin in 1961, White tried *19 R×d7*, but Black replied *19 ... B×f3!*, and *20 Rd8+ K×d8 21 Qb6+ Ke7 22 B×f3 Nd7 23 Qb7 Qd4+ 24 Kh1 Qb6 25 Qe4 Bg7* left him a piece up; Black stands equally well after *22 Qc5+ Kd7 23 Qa7+ Kc8*) 19 ... Bd6! 20 Bd3 Rg8 21 Rd2 h5!, and one gains the impression that, apart from an extra pawn, Black has also gained the initiative.

The refutation of Black's 'pawn-grabbing'—15 ... Q×b2—is not to be found in 17 Rad1.

White also fails to achieve his aim by 17 f×g7, as occurred in the game Shmit-Kovacevic (Match USSR-Yugoslavia, Belgrade 1961)—White incorrectly assists the development of the black pieces. After the practically forced 17 ... B×g7 18 Bd3 Bd4 19 N×d4 Q×d4 20 Q×d4 R×d4 21 Nf6+ Ke7 22 Rf2 Nd7 23 Raf1 Ne5! 24 B×h7 Rh4 Black gained the advantage.

Finally, the apparently logical move 17 c4, as occurred in the above-mentioned game Simovich-Vitolinsh, was parried by Black by 17 ... B×e4 18 Q×e4 Q×f6 (in the event of *19 ... g×f6*, after *20 c×b5 a×b5 21 Rab1 Bc5+ 22 Kh1 f5 23 Q×e6+ f×e6 24 R×b2* White gains the advantage — *24 ... Ke7 25 B×b5*), and after 19 Ne5 (on *19 c×b5* Black had evidently prepared *19 ... Bc5+ 20 Kh1 0-0*, and if now *21 Ne5*, then *21 ... Rd4!*) 19 ... Bc5+ 20 Kh1 Rd4 21 Qe3 Rd5! 22 Qg3 (if *22 Qh3*, then *22 ... Q×e5 23 c×d5 Q×d5*, and after castling Black stands well) 22 ... Q×e5 33 c×d5 Q×g3 24 h×g3 Ke7 25 d×e6 f×e6 an ending arose, in which White's advantage could be discerned only under a microscope. In the game Simovich even managed to lose, but this result had no connection with the opening stage (White blundered with *26 a4??*, and after *26 ... b4 27 Bc4 Rd8* Black seized the initiative).

So that Black has to reckon with the move 17 c4, but after it he again apparently has chances of emerging unscathed.

The two continuations which are most dangerous for him are 17 a4 and 17 Rab1. It is in these variations that the capture by the queen on b2 has not stood up to practical testing. The game Estrin-Vitolinsh (Semi-Final USSR Championship, Moscow 1963), for instance, concluded rather quickly:

17 Rb1 Q×c2 18 Nfg5 g6 19 Rbc1 Q×a2 20 N×f7! (destroying the black king's pawn cover; on *20 ... K×f7, 21 Ng5+* is decisive) 20 ... R×f7 21 Nc3 (White continued even more strongly in the game Goikhman–Petrushkin, 1965: *21 Qa7! Nc6 22 B×b5!*) 21 ... Qb3 22 Rb1, and Black was unable to defend e6. He attempted to resort to tactics by 22 ... Bh6, but 23 Qg3! Bf4? 24 Qh3 Qa3 25 Q×e6+ Kf8 26 R×f4 gave White a marked advantage.

True, the picture became rather less clear after the game Parma–Tatai (Athens 1967), when instead of 18 ... g6 Black replied 18 ... Qc7!, and White's attacking forces proved insufficient to break down his opponent's defence, now reinforced by the queen. Parma chose 19 f×g7 B×g7 20 N×e6 f×e6 21 Ng5, but after 21 ... Qe5! 22 Bh5+ Kd8 23 Qb6+ Kc8 24 N×e6? (*24 Rbc1+ Nc6 25 R×c6+ Kb8!*, and Black wins) 24 ... Qd4+! Black went on to win.

This line was never tested again in practice, but I consider nevertheless that it is favourable for White. In my opinion, he should not be in a hurry to capture on g7.

Black, it is true, once achieved a stunning success, when after 15 ... Q×b2 16 Qe3 Bb7 17 Rab1 Q×c2 18 Nfg5

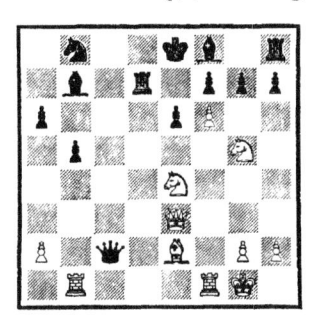

he made the paradoxical move 18 ... Rg8, which *Chess Informator* No. 3 promptly accompanied with two exclamation marks.

Indeed, in the correspondence game Reynolds–Boese, 1967, after 19 Rbc1 Q×a2 20 N×f7 R×f7 21 Nc3 g×f6! 22 Rf2 Qa3 23 Bh5 R×g2+! 24 R×g2 Bc5 White had to resign.

However, Black's 'improvement' does not alter the assessment of the capture on b2, and if it had been a strong player playing White in this game, I am sure that, not only in correspondence play, but also at the board, he would have found the refutation of Black's 18th move. After 19 Rbc1 Q×a2 White only had to find 20 Qg3!, and Black would have been defenceless. A possible conclusion would be 20 ... Nc6 21 R×c6! B×c6 22 Qb8+ Rd8 23 Qc7 Bd7 24 Bh5! g6 25 Nd6+ B×d6 26 Q×d6, and mate next move.

It remains for us to consider the main continuation 17 a4.

This is what A. Novopashin played against A. Volovich (Sochi 1961), tackling the problems in the diagram position by quiet, purely positional means, which, incidentally, are highly unpleasant for Black. White's idea is simple: 18 a×b5 and 19 Rab1. Black's attempt to prevent the opening of lines by 17 ... b4 was unsuccessful: 18 c3! B×e4 (*18 ... b×c3 19 f×g7 B×g7 20 Rfb1 Qc2 21 R×b7 R×b7 22 Nd6+*) 19 Q×e4 Bc5+ 20 Kh1 g×f6 21 Rfc1 (shutting out the black queen) 21 ... 0–0 22 Rab1 Qa2 23 c×b4

Be7 24 b5, and despite being a pawn down, White has the better position. After 24 ... f5 25 Qe3 a×b5 *(25 ... Q×a4 26 b×a6 N×a6? 27 Ra1)* 26 B×b5 Rdd8 27 Qh6! Kh8 28 Ne5 White went on to win, since to the very end of the game Black was unable to move his knight from its initial post at b8.

If, in addition, one adds that after 17 Rab1 Black also has considerable difficulties, it is not difficult to realize just how antipositional the capture with the queen on b2 is.

Thus on finding the move 15 Nf3, I immediately decided that I would retreat —15 ... Qc7, and thought to myself: "The knight move didn't occur to me straight away, so perhaps others too won't hit upon it so quickly!" But shortly after this Mikhail Tal was in Moscow for some reason, and in conversation with me remarked in passing:

"You know, in your Variation after 13 ... Rd7 14 Ne4 Qe5 White can retreat his knight."

And he gave 15 Nf3 ....

"I know, Misha", I replied dispiritedly, "and I'm very concerned about it."

Our conversation dispelled all my illusions: anything that is known by two people soon becomes the property of everyone. This meant that I would have to do battle against 15 Nf3 in the very near future.

And that is what happened. The first to employ it in a game with me was **A. Novopashin** in that same year, 1960, in the USSR Championship Semi-Final in Vilnius. I replied **15 ... Qc7**, and the dispute began.

16 Qe3 g6

In opening books this move was subsequently considered to lead to equality, but in fact all Black's troubles lie ahead. The alternative, 16 ... Bb7 17 Nfg5 B×e4 18 N×e4 Qa7 19 Q×a7 R×a7 20 c4, which occurred in the game Murei-Feldman (Match Moscow-Leningrad, 1965) also maintained for White a marked advantage.

17 c4

In a slightly later game Kuindzhi-Vasilchuk, from a junior tournament in 1960, White played 17 Kh1, which despite its slow appearance is also fairly good. After 17 ... Bb7 18 a4 Black played the extremely risky 18 ... Q×c2 *(18 ... b4 is correct)* 19 Nfg5 h6, when White's attack became spectacularly decisive: 20 Rac1 Q×b2 21 Qa7 Nc6 22 Q×c6! Q×e2 23 Qb8+ Rd8 24 R×e6+ f×e6 25 f7+ Ke7 26 Qc7+ Rd7 27 Qc5+, and Black, threatened with inevitable mate, resigned.

17 ... b4

To allow White to open the 'c' file would be equivalent to suicide.

18 Kh1

This allows Black the chance to draw breath.

18 ... Bb7 19 Rad1 h5!

A tactical nuance—on 20 Nfg5 Black replies 20 ... Bh6, with the threat of 21 ... B×e4—enables him to stand firm on the edge of the abyss. It appears that at any moment White will carry out a thematic blow, sacrificing at f7 or e6, but for this he is always one tempo short.

20 Neg5 Bc5 21 Qe5 Bd6!

It was for the sake of this move that the black bishop changed direction a move earlier. White is forced either to repeat moves, or, as occurred in the game, to sacrifice the exchange, which however is sufficient only for a draw.

22 R×d6 Q×d6 23 N×f7 K×f7

The attempt to avoid perpetual check is clearly in White's favour: 23 ... Q×e5 24 N×e5 Rc7 25 f7+.

24 Ng5+ Kf8 25 N×e6+ Kf7 26 Ng5+, and the players agreed to a **draw**.

Straight away Novopashin and I made a fairly thorough analysis of the critical position

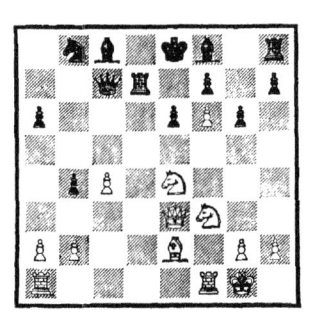

and established that, instead of 18 Kh1, by 18 Bd1 White could have gained a marked and possibly decisive advantage. This move became known in the circle of leading Russian Federation players, and was later tested in the 1961 Championship of the Voronezh region in the game Zagorovsky-Kaverin.

This game went 18 Bd1 Bb7 19 Ba4 Bc6 20 B×c6 N×c6 21 Rad1, and Black's position began to crack up. He was not even saved by the 'patent' 21 ... h5 22 c5 Bh6 23 Qe2 0-0 24 Q×a6, when White had an extra pawn and the better position. But by that time, to me (after the game with Novopashin I didn't spare a single day more analyzing the resulting position) it was already clear that the move 15 ... Qc7, just like 15 ... Q×b2, did not solve the problems facing Black.

To be frank, at this point I felt really dejected. Could it be that this modest move 15 Nf3 would completely refute Black's plan and bury The Variation, which had endured and suffered so much? The Variation, on which had been spent such masses of effort, time and nervous energy, and with which so few games had yet been played? It is true that with cold reasoning, which had been pushed somewhere into the background, I realized that The Variation could not be completely irreproachable, that it had its deficiencies, and that sooner or later the logic of chess would triumph. But that the refutation should come so soon ... My entire nature protested against this, and, regardless of common sense, the decision was made: to seek again! To seek and seek until I found that fresh idea which in the critical position would instill the despondent black pieces with life, and enable the situation on the board to be assessed differently.

A GLANCE FROM THE SIDE

A large part of the time spent on preparing for the 1961 USSR Championship had to be given over to The Variation. And the impossible came to pass. I recall how then, on the completion of my work, two thoughts stayed with me for a long time. One was of the boundless and inexhaustible nature of chess, which is in no way associated with the astronomical number of moves present in every position. The depth of chess lies in the wide variety of ideas and methods by which any position on the board is characterized, and in those exceptions which are almost always present in any particular piece arrangement.

And the second thought: how fortunate chess was to have the harmonious coexistence between, on the one hand, Steinitz, Capablanca and Botvinnik, who by their games and analyses discovered the general laws and logic of chess, and, on the other hand, Chigorin, Lasker and Simagin, those 'rebels', who sought and found exceptions to these general rules. Complementing one another, these two streams—classical and romantic—have created and will continue to create a form of chess which no man of any era or generation will fully comprehend or exhaust. And, proceeding from such a proximity of rules and exceptions, one should perhaps not be so frightened by the thought that, in opening theory too, the classical schemes of the Queen's Gambit are to be found alongside the at times completely unassessable labyrinths of the Sicilian Defence.

Here I will permit myself one further digression. I trust the reader will not find too far-fetched and bombastic these arguments about questions which are far broader than the analysis of any variation, however complex.

At times a chess player cannot get by merely by working out moves and continuations. Just as an artist painting a picture should from time to time break off from making individual brush strokes, and, taking a step back, take in the complete canvas at a glance, so a chess player, by simply resorting to an abstract approach, is able as if from the side to assess his ideas and calculations, examine the impasse lying in wait for him, and find that turn which is able to lead the position out onto the highway of chess practice. And if one fails to think from time to time over the course of the chess process as a whole, if one does not pay attention to its nuances, to the precedents existing in the assessment of this or that position, then most of the 'concrete' searching will be doomed to failure.

As an analogy, one can recall that today the mathematical apparatus is used by virtually all sciences, but that without philosophy, mathematics itself would have reached an impasse in the study of 'unusual' worlds, concepts and characteristics.

I would say that it was this complex of philosophical thoughts about the essence of my searching which suggested to me a paradoxical idea: why had I been drawn, as if by a magnet, to base the whole of my analysis on the manoeuvre ... Ra7–d7, which I considered the flesh and blood of The Variation, and its basic strategical backbone? Why had I not sought the truth on a different path, even if it were not a parallel one? And it was then that I found a move which, I must admit, at first shocked me in the full sense of the word.

2. The Birth of a Variation

12 ... Qe5

Surely the safety margin in chess can't be so great, I asked myself in astonishment, that in the opening, with one's pieces completely undeveloped, one can make a fourth successive move with the queen, and escape unpunished?

All the accepted—or inborn(?)—classical examples told me that this was a Utopianism. In chess such a thing doesn't, and cannot happen, just as in nature the law of conservation of matter cannot be broken. I was very close to rejecting this move, without bothering to analyze it, and what restrained me, I must confess, was by no means intuition or acute chess perception.

"In the end, this isn't a tournament game, but only analysis", I argued, and perhaps even tried to persuade myself. "So much effort has been devoted to The Variation, that it won't do any harm to waste a little more, before admitting defeat."

But the more that I looked into the idea I had discovered, the more that its paradoxical correctness became apparent. It turns out that 12 ... Qe5 is by no means a loss of time! After all, the black queen is all the same forced to move to e5 after Ne4, and by moving there beforehand it denies White this useful activation of his knight. Also, after 12 ... Qe5, 13 ... Bc5 is threatened, and this deprives White of a significant part of his lead in development. Finally, by returning in case of necessity to c7, the black queen defends d8, and, having moved out of range of a possible attack, economizes on the time required for the manoeuvre ... Ra7-d7.

Now all this appears obvious to me, and hardly worth mentioning, but at the time weeks were spent on grasping these truths, backed by a mass of variations. And when the analysis was complete, I realized this: The Variation was alive!

This work was done, as I recall, in 1960, but I was able to try out my new idea only a year later, in the RSFSR Championship in Omsk, against a local master, **A. Byelov**, an excellent tactician.

After **12 ... Qe5** my opponent continued **13 f×g7 B×g7 14 Nf3 Qc5+ 15 Kh1 Bb7**. I considered this position to be level. However, the further course of the game, although it did not shake this general assessment, showed that the resulting position was so complex and intricate that it required additional analysis.

The game continued:

16 Qd3 (a very interesting move, by which White initiates complications) **16 ... 0-0 17 Rad1 Nc6 18 Ne4 Qe7 19 Neg5 f5 20 Qe3 Rae8 21 c4! h6 22 c×b5 a×b5 23 Nh3 e5! 24 B×b5 Kh8 25 Rc1 Rc8**, and for the pawn Black obtained counterplay in the incredible complications after

26 Rfe1 Nb4 27 Bc4 Be4. The game finally ended in a **draw: 28 Qe2 Rcd8 29 Nf2 B×f3 30 g×f3 Nc6 31 Nd3 Nd4 32 Qg2 Qd6 33 Rg1 Rd7 34 Nf2 Qf6 35 Qh3 Qc6 36 Rc3.**

36 ... N×f3 37 Q×f3 e4 38 Qe3 Bd4 39 Bd5 Qb6 40 Qc1 B×f2 41 Rc6 Be3 42 Qc3+ Qd4 43 Qa3 Rb8 44 Qa6 B×g1 45 R×h6+ Rh7 46 Qg6 Qg7 47 R×h7+ Q×h7 48 Qf6+ Qg7 49 Qh4+, but I gained the feeling that 14 ... Qc5+, which I had analyzed beforehand, was neither obligatory, nor the strongest, and that 14 ... Qe3+ was perhaps to be preferred.

However, White too did not have to force matters. In the initial position, if one can call it that,

he has a number of continuations, which cannot be disregarded.

E.g. 13 Kh1. After this I didn't care for 13 ... g×f6, on account of 14 Bf3 Ra7 15 Re1, and 15 ... Qc7 looks unattractive in view of 16 Nd5 Qd8 17 Qd2, with the threat of 18 Qf4, while the black queen has no other convenient retreat square.

But on 13 Kh1 Black can reply with an immediate 13 ... Ra7, and the threat of 14 ... Rd7 forces White to retreat his knight from its central square. Black is not likely to be smashed by such tactics.

This was confirmed, incidentally, by the game Estrin–Korzin (Moscow 1961): 14 Qd3 (a dubious move; *14 f×g7 B×g7 15 Nf3* is preferable) 14 ... Rd7 15 Nf3 Q×f6 16 Qe3 Bd6 17 Ne4 Qf4 18 N×d6+ Q×d6 19 Ne5 Re7! 20 Rad1 Qc7, and Black repelled the attack, while maintaining his material advantage: 21 Qg3 0-0 22 Bd3 f6 23 B×h7+ K×h7 24 Qh4+ Kg8 25 Ng6 Ree8! 26 Qh8+ Kf7 27 R×f6+ K×f6.

I also had to study energetic variations of the type 13 Re1 Q×f6 14 Bf3 Ra7 15 Nd5 Qd8 16 Nf5 Bc5+ 17 Kh1 0-0, but nothing definite for White emerged.

The continuation which caused me the most concern was 13 Bf3 Ra7 14 Nc6!? (if *14 Ne4, then 14 ... Rd7 15 c3 g×f6*, and Black has nothing to fear; the game Ortega–Polugayevsky, Havana 1962, went *14 Re1 Q×f6*, and *15 Bc6+?*, as played by White, led to his rapid defeat: *15 ... N×c6 16 N×c6 Rd7 17 Nd5 Bc5+ 18 Kh1 Qh4 19 Qf3 0-0 20 Re4 Qh6*, and White's pieces were left hanging. After *21 Nf4 Bb7 22 Ne5 B×e4 23 Q×e4 Rd4* he resigned), and I did not care for 14 ... N×c6 15 B×c6+ Bd7 16 B×d7+ R×d7 17 Qf3. Naturally, I therefore considered 14 ... Qc5+ 15 Kh1 Rd7.

If 15 ... N×c6, then 16 Ne4 Qb6 (equally bad is *16 ... Qd4 17 Nd6+!! Q×d6 18 f×g7* and wins, or *16 ... Qe5 17 f×g7 B×g7 18 Nd6+ Ke7 19 B×c6 Q×d6 20 R×f7+*) 17 f×g7 B×g7 18 Nd6+ Ke7 19 B×c6, and after 19 ... f5 20 N×f5+ e×f5 21 Re1+ Kf7 22 Qd5+

Kg6 23 Qd6+ White gains a decisive attack, since 23 ... Bf6 fails to 24 Be8+, while on 19 ... f6 the quiet 20 N×c8+ R×c8 21 Bf3 is sufficient, with an overwhelming position for White, since the black king is stuck in the centre; in this last variation there is an interesting but unclear continuation of the attack by 20 Nf5+ e×f5 21 Qd5.

16 N×b8!! R×d1 17 Ra×d1 (*17 Bc6+? Q×c6 18 N×c6 R×a1 19 R×a1 g×f6*, with advantage to Black).

18 Bc6+ is threatened, and therefore 17 ... g×f6 is practically forced, when White replies 18 Ne4.

Black is faced with a dilemma: where is he to move his queen? 18 ... Qe5 loses to 19 Nc6, while 18 ... Qb6 meets with a brilliant refutation—19 N×f6+ Ke7 20 Bh5!—and if 20 ... Q×b8, then 21 Ng8+ R×g8 22 R×f7+ Ke8 23 Rg7 mate, while on 20 ... Bg7 or 20 ... Bh6 White continues 21 Nc6+!!, diverting the queen from the defence of d8. After 21 ... Q×c6 Black is mated by 22 Ng8+ Kf8 23 R×f7+ K×g8 24 Rd8, while after 21 ... Kf8 (following *20 ... Bh6*), by 22 Rd8+ Kg7 23 Ne8+ R×e8 24 R×f7+ Kg8 25 R×e8. A fantastic finish!

On 18 ... Q×c2, 19 Rc1 concludes the game, and on 18 ... Qc4—19 b3.

I must ask the reader to believe that all these unusually beautiful variations were neatly written down in one of my notebooks, dated 1960, when I can say without exaggeration that I studied literally day and night the new problems which constantly emerged. It was bound to happen that, seven years later in the game Parr-Klibor (West Germany 1967), the move 13 Bf3 occurred, with all the 'details' given above! The game reached the position shown in the diagram, when Black chose 18 ... Qb6 19 N×f6+ Ke7 20 Bh5, and only here was a deviation made—20 ... Qc5, but it made essentially no difference: 21 Nc6+! led to his immediate capitulation.

Does this mean that I was bluffing? Being fully aware that Black loses by force, did I nevertheless continue to adopt The Variation, hoping for a mistake by my opponent? A thousand times no! In the depths of the maze into which 13 Bf3 had led me, I nevertheless found a narrow saving path: in the position in that same diagram there is one and only one move that comes to Black's rescue: 18 ... Qf5!.

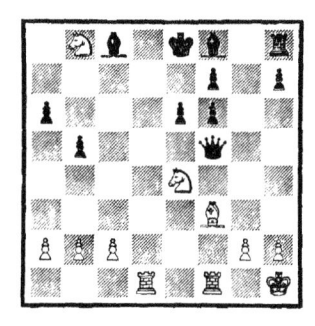

Now nothing is gained by 19 Nd6+ B×d6 20 Bc6+ Ke7 21 R×f5 e×f5, when Black stands well, while on 19 g4 he replies 19 ... Qf4. Regaining the sacrificed queen by 19 N×f6+ Q×f6 20 Bc6+ Ke7 21 R×f6 K×f6 leads apparently to an equal ending: 22 Nd7+ Ke7 23 N×f8 R×f8, or 22 ... B×d7 23 R×d7 Be7 24 Be4 (*24 Ra7 Rd8*) 24 ... h6

25 Bd3 Rd8. Although this variation, which is close to a draw, did not completely impress me, on finding it then, in 1960, I accepted it as a first approximation. The main thing was that I had managed to avoid the danger of a forced loss, and of course I hoped to return again to the move 13 Bf3 to seek new defensive resources for Black.

But it so happened that other continuations in The Variation diverted my attention, and this work was successfully carried out by the Soviet master G. Fridstein, who in 1971 found the strongest continuation for Black, and demonstrated the complete harmlessness of the move 13 Bf3. He established that after 13 ... Ra7 14 Nc6 Black should go in for 14 ... N×c6 15 B×c6+ Bd7 16 B×d7+ R×d7, and in the event of 17 Qf3 reply not 17 ... Bc5+ 18 Kh1 0-0 19 Ne4, which gives White the advantage, but 17 ... Bd6!.

An important finesse. Black keeps the check in reserve, and here are the variations considered by Fridstein:

A. 18 g3 (*18 Qa8+ Bb8*) 18 ... Q×f6 19 Qa8+ Qd8 20 Q×a6 b4 21 Ne4 0-0. This position was tested in the game Mariotti–Ribli (Manila 1976): after 22 Qb5 Be7! 23 c4 Rd4 24 Nf2 Qa8 25 b3 Rfd8 26 Qh5 Bf6 Black stood better.

B. 18 Qh3 b4! (if Black had first given check—*17 ... Bc5+*, then after *18 Kh1 Bd6 19 Qh3* the move *19 ... b4* would have been refuted by the surprising rejoinder *20 Nd5!*, when *20 ... Q×d5* fails to *21 f×g7* and *22 Q×h7*) 19 f×g7 (now *19 Nd5* does not work, since after the capture of the knight Black has a check with his queen at d4) 19 ... Rg8 20 Q×h7 Q×h2+ 21 Q×h2 B×h2+ 22 K×h2 b×c3. These variations are favourable for Black.

C. Black has more difficult problems after 18 Ne4, but even in this case, by continuing 18 ... Q×h2+ 19 Kf2 Qe5! he can be satisfied with his position. E.g. 20 g3 (after *20 f×g7 Bc5+! 21 Ke2 Rg8* the advantage is with Black; he threatens *... f7-f5*) 20 ... 0-0. In this sharp position each side has his trumps.

But let us go back ten years.

At that time, at the cost of many weeks of analysis, I had succeeded in reinforcing The Variation, which had seemed on the point of collapse. It appeared that all was quiet on the Western front, but danger, as it turned out, was already approaching from another side.

A TRAP

Yes, I remember the relief I experienced, and the happy thought which was constantly with me: The Variation was alive! But the period of 'well-being' did not last long. In 1961 new complications began, and by theorists The Variation was again numbered among the ill, and if not fatally, then extremely seriously.

In January 1961, in the 8th round of the Championship of the Country, I met David Bronstein, possibly the most resourceful grandmaster in the world. The first few moves of the game immediately took me rather by surprise: Bronstein, who had usually avoided this opening, suddenly gave me the opportunity to play

2. The Birth of a Variation

The Variation. Naturally I couldn't refuse the challenge, otherwise for a long time I would have reproached myself for my cowardice and for not sticking to my principles. And so, after quickly playing the 'introduction'—**1 e4 c5 2 Nf3 d6 3 d4 c×d4 4 N×d4 Nf6 5 Nc3 a6 6 Bg5 e6 7 f4 b5 8 e5 d×e5 9 f×e5 Qc7 10 e×f6 Qe5+ 11 Be2 Q×g5**, Bronstein thought for some 30-40 seconds, gave me a rather crafty glance, and slowly moved his queen to d3. Following this he got up from the board, and his whole appearance said (or possibly this was how I interpreted for myself the resulting situation): "Now try and work out that little lot!"

Bronstein had hit the nail on the head! However much I had analyzed The Variation in the past, and whatever the possibilities for White I had considered, for some strange reason the move 12 Qd3 had not come within the range of my searching. Nowadays it seems simple, even obvious, but at the time, when only a first approximation to the truth was being made, everything seemed far from clear.

Jumping ahead, I should mention that, after the game, Bronstein said that the idea of the move did not belong to him, but to his old friend Kh. Muchnik, together with whom Bronstein used to constantly examine the topical opening systems which interested him.

But let us return to the game. When the move **12 Qd3** appeared on the board, I immediately realized that I had been 'caught': I was too well familiar with the manner of my opponent's preparation for it to be otherwise. I had to literally force myself out of a minute's bemusement, and to concentrate fully. I recall how I tried to assume a calm expression, and by my entire appearance demonstrate that nothing extraordinary had happened. Nevertheless, I consider it unlikely that this outward impassivity could have deceived Bronstein, with all his experience....

At the board my study of the new problems which had unexpectedly arisen did not begin, strangely enough, with the calculation of various continuations, but with a thought which was ... abstract, but essential for my spiritual peace of mind. It can be formulated roughly as follows: "How much time have I spent on this one single Variation, and on how many occasions have I found a defence for Black! It would simply be unjust if all this work were in vain! Something will also turn up against 12 Qd3. I must search, search!"

Having thus 'calmed' myself—incidentally, the time spent on this was less than it takes to read these lines—I began to work through the specific variations. The idea of 12 Qd3 was perfectly clear: to play Ne4, if Black should not prevent it, but in particular—to prepare Q-side castling. In this case the threats along the 'd' file would appear much more quickly, and would be much more dangerous, than after K-side castling.

I do not remember, unfortunately, how long I spent at the time in search of a plan. On the other hand, I will never forget how after the game the 'computing machine', as I was sometimes called in those days, felt as though for a long time it had been working under great stress, for which it had not at all been prepared....

Be that as it may, but the reply was **12 ... Qh4+**. It is difficult to penetrate into such a 'supernatural' field of chess as intuition, but for some reason I felt firmly convinced that if Bronstein had in fact examined this check beforehand, it would only have been highly superficially, in passing. By that time it was clear to me that I would have to capture the pawn on f6, but in whose favour was the opening of the long white diagonal? It could hardly be hoped that the rook at h1 would fall victim to Black's white-squared bishop, but nevertheless the check on h4 was made!

Now, with the benefit of hindsight, I realize that my brain was so accustomed to The Variation, and I believed so sincerely, one might even say religiously, in its viability, that at the board I managed to discover a path along which dangers and pitfalls threatened not only Black, but also White.

Our game continued as follows:

13 g3 Q×f6 14 Qe4

Here it was Bronstein's turn to think at length over his move, but it nevertheless proved to be a poor one, and Black, after completely neutralizing White's pressure, gained a slight advantage.

14 ... Ra7 15 Rf1 Qg6!

The beginning of a tactical operation, on which Black's whole defence is founded. White assumed that forcing the black rook off the back rank would enable him to create serious threats, but in reply to **16 Qf4 Nd7 17 Nc6** there followed **17 ... e5!**.

And suddenly the harmony became apparent among the black pieces (even those as widely-separated as the queen at g6 and the rook at a7), fulfilling a single common aim: control over the centre and the defence of their king. Incidentally, it is on this harmony of Black's pieces, which gradually emerges as if on a photographic print, and on their amazing co-ordination, that the entire Variation as a whole is based.

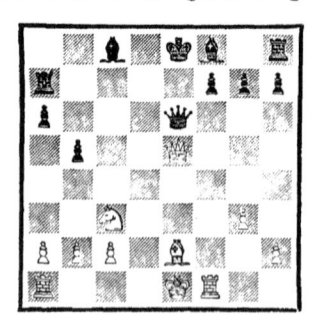

18 N×e5 N×e5 19 Q×e5+ Qe6

and White has nothing better than to exchange queens, since 20 Qb8 would be answered by 20 ... Bc5, then 21 ... 0-0, and the white queen would soon feel like a fish out of water.

20 Q×e6+ B×e6 21 0-0-0 Be7 22 Nd5 Bg5+ 23 Kb1 0-0 24 h4 Bd8 25 Nf4 Bc8, and the black bishops, although they have retreated onto the back rank, will sooner or later make their presence felt. There is no disputing Black's persistent, although minimal advantage.

26 Bf3 g6 27 Bd5

Simultaneously with this move Bronstein offered a **draw**, which, to the surprise of the spectators and the other competitors, was accepted. Of course, Black can play for the set-up ... Kg7, ... Bf5, ... Bc7–b8 and ... Rc8, which would give him the initiative. But, firstly, I had used up a tremendous amount of effort on the opening stage of the game, and secondly, the maximum possible satisfaction (creative, not competitive) from the game had already been obtained. After all, my 'brainchild' had survived yet another test!

After the game, David Ionovich was quite seriously upset. And this was not surprising, because he had caught his opponent in a prepared variation, but had failed to win the game, and in addition had used up his innovation! "I trusted Muchnik", Bronstein grieved, "but 12 Qd3 doesn't win!"

About my happiness at that moment I have already spoken, but gradually, on the way to the hotel, it began to be replaced by uneasiness. The night was spent at the chess board: had 12 Qd3 been refuted, or was this move in fact the refutation of The Variation? Or perhaps neither the one nor the other? It is true that, instead of 14 Qe4, Bronstein could have made the move which at the board I was most afraid of—14 Rf1. Then on 14 ... Qg6 White has the reply 15 Qf3, and none of the variations that I examined was acceptable for Black.

I had to switch to the alternative queen move—14 ... Qe5. On 15 0-0-0 Black now has 15 ... Bc5, and whatever White plays, for instance 16 Nd×b5 or 16 N×e6, Black has an intermediate check with his queen at e3.

And I calmed down.

But then, roughly a day later, after the following round, I again began to have doubts. All the time Black was balancing on the very edge of the abyss. It only required the white king to stand slightly to one side—at b1, and Black could resign. Or if White were to find some intermediate move, catastrophe would be inevitable. A presentiment of danger in this position tormented me, and would not leave me in peace. On the one hand everything seemed all right, but on the other....

In this way some six months went by. The time came for me to prepare for a new USSR Championship, the second in that year. Together with M. Yudovich (Junior) I analyzed several times the continuation 12 Qd3, did not find anything for Black to be afraid of, and at that set off for Baku...

MEMORANDUM FROM MOSCOW

Literally only a couple of rounds had passed, and, after the November slush of their home towns, the competitors in the Championship had not yet had time to become accustomed to the warmth of the Caspian Sea, when I received a note from Moscow from Mikhail Yudovich. After a few warm words of introduction, dictated by sympathy, it was shown in an extremely accurate and scrupulous analysis that in the above variation after 15 ... Bc5 White wins by force! And although, apart from us two, no one then knew about this, it is not at all difficult to imagine my feelings at that moment.

Yudovich, it turned out, had found that after 16 N×e6 Qe3+ White replies 17 Rd2!!, when Black is lost. On 17 ... Q×d3 there follows 18 Nc7+ Kd8 19 R×d3+ K×c7 20 R×f7+, and both after 20 ... Kb6 21 b4! B×b4 22 Nd5+

Ka5 (also bad is *22 ... Kc5 23 N×b4 K×b4 24 Bf3*, with a big material advantage) 23 Rff3!, with the threat of mate on a3, and after 20 ... Nd7 21 Bg4 Rd8 22 Ne4! Bf8 23 Ng5, Black cannot save the game.

All this is also possible with the white king at b1, i.e. in the event of 17 Kb1, and not 17 Rd2. But in the variation 20 ... Bd7 21 Bg4 Rf8 the strength of White's 17th move is disclosed. He can play simply 22 R×g7, without having to worry about back-rank checks—22 ... Rf1+ 23 Kd2. If the white king were at b1, after the forced 23 Nd1 Bd6! Black would beat off the attack, while maintaining his material advantage. But here 23 ... Bd6 fails to 24 Ne4!.

If on the other hand Black plays 21 ... Rd8, then White attacks in similar fashion to that given above: 22 Ne4 Bf8 (on *22 ... Bb6* White has the calm reply *23 R×g7*, and how Black can free himself is not apparent) 23 Ng5.

I tested and retested most painstakingly the analysis in my friend's letter, and realized that The Variation had been floored. The move 15 ... Bc5 wasn't playable, and this meant that Black had once again to seek an answer to Hamlet's eternal question: "To be or not to be?" I must admit that, at the start of the 1961 USSR Championship in Baku, I was certainly no happier as a result of this.

I repeat: no one knew about this, and for the time being I had to battle against an unseen opponent. But imminent questions do not hover about for long, and the opponent could at any time become a quite specific person. And besides, in general I did not have the moral right to adopt The Variation, relying merely on my opponent's possible ignorance. What was needed, indeed essential, was spiritual confidence, but this could be generated only out of a host of variations on the board.

Fate granted me something of a postponement. In the Championship only once did I have to uphold The Variation, against that brilliant tactician Rashid Nezhmetdinov, but there it was a quite different line that was tested.

But after the tournament I had ample time for analysis. Once more—for the umpteenth time!—I began studying the position after 12 Qd3. I worked through—in great detail—Black's various replies. In the end I chose what seemed to be the least evil, and settled on 12 ... Qh4+ 13 g3 Q×f6 14 Rf1 Qe5 15 0-0-0 Ra7, although Black's position after 16 Nf3 did not greatly impress me. The account of this analysis will be given a little later, but now I wish to confess that it was after this enormous amount of work, that I began to be seized more and more with a feeling of apathy towards The Variation.

The point was that, apart from the highly unpleasant Bronstein–Muchnik move 12 Qd3, misfortune had also stolen up on The Variation from another side. Grandmaster V. Simagin, a highly original and non-routine thinker, proposed two moves earlier the highly interesting 10 Qe2!?, with the idea of maintaining the forepost at e5, quickly castling Q-side, and mounting an attack on the black king which is stuck in the centre.

To wage war on two fronts, to find a defence simultaneously against two, equally dangerous systems, was a task that at the time was beyond me. I was lacking both in energy, and in peace of mind. While working on one move, I could not avoid thinking that the labour might be in vain, since it was possible that a defence wouldn't be found against the other. And suddenly it began to appear to me that The Variation had contracted radiculitis: the pain would ease in one place, only to appear the following day in another. It was then that the idea came to me of abandoning The Variation....

"Enough! I'm tired of this eternal searching, of this constant anticipation of further unpleasant surprises! It's time to decide!"

After the USSR Championship in Baku, from inertia I played it again in two 1962 games, against Ortega in Cuba and against Nikitin in the Championship of the 'Burevestnik' club, and that's all.

"My thanks to you, Variation. I don't condemn you for your betrayal, and I bid you farewell!"

And it was just as well that this happened! At that point, when disillusionment had overtaken me, The Variation was suddenly taken up by a number of players. It began to be met in every tournament of any rank, and to fill the pages of magazines and bulletins. The Variation had become fashionable!

On the one hand, such an unspoken general recognition flattered my self-esteem—after all, for three long years, essentially I alone had constantly upheld The Variation for Black. But on the other hand it provoked a mixture of feelings of offence and bewilderment. It would have been one thing to play The Variation earlier, when it consisted purely of blank pages, and when every game represented 'a venture into the unknown'. But now, when such difficult experiences had befallen Black...!

This was the reason for my bewilderment. The offence I felt was for The Variation, which one new player after another would play rather light-heartedly, without going carefully into the already-published examples, comments and analyses, without taking the trouble to investigate this unusual opening scheme which did not yield to general assessments, and as a result would suffer one crushing defeat after another. Contrary to the voice of reason, I took each such defeat to be a personal failure, and my heart sank each time I saw in print a new 20–25 move game, with the laconic 'Black resigns' at the end.

Many a time the thought flashed through my mind: shouldn't I once again throw myself into the battle, and put literally all my efforts into rehabilitating The Variation, to 'cleaning up' its badly damaged reputation? But the strength was no longer there, and my impulsive decision to abandon The Variation was confirmed roughly as follows:

"Let Black go on suffering defeats, only not in 'my' Variation, but in someone else's. I have had enough!"

THE RETURN

And for many years I didn't 'touch' The Variation at all, either in analysis, or in practice. Even now I don't know whether I would ever have returned to it, had it not been for the conversation with Botvinnik given at the very beginning of this book. Having merely become firmly convinced that it was about The Variation that I would write, I began examining old games, both my own and other players', and started lingering over what were apparently thoroughly-studied positions, checking once again things which had been tested many times. And a miracle occurred: after an interval of ten years The Variation suddenly took on for me a new aspect, and appeared in a completely different light. A sensation, hidden in the depths of my emotional memory, was suddenly revived: what if... What if for me The Variation is not dead? If The Variation is alive?!

It was as if a dam had burst. To my relief, I began to discover that lines, of which formerly I had been so afraid, were in general perfectly feasible, and that far from the last word on them had been said. Feverishly, without a board, I worked from memory through the dozens of games that had been played in the intervening years... It appeared that the majority of them merely repeated what had gone before, or else were not of great importance. So that couldn't I search for this last word myself?!

My searching began in the first instance around the move 12 Qd3. To be honest, to some extent I had to 'overcome' myself, and to pluck up courage, so as after an interval of so many years to begin stirring up the past, and try to solve the eternal dilemma: what to do?

Back in 1961, after the USSR Championship in Baku, I had attempted in this position

to play differently, and instead of 12 ... Qh4+ tried various other continuations. These were the possibilities that I checked at that time:

A. 12 ... Nd7? This move is bad in view of the virtually forced 13 Qf3 Ra7 14 Ne4 Qe5 (no better is *14 ... Qd5 15 Rd1 Bb7 16 f×g7 B×g7 17 Nf5!*; both white knights are taboo in view of the check at d6, and in any case Black loses material) 15 Nc6 Q×b2 16 Rd1 Rc7 17 f×g7 Q×g7 (not *17 ... B×g7 18 Nd6+, and mate next move*) 18 R×d7!. White exploits his lead in development by combinative means. Neither 18 ... B×d7, nor 18 ... R×d7, nor 18 ... R×c6 is possible, on account of 19 Nf6+, when Black has to give up his queen, while after 18 ... K×d7 White has the decisive 19 Nf6+ Kd6 20 Ne8+.

B. 12 ... g×f6?!. An interesting game Bobkov-Vitolinsh (USSR Championship Semi-Final, Riga 1962) continued: 13 Ne4 Qe5 14 0-0-0?!, and after 14 ... Be7 15 Nf3 Qf4+ (gaining a very important tempo for the defence, and thereby succeeding in blocking the main avenue of attack—the 'd' file) 16 Kb1 Bb7 17 Nc5 Bd5 18 Nb3 Nc6 Black gradually repulsed the attack while keeping his extra pawn.

However, it was promptly established that, instead of castling Q-side, at the cost of another pawn White could gain a probably irresistible attack: 14 Nf3 Q×b2 15 0-0! f5 (essential, so as to assure the queen of the square f6, from where it can take part in the defence, in particular of d8; on *15 ... Be7*, for instance, decisive is *16 a4!*, with the terrible threats of *17 a×b5* and *17 Rfb1*, trapping the queen) 16 Nd6+ B×d6 17 Q×d6 Qf6 (if *17 ... Nd7, then 18 Nd4*, with numerous threats: *19 Bf3, 19 Nc6* and *19 N×e6*), and after the continuation suggested by Boleslavsky, 18 a4 Qe7 19 Qg3, Black's position is unenviable: his king is forced to live out its days in the centre.

In a later game Matulovic-Ermenkov (Sombor 1972) White continued the attack differently, with 18 Nd4, and on 18 ... Nd7 (if *18 ... Qe7*, then, as shown by Velimirovic, *19 Qe5 f6 20 Bh5+ Kf8 21*

Qe3 Rg8 22 Rae1, and *23 N×f5*, with a subsequent mate at e8, is very difficult to parry) he played 19 Bf3 Ra7 20 Bc6, when White won easily, as there is no defence against the simultaneous threats of N×f5, Rad1 and Qb8 etc.

C. 12 ... Ra7. At first I had some hopes of this move, but soon it had to be rejected. White continues 13 Ne4 Qe5 14 0-0-0 Rd7 15 Qc3.

15 Qg3 Q×g3 16 h×g3 Bb7 has also occurred in practice; in the game Ribli-Szabó, Hungarian Championship 1967/68, White sacrificed a piece by 17 N×e6 f×e6 18 R×d7 K×d7!, but Black beat off the attack—19 f×g7 B×g7 20 Nc5+ Kc6 21 Rh5 Kb6 22 N×e6 Re8, and went on to win. Also of great interest for Black is the idea employed by Fischer in a game with Minic, Skopje 1967: 15 ... g×f6 16 Q×e5 f×e5 17 Nf6+ Ke7 18 N×d7 B×d7 19 Nb3 Bc6! 20 Bf3 e4 21 Be2 Nd7, and it is clear that Black's strong central pawns and two bishops are more than sufficient compensation for his slight material deficit. It is interesting to follow how, without any apparent effort, Black increases his advantage: 22 Na5 Ba8 23 Rhf1 f5 24 Kb1 Bh6 25 a4 b×a4 26 Rd4 a3 27 Rfd1 Nf6, and the threat of ... f4-f3, plus the weakness of White's c2, make Black's position clearly preferable.

15 ... Bb7

15 ... Q×e4 is bad on account of 16 Q×c8+ Rd8 17 Q×d8+! K×d8 18 N×e6++ Kc8 19 Rd8+ Kb7 20 Bf3 Q×f3 21 g×f3 f×e6 22 f7, and White won easily (Prodanov-Ayansky, Bulgarian Championship 1965) while after 15 ... Qc7 16 N×b5 a×b5 17 f×g7 Q×c3 18 g×f8=Q+ K×f8 19 N×c3 Black is quite simply a pawn down with an inferior position (Turunen-Teirlinck, Groningen 1968/69).

16 N×b5

This thematic blow enables White to win a pawn; weaker is 16 Bf3 g×f6 17 N×f6+ Q×f6 18 B×b7 Bh6+ 19 Kb1 0-0, and Black is all right; he can also play 16 ... b4 17 Qd3 g×f6 18 Rhe1 Be7 19 Ng3 Qf4+ 20 Kb1 B×f3 21 g×f3 0-0, and after a complicated struggle the correspondence game Gora-Novak, Czechoslovakia 1973, ended in a draw.

16 ... Q×c3 The temptation to accept the 'Greek gift' and capture the 'Trojan horse'—16 ... Q×e4, cost Black dearly in the game Browne-Osban, USA Open Championship 1971: 17 f×g7 Rg8 18 Nc7+ Kd8 19 g×f8=Q+ R×f8 20 N×a6, and there is no arguing with White's three passed pawns, especially in view of the vulnerable position of the black king with heavy pieces on the board.

17 Nb×c3 R×d1+ 18 R×d1 g×f6 19 N×f6+ Ke7 20 Nfe4 f5, and for the pawn (*21 Nc5 B×g2 22 N×a6*) Black, in the opinion of A. Matsukevich, has some counter-play.

But, although it may seem strange, in my analysis of 12 ... Ra7 I paid little attention to these complicated variations, since it was obvious that after 12 ... Ra7 13 Ne4 Qe5 White could play much more simply—14 0-0! (or *14 Nf3* immediately), and in the event of 14 ... Rd7 15 Nf3 Q×b2 16 Qe3 a position is reached with which we are already familiar (arising from the move order *12 0-0 Ra7 13 Qd3 Rd7 14 Ne4 Qe5 15 Nf6*), and which I considered completely unacceptable for Black. It was for this reason, that the position arises literally after only 2-3 moves, and hat Black cannot avoid it, that there was simply no point in making a detailed analysis of 12 ... Ra7.

Thus the range of possibilities had been markedly reduced. A natural and apparently logical continuation suggested itself:

D. 12 ... Bb7. It should be mentioned that I had analyzed this bishop move very thoroughly ten years earlier. However, this analysis did not see the light of day, and all this time lay neatly written in a notebook. The point was that then, after the 1961 Championship of the Country, I had given a categorical verdict on the bishop move: it's no good! And I must admit that I was pretty astonished when, first in a monograph by A. Matsukevich, and then in a monograph by I. Boleslavsky published in East Germany, I saw that they had given the move 12 ... Bb7 a positive assessment. They based their opinion on the following variations:

13 Bf3 B×f3 14 Q×f3 Ra7 15 Ne4 Qe5 16 0-0-0 Rd7 17 Rhf1 g6! (but not *17 ... R×d4 18 f×g7 R×d1+ 19 R×d1 Q×g7 20 Nf6+ Ke7 21 Rf1! Kd8 ɐ22 Qb7 Bd6 23 Rd1 Q×f6 24 Q×b8+ Ke7 25 Q×d6+ Ke8 26 Q×a6*, and White wins; if on his 18th move Black tries *18 ... B×g7*, then *19 R×d4 Q×d4 20 c3 Qd7 21 Qg3* —attacking two pieces—*21 ... f5 22 Nc5 Qa7 23 N×e6*, with a swiftly decisive attack), and they consider that White has no advantage, despite the strong pawn at f6, which has penetrated into the black position like a wedge. There can follow, according to Boleslavsky, 18 c3 Bh6+ 19 Kb1 0-0 20 g4 Rfd8 21 h4 b4, with a double-edged game.

All this looks convincing enough, but nevertheless a whole series of questions arise on the way. Why should White play 17 Rhf1, which is not altogether logical in this position, since to develop his king's bishop Black will all the same play ... g7-g6, when White's rook at f1 will be rather stupidly blocked by his own pawn at f6? Instead of this, White has several other ways of maintaining his initiative.

For instance, 17 c3, or even better, 17 Nb3. All the same Black has nothing better than 17 ... g6, but then comes 18 Kb1, and White retains all the advantages of his position: he has control of c5, and on 18 ... Bh6 there can follow 19 R×d7 N×d7 20 Rd1, when White's position is highly menacing. But these are minor problems.

The real trouble is that several moves earlier, after 12 ... Bb7 13 Bf3 B×f3 14 Q×f3 Ra7, White has an obvious move, not mentioned by the theorists: 15 Nc6!, when with a clear conscience Black can already resign. Thus on 15 ... Rb7 (with the idea after *16 N×b8* of playing not *16 ... R×b8 17 Qc6+*, but *16 ... Qe5+*) White replies 16 Rd1! (however, *16 Ne4* is also suggficient) 16 ... Nd7 (there is nothing else) 17 Ne4 Qg6 (*18 f×g7* was threatened, and therefore Black must defend g7, so as not to 'overload' his bishop, which is occupied with guarding d6) 18 f×g7 Q×g7 19 Nf6+! Q×f6 20 Q×f6 and 21 Rd8 mate. There remains 15 ... N×c6 16 Q×c6+ Rd7 17 Rd1 Qe5+, but then 18 Ne4! Qc7 19 Q×a6, and the win for White is merely a matter of time.

And so, this exhausted all the possibilities for Black which were in the slightest degree logical on his 12th move. All were unsatisfactory. And, willy-nilly applying to chess the saying 'All roads lead to Rome', I had to return to that game with Bronstein, in which the move 12 Qd3 first saw the light of day. In the end it became clear that the idea of capturing the pawn on f6 with the queen was correct: this 'precocious infantryman' had already caused the black king too much trouble in combination with the attack on the 'd' file! But if the idea was correct, and the problem facing Black was nevertheless unsolved, it meant that the errors in the execution of this plan had to be found....

And, like an electrician searching for a fault in a circuit, I began testing section by section, move by move, in the play for both White and Black after 12 ... Qh4+ 13 g3 Q×f6 14 Rf1!.

Now on 14 ... Qg6, as I have already remarked, very unpleasant for Black is 15 Qf3 Ra7 16 Nc6, when on 16 ... Bb7 there follows 17 Bd3, and if 17 ... B×c6, then 18 Qe3. Therefore I concentrated all my attention on 14 ... Qe5, and tried to find a defence against 15 0-0-0.

A number of moves were rejected straight away. Thus 15 ... Be7 is refuted by 16 Qf3, with an attack on the rook at a8 and the pawn at f7. For the same reason, neither the knight nor the bishop can be developed at d7, 15 ... Bb7 fails to the thematic sacrifice 16 N×e6! (but not *16 Nd×b5? Qg5+ 14 Kb1 a×b5*), while 15 ... Bc5 is unfortunately ruled out by the analysis of M. Yudovich given above. There remained only 15 ... Ra7, avoiding the double attack after Qf3, and securely defending f7.

At first I saw to my relief that here the troublesome pseudo-sacrifice 16 N×e6 becomes a real sacrifice, on account of 16 ... Rd7, and does not bring White any joy. On 16 Nd×b5, Black has the following rather elegant defence: 16 ... Rd7 17 Qc4 Bc5! 18 Ne4 Be3+ 19 Kb1 R×d1+ 20 R×d1 0-0, and if 21 Nbd6, then 21 ... Bd7, and after completing his development, Black, thanks to his two bishops and open files on the Q-side, can hope for more than a draw.

In the event of 16 Nf3 I at first decided to content myself with 16 ... Qc7, and if 17 Qd4, then 17 ... Nc6 18 Qg4 h5! followed by 19 ... g6, holding the position. While on 17 Ng5 (or *17 Ne5*) I planned 17 ... Be7 18 N×f7 0-0, when Black at least is still alive!

However, I was left with a certain feeling of dissatisfaction, and a little later, on closer examination, the situation suddenly clarified: one only has to continue this last variation for a few more moves, and Black begins to feel uncomfortable. For example, 19 Nd6 Rd8 20 Nce4 Nc6 21 Qf3 Ne5 22 Qe3, with a clear advantage. In this and similar lines White's superiority lies not in a dashing attack on the king, but in his solid positional pressure and in the complete disharmony among the black pieces, which in addition are very cramped. If after 19 Nd6 Black should try to weaken White's pressure down the 'f' file by 19 ... R×f1, then 20 B×f1, with a big positional advantage—20 ... Bd7 21 Bh3 Nc6 22 Qe3!.

Thus, here too I was unable to find an equalizing line.

Could it be that the circle had closed and there was no way out?

I should remind the reader that all this was analyzed back in 1961/62. And then one memorable evening many years later, during my regular wanderings through the labyrinths of The Variation, it suddenly dawned on me: the pawn standing at g3 deprives the black queen of the valuable square f4! And in a game with that splendid tactician **Ljubomir Ljubojevic** in the 1973 international tournament at Hilversum, I now boldly went in for the entire Variation, being aware of the error found in the execution of the correct idea.

It turns out that after **12 Qd3** one should not give an intermediate check at h4, but immediately capture the pawn—**12 ... Q×f6**. Then after **13 Rf1 Qe5**

14 0-0-0 Ra7 15 Nf3 Black now has the intermediate **15 ... Qf4+** (that white pawn is at g2!) **16 Kb1**, and **16 ... Rd7**, enabling him to escape from all his troubles!

Such is the unusual logic of chess. I am convinced that if the position after White's 12th move were shown to a beginner, he would without thinking play **12 ... Q×f6**. Black in fact wins a pawn, and in doing so does not spoil his pawn formation! But for us to reach this truth, more than ten years, alas, was required!

Of course, at the board Ljubojevic foresaw the intermediate check at f4, and so instead of castling long played **14 Rd1**. This move is not without its dangers for Black, but I think it will be agreed that the fact that White's king has remained in the centre cannot help him in developing his initiative against his black opposite number. After **14 ... Ra7 15 Nf3 Qc7 16 Ne5 Be7** (16 ... f5 fails to 17 Bh5+ g6 18 N×g6 h×g6 19 B×g6+ Ke7 20 Qe3, and White wins, since 20 ... Kf6 is decisively met by 21 B×f5, Lipiridi–Sanakoyev, Semi-Final RSFSR Championship, Rostov-on-Don 1961, with the inclusion of the moves 12 ... Qh4+ 13 g3) **17 N×f7 0-0**

the variations given above are no longer so strong.

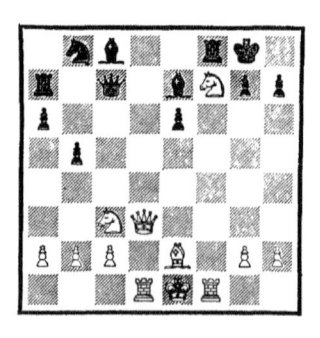

White continued **18 Nd6**, and after **18 ... R×f1+ 19 K×f1 Bd7 20 Nce4 Nc6** Black was out of danger. The game continued **21 g3 Nd8 22 c4 b×c4 23 Q×c4 Q×c4 24 B×c4 Nf7**, when Black maintained the balance. In a subsequent commentary on this game, Ljubojevic suggested for Black, instead of 17 ... 0-0, the highly interesting possibility of 17 ... Q×h2!? (another reason why Black shouldn't give the queen check at h4 on move 12!). Now 18 N×h8 fails to 18 ... Bh4+ 19 Kd2 Rd7, while on 18 g3 Ljubojevic recommends 18 ... 0-0, and in the event of 19 Qf3 (with the threat of 20 Rh1)—19 ... Bb7 20 Qe3 R×f7!, when for the exchange Black obtains two pawns and the better position.

Here I must break to some extent the chronological order of my account.

The point is that, two years after our game, Ljubojevic once again had White against The Variation, this time in a game with Mecking in the tournament at Las Palmas. The Yugoslav chose the continuation 12 Qd3, but in reply to 12 ... Q×f6 13 Rf1 Qe5, unexpectedly played 14 0-0-0, from which he had refrained in the game with me.

There followed **14 ... Ra7 15 Nf3 Qf4+ 16 Nd2 Qe5**, and White made a tacit offer of a draw—**17 Nf3 Qf4+ 18**

Nd2. But Mecking decided to try for more, avoided the repetition of moves—18 ... Qd6?! 19 Qf3 Qc6 20 Nde4, and jauntily played 20 ... b4, thinking that he had seized the initiative. Later, to my question as to what he had been guided by, the young Brazilian grandmaster declared somewhat categorically:

"Oh, I always play only for a win!"

Ljubojevic responded with the very subtle 21 Qf2!!, and it turned out that on 21 ... Rb7 or 21 ... Rc7 there follows 22 Bh5!, characteristic of The Variation, with deadly threats. As the lesser evil Black chose 21 ... Rd7, although, naturally, he was unable to save the game: 22 R×d7 N×d7 23 Q×f7+ Kd8, 24 Ng5 Kc7 25 Bf3.

Ljubojevic conducts the attack in his customary manner. White does not require the 'f' file any more; his rook will continue its activity on the 'd' file.

25 ... Qd6 26 N×e6+ Kb6 27 Rd1 b×c3.

Black has to part with his queen, since 27 ... Qb8 is adequately met by 28 Na4+, with mate in a few moves. However, in the game too Black does not resist for long.

28 R×d6+ B×d6 29 Q×g7 Be5 30 Qe7 c×b2+ 31 Kb1 a5 32 Nc5 N×c5 33 Q×e5.

Further loss of material is inevitable, and Black resigned.

But of course, this encounter did nothing to refute the system of defence worked out by Black, and indirect evidence for this was provided by, among others, a game played by Ljubojevic two months after his meeting with Mecking. At the IBM Tournament in that same year, 1975, against F. Gheorghiu the Yugoslav grandmaster chose this same system, but ... this time with Black. The following position was again reached.

But here, without even offering a repetition of moves (*16 ... Qe5*), Ljubojevic introduced an innovation—16 ... Qc7. This appears to be very dangerous for Black, since he blocks the path of his rook from a7 to d7. White naturally attempted to prevent his opponent from castling, and played 17 Bh5, which was coolly answered by 17 ... g6. Not fearing the weakening of his black squares, in particular f6, Black excludes the white bishop from the attack and prepares to castle, after which he will have everything in order.

18 Qd4 e5!. Although Black loses control over d5, his defence nevertheless holds, since his king escapes from the danger zone in the centre.

19 Qf2.

19 Qd3 Be6 was also possible (too dangerous is *19 ... g×h5 20 Nd5* and *21 Nf6+*), but White plans an intrusion at f6.

19 ... Bc5 20 Qf6 0-0 21 Nd5.

Black appears to be in a bad way. On 21 ... Qd6 White gains an advantage by 22 Ne4 Q×f6 23 Nd×f6+ Kg7 24 N×c5 g×h5 25 N×h5+, for the same reason 21 ... Qc6 does not work, and all other queen moves are unsatisfactory. But, it turns out, Black's defence is held together by an elegant tactical resource, and it cannot be ruled out that this was found by Ljubojevic not at the board, but beforehand....

21 ... Be7!!

Now after 22 N×c7 B×f6 Black has an extra pawn, even though it is doubled, while in the event of 22 Qf2 the chasing of the white queen continues: 22 ... Bc5.
22 Qf3 Bb7! 23 N×e7+ Q×e7 24 Qf2 Bd5.

The picture has clarified: Black assumes the attack, in accordance with the classical canons of the Sicilian Defence in general, and of The Variation in particular. There is no salvation.

25 Bf3 B×a2 26 Ne4 Re7 27 Qb6 Rfc8 28 Nf6+ Q×f6, and White resigned.

It was thus that a defence appeared against the formidable Bronstein-Muchnik innovation 12 Qd3. Earlier, in a game with **M. Matulovic** (Belgrade 1974), I tried out an alternative method of defence, which formerly I had rejected: after **12 Qd3 Q×f6 13 Rf1** I played **13 ... Qg6**, so as to test the continuation 14 Qf3 Ra7 15 Nc6 Bb7 16 Bd3 B×c6 17 Qe3 Qh5 18 Q×a7 Bd6. And at once the Yugoslav grandmaster made a move which was completely new to me.

14 Qe3! It turned out that this variation, in which 14 ... Ra7 is not possible on account of 15 Nd×b5, had been tried in some Yugoslav tournaments, but had not been noticed by the theorists, and therefore had not appeared in chess literature. At the board I was forced to solve some difficult problems.

14 ... Bc5 15 Bf3 Ra7 16 Ne4 Bb4+!

At first sight the idea of this check is not clear. The point is that Black, having decided to sacrifice the exchange, considered it useful to weaken the white king's future castled position, and also the square d3. The direct attempt by Black to maintain material equality, and even his advantage of one pawn, 16 ... Rc7, would have allowed White to gaini by simple means a considerable superiorety: 17 Qf4! Bb6 (there is nothing else) 18 Nd6+ Ke7 19 Rd1, and the storm clouds are beginning to gather over the black king, .g.a 19 ... Rd8 20 Nc6+! N×c6 21 B×c6, und the threat of mate at f7 is extremely unpleasant.

In the game White continued **17 c3 Be7 18 N×e6** (if 18 Nd×b5, then 18 ... Rd7, with a double-edged game) **18 ... Q×e6 19 Q×a7 Nc6** (gaining a further tempo for development, and planning in some cases to play the knight via e5 to d3) **20 Qc7** (at the board I was afraid of

20 Qa8, although it is true that here too Black has the move 20 ... f5; in general it must be said that, since both players were forced to improvize all the time, this game is of an obviously experimental character, and it raises a number of new questions, for the solving of which additional analysis and practical testing are required) **20 ... f5 21 0-0-0 f×e4 22 Bh5+**.

Interesting, of course, was 22 Rfe1, with the possible follow-up 22 ... Qh6+ 23 Kb1 Bf5! 24 B×e4 B×e4+ 25 R×e4 0-0 26 R×e7 N×e7 27 Q×e7 Q×h2, or 27 ... Qg6+ 28 Ka1 Q×g2, with a sharp endgame, which is nevertheless more favourable for White.

It is possible that, at the board, Matulovic did not care for 22 ... 0-0 23 B×e4 Bg5+ 24 Kb1 Ne7 25 B×h7+ K×h7 26 R×e6 B×e6, and so therefore he forced a **draw: 22 ... g6 23 Bg4 Q×g4 24 Q×c6+ Bd7 25 R×d7 Q×d7 26 Qa8+ Qd8 27 Qc6+ Qd7 28 Qa8+**.

I have given this game, so as once again to emphasize the diversity of the methods of defence to which Black can resort, and so as to provide a stimulus for research by probably more than one generation of chess players. Experience tells me that there is no simple answer here, and the possibilities for both sides in the open piece battle are very considerable.

I can merely again draw the reader's attention to the fact that, ten years after the initial analysis, the move 13 ... Qg6 seemed to me to have far from exhausted its resources.

ON THE RACK

Thus an antidote was found against the last and most dangerous method of attack associated with the capture on f6—10 e×f6. But the reader may recall that an important part in my earlier decision to abandon The Variation was played by the move suggested by V. Simagin—**10 Qe2**. Or, to be more exact, not the move, but the entire system. By defending his e5 pawn, White gains time for castling on the Q-side, and since his bishop at g5 survives, which together with the rook from d1 will be aimed at the square d8, White has the preconditions for an attack. His queen will later take its place at g4 or h5, and in combination with the threat of N×e6 the pressure on the black king's position will become highly intense. It will be seen that this scheme has a number of advantages over the alternative, formerly current, defence of the 'e' pawn—10 Nf3. There a piece was moved away from the centre, whereas here White achieves an optimal and highly rapid centralization of his forces.

After 10 Qe2, apart from 10 ... Nfd7, all other continuations, such as 10 ... Bb4 or 10 ... b4, have suffered a fiasco.

In the first case White gains a deadly attack: 10 ... Bb4 11 e×f6 B×c3+ 12 b×c3 Q×c3+ 13 Qd2 Q×a1+ 14 Kf2, and now 14 ... Bd7 (15 B×b5+, winning the queen, was threatened) 15 f×g7 Rg8 16 Qb4 (Mende-Pershonu, Rumania 1963), or 14... 0-0 15 f×g7 Re8 16 B×b5 Q×h1 17 B×e8, and Black is hopelessly behind in development. E.g. 17 ... e5 18 Qb4 (threatening mate at f8) 18 ... Nd7 19 Qe7.

The second continuation, 10 ... b4?, is dubious because it does nothing to solve Black's development problems. By straightforward play White gains a strong attack: 11 Ncb5 a×b5 12 e×f6. Now none of the following continuations is able to save Black:

A. 12 ... b3 13 N×b5 Qa5+ 14 c3 g×f6 (if *14 ... Nd7*, then *15 Qf3* with the threat of *16 Q×a8* and *17 Nc7+*) 15 B×f6 Rg8 16 Qc4, and wins (Estrin-Bukhtin, USSR 1968).

B. 12 ... h6 13 N×b5 Qc6 14 Qe5! h×g5 15 f×g7 B×g7 16 Q×g7 Rf8 17 0-0-0 Nd7 18 Nd6+ Kd8 19 Bb5, with a decisive offensive (Majstorovic-Little, Corr. 1967).

C. 12 ... Ra5 13 N×b5 Qb6 14 Qe5! g×f6 15 B×f6 Rg8 16 Nc7+ Kd7 17 Rd1+ Kc6 18 Qe4+ Rd5 19 N×d5, winning (Gordienko-Kulakov, Central Chess Club Championship Semi-Final, Moscow 1961).

D. 12 ... Bd7 13 Qe4 Qa5 14 b3 h6 15 Bh4 g5 16 Bg3 Bc5 17 Rd1 h5 (what else can one suggest for Black?!) 18 N×b5 Kf8 (or *18 ... Bc6 19 Qe5*, if there is nothing better) 19 Qb7, with a crushing attack (Musil-Antal, Match Yugoslavia-Hungary, 1962).

E. 12 ... Nd7, and now instead of 13 N×b5 Qc5 14 Be3 Qc6 15 Qc4! (exchanging off the sole defender of Black's Q-side—his queen) 15 ... Q×c4 16 B×c4 Rb8 17 Ba7 Rb7 18 f×g7 B×g7 19 Nd6+, winning (Kuprijanov-Jovcic, Yugoslav Championship 1962), White could have won even more quickly by 13 N×e6!, which immediately decides the game.

There was no need for us to quote all these games, which are devoted to secondrate, clearly defective variations. But it is remarkable how many players in different tournaments and at different times have tried to find a defence against Simagin's continuation! And this has all shown that to 10 Qe2 there is only one reasonable reply—**10 ... Nfd7**.

11 0-0-0

We have reached the basic position analyzed by Simagin. He considered that after 11 ... Bb7, which is Black's main continuation, by Qg4 or Qh5 and subsequent sacrifices on e6 or b5 White would gain a very strong attack, since it is rather difficult for Black to evacuate his king from the centre. Clearly, Black can play neither 11 ... Q×e5 12 Q×e5 N×e5, because of 13 Nd×b5, nor 11 ... N×e5 on account of the same idea, only in more spectacular form—12 Nd×b5 a×b5 13 Q×e5, and the queen is taboo in view of mate by the rook at d8.

Apart from 11 ... Bb7, Black also has other, less important continuations, in particular 11 ... Bb4. This move occurred in the very first game played with the 10 Qe2 variation, between Giterman and Stein (USSR Championship Semi-Final 1960). The future USSR Champion was clearly taken unawares by Simagin's move, for after the impromptu reply, 11 ... Bb4, Black stood badly. By the sacrifice of a pawn, White gained everything that he could have been dreaming of: 12 Ne4!, and in every case the bishop at b4 remains out of play, while at the same time presenting a target for attack. The game developed as follows: 12 ... Q×e5 13 Nf3 Qc7 14 a3 Bf8 (not from choice, but the bishop has no other square) 15 g4! Bb7 16 Bg2.

The two sides' forces have not yet come into direct contact, but White's lead in development is so great that the storm is likely to break at any moment. Anticipating this, Black offered the exchange of queens, but this did not weaken White's attack: 16 ... Qc4 17 Q×c4 b×c4 18 Ne5!, and it turned out that 18 ... Be7 would now fail to 19 B×e7 K×e7 20 N×d7 N×d7 21 R×d7+ K×d7 22 Nc5+, when Black loses two pieces for a rook, while on the plausible 18 .. f6, simply 19 N×c4 is highly unpleasant.

The attempt to block the X-ray action of the white rook on d8 by 18 ... Bd5 is similarly unsuccessful, since there follows 19 N×c4 (*19 N×d7 N×d7 20 Rhe1*, with the threat of mate in two moves, is insufficiently tempting, since by *20 ... Nb6* Black can hold on), and if 19 ... B×c4, then 20 Nd2!, re-establishing material equality and continuing the attack on the king—20 ... Bd5 21 B×d5 e×d5 22 Rhe1+ and 23 R×e7+.

On the other hand, after the continuation in the game, 18 ... c3 19 N×d7 N×d7 20 Nd6+ B×d6 21 B×b7 Be7 (*21 ... Ra7 22 Bc6*) 22 Bf4, White not only maintained his positional advantage, but also won material.

Besides, on 11 ... Bb4, apart from the move made by Giterman, Black must also reckon, in my opinion, with the sharp and aggressive 12 Nf5!?. It has occurred only once in practice, and there Black succeeded in beating off the attack—12 ... 0-0 13 Ne7+ Kh8 14 N×c8 R×c8 15 Qe4 Nc6 16 Bd3 Nf8 17 Bf4 B×c3 18 b×c3 Ng6 19 Rde1 f5 (Rozinatovsky–Yonshlescu, Corr. Rumania 1966). But White could probably have played more strongly.

However, since the continuation 12 Ne4 gives White a clear advantage, interest in the move 12 Nf5 is really of a purely academic nature.

And now a short excursion into history. When, early in 1961, I first learned of Simagin's idea, I decided without due preparation that I would play 10 Qe2 Nfd7 11 0-0-0 Nc6, since in the resulting position I considered one of Black's main enemies to be the white knight at d4.

But in the spring, I think it was in May, that brilliant teacher and analyst G. Ravinsky suggested, in reply to this, 12 N×c6 Q×c6 13 Qd3! (this is much stronger than my suggestion of *13 Ne4 Bb7 14 Nd6+ B×d6 15 R×d6 Qc7* followed by ... *Nc5*, depriving White's white-squared bishop of the square d3). White improves the position of his queen, and opens the way for his bishop at f1. After this, Black's position gradually ceased to appeal to me, and by the summer of the same year in the RSFSR Championship I had already decided on 11 ... Bb7.

To return to Ravinsky's continuation, one of the moves tried was 13 ... Bc5, which allows White the possibility of attacking this bishop with his knight, and after 14 Be2 Qc7 15 Ne4 0-0 16 Qg3! Kh8 (forced, in view of the threat of *17 Nf6+*, which is also decisive after *16 ... Q×e5?*, since *17 ... g×f6 18 Bf4+* leads to the loss of the queen, and *17 ... Kh8 18 N×d7* to the loss of a piece) 17 Bf4 Be7 18 Nf6! Qd8 (obviously the knight cannot be captured in any of the possible ways, since *19 e×f6* threatens both mate at g7, and also the black queen) 19 Bf3 Ra7 20 Be3 White won the exchange in the game Tomson–Kovacevic (Lvov 1961).

Of course, 13 ... Bc5 is a poor move, but even analysis of what is in my opinion the best continuation, 13 ... Bb7 14 Be2 Qc7, did not produce anything resembling equality, however much I searched. And this is not surprising! After all, Black's K-side is undeveloped, and his king is in the centre. White can, for instance, build up his heavy pieces on the 'd' file, and

74   *Grandmaster Preparation*

happily part with his 'e' pawn, which opens additional lines for the attack: 15 Rd2 N×e5 16 Qg3! Bb4 17 Bf4 B×c3 18 b×c3 f6 19 B×e5 f×e5 20 Bh5+ g6 21 B×g6+ h×g6 22 Q×g6+ Qf7 23 Q×f7+ K×f7 24 Rd7+. So that 11 ... Nc6 does not lead to a 'change of values'.

On one occasion Black also played 11 ... Be7, which, to be honest, I had not analyzed at that time, so hopelessly bad did it appear to me. Black did indeed suffer a swift and severe debacle: 12 B×e7 K×e7 13 Qg4 Q×e5 (or *13 ... Kf8 14 Q×e6! N×e5 15 Nd5!*) 14 B×b5! (intending to answer *14 ... a×b5* with *15 Rhe1 h5 16 Qf3 Qg5+ 17 Kb1 Ra7 18 Nf5+ Kf8 19 Nd6 Nb6 20 Qf2*, regaining the piece and winning the game) 14 ... Bb7 15 Rhe1 h5 16 Nf5+ Kd8 17 Qh4+, and Black shortly resigned: 17 ... g5 (on *17 ... Qf6* White wins by *18 Q×f6 g×f6 19 Nd6* and *20 B×d7*) 18 Q×g5+ f6 19 B×d7 f×g5 20 B×e6+ (Kupper-Walther, Zurich 1961).

That was how, practically by the method of elimination, my choice came to fall on **11 ... Bb7,** although from the very start I regarded it with some scepticism. The combinative possibilities that White acquires (after 12 Qg4) are too extensive, particularly in connection with the weakening of e6! And when between 1961 and 1962 I took the decision to part with The Variation, an important role in this was played by the position in the diagram.

At that time Simagin's idea was only just beginning to gain acceptance (it is true that it did this fairly rapidly and confidently), and therefore I had hardly any personal experience of playing this position. But a vast number of games were played on this theme, and they provided material for a rather surprising conclusion: it was too early to come to a conclusion! The position was so complicated that here too there was a whole wealth of possible work for chess players!

And so, it is White to make his 12th move. In the first game where Simagin's idea was employed against me, M. Yudovich played a poor move—**12 Bf4.**

White has unexpectedly betrayed the basic demand of the position, which is to be prepared to make sacrifices in general, and of the 'e' pawn in particular, so as to attack, attack and attack. Black replied **12 ... Nc6,** when White has nothing better than **13 N×c6,** since the pressure on the 'e' pawn is becoming unpleasant, and by ... Bc5 Black plans to complete his development.

The game continued **13 ... Q×c6,** and in order to clear the way for his king's bishop, White was forced to waste a tempo: **14 Qd3.** But now **14 ... Nc5 15 Qe3** (in the event of 15 Qg3 Black acquires the square e4 for his knight with gain of tempo by 15 ... b4) **15 ... Be7 16 Be2 0-0** led to a position in which

Black was fully mobilized and had seized the initiative; the white king is clearly less happily placed than his black opposite number. The overall idea of the Sicilian Defence—counter-attack on the Q-side—has developed into an attack, and it is now White who must think in terms of defence.

17 Bf3 Qc7 18 Rd2 Rac8 19 Rhd1

White has seized the open 'd' file, but since there are no squares of intrusion on it, Black does not intend to contest it. His main avenue of attack is the 'c' file.

19 ... b4 20 Ne4

20 ... B×e4!

A crucial and correct decision. White is unable to utilize the advantage of the two bishops, while the knight at c5 is needed by Black to support his Q-side pawn offensive, and also to defend the d7 square against the possible intrusion of the white rooks.

21 B×e4 a5 22 Bf3 a4 23 Kb1 Qa5

The storm clouds are gathering over the white king. Black threatens both the breakthrough ... b4–b3, as well as the further concentration of his forces by ... Rc7 and ... Rfc8. It is already too late for White to think of a similar advance of his 'g' and 'h' pawns. Even so, he should have avoided the following move, which leads to an exchange of bishops.

24 Bg5 B×g5 25 Q×g5 b3 26 a3

Of course, on 26 c×b3 Black would not have replied 26 ... a×b3 27 a3, when his attack is repulsed, but 26 ... N×b3, and if 27 Rd7 (*27 a×b3??* loses immediately to *27 ... a×b3*, when there is no defence against mate at a2) then 27 ... Nc5, with subsequent pressure now down the 'b' file.

26 ... b×c2+ 27 R×c2 Nb3

The end draws close, since White loses control of the 'c' file, and with it the square c1.

28 R×c8 R×c8 29 Be4

Intending to post the bishop at c2, since the 'active' 29 Qe7 loses instantly to the thematic 29 ... Qd2.

29 ... f6!

Driving the queen off the c1–h6 diagonal.

30 Qh4 f5 31 Bc2 Nd2+ 32 Kc1 Nc4

Black has too many threats (against the 'e' pawn, the square b2, and the white king) for White to be able to parry them all.

33 Qd4 Qc7

Black has no intention of limiting himself to the capture of the 'e' pawn, and now threatens 34 ... N×a3.

34 Qd7 Ne3

Black has calculated a lengthy, but straightforward variation, which wins by force.

35 Q×c7 R×c7 36 Rd2 Rc5 37 Kb1 N×c2 38 R×c2 R×e5 39 Rc4 Re2 40 R×a4 R×g2

The point, of course, is not that Black has an extra pawn, but that the passed pawn at f5 plans to become a queen within four moves.

41 Rc4 e5

This move was sealed by Black. On resumption White replied **42 Rc5**, and after **42 ... Re2** he **resigned**.

Thus the passive move 12 Bf4 suffered a fiasco.

Two other moves are also not especially terrible for Black: 12 Nf5 and 12 N×e6. Both have the immediate aim of destroying by combinative means the pawn cover of the black king in the centre.

12 Nf5 is to some extent dangerous, but Black nevertheless succeeds in maintaining the balance.

12 ... e×f5 (otherwise on *12 ... Nc6* White replies *13 Ne4*, with an intrusion on d6) 13 e6 Nf6 14 B×f6 g×f6 15 Qh5. White's specific intention takes shape: to open the 'e' file, and, by the further sacrifice of his bishop on b5, to strike at the black king after Rhe1.

15 ... Bb4!

Without doubt the strongest. In the game Belokurov-Sanakoyev (Lipetsk 1962) Black played the weaker 15 ... Bg7?, and quickly came under a crushing attack: 16 B×b5+ a×b5 17 e×f7+ Kf8 (if *17 ... Q×f7*, then *18 Rhe1+ Be4 19 N×e4! Q×h5 20 Ng5+*, and it is the position of the bishop at g7 that is Black's undoing, cutting off the escape of his king) 18 Rhe1 Be4 19 N×e4 Nd7 20 Nc5!, and Black resigned, since he cannot play 20 ... Ne5, covering the square e8 — 21 Ne6+.

By 15 ... Bb4! Black prepares for castling, and White, so as not to lose the initiative, has to go in for further sacrifices.

16 B×b5+ (White cannot avoid this, since the immediate *16 e×f7+* allowed Black in the game Pimonov-Kremenetsky, Moscow Championship Semi-Final 1969, to beat off the attack: *16 ... Kf8! 17 Qh6+ K×f7 18 Be2 B×c3 19 Bh5+ Ke6 20 b×c3 Be4*, and the black king is very comfortable in his fortress in the centre) 16 ... a×b5 17 e×f7+ Kf8!.

For rather a long time this was thought to be a losing move, this opinion being based on what was a virtually unique case of 'twin' games. In Boukal-Ptak (Czechoslovakia 1969) after 18 Rhe1 Na6 19 Re8+ Kg7 20 Q×f5 Q×f7 21 Qg4+! Qg6 (after *21 ... Kh6 22 Re3*, mate or loss of the queen is inevitable) 22 Rd7+ Kh6 23 Qh4+ Qh5 the players agreed a draw, assuming that White had nothing more than perpetual check. But a year later in the game Gubolini-Palmiotto

(Italian Championship 1970) in this position White announced mate in three moves: 24 Q×f6+ Qg6 25 Qh4+ Qh5 26 Re6 mate.

Therefore, instead of 17 ... Kf8, the theorists recommended 17 ... Q×f7, which, according to analysis by Belokurov, leads to perpetual check after 18 Rd8+ Ke7 19 Re1+ Be4 20 Nd5+ Ke6 21 Nf4+. True, if on the previous move Black had played 20 ... Q×d5!, then after 21 R×d5 B×e1 it would be White, not Black, who would have had to think in terms of saving the game. Therefore, Belokurov's analysis is correct only with the following transposition of moves: first 20 R×e4+ f×e4, and only now 21 Nd5+ Ke6 22 Nf4+, with a draw.

Later, however, Boleslavsky established that it was not 17 ... Kf8 that was wrong, but the move following it in reply to 18 Rhe1—18 ... Na6?. After the superior 18 ... Nd7! White's attack is insufficient, e.g. 19 Q×f5 Ne5 20 Q×f6 N×f7, or 19 Re8+ Kg7 20 Q×f5 Ne5.

The other 'violent' possibility—12 N×e6 f×e6 13 Qg4—can also be repulsed by Black, but not without some difficulty.

True, the poor move 13 ... Qb6 leads to a forced loss: 14 Rd6! B×d6 15 Q×e6+ Kf8 16 Bc4! b×c4 17 Rf1+ Nf6 18 R×f6+ g×f6 19 Bh6 mate. Black also has other ways of losing. Thus Boleslavsky and Matsukevich, who have devoted much analysis to this variation, consider three further instances in which White gains an irresistible attack. Here they are:

A. 13 ... N×e5 14 Q×e6+ Be7 15 B×b5+ Kf8 16 Rhf1+ Bf3 17 R×f3+ N×f3 18 B×e7+ Q×e7 19 Qf5+ Qf6 20 Rd8+, winning.

B. 13 ... Nc6 14 Q×e6+ Ne7 (on *14 ... Be7, 15 Nd5* is decisive) 15 B×b5 a×b5 16 N×b5 Qc6 17 Nd6+ Kd8 18 N×b7+ Q×b7 19 R×d7+ Q×d7 20 Rd1, and White wins. E.g. 20 ... Ra7 21 R×d7+ R×d7 22 Qb6+ Rc7 23 Qb8+ Rc8 24 Qd6+ Ke8 25 e6 Rd8 26 Qf4 Ra8 27 Qd4; no better is 20 ... Q×d1+ 21 K×d1 Rc8 22 Qb6+ Ke8 23 e6 h6 24 Qb5+ Nc6 25 Qb7, with similar effect.

C. 13 ... Nc5 (this sets White slightly more problems, but does not save the game) 14 Rd8+ Q×d8 15 B×d8 K×d8 16 b4 Ncd7 17 a3 Nc6 18 Q×e6 Nc×e5 19 Be2 (possibly even stronger is *19 B×b5 a×b5 20 Rd1 R×a3 21 Q×e5 Ra1+ 22 Nb1 Ra8 23 Q×b5*, with a decisive attack) 19 ... Rc8 20 Rd1 R×c3 21 Q×e5 Rc7 22 Bg4, and although Black has kept his material advantage, his king is badly placed, and White's chances are markedly preferable.

However, instead of 17 ... Nc6 Black has a stronger reply: 17 ... g6, and after 18 Q×e6 Bg7 his pieces become very active. 17 a3 looks rather slow, and for this reason the path chosen by White in the game Winslow–Browne (USA 1976) is much more dangerous for Black: 17 Be2!? h5 (*17 ... Nc6 18 Rd1 Nc×e5 19 Q×e6 Kc7 20 B×b5 a×b5 21 N×b5+ Kb8 22 R×d7*, or *17 ... g6 18 Rd1 Bg7 19 Q×e6 Re8 20 Qb6+ Kc8 21 Bg4 Re7 22 Qd6 Kd8 23 e6 B×c3 24 Qb6+*) 18 Q×e6 B×b4 19 Qb3 B×c3 20 Q×c3 Re8 21 Rd1 Nbc6 22 B×h5 R×e5 23 Bf3

(Winslow considers that *23 Bg4 Re7 24 B×d7 R×d7 25 Q×g7* also gives good winning chances) 23 ... Re6 24 Q×g7 Re7, and now, in Shamkovich's opinion, 25 Qg5 Rc8 26 Rd6! gives White a decisive advantage.

But Black has at his disposal a possibility of repelling his opponent's menacing offensive: 13 ... Q×e5.

14 Bd3.

The strongest. In the event of 14 B×b5 a×b5 15 Rhe1 there follows a counter-blow typical of positions in this plan: 15 ... h5! 16 Qh4 Qc5! 17 R×e6+ Kf7 18 Rde1 Qf5 19 g4 Q×g4 20 Qf2+ Kg8 21 Be7 Nc6, and Black wins (A. Zaitsev-Byelov, RSFSR Championship 1960). In this line 16 ... Qc7 is weaker in view of 17 N×b5 Qc5 18 Qf4!, but not 17 R×e6+ Kf7 18 N×b5 Qc5.

14 ... Be7 (inadequate is *14 ... Nf6 15 B×f6 g×f6 16 Kb1 Kf7 17 Rhe1 Rg8 18 Qh3 B×g2 19 Q×h7+ Rg7 20 Bg6+ Ke7 21 Qh4*, and wins—analysis by Browne) 15 B×e7 K×e7 16 Rhe1 h5!?.

On 16 ... Qf6 White has several possible replies. Winslow examines 17 Qb4+ Kd8 18 Be4 B×e4 19 N×e4 Qf4+ 20 Kb1 Ra7 21 Qd4 Rc7 22 Q×g7 Qf8 23 Q×f8+ R×f8 24 Ng5. Shamkovich suggests 17 Kb1 Ne5 18 Qb4+ Ke8 19 Ne4 B×e4 20 B×e4 Ra7 21 Qd6 Nbd7 22 Bc6, or 17 ... Nc5 18 Qb4 Nbd7 19 Be4, and recommends as the best defence for Black 17 ... Rc8!, and if 18 Qb4+, then 18 ... Rc5 19 Be4 a5. In my opinion, the most forceful move for White is 17 Be4, when Boleslavsky's recommendation of 17 ... Nc6 is met by the quiet 18 Qg3! creating irresistible threats.

17 Qb4+ Qc5 18 Qh4+ Nf6! (the only way; in the event of *18 ... g5 19 Qh3* White's initiative is very dangerous) 19 Qg3 Rg8 20 Re5 Qb6 21 Bf5 Nbd7 22 R×e6+ Q×e6 23 B×e6 K×e6 24 Qd6+ Kf7 25 Qc7 Bc8 26 Nd5 N×d5 27 R×d5 Re8 28 R×d7+ B×d7 29 Q×d7+ Kg6, with a draw, Olafsson-Polugayevsky, Reykjavik 1978.

We can thus draw an intermediate, as it were, conclusion: in the position given in the last diagram, neither the timid 12 Bf4, nor either of the wild knight charges, promises White any real advantage. There remain the two 'pressurizing' queen moves—12 Qh5 and 12 Qg4.

After 12 Qh5

in view of the threat of 13 N×e6 (note that in all variations White aims to mount his attack against the square e6, which has been weakened by the departure of the bishop from c8) Black has three replies. Two of these lose:

12 ... Q×e5 13 B×b5 a×b5 14 N×e6 (nevertheless!) 14 ... Q×e6 (if *14 ... g6, then 15 Nc7+ Q×c7 16 Qe2+ Ne5 17 Q×e5+ and 18 Rd8 mate*) 15 Rhe1 g6 16 N×b5, with decisive threats.

Or 12 ... Qb6—here the refutation is more difficult to find, but it is there— 13 B×b5 a×b5 14 Nd×b5 g6 (if immediately *14 ... R×a2, then 15 Rd6! Ra1+ 16 Nb1*, and Black cannot meet the threat of *17 R×e6+*, since *16 ... B×d6* loses to *17 N×d6+*) 15 Qh3 (renewing the threat to e6 after *16 Nd6+ B×d6 17 R×d6*) 15 ... R×a2! 16 Rd6! Ra1+.

All this occurred in the game Kondratiev–Ermilov (Central Chess Club Championship Semi-Final, Moscow 1962). Here the players 'exchanged compliments'—17 Nb1? B×d6? 18 N×d6+ Kf8 19 Qh6+ Kg8 20 Ne8, and Black resigned. He had a defence in 17 ... Be7! 18 B×e7 (or *18 R×b6 B×g5+ 19 Kd1 N×b6*, when Black has a material advantage, and it is the white king that is more likely to come under attack than his black opposite number) 18 ... Q×b5 19 Bf6 N×f6 20 R×e6+ f×e6 21 Q×e6+ Kd8 22 Q×f6+ Kc7 23 Q×h8 Qe2, and Black starts a decisive counter-attack. But the move earlier White, too, could have won, by continuing 17 Kd2!, and if 17 ... B×d6 (activating the queen does not help—*17 ... Qf2+ 18 Ne2 B×d6 19 N×d6+ Kf8 50 Qh6+ Kg8 21 Ne8*), then 18 N×d6+ Q×d6 19 e×d6 R×h1. Despite Black's material advantage, it is the white queen that dominates the position. Black cannot hold out for long: 20 Qh6 Nc6 21 Qg7 Rf8 22 Nb5, or 20 ... Ba6 21 Qg7 Rf8 22 Be7 Nc6 23 B×f8 N×f8 24 Ne4.

On the other hand, Black's third reply in the diagram position—12 ... g6!—is perfectly adequate to successfully repel White's onslaught. One possibility here which has occurred in practice is 13 Qh4, when Black has a choice between two alternatives.

One is a double-edged and, in my opinion, unreliable continuation, in which Black's position all the time hangs literally by a thread: 13 ... Q×e5 14 B×b5 a×b5 14 Rhe1 Qc5, and if 16 Qf4 (the rook sacrifice *16 R×e6+*, as played in a certain correspondence game, did not prove successful: *16 ... f×e6 17 N×e6 Qf5! 18 N×b5 h6! 19 Nec7+ Kf7 20 Qc4+ Kg7 21 Ne6+ Kh7*, and Black beat off the attack), then 16 ... Bd6! 17 N×e6 B×f4+ 18 N×f4+ Kf8 19 Bh6+ Kg8 20 Re8+ Nf8 21 Ncd5 B×d5 22 R×d5 Nd7! 23 R×a8 Qg1+ 24 Kd2 Q×h2, and in the game Berkovich–Minakov (Moscow Championship Quarter-Final 1970) Black won.

The alternative is the quieter and more reliable 13 ... Nc6 14 N×c6 (certain specialists in sharp play have expressed the opinion that White has a promising piece sacrifice here—*14 B×b5 a×b5 15 Nd×b5 Qb6*, but in my opinion it is hardly possible to demonstrate that White has full compensation for it; thus if *16 Bf6*, then *16 ... N×f6 17 Q×f6 Bh6+* and *18 ... 0-0*) 14 ... B×c6 15 Ne4 B×e4 16 Q×e4 Rc8 17 Bf6 (otherwise the e5 pawn cannot be saved) 17 ... N×f6 18 e×f6 Bh6+ 19 Kb1 Bg5!, and after the elimination of the pawn at f6, the difference in strength of the opposite-coloured bishops is clearly in Black's favour: 20 a4 0-0 21 a×b5 a×b5 21 B×b5 B×f6, and the position of White's king on the Q-side is hardly defensible (Razuvayev–Unanyan, Baku 1961).

Nevertheless, it cannot be considered that the study of the move 13 Qh4 is complete, and this was confirmed in a game played in the 1975 USSR Spartakiad in Riga between **G. Kuzmin** and myself.

When in this game the following position was reached,

I was afraid to play 13 ... Q×e5, since, in comparison with the afore-mentioned Berkovich-Minakov game, White could have prepared some improvement. Of course, there were arguments for playing the already approved 13 ... Nc6, or 13 ... h6, which had not yet occurred in practice. But I thought it useful to try another new continuation.

13 ... Bg7

It turns out that, for the moment, the weakening of the d6 square is not so dangerous, since on the thematic 14 B×b5 Black replies 14 ... 0–0!, and promptly seizes the initiative. The sacrifice 14 Nd×b5 a×b5 15 N×b5 is parried by the simple 15 ... Q×e5 16 Nd6+ Kf8, when White cannot meet the threats against b2 and a2.

But if Black should succeed in castling, the weakening of the white 'e' pawn and the possibilities of an attack on the Q-side will give him a marked advantage, and after prolonged thought Kuzmin took the decision to utilize at any cost his single trump—to try to keep the black king in the centre.

14 Be7 Q×e5

During the game I could see no specific refutation of 14 ... B×e5, and nor do I see one now. I avoided the move on the grounds that the place for the bishop is at g7, where it is 'solidly' placed, and where it cements together all the weakened black squares on the K-side.

In the resulting position White is obliged to play forcefully: he has no time for the quiet completion of his development by 15 Be2 and Rhe1, since he has to reckon with the imminent threat of 15 ... h6 and 16 ... g5. The retreat of the bishop, 15 Ba3, can be neutralized by 15 ... Bf6 followed by 16 ... Nc6, or even by 15 ... g5!?.

15 B×b5 a×b5

Black accepts both the challenge, and the sacrifice. After the game I established that it would have been much more practical to decline the sacrifice, by playing 15 ... Qh5. Then after 16 B×d7+ N×d7 17 Q×h5 g×h5, firstly, White's 'g' pawn is weak, and secondly, the two black bishops sweep the entire board.

It is interesting to note that the improvement I found did not go wasted. Knowing my game with Kuzmin, grandmaster Quinteros was not averse to repeating it when we met in the 1976 Interzonal Tournament at Manila. Unfortunately for the trusting Argentinian, the present book with the innovation 15 ... Qh5 was still at the printer's in Moscow, and at the board Quinteros was literally flabbergasted by the queen manoeuvre. The effect of the innovation quickly showed itself: after 18 Bg5 (better, of course, is *18 Bh4*, but even then Black gains an excellent position by continuing *18 ... Ne5*) 18 ... Rg8! 19 Bh4 Be5 20 Bg3 B×g2 21 Rhe1 B×g3 22 h×g3 R×g3 23 Nf5 Rg6 24 Nd6+ Ke7 White found himself in a lost position.

Evidently White should play 16 **Ba4**, but the simple 16 ... Q×h4 17 B×h4 0–0 gives Black a good game. And if White should be tempted by the variation 18 N×e6 f×e6 19 B×d7 N×d7 20 R×d7, he ends up in a somewhat inferior position: 20 ... B×g2 21 Rg1 B×c3 22 b×c3 Bd5.

16 Nd×b5 g5 17 B×g5

17 Qb4 will not do, because of 17 ... Nc6 18 Nd6+ K×e7 19 Nf5++ Kf6 20 Q×b7 Nc5 21 Q×c6 Rhc8.

17 ... 0–0 18 Rhe1

The black king is at last out of the firing line; Black has an extra piece, but his position is extremely precarious. To a considerable extent this is due to the insecure position of his queen in the centre, while in addition one of the white rooks can be transferred along the third rank to the K-side, whereupon White's attack will become decisive. I therefore decided to return the piece, and by conceding material to attempt to seize the initiative.

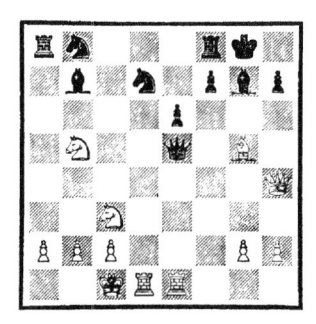

18 ... Qf5 19 Nd6 Qg6 20 N×b7 B×c3

This is the point of Black's plan: after defending the K-side with his queen, he breaks up the pawns in front of the white king. At the same time the black queen also takes part in the attack, at any rate for the time being. The idea is not bad, although objectively speaking it is hardly sufficient to achieve equality.

21 b×c3 R×a2 22 Rd3 Nc6

Opening the way for the second rook to the Q-side. The alternative—22 ... Kh8 23 Re2—leaves White with the advantage. It would appear that now too White will gain a material advantage, but ....

23 Bh6 Rfa8!!

An unexpected continuation, but the only correct one. The plausible 23 ... Rb8? 24 Rg3 R×c2+ 25 Kd1 leads to an immediate loss for Black.

24 Rg3 R×c2+ 25 Kb1

This is the point! The king cannot go to d1 in view of mate on the move, but now the fact that it is on the same file as the white knight enables Black to maintain approximate material equality.

25 ... R×c3+ 26 R×g6+ h×g6

An amazing position! Despite the loss of his queen, Black's threats are very real.

In particular, 27 ... Raa3 (on *27 Kb2*) guarantees him at least a draw. Therefore White, who has a queen for a rook (!), is forced to reconcile himself to the loss of a piece.

27 Bc1 Rb8 28 Bb2 R×b7 29 Rc1

On account of the mate at h8 Black is unable to retain his second rook for the attack (*29 ... Rcb3*), and he is therefore forced to exchange it and begin searching not for counter-play, but for a drawing line. However, he has perfectly adequate compensation for the queen, and he merely has to ensure the safety of his king by neutralizing the pressure along the a1–h8 diagonal. This aim is best met by 29 ... Rb4, driving back the queen, then exchanging on c1, and posting one of his knights at e5. In this way Black could have been confident of a draw.

An alternative was to exchange on c1 and then sacrifice the exchange on b2. During the game I was afraid to go in for this continuation, but later in analysis I discovered a whole series of positions where no win for White is apparent.

However, the set-up planned in the game also does not yet lose.

29 ... R×c1+ 30 K×c1 e5

Hoping somehow to give up the 'e' pawn and one of the knights for the bishop. But now White sharply activates his forces.

31 Qc4 Rb6

Black immediately deviates from the correct path. He should have played 31 ... Ne7, and then endeavoured to transfer his rook to b6. True, even the move order chosen does not yet rule this out.

32 h4 Nf6

But now 32 ... Ne7 was virtually obligatory. After the move played White's queen literally plunges in among the black pieces, and my position definitely ceased to appeal to me.

33 Qc5 Nd7

An admission of guilt!

34 Qd6 Ncb8 35 Qe7 Rc6+ 36 Kd1 Re6 37 Qd8+ Kg7 38 g4 Rf6 39 h5

Although it is not particularly desirable for Black to play his rook to f1, White should perhaps have delayed forcing matters, and for the moment played 39 Ke2.

Now Black at least gains some play with his rook.

39 ... Rf1+ 40 Ke2 Rh1 41 Ba3

This obvious move—the bishop cannot be maintained on the long diagonal—was sealed by White, and I was faced with the eternal question: what to do?

Neither now nor later is the exchange on h5 possible, since after a check on g5 the recapture on h5 is decisive. At the same time White has a mass of possibilities for strengthening his position.

I will not now describe how my analysis proceeded: the reader can familiarize himself with examples of adjournment analysis in much more detail in the third chapter of this book. I will merely say that, when I was already inclined to regard Black's position as hopeless, an idea came into my head...

On the resumption there followed:

41 ... Ra1 42 Bd6

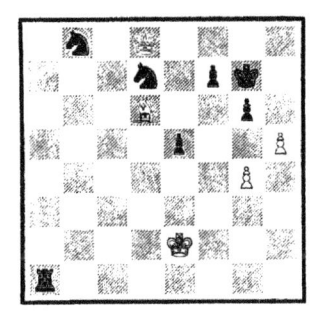

42 ... Ra6!! 43 B×b8

White fails to see through his opponent's intention—to take play into a drawn ending with queen and pawn against rook and pawn, otherwise he would have preferred 43 Qe7, maintaining the tension. Black would then have been faced with considerable difficulties.

43 ... N×b8 44 Q×b8 g×h5

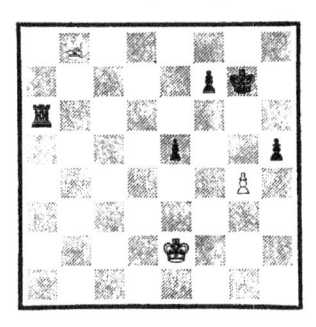

And here I saw from my opponent's face that he had realized his irreparable mistake. Black has achieved an impregnable fortress, or in other words, a positional draw.

The remainder is therefore simple:

45 Q×e5+ Kg8 46 Qb8+ Kg7 47 Qb2+ Kg8 48 g×h5 Re6+ 49 Kf3 Kh7 50 Kf4 Rh6 51 Kg5 Re6 52 Qh2 Rh6 53 Qf4 Kg7 54 Q×f7+ K×f7 55 K×h6 Drawn.

However, after 12 Qh5 g6! the move 13 Qg4 occurs more frequently in practice. White continues his thematic attack on e6, but it soon becomes clear that, in comparison with the position examined below after 12 Qg4, the inclusion of the move ... g7–g6 is to Black's advantage. He continues 13 ... Q×e5 14 B×b5 h5 (also possible, however, is *14 ... a×b5 15 N×e6 f×e6 16 Rhe1 h5! 17 Qh4 Qf5*, when it very much appears as though White's attack is on its last legs) 15 Qh4 Q×g5+! (here is the advantage of ... g7–g6!) 16 Q×g5 Bh6 17 Q×h6 R×h6 18 Bf1 (similarly after *18 B×d7+ N×d7* Black stands better, thanks to his strong bishop and imposing pawn mass in the centre and on the K-side) 18 ... h4! 19 Rg1 Ke7 20 Nb3 Nc6, and Black gained a positional advantage (Bojkovic–Vitolinsh, Match Yugoslavia–USSR, 1963).

But in the event of 12 Qg4, which is considered the main continuation,

colossal complications with numerous possibilities arise. Here Black has two radically different plans. The first of these—12 ... Qb6, is a kind of flank defence of e6, which at any rate seriously hinders White's vigorous intentions. Black's second plan is associated with the aggressive, but also highly dangerous 12 ... Q×e5, and has the aim of eliminating the annoying pawn at e5, and, correspondingly, the possible intrusion of the white pieces at d6.

It is true that the black queen is prematurely advanced into the centre, and that White can, with gain of time, begin a frontal assault on e6 and on the black king's position.

We will consider these two plans in turn, but before doing so we should point out that neither of the two following possibilities is playable for Black: 12 ... N×e5 13 N×e6! f×e6 14 Q×e6+ Be7 15 B×b5+ a×b5 16 N×b5, or 12 ... Nc6 13 B×b5! a×b5 14 Nc×b5 and 15 N×e6, with a swiftly crushing attack.

After 12 ... Qb6

White must either continue the purposeful mobilization of his forces, or attempt to combine the development of his K-side with an immediate attack on e6, and, consequently, on the black king stranded in the centre. The latter plan gives rise to the idea of a typical sacrifice, which is always in the air: 13 B×b5 a×b5 14 Nd×b5.

The threat of 15 Nd6+ B×d6 16 R×d6 (attacking e6 with gain of time) is unpleasant, but it is Black to move, and he can effectively parry it by playing 14 ... N×e5.

Weaker is 14 ... Nc6 15 Rd6!, with the same threat, and now either 15 ... Nc5 16 b4 B×d6 17 N×d6+ Kf8 18 Rf1 N×e5 19 b×c5 Q×d6 20 R×f7+ Ke8 21 c×d6 N×g4 22 R×b7 (Gumerov-Tatarintsev, Bashkir Championship 1961), or 15 ... B×d6 16 N×d6+ Kf8 17 Rf1 Nc×e5 18 Q×e6 f6 19 B×f6 (a game Tskhai-Bogomyachkov, Chita 1965, went *19 Bh6 B×g2 20 R×f6+*, and Black resigned) 19 ... g×f6 20 R×f6+ N×f6 21 Q×f6+ Kg8 22 Qe6+ Kf8 23 Q×e5!, and, as pointed out by Boleslavsky, the threat of mate in two prevents Black from keeping his enormous material advantage. 23 ... Qf2 24 Q×h8+ Ke7 25 Qe5+ Kd7 26 N×b7—this is all in White's favour.

After 14 ... N×e5 Boleslavsky gives the following variation: 15 Qf4 (obviously the main continuation of the attack) 15 ... Nbc6! (in the game Simovich-Vitolinsh, Moscow 1962, Black played the weaker *15 ... Nbd7?*, and after *16 R×d7* Black loses after either *16 ... f6 17 R×b7 Q×b7 18 B×f6 Ng6 19 Qc7*, as occurred in the game, or *16 ... K×d7 17 Rd1+ Ke8 18 Q×e5*) 16 Rhe1 h6 17 Qf2 Qa5 18 Bf4 h6, where in his opinion it is completely unclear as to whether White's initiative compensates for the sacrificed piece.

Along with this aggressive bishop sacrifice, it is also hardly expedient for White to switch to the defence of his 'e' pawn by 13 Bf4 or 13 Qg3. Both these moves can be classed as deviations from the overall policy of The Variation: after all, at a very early stage of the opening (on the 8th move) White as it were took it upon himself to play boldly, utilizing his lead in development for an attack.

But here after 13 Bf4 the simple 13 ... Nc5, with the idea of ... b5-b4, gives Black, as pointed out by Boleslavsky, good counter-play, e.g. 14 Bd3 b4 15 Nce2 Nbd7 16 Rhf1 N×d3+ 17 R×c3 Nc5 18 Rdd1 Rc8 19 Kb1 Be4, or 14 a3 Nc6 15 Nf3 b4 16 a×b4 Q×b4.

In the event of 13 Qg3 White removes an attack from e6: 13 ... Nc6 14 Nf3 h6

2. The Birth of a Variation

15 Bd2 0-0-0 16 Ne4 Nc5 17 N×c5 Q×c5 18 Be2, and in the game Spasjoevic-Stanculescu (Student Olympiad 1967) Black could now have attained a good game by advancing his 'g' pawn—18 ... g5.

Clearly White must seek a golden mean between the risky 13 B×b5 and the excessively cautious defence of his 'e' pawn. This aim is ideally answered by 13 Be2.

By sacrificing not a piece, but his 'e' pawn, in the majority of games played with this variation White has gained a dangerous attack. Black is practically forced to venture into 13 ... N×e5, which is of course risky, but what can one suggest instead?

Thus to 13 ... Bc5 White has the good reply 14 Be3 (the immediate *14 Ne4!* also looks very strong to me) 14 ... g6 15 Ne4 B×e4 16 Q×e4 Nc6 (if *16 ... Ra7*, then *17 b4! B×b4 18 N×b5*, winning literally everything in sight) 17 N×c6 B×e3+ 18 Kb1 Bc5 (*18 ... Rc8* fails to *19 Rd6! Bc5 20 Ne7*, when the rook at d6 is invulnerable) 19 b4 Bf8 (no better is *19 ... Be7 20 Bf3 Rc8 21 N×e7 K×e7 22 Rd6 Qc7 23 Rhd1 Rhd8 24 Qh4+ Ke8 25 Bc6*, and the 'mortal' pin on the knight proves decisive) 20 Qf3! (threatening *21 Rhf1*) 20 ... Qc7 21 Rhf1 Nb6 22 Ne7!, and wins.

After 13 ... Nc6 14 N×e6! Nc×e5 15 N×f8! N×g4 16 N×d7 the position reached is worthy of a diagram.

White's two minor pieces are much stronger than the queen, since the black king is quite simply unable to escape to either flank. On the only reasonable move, 16 ... Qg6 (otherwise White captures the knight, and obtains in addition a sufficient material equivalent) there follows 17 h4! Nf6 (or *17 ... Nf2 18 Rhe1! N×d1 19 Bg4+ Qe6 20 B×e6*, and White has a winning advantage) 18 Bd3! (by this attack on the queen White gains a tempo for his offensive, since Q-side castling was now prepared) 18 ... Ne4 19 N×e4 B×e4 20 Ne5 B×d3 21 N×g6 B×g6 22 Rde1+! Kf8 (if *22 ... Kd7*, then simply *23 h5 f6 24 h×g6 f×g5 25 R×h7*) 23 h5 Bf5 24 Rhf1 Bg4 25 h6 f5 26 Re4! Kg8 27 Re7, and Black stands badly.

After 13 ... N×e5, events normally develop as follows: 14 Qg3 (*14 Qh5*—as played in the game Spassov-Ajanski, Bulgarian Championship 1965—is weaker: *14 ... Nbd7 15 Rhe1*, and now by *15 ... g6* Black could have attained a reasonable position, plus an extra pawn; however, *14 Qh3* is worth considering) 14 ... Nbd7 15 Bf4 (if *15 Rhe1*, then *15 ... Bc5! 16 Be3 0-0-0*, and Black can breathe a sigh of relief) 15 ... f6.

This move, which occurred in the correspondence game Popescu-Betsech (Rumania 1973), looks highly risky. The only justification for it, and a highly dubious one at that, is the fact that 15 ... Ng6 (incidentally, when analyzing this position I came to the conclusion that *15 ... b4?* is also doubtful, on account of *16 Na4! Qa5 17 Nb3 Q×a4 18 B×e5 0-0-0 19 Rd4*, with advantage to White) is similarly unpromising for Black: 16 Bc7 Qc5 17 Nb3 Qa7 18 R×d7 K×d7 19 Rd1+ Ke8 20 N×b5, and the king is defenceless.

But after 15 ... f6 White should have played not 16 Qh3, although even here 16 ... Kf7 17 Rhf1 g6 18 Nf3 B×f3 19 B×f3 Ra7 20 Be4 left Black with a dubious position, but 16 Bg4, or first 16 Bh5+. The impression gained is that White's attack is highly formidable.

In tracing the fate of the move 12 ... Qb6, when I was already working on this book I checked all the more or less reasonable possibilities for Black after 13 Be2, trying to find that support on which one might construct a defence. One day the thought occurred to me: why not drive the white bishop away from its good position before starting 'pawn-grabbing'?

Translated into chess language, this idea is very simple: Black can include the preliminary 13 ... h6, when on 14 Bf4 he has the possibility of the bayonet thrust 14 ... g5. Of course, I realized that it wasn't immediately possible to 'pass a verdict' as to whom it favoured, and that only practical testing could give the answer. And after a short analysis had convinced me that it was worth trying, fate afforded me the opportunity to employ my new idea.

THE VARIATION LIVES!

In the 1974 International Tournament at Las Palmas, the pairings gave me the black pieces against **L. Kavalek**. It was highly probable that my opponent would begin the game by advancing his king's pawn, and that in reply to the Najdorf Variation of the Sicilian would play 6 Bg5, and I could not resist the temptation to 'revive the good old days'. Especially since the true worth of my idea had of course to be tested in a game with a strong opponent.

And so, **13 ... h6**.

It was apparent that Kavalek had not expected this move, and he spent a long time in thought. But immediately after his reply it was my turn to bend over the board: the rejoinder **14 Qh3!** proved very effective, and took me quite unawares. In my preliminary calculations I had underestimated it, and only during the game did I see that 14 ... Bc5 would not work, on account of 15 N×e6! Q×e6 16 Bg4 Qg6 17 B×d7+ Kf8 18 Be3!, when White wins.

Black therefore chose **14 ... N×e5 15 Rhe1 Nbd7 16 Bh4** (White already had to reckon with the possible exchange sacrifice 16 ... h×g5 17 Q×h8 0-0-0) **16 ... g6 17 Bg4 h5!** (the only move, after which the play takes on a forced aspect) **18 B×e6 B×h6+ 19 Kb1 f×e6 20 N×e6 Rh7?** (this could have cost Black dearly; he should have played 20 ... Kf7!) **21 Bg3?** (a mistake in reply; 21 R×d7!, luring the black king into a discovered check, would have given White a decisive attack) **21 ... Re7 22 B×e5 Q×e6** (it was not yet too late for Black to lose, by 22 ... R×e6

23 Bd4!) 23 Q×e6 (the tempting 23 Bd6? fails to 23 ... Q×e1) 23 ... R×e6 24 Bf4! R×e1+ 25 R×e1+ Kf7, and with complete equality—and opposite-coloured bishops!—on the board, the opponents in this long-suffering game agreed to a draw.

Of course, this game did not by any means shake completely the reputation of the move 13 Be2. Couldn't White have played more energetically at some point? And didn't Black have an improvement somewhere along the way? These questions remained open, and, as before, the situation in this line remained 'terra incognita'.

Naturally, I could not rest content at that, and before my next meeting with Kavalek, at Manila in the autumn of 1975, I found an improvement which, however, did not pretend to be a final assessment of the resulting position

Here Black deviated, having prepared instead of 16 ... g6, a surprise: **16 ... g5!.**

This move proved to be so paradoxical that my opponent spent a long time in thought, and then became somehow rather sad. Indeed, the white bishop has only just left g5, and now Black once again entices it there, for the sake of which he parts with his extra pawn.

But meanwhile after **17 B×g5** (the thematic 17 N×e6 fails to 17 ... f×e6! —*17 ... Q×e6 18 Bg4* weaker—and if now 18 B×g5, then simply 18 ... h×g5 19 Q×h8 0-0-0, when Black has both a material and a positional advantage) **17 ... Rg8!** the overall idea of The Variation is revealed in its purest form. Without concerning himself over the safety of his king or keeping a material advantage, Black aims for active counter-play with his pieces. Here he obtains this, since his formerly inactive king's rook is included in the counter-attack. White is evidently forced to gamble on his attack, since after the retreat of the bishop to h4 Black has a mass of tempting possibilities, such as 18 ... B×g2 or 18 ... Bc5.

After spending a mass of time in thought, Kavalek embarked on a sacrificial path.

18 N×e6 h×g5 19 Bh5

Here I made a blunder of a psychological nature. At home, for all the sharpness and complexity of the position, I had satisfied myself that White must not play 19 Bh5 on account of 19 ... g4!, and after 20 B×f7+ (there is nothing else, since *20 ... Q×e6* is threatened) 20 ... K×f7 21 Qh7+ Rg7! (but not *21 ... K×e6 22 R×d7*, or *21 ... Bg7 22 Ng5+*) White's attack is beaten off. Thus neither 22 N×g7 B×g7 23 Rf1+ Nf6, nor 22 Rf1+ K×e6 leads White anywhere—black pieces alone are to be seen on the board.

But during the game, as I was checking these variations, I suddenly discovered an additional attacking resource for White: 22 R×d7+ N×d7 23 Ng5+. Of course, I saw that I could advance my king—23 ... Kf6, and now the win of the queen by 24 Re6+ (on *24 Nce4+* Black has *24 ... Ke7*, and his king escapes safely to the Q-side via d8) costs White too much. But what I didn't care for was 24 Qh6+ Rg6 25 Rf1+. The fact that here the king can calmly retreat to e7, when the rook at g6 remains defended by the queen from b6, I quite simply overlooked!

After calculating for the first time these variations at the board—and miscalculating!—I somehow promptly lost confidence in the whole of my prepared analysis, and instead of checking once more the resulting position, I decided not to play 19 ... g4. And as a result I made not just a pseudo-blunder, but a real one.

19 ... Bd6?

Overlooking that White can strengthen decisively his attack on f7.

20 Qf5

It is now that things become really bad for Black. The threat is 21 B×f7+ N×f7 22 Nc5+ Nde5 23 R×e5+ N×e5 24 Qe6+, against which, incidentally, 20 ... Ke7 does not save Black. After mobilizing literally all of my composure, I found the only saving chance—the amazing

20 ... Rh8?!!

The idea of this move is very soon revealed.

21 B×f7+ Ke7

Black couldn't of course play 21 ... N×f7 22 N×g5+ Nfe5, since White has a mass of attractive ways of continuing the attack. Perhaps the most suitable is 23 Nf7 Rf8 24 N×d6+, when 24 ... Q×d6 is not good in view of the *zwischenzug* 25 Qh5+.

22 N×g5 Rh6?!

This is the idea: for the time being at least the critical e6 square is defended.

But even so, this would have been insufficient, had White now calmly played 23 Nge4, threatening a queen check at g5, and also threatening Black's 'central defender'—his bishop at d6. In this case Black's position would have been indefensible.

Instead White attempts to break through to the key square e6, using the idea of interference.

23 Bg6?

Threatening 24 Qe6+ and 25 R×d6, but it is Black's turn to move.

23 ... Kd8!

By returning a part of his extra material, Black's king slips away from the epicentre of the 'earthquake'.

24 R×e5

White has nothing better. If 24 Ne6+, then 24 ... Kc8 25 Be8 Rf6, and the black pieces group together powerfully.

24 ... N×e5 25 Qf8+

White avoids a transparent trap: 25 Q×e5 R×g6 26 Nf7+ Kd7 27 Qf5+ Kc7 28 Q×g6 Bf4+.

25 ... Kc7 26 Ne6+ Kd7 27 Q×h6 N×g6 28 Qg7+

It turns out that, although with his 26th move White has parried the bishop check at f4, he still cannot capture the knight at g6, on account of the queen check at e3. But 28 Qh7+ was correct.

28 ... Ne7 29 Nd4

Had White's queen been at h7, he could have continued the attack with 29 Qh3. Here he does not have the analogous move 29 Qg4, on account of that same check—29 ... Qe3+. After the retreat of the knight, the position is rather in Black's favour, although he still has to meet certain threats, and in particular 30 Nf5.

29 ... Rg8 30 Qf7

Perhaps White should again have tried going the other way—30 Qh7—to which I was planning to continue as in the game.

30 ... Qc5 31 Qe6+ Ke8

Of course, not 31 ... Kc7? 32 Q×g8. Now Black's pieces, and in particular his bishops, control virtually the entire board.

2. The Birth of a Variation   89

White has to play precisely to avoid an inferior position, and to this end 32 Nd×b5 a×b5 33 R×d6 Bc8 34 Qh6 R×g2 deserved consideration, reducing the number of black pawns to the minimum.

The subsequent stage of the game took place in a mutual time scramble.

32 Ne4 B×e4 33 Q×e4 Qg5+ 34 Kb1 Q×g2

Black once again has a material advantage, but nevertheless he is unable to realize it. Although an attack is not threatened, the black king feels rather uncomfortable in the centre of the board.

35 Qd3 Qd5 36 a4

A draw becomes practically inevitable: Black has simply nothing left with which to win.

36 ... b×a4 37 Q×a6 a3

Black utilizes his last chance—he breaks up the pawn screen in front of the white king, and tries somehow to worry it. But....

38 Qb5+ Q×b5 39 N×b5 B×h2 40 N×a3 Rg4 41 c3 Kf7 42 b4

This move was sealed by White. Strictly speaking, there was no need and no point in adjourning the game...

42 ... Be5 43 Kc2 Ke6 44 Rd3 Nd5 45 Nb5 Rg2+ 46 Kb3 Bf6 47 Nd4+ Ke5 48 Nc2 Nf4 49 Re3+ Kd6 50 Nd4 Nd5 51 Nb5+ Kd7 52 Rd3 Ke6 53 Nd4+ Drawn.

A year after this game, another important development confirmed the viability of The Variation. In his game with Balashov at Manila, 1976, E. Mecking chose as Black 13 ... N×e5 14 Qg3 Nbd7 15 Bf4 b4!? 16 Na4 Qa5 17 Nb3 Q×a4 18 B×e5, and reached a position which I had formerly rejected (cf. p. 86). Only instead of 18 ... 0-0-0 19 Rd4 with advantage to White, Mecking continued 18 ... Rc8! 19 Rhe1 N×e5 20 Q×e5 Qc6 21 Kb1 Qc7, with a good game. It is difficult to say whether or not White can play better at any point (some theorists have suggested, for instance, *17 b3*), but in any case Mecking's idea deserves serious consideration.

On his 12th move Black has an alternative, which is radically different in character: 12 ... Q×e5.

This move has attracted the attention of numerous chess minds, if only for the reason that it is the most uncompromising. Its virtues and drawbacks have already been mentioned in passing: Black gets rid of the e5 pawn, and for a certain time includes his queen in the defence of e6. In a number of instances the bishop at g5 is hanging, but on the other hand the 'e' file is opened, and White can very soon make a frontal attack on e6 with a rook from e1.

For a long time it was thought that Black's 12th move could be refuted directly by that same sacrifice 13 B×b5 a×b5 14 Rhe1 (a tempo is worth more than a bishop!), but the reply 14 ... h5!! was found, when, by removing one of the attacks on e6, Black can defend successfully: 15 Qh4 Qc5!.

It is illogical to play 15 ... Qc7, since this allows White to capture on b5 with gain of tempo. Nevertheless this move has been played, and here are the variations given by the Soviet master S. Selivanovsky: 16 Nc×b5, and now:

A. 16 ... Qa5 (Black loses after *16 ... Qc4 17 N×e6*, or *16 ... Qc8 17 Qf4*, with the threats of *18 Nc7+* and *18 N×e6*) 17 N×e6 f×e6 18 R×e6+ Kf7 19 Qc4!, and in the correspondence game Ljiljak–Goddard, 1968, White won.

B. 16 ... Qb6 17 Qf4 (bad is *17 Bd8? Q×d8 18 N×e6 f×e6 19 R×e6+ Be7 20 Qf4 Ra6*, when after *21 Nc7+ Q×c7 22 Q×c7 R×e6 23 Q×b8 0-0* Black has a big material advantage) 17 ... Na6 18 N×e6 f×e6 19 Rf1, and Black's defensive resources are exhausted, e.g. 19 ... Nf6 20 B×f6 Bc5 21 Nd6+ B×d6 22 R×d6.

C. 16 ... Qc5 17 R×e6+! f×e6 18 N×e6 Qe5 (if *18 ... Qf5, then 19 Qc4 Nf6 20 N×g7+ B×g7 21 Nd6+* and wins, while on *18 ... R×a2* there follows *19 N×c5 Ra1+ 20 Kd2 R×d1+ 21 K×d1 N×c5*—or *21 ... B×c5 22 Qf4 Na6 23 Nd6+ B×d6 24 Q×d6*—*22 Qf4 Nba6 23 Nd6+ Kd7 24 N×b7 N×b7 25 Qa4+*, with a winning advantage) 19 Qc4! Nf6 (after *19 ... Be7 20 Nbc7+ Kf7 21 Nf4+* White wins by force) 20 Nbc7+ Ke7 21 Bf4 Qe4 22 Bd6+.

Therefore after 15 Qh4 the only correct move is 15 ... Qc5, when White has several possibilities:

16 N×e6 (here this sacrifice does not achieve its aim) 16 ... f×e6 17 R×e6+ Kf7 18 Rde1 Qf5 19 g4 Q×g4 20 Qf2+ Kg8 21 Be7 Nc6, and in the game A. Zaitsev-Byelov (RSFSR Championship 1966) which has already been given earlier, White had achieved precisely nothing.

It remains for us to check the variations where White refrains from the second sacrifice—on e6: 16 Nc×b5 R×a2.

Evidently the strongest. The game Torre-Mariotti, Manila 1976, went 16 ... Bd5 17 Rd3 Na6 18 a3 Qb6 19 N×e6! B×e6 20 R×e6+! Q×e6 21 Re3 Q×e3+ 22 B×e3, when it was difficult for Black to co-ordinate his scattered forces.

16 ... e5?!, as occurred in the game Martinovic-Rajkovic, Vrnjacka Banja 1975, looks highly suspect. White should have replied either 17 b4 Qb6 18 Bd8! Q×d8 19 R×e5+! Be7 20 Nc7+ Kf8 21 Nde6+ f×e6 22 N×e6+ Kg8 23 Qg3 Qf8 24 Rf5, or, according to analysis by Honfi, 17 R×e5+!? N×e5 18 Nb3 Qb6 19 Rd8+ Q×d8 20 B×d8 Na6 21 Na5.

17 Kb1 Bd5 (*17 ... Ra5* is bad on account of *18 Qf4! R×b5 19 N×b5 Q×b5 20 Q×b8+*). Formerly this position was considered favourable for Black, but the game Velikovic-Sahovic (Yugoslavia 1973) appeared to shake this opinion: 18 Rd3 (with the threat of *19 Rc3* and *20 Rc8* mate) 18 ... Qb6 19 N×e6+ B×e6 20 Qc4, and wins. I myself do not find this game convincing, if only because of 19 ... R×b2+! 20 K×b2 (bad is *20 Kc1 f×e6! 21 R×d5 R×b5*) 20 ... Q×b5+ 21 Rb3 Q×b3+! 22 c×b3 f×e6, and with the resulting material balance I would prefer to play Black.

Also possible on the 16th move is 16 Nd×b5, which has caused Black considerable trouble: 16 ... Na6 17 Qf4 (on *17 Bf4* Black again replies *17 ... Bc6*) 17 ... Bc6, and in the game Lukovnikov-Manukovsky, Voronezh 1971, after 18 b4 Q×b4 19 Rd4 Qa5 20 Ra4 Qb6 21 R×a6! and 22 Nc7+ White achieved his goal.

But Black could have played 19 ... Qc5! (the immediate queen sacrifice *19 ... Q×b5 20 N×b5 B×b5* runs up against a strong reply in *21 Qf3!;* White threatens *22 a4*, and Black loses after *21 ... Nb6 22 Q×a8+*, or *21 ... Nc7 22 Qb7*, while on *21 ... Rc8* there follows *22 Qb7 Rb8 23 R×d7 Ba3+ 24 Kd1 0-0 25 Qf3*) 20 Rc4 (*20 Rd6 e5*), and only now sacrificed his queen—20 ... Q×b5! 21 N×b5 B×b5 22 Qf3 Rb8 23 Rf4 Nb4 (*23 ... Nf6 24 R×f6*) 24 R×f7 N×a2+ 25 Kd1 Bc4. In this complex position, which can hardly be subjected to exact analysis, Black appears to have dangerous threats.

It seemed that all the possibilities for White had been studied, but a game Berezyuk-Izhnin, played in the 1976 USSR School Children's Spartakiad, added a fresh portion of fuel to the fire. In it White played 14 Nc×b5 immediately (instead of *14 Rhe1*), and with a cascade of sacrifices mated his opponent: 14 ... h5 15 Nc7+! Q×c7 16 N×e6 Qe5 17 Nc7+ Q×c7 18 Qe2+.

Certain experts saw in this innovation the refutation of 12 ... Q×e5, but such a conclusion was clearly over-hasty. The cause of Black's crushing defeat was the erroneous move 14 ... h5?. If he plays 14 ... f5! (D. Minic recommends *14 ... Be7*, with an unclear position) it is not clear whether White's initiative compensates for his material deficit. Thus on 15 Qh3 Black has an adequate reply in 15 ... Kf7 16 Rhe1 Be4, while in the event of 15 N×f5 e×f5 16 Qc4 Na6 17 R×d7 K×d7 18 Rd1+ Ke8 he beats off the attack.

In general, from the analysis of variations one gains the impression that 13 B×b5 is rather premature, although Black is caused many anxious moments, and he must play exactly.

However, White has at his disposal a much more dangerous, although apparently less energetic move: 13 Bd3!.

It is this move that enables White to utilize most favourably his attacking possibilities. While completing the mobilization of his forces, White as it were asks his opponent: "Well now, can you do the same?" Meanwhile the familiar attack on e6 is on the agenda after 14 Rhe1, and it is obvious that Black has no time for quiet development.

Since this book is not only about The Variation, but also about the search for the truth in it, I should mention that earlier, in 1961, the move 13 Bd3 did not appear dangerous to me. Black has 13 ... Nf6, when, I decided, he can survive. And it was only on returning to The Variation that I realized that it was here that the most severe tests awaited Black, tests which at times have appeared virtually insoluble....

13 ... Nf6

One gains the impression that this is the only move. 14 Rhe1 is threatened, and it is essential to disturb the co-ordinated attack of the white pieces on e6. To this end 13 ... h5? does not work; in the game Shaks-Bilchuk, Poland 1969, there followed 14 Q×e6+ Q×e6 15 N×e6, and White re-established material equality with a winning position, since on 15 ... f×e6?? he gives a 'linear' mate with his two bishops by 16 Bg6.

14 B×f6!

In 1961/62 a correspondence match was held between the Ukraine and France. In one of the games Rooz played against Yu. Sakharov 14 Qh4 Nbd7 15 Rhe1 Qc5 16 Bf5 (increasing to the maximum the pressure on e6) 16 ... 0-0-0!, and Black managed to beat off the attack, retain a material advantage, and win. On the basis of this game the whole line with 13 Bd3 was considered inadequate.

But then in 1969, in his game with Anikayev from the USSR Championship Semi-Final in Kiev, Tukmakov exchanged on f6, not begrudging his strong bishop for the sake of maintaining the tempo of the attack. Now on 14 ... Q×f6 White replies 15 Rhe1, and the sacrifice on e6 takes place under highly favourable conditions. E.g. 15 ... h5 16 N×e6!! h×g4 17 B×b5+! Ke7 (on *17 ... a×b5* White gives mate by *18 Nc7*) 18 N×f8+ Qe6 (not *18 ... K×f8 19 Re8* mate) 19 N×e6 f×e6 20 Bc4, and White is material up with a won position (Felling-Lindblom, Geustal 1971).

14 ... g×f6

Now the threat of 15 ... Qg5+, with the exchange of queens, does not allow White time for Rhe1. But in his arsenal he has what is virtually his main weapon in this variation—interference.

15 Bf5!

There can be no doubt that this quintessence of the whole 13 Bd3 line was found by Tukmakov in his preparations, and was merely 'published' in the afore-mentioned game with Anikayev. Now Black is lost after 15 ... Qe3+ 16 Kb1 h5 17 N×e6!!, when on 17 ... h×g4 there follows 18 Nc7+ Ke7 19 N7d5+, regaining the queen with a big advantage, while if 17 ... Q×e6 (S. Kogan-Kotenko, USSR Correspondence Championship 1970-73), then 18 Qd4 Nc6 (the only defence against mate) 19 Qd7+! Q×d7 20 B×d7+ Kd8 (*20 ... Ke7* fails to *21 B×c6*, with the threat of *22 Rhe1+* and mate) 21 B×c6+ Kc7 22 B×b7 K×b7 23 Rd7+, with a won ending.

Black is similarly defenceless after 15 ... e×f5 16 N×f5, when the threat of Rhe1 cannot be met, while on 15 ... Bh6+ Tukmakov gives the following variation: 16 Kb1 Qf4 17 N×e6! (for the umpteenth time!) 17 ... Q×g4 (if the sacrifice is accepted—*17 ... f×e6*, then *18 Qh5+ Ke7 19 B×e6 Rf8 20 Rhe1*, and all the same the black king cannot escape) 18 Nc7+ Kf8 19 B×g4 Ra7 20 Rd8+ Kg7 21 Ne8+, winning material.

Therefore Anikayev found what is probably the strongest defence.

15 ... h5

Now the sacrifice on e6 is not possible: 16 N×e6? h×g4, and the square c7 is defended.

16 Qh3 Bc5 17 Rhe1 Qf4+ 18 Kb1 B×d4

So as to at least learn the worst....

19 B×e6! B×c3

Black rids himself of one potential white attacker. This would appear to be necessary, since on the immediate 19 ... f×e6 there follows 20 Q×e6+ Kf8 21 Qe8+ Kg7 22 Re7+, and on 19 ... Be5—20 Nd5 Qg5 (equally bad is *20 ... B×d5 21 B×d5 Ra7 22 Qc8+*) 21 Qa3! Nc6 (White concludes the game elegantly after *21 ... B×d5 22 B×d5 Ra7 23 Qd6 Nd7 24 Bc6 Qf5 25 Qb8+*) 22 Nc7+ B×c7 23 Bd7++ Kd8 24 Bf5+, announcing mate in three. I must mention that all these variations are given by Tukmakov, and that in the attack which began back on the 14th move the white pieces develop tremendous energy.

20 b×c3 0-0

But here White went wrong. He played the natural move 21 Rd4, including his rook in the attack, but after 21 ... Qg5 22 Re3 B×g2 Black managed to beat it off. As Tukmakov himself later pointed out, he could have won here by either 21 Re3, or the even stronger 21 B×f7+!, which wins by force:

On 21 ... K×f7 White quickly reaches his goal: 22 Q×h5+ Kg8 23 Qg6+ Kh8 24 Re7, and there is no defence against the mate. The black king has a slightly longer life after 21 ... R×f7, but here again after 22 Re8+ Kg7 (if *22 ... Rf8,* then *23 Qe6+ Kg7 24 R×f8 K×f8 25 Rd8+ Kg7 26 Rg8+ Kh6 27 Qf7*, mating) 23 Rdd8, despite being two pieces down, White's attack concludes successfully: 23 ... Nc6 (there is nothing more sensible; on *23 ... Be4* White can play, for instance, *24 Q×h5 Bh7 25 Rh8 Qf5 26 Rdg8+ B×g8 27 Qh6* mate) 24 Rg8+ Kh6 25 Rh8+ Rh7 26 R×h7+ K×h7 27 Q×h5+ Kg7 28 Rd7+, and mates.

Had this occurred, Tukmakov's excellent preparation would have received an adequate and worthy reward.

I have to admit that my attempts to find a 'hole' in White's plan were unsuccessful, and however much I tried to deviate after 14 B×f6, nothing real came of it.

It turned out that an improvement had to be sought earlier, immediately in reply to 13 Bd3, and A. Planinc succeeded in doing this in a game with V. Mestrovic. On the 13th move he introduced an important improvement, choosing, instead of 13 ... Nf6, which is apparently the only reasonable move, 13 ... h6!.

Mestrovic attempted to refute the innovation by the standard sacrifice 14 N×e6, but after 14 ... h×g5 15 Rde1 (if *15 Rhe1*, then *15 ... Rh4!*, and the white queen is trapped; the game Winston–Dieks, World Junior Championship, Manila 1974, continued for a few moves more: *16 Q×h4 g×h4 17 R×e5 N×e5 18 Nc7+ Ke7 19 N×a8 B×a8*, and Black easily realized his advantage; in the event of *16 Nc7+ Kd8 17 R×e5 R×g4 18 N×a8 B×a8* White again stands badly) 15 ... Rh4 16 Qd1 f×e6 17 R×e5 N×e5 Black had nothing to worry about. The game continued 18 Qe2 Nbd7 19 Be4 0–0–0 20 g3 R×e4 21 N×e4 Nf6 22 N×g5 B×h1, and after a lively battle, ended in a draw, although I consider that in the position after his 17th move Black could have hoped for more.

Thus White's cavalry attack proved unconvincing, and what's more, in this game the main idea behind Planinc's innovation did not see the light of day. This happened later, in several games from the years 1972 and 1973, when White made what is undoubtedly the strongest move.

14 Bh4 g5!

It suddenly turns out that the menacing white queen is short of squares after both 15 Bg3 Qe3+ 16 Kb1 h5, and 15 Rhe1 h5!. White is therefore forced into a tactical mêlée.

15 N×e6

A cursory glance at the position is sufficient to create the impression that, although White has two pieces *en prise*, the black king is bound to perish very shortly. Its fate hangs by a thread, but unexpectedly this thread proves to be made of highly durable material.

15 ... h5!!

A most unusual position, in which the main 'dramatis personae' of both sides are under attack. Three white pieces are simultaneously attacked by pawns, and if on the previous move Black had decided to 'treat himself' to the knight or the bishop, he would have lost immediately on account of the catastrophe on the 'e' file.

Here in the game Luczak-Schmidt (Team Championship of Poland, 1973) White played 16 Qh3, and after 16 ... f×e6 17 Rhe1 Qf4+ 18 Kb1 g×h4 19 Q×e6+ the resulting complications were difficult to assess.

However, in my opinion this continuation is by no means obligatory for Black. He should have continued playing in the same manner, and instead of capturing pieces should have created threats. Highly suitable to this end is 16 ... Bh6!.

The immediate 16 ... g4 does not work, in view of 17 Nc7+ Q×c7 18 Rhe1+, with very dangerous threats, such as 18 ... Ne5 19 R×e5+! Q×e5 20 B×b5+ a×b5 21 Rd8 mate. Of course, in this line Black could have avoided mate, but White obtains a very strong attack.

But now (after *16 ... Bh6!*) the advance ... g5-g4 becomes highly unpleasant for White, since his queen is threatened, while the black king obtains a saving escape square at f8. White no longer has time for 17 Rhe1, and Black, in my opinion, can feel perfectly content.

Thus on 17 B×g5 he replies simply 17 ... B×g5+ (and if *18 N×g5*, then *18 ... Q×g5+ 19 Kb1* and possibly even *19 ... 0-0*, as it were leaving the capture on g2 in reserve, while after *18 Kb1* he has *18 ... f×e6! 19 Rhe1 Ke7! 20 R×e5 N×e5*, and, firstly, Black has a lot of pieces, and secondly, they are very harmoniously placed, particularly after ... Nd7). In the event of 17 Kb1 Black again wins an important tempo for the evacuation of his king, and can continue 17 ... g4 18 Nc7+ Kf8 or 18 ... Q×c7.

It seems fairly certain that, by retreating his queen to h3 on move 16, White loses the initiative. For this reason 16 Q×g5 has been tried in other games. After this, against Dueball (Skopje Olympiad 1972) Kerr continued 16 ... Bh6, and on 17 Rhe1—17 ... f×e6! (*17 ... Q×e1* is dangerous on account of *18 R×e1 B×g5+ 19 N×g5+*, when for the exchange White has a pawn, two strong bishops, and even without the queens his attack persists) 18 Bg6+ Kf8 19 Rf1+ Kg8 (Black cannot play either *19 ... Nf6 20 Q×h6+ R×h6 21 B×f6 Qe3+ 22 Kb1*, with advantage to White, since the threats of *23 Rd8* mate and *23 Bd4+* cannot both be parried, or *19 ... Kg7 20 Rf7+ Kg8 21 Bh7+!*, with a very strong attack), and White forced perpetual check—20 Bf7++ Kh7 21 Bg6+ Kg8 etc. However, after 19 Rf1+ Boleslavsky and Kapengut then found an amazingly beautiful move—19 ... Qf6!!.

Now Black wins: 20 R×f6+ N×f6 21 Rd8+ Kg7 22 R×h8 B×g5+ 23 B×g5 K×g6, and he comes out a piece ahead.

In the game Ljubojevic–Mariotti, Manila 1976, after a slightly different move order—14 ... g5 15 Rde1 h5! 16 Q×g5 Bh6 17 N×e6—a position from the Kerr–Dueball game was reached, with the difference that White's queen's rook was at e1; this is of no great significance. By continuing 17 ... f×e6! (instead of *17 ... B×g5*) 18 Bg6+ Kf8 19 Rhf1+ Qf6! Black could have gained the advantage. Minic has suggested 20 R×f6+ N×f6 21 R×e6 Nbd7 22 Ne2, supposedly leading to an unclear position, but it is difficult to agree with this. Thus Black appears to have a good continuation in 22 ... Rc8 (instead of *22 ... B×g5*, as suggested by Minic) 23 Nf4 B×g5 24 B×g5 Rc6 25 Re1 Rd6 26 Bf5 Rg8.

But following the discovery of 19 ... Qf6!! the arguments around Planinc's continuation did not cease, and soon a game was played which added much fuel to the fire. In a 1973 Soviet tournament, after 13 ... h6 14 Bh4 g5 Litvinov chose against Zarenkov the seemingly impossible 15 Bg3, and in reply to 15 ... Qe3+ 16 Kb1 h5—17 Rhe1!. Attack for attack! Blow for blow!

Naturally, Black attempted to win material—17 ... Q×e1, but 18 Q×g5 Bh6 19 Q×h5 Qe3 20 N×e6!! presented him with difficult problems. He chose 20 ... Q×e6, since the threats of Nc7+ and Re1 demand a clarification of the situation, and on 21 Re1—21 ... Q×e1+ 22 B×e1 Bg7!, attacking the queen and consolidating his forces. But in reply to 23 Qg4 he went wrong with 23 ... 0–0?. Black assumed that everything was in order, and that after the completion of his Q-side development his material advantage should tell, but 24 Qh4! reminded him that the middlegame and White's attack were still in progress. Better, according to Boleslavsky and Kapengut, whose opinion I fully share, is 23 ... Kf8, when a highly complicated position is reached.

But besides 19 Q×h5 White has another interesting possibility: 19 Qh4!. Having adopted it in a correspondence game, M. Rudnev considers this move to be stronger than the capture of the pawn. After 19 ... Qe3 20 N×e6 Q×e6 (Black loses after *20 ... f×e6 21 Bg6+ Kf8 22 Rf1+ Kg8 23 Qe7*) 21 Re1 Q×e1+ 22 B×e1, a position is reached where, in comparison with the previous game, the white queen is better placed. Which is more important: Black's material advantage, or White's initiative? It is highly possible that the fate of this whole scheme of play depends upon the answer to this question.

The reader will no doubt already have noticed that, in this line, the play of the two sides proceeds as if according to the principle of constant counter-blows. "What happens if one tries at some point to deviate from this exchange of blows?", I thought to myself one day, and soon discovered that a convenient moment for this did exist. In reply to Litvinov's innovation of 17 Rhe1, Black can calmly play 17 ... h×g4 18 R×e3 Nc5!, if possible exchanging off White's white-squared bishop, or, if it should retreat, say, to e2, then preparing the counter-blow 19 ... b4.

If, in addition, account is taken of the fact that Black has an extra pawn and is threatening to complete his Q-side development, it is clear that any delay by White will be equivalent to suicide. And in fact he has a piece sacrifice, leading to a highly unclear position; but if he plays the routine 19 B×b5+ a×b5 20 Nd×b5, then 20 ... Nba6, and how White can develop his initiative is not apparent. There remains 19 Nc×b5 a×b5 20 B×b5+ Nbd7 21 b4 0-0-0 (dangerous is *21 ... Ne4 22 N×e6 f×e6 23 R×d7*, with an attack) 22 b×c5 N×c5, and at first sight Black's K-side pawn phalanx appears more attractive than White's three pawn islands. On the other hand, White's pieces are much more active; but, I repeat, the position is highly unclear.

These latest games have shed new light on the system of play proposed by Simagin. Black, although forced to balance on the edge of the precipice, appears to be able to hold on, and one gains the impression that it is now White's turn to come up with something new. Of course, this may well happen: the positions arising are so sharp and complicated, so rich in double-edged possibilities for both sides, that improvements for White are perfectly possible. As, however, are further improvements for Black.

And the first signs have already appeared. At the 1976 Interzonal Tournament in Manila, the Soviet grandmaster Y. Balashov employed an innovation in his game against the Argentinian Quinteros, playing 13 Be2!. The idea of the move is to avoid blocking the 'd' file, and to counter Black's plan of 13 ... h6, on which there would now follow 14 Bf4 (after *13 Bd3* this is not possible, since the knight at d4 is undefended). In addition, White plans the exchange of bishops, after, for instance, 13 ... b4—14 Bf3.

The attempt by Quinteros to play actively proved unsuccessful: 13 ... h5 14 Qh4 f6 15 Bf4 g5 16 Q×h5+! R×h5 17 B×h5+ Ke7 18 B×e5, and it is unlikely that anyone will wish to play this position again.

A little later, in the game Balinas-Tarjan, Odessa 1976, Black defended differently, but again unsuccessfully: 13 ... Nf6 14 B×f6! g×f6 (after *14 ... Q×f6 15 Rhf1 Qg6 16 Qf4* White clearly stands better) 15 Rhe1 Qg5+ (or *15 ... h5 16 Qh3 Qg5+ 17 Kb1 B×g2 18 B×b5+ a×b5 19 N×e6!*, and things are bad for Black) 16 Q×g5 f×g5 17 Bh5 Ke7 18 Rf1 f5 (or *18 ... f6 19 Nf5+! e×f5 20 Rfe1+*, and wins) 19 Rfe1 B×g2 20 R×e6+, and White soon won.

But Black, in his turn, was not long in replying. In the 1977 England–Iceland Telechess Match, Sigurjonsson employed an interesting improvement against Stean: 13 ... Bc5!. The game continued 14 Bf3 (on *14 Rhe1* Black would have replied as in the game) 14 ... B×d4! 15 B×b7 B×c3 16 b×c3 (*16 B×a8 B×b2+* is clearly advantageous for Black) 16 ...

Ra7 17 Rhe1 h5! 18 Qh4 Q×c3 19 Re3 Qa1+ 20 Kd2 Q×a2 21 Qb4 f6 22 Qd6 R×b7, and Black successfully passed the examination.

A NEW IDEA

It was found very recently by White. The Moscow master V. Lepeshkin has published an interesting piece of research, in which he demonstrates the correctness of the knight sacrifice on White's 12th move in the position after 11 ... Bb7.

He attaches an exclamation mark to the continuation 12 N×e6!, and gives the following evidence.

12 ... f×e6

13 Qh5+

This check is the point of the idea found by Lepeshkin.

13 ... g6 14 Qg4 Q×e5

The tactical operation 14 ... Be7 15 B×e7 N×e5 is interesting. But after 16 Qg3 Q×e7 17 Q×e5 0–0 18 Rd6, or 18 Bd3, White has a solid advantage. Equally unsatisfactory is 16 ... K×e7 17 B×b5 a×b5 18 Qh4+ Kf8 19 Rhf1+ Kg7 20 Qf6+ Kh6 21 Rd4, or 18 ... Ke8 19 N×b5 Qe7 20 Nd6+.

15 Bd3

Here Lepeshkin considers two possibilities.

A. 15 ... Be7 16 B×e7 K×e7 17 Rhe1 h5 (other continuations are weaker: *17 ... Nf6 18 Qb4+ Qd6 19 R×e6+ K×e6 20 Bf5+ g×f5 21 Q×d6+*, or *17 ... Qf6 18 Be4 B×e4 19 Q×e4 Qg5+ 20 Kb1 Ra7 21 Q×e6+ Kd8 22 Qb6+ Rc7 23 Q×b8+*, or *17 ... Qc7 18 Q×e6+ Kd8 19 B×b5*) 18 Q×g6 Qf6 19 Qg3 Rf8 (*19 ... Kd8 20 Be4!*) 20 Be4 B×e4 21 R×e4 Kd8 (Black has to defend against the threats of *22 Nd5+* and *22 Qc7*) 22 a4 Kc8 23 Kb1.

23 ... Nc5 24 a×b5! Nbd7 (bad is *24 ... N×e4 25 N×e4 Qf4 26 Qc3+ Kb7 27 Qg7+ Kb6 28 Rd6+*, or *26 ... Qc7 27 Nd6+ Kd7 28 Ne8+*) 25 Rc4 a×b5 26 N×b5, with a powerful attack.

B. The alternative: 15 ... Nc5.

Now 16 Rhe1 achieves nothing after 16 ... N×d3+ 17 c×d3 Qf5 18 R×e6+ Kd7!. Similarly unsuccessful is 16 B×g6+ h×g6 17 Rd8+ Kf7 18 Rf1+ Kg7 19 Bf6+ Q×f6 20 R×f6 K×f6 21 Qf4+ Ke7 22 Qd6+ Kf7 23 Qc7+ Kf6 24 Qf4+, and White is obliged to force a draw.

After 15 ... Nc5 Lepeshkin analyzes three basic continuations:

2. The Birth of a Variation

B(i). 16 Rhf1 Be7 (after *16 ... Nbd7* White's initiative develops unhindered: *17 Rde1 Qd6 18 B×b5! Bg7 19 b4! a×b5 20 N×b5 Qb6 21 Nc7+! Q×c7 22 R×e6+ N×e6 23 Q×e6* mate, or *18 ... a×b5 19 N×b5 Qc6 20 Nc7+ Q×c7 21 R×e6+*, or *18 ... Bc6 19 B×c6 Q×c6 20 Qf4*) 17 B×e7 K×e7 18 Rfe1 N×d3+ 19 c×d3 Qd6! 20 Qg5+ (*20 d4 Bd5!*) 20 ... Kf7 21 Rf1+ Ke8, and Black beats off the attack.

B(ii). 16 B×b5+!? Nc6!

Weaker is 16 ... Kf7 (*16 ... a×b5 17 Rd8+ Kf7 18 Rf1+ Kg7 19 Qh4*, or *16 ... Nbd7 17 Rhe1 Qf5 18 B×d7+ N×d7 19 R×e6+ Kf7 20 Qc4*, and wins) 17 Rd8 Nbd7 (*17 ... a×b5 18 Rf1+ Kg7 19 Qh4*) 18 R×d7 N×d7 19 Rf1+ Ke8 (*19 ... Kg7 20 B×d7*, and White maintains very strong pressure) 20 B×d7+ K×d7 21 Rf7+ Kc8 22 Qc4+ Kb8 (*22 ... Qc5* loses immediately to *23 R×f8+*) 23 Bf4 Bh6 24 B×h6 Rc8 (*24 ... Qe1+ 25 Nd1 Rc8 26 Bf4+ e5 27 Qb3 Rc7 28 R×c7*, with a won position) 25 Qf4 Q×f4 26 B×f4+ Ka7 27 Be3+ Kb8 28 Na4, with advantage to White.

17 Rhe1 Qf5 (*17 ... h5 18 Qh4 Q×g5+ 19 Q×g5 Bh6 20 Q×h6 R×h6 21 B×c6+ B×c6 22 b4 Ke7 23 B×c5*, and an endgame is reached where White has an extra pawn and the initiative. He also has the advantage after *18 ... Qf5 19 Nd5 a×b5 20 Nc7+ Kf7 21 N×a8*).

18 Qg3 a×b5 19 Rd5 Qf7 20 N×b5 Rc8 21 Qc3 Rg8 22 R×c5 Be7 (bad is *22 ... B×c5 23 Q×c5*, when there is no defence against *24 Nd6+*, or *22 ... Qd7 23 Rd1*) 23 Kb1!, and Black is helpless against the threats of 24 B×e7 and 24 Qc4.

B(iii). 16 Qh4 Nbd7 17 Rhe1 Qg7 18 Be4 B×e4 19 N×e4

19 ... Rc8 (*19 ... Kf7 20 N×c5 N×c5 21 b4*) 20 Qh3! Be7 (bad is *20 ... Rc6 21 N×c5 B×c5 22 R×e6+*, or *20 ... Kf7 21 R×d7+ N×d7 22 Nd6+*) 21 Nd6+ B×d6 22 R×e6+ Kf7 23 Re×d6 Rc7 24 Rf1+ Kg8 25 Bh6 Qe7 26 Qf3, and Black is helpless.

Black is also faced with difficult problems in the event of 16 ... N×d3+ 17 R×d3 Nd7 18 Re1 Qf5 19 g4 Qf7 20 Red1 Bc6 (after *20 ... Bg7 21 R×d7 Q×d7 22 R×d7 K×d7 23 Bf6 B×f6 24 Q×f6* the co-ordination between White's queen and knight guarantees him the advantage) 21 R×d7! B×d7 22 Ne4 Be7 23 B×e7 Qf4+ (*23 ... Q×e7 24 Nf6+*) 24 Kb1.

Despite being the exchange up, Black's position does not inspire confidence. E.g. 24 ... Q×e4 25 Bd6 Kf7 26 Qe7+ Kg8 27 Rf1.

I have given in full the analysis made by Lepeshkin. If one unconditionally takes on trust the variations indicated, then it may seem at first that Black's entire opening system has been struck a serious blow. But after checking the analysis in detail, I discovered in it several mistakes and areas of unexplored territory, which, in my opinion, must shake seriously the conclusions drawn by Lepeshkin:

I. In variation *A* (*15 ... Be7*), the position on p. 98, which is assessed by Lepeshkin as won for White, is still far from clear. Only one possibility, 23 ... Nc5, is analyzed, but Black also has other resources. In particular, 23 ... Qf2 deserves consideration, with the follow-up 24 Qd6 Qb6 25 Qe7 Ra7 26 R×e6 Qc5.

II. In variation *B* (ii)—p. 99—after 15 ... Nc5 16 B×b5+ Nc6 17 Rhe1 h5 18 Qh4 Qf5 19 Nd5 a×b5 20 Nc7+ Kf7 21 N×a8 Lepeshkin considers that White has the advantage. But Black can continue 21 ... Q×g5+ 22 Q×g5 Bh6, when both 23 Rf1+ Kg7 24 Q×h6+ K×h6 25 Nc7 b4 26 Rd6 (*26 Rf6 Kg7*) 26 ... Rc8 27 N×e6 N×e6 28 R×e6 Nd4, and 23 Q×h6 R×h6 24 Nc7 b4 25 Rd6 g5 are favourable for him.

Besides, in the main line, 17 ... Qf5 18 Qg3 a×b5 19 Rd5 Qf7 20 N×b5 Rc8 21 Qc3, Lepeshkin considers only 21 ... Rg8, and overlooks an excellent tactical possibility for Black: 21 ... Nb4!!, and now 22 Q×h8 Ncd3+ 23 R×d3 (if *23 Kd1*, then *23 ... N×b2+ 24 Ke2 Ba6! 25 c4 N×c4*, and Black wins) 23 ... N×d3+ 24 Kb1 (*24 Kd1 Nf2+*) 24 ... Qf2! 25 R×e6+ Kd7 26 Q×h7+ K×e6 27 Q×g6+ Ke5! 28 Q×d3 Qe1+ 29 Bc1 Be4, and White is defenceless.

After 23 Kb1 B×d5 24 Nd6+ Kd7 25 N×f7 B×a2+ 26 Ka1 Black can, if he wishes, force a draw by 26 ... Ra8 27 Re2 (*27 Qd4+ Bd5+ 28 Kb1 Ra1+!*) 27 ... Bd5+, but he can also attempt to play for a win by 26 ... N×e1, meeting 27 Ne5+ by boldly advancing his king: 27 ... Kd6 28 b3 Ne×c2+ 29 Kb2 Kd5! 30 Qf6 Nd4.

III. In variation *B* (iii)—p. 99— Lepeshkin concentrates on 19 ... Rc8, and totally disregards the stronger 19 ... Be7!, when it is doubtful whether White has more than a draw: 20 B×e7 Q×e7 21 Nd6+ Kd8 22 Nf7+ (*22 Qd4 Rf8*) 22 ... Ke8.

IV. And, finally, Lepeshkin does not consider at all the important continuation 14 ... Nc5, where after 15 Rd8+ Q×d8 16 B×d8 K×d8 the move 13 ... g6 proves very useful for Black. In this case it is doubtful whether White can hope for an advantage.

Thus Lepeshkin's analysis does not bury the entire Variation, but merely provides additional material for reflection and creative argument.

Finally, only one conclusion can be drawn: the wealth of ideas and the number of variations here are so great, that all lovers of so-called 'fighting play' will always be able to find in The Variation a boundless and fruitful field for exploration, experiment and discovery.

And so, the fate of The Variation is on the agenda. Will White be able to find a new antidote against Black's undoubtedly daring plan? It is doubtful whether the coming years or even decades can give a more or less complete and definite answer to this simple question....

The latest word (June 1980) by the Translator

With this book at the proof stage, it seems entirely appropriate to comment on four important games played by the author during the past 12 months. In the first of these, against **Belyavsky** in the USSR Spartakiad, Moscow 1979, The Variation suffered a temporary setback:

After the initial moves 1 e4 c5 2 Nf3 d6 3 d4 c×d4 4 N×d4 Nf6 5 Nc3 a6 6 Bg5 e6 7 f4 b5 8 e5 d×e5 9 f×e5 Qc7 10 e×f6 Qe5+ 11 Be2 Q×g5 12 0-0 Qe5 (pp. 55-56) White introduced the innovation **13 Nf3**. The following comments are by Belyavsky in *64*.

13...Bc5+ (The immediate capture on f6 is clearly unfavourable in view of 14 Ne4.) **14 Kh1 Q×f6 15 Ne4 Qe7 16 Nfg5.**

16...0-0 (16...f5 is refuted by 17 Bh5+ g6 18 N×h7! g×h5 19 Nef6+ Kf7 20 Q×h5+ Kg7 21 Rf3.) **17 N×f7! R×f7 18 R×f7 K×f7 19 Bh5+ Kg8** (The tactical justification for the capture on f7 lies in the variation 19...g6 20 N×c5 Ra7 21 Ne4 g×h5 22 Nd6+ and 23 N×c8.) **20 N×c5 Nd7?** (This loses a pawn. It is true that 20...Q×c5 fails to 21 Qd8+ Qf8 22 Bf7+!, but after 20...Ra7 Black could still have just about held on.) **21 N×e6! Bb7** (The knight cannot be taken, because of 22 Bf3, with the threats of 23 B×a8 and 23 Bd5.)

White went on to win after a stubborn battle lasting 78 moves. However, correspondence published shortly afterwards in *64* suggested that Belyavsky's idea was neither as new, nor as dangerous as it appeared. The position after White's 16th move (see diagram) had evidently already occurred in a correspondence game back in 1977, which went 16...f5 17 Bh5+ g6 18 N×h7 Kf7! (rather than *18...g×h5*, as given by Belyavsky), when it would seem that Black should at least be able to hold his own.

At any rate, Polugayevsky himself must have found a satisfactory counter, for a few moths later, against **Grünfeld** at the Interzonal Tournament, Riga 1979, he again employed the Variation, only this time it was he who introduced an innovation.

In the Simagin line (pp. 72-73) Black chose **11...Nc6**, a move which formerly was condemned, because of the continuation **12 N×c6 Q×c6 13 Qd3**, but Polugayevsky's new move **13...h6!?** gives Black additional defensive resources based on ...g7-g5. The game continued sharply

14 Bh4 Bb7 15 Be2 Qc7 16 Rhe1 Nc5 17 Qh3 b4 (very risky; 17...Rc8 appears sounder) 18 Nb5 a×b5 19 B×b5+ Bc6 20 Qf3.

In this apparently desperate position Polugayevsky had foreseen the spectacular counter **20...Nb3+!!** The reply **21 Kb1?** allowed Black to retain his extra piece by **21...Na5**, and eventually he was able to realize his material advantage. After 21 a×b3, on the other hand, a maze of complications result, in which we can merely indicate the first few possible steps: 21...Ra1+ 22 Kd2 Qd7+ 23 Ke3 Bc5+ 24 Kf4 g5+ 25 Kg3 R×d1 26 B×c6 R×e1 27 B×d7+ Kf8, and analysis by Averkin suggests a draw as the likely outcome.

The fact that 11...Nc6 may after all be playable opens up a whole new field for experimentation and research!

In his introduction to the Russian edition of this book, **Mikhail Tal** expressed the opinion that "some day White will succeed in casting doubts on the theoretical correctness of Black's set-up". In his recent Candidates Quarter-Final Match against Polugayevsky, Alma-Ata 1980, the former World Champion attempted to do just this in the very first game in which he was White.

In the basic position of The Variation after 9...Qc7, Tal essayed a new sacrificial idea: **10 B×b5+!? a×b5 11 e×f6 Qe5+ 12 Qe2 Q×g5 13 Nd×b5**, but now the fine defensive manoeuvre **13...Ra5!** enabled Black to maintain the balance. Following a typically sharp middlegame, Tal went wrong in a level ending, and lost. Tal made a further attempt in the 4th game of the match, which followed the Ljubojevic-Polugayevsky game given on p. 68 up to the 16th move, when White deviated with **16 Ng5**. Black answered **16...f5 17 Qd4 h5** (intending to bring his rook into play via h6).

Here White attempted to seize the initiative by the sacrifice of a 'whole' rook: **18 R×f5!? e×f5 19 Nd5 Qd7 20 Qh4 Be7 21 Kf1 B×g5 22 B×h5+ Kf8 23 Q×g5**. The threat of 24 Nf4 now forced Black to give back the exchange, and White's initiative eventually sufficed to regain his piece, but by then Black's counter-attack was under way, and only a mistake on move 31 robbed Polugayevsky of a second victory with The Variation. The game ended in a draw by perpetual check.

And so, having survived two new sacrificial attempts by the greatest attacking player of our time, The Variation still looks in good shape!

Addendum*

(cf. p.38)

In our World Championship Quarter-Final Candidates' Match in Alma-Ata, 1980, Ex-World Champion Mikhail Tal made a direct attempt to refute The Variation. In just the second game of the Match, i.e. the first in which he had White, after the initial moves 1 e4 c5 2 Nf3 d6 3 d4 c×d4 4 N×d4 Nf6 5 Nc3 a6 6 Bg5 e6 7 f4 b5 8 e5 d×e5 9 f×e5 Qc7 there followed **10 B×b5+**, which came as a complete surprise to me.

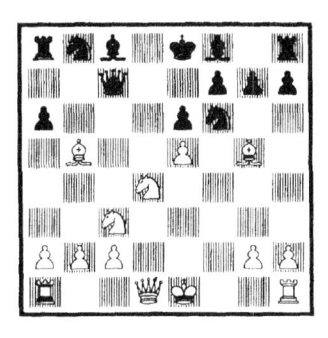

I must confess that, when I was earlier working on The Variation, I had regarded this continuation as sheer folly, and had never made a special examination of it. And suddenly—this innovation, and moreover, in a highly important encounter! Incidentally, Tal later said that the idea belonged to his second, the Latvian master Vitolinsh.

*Added September 1980 by the Author

The game continued **10 ... a×b5 11 e×f6 Qe5+ 12 Qe2 Q×g5 13 Nd×b5**, when I became absorbed in thoughts of a highly serious and not altogether pleasant nature (at the board who likes having to try to refute a prepared variation by the opponent?). Much time was spent on them, but on the other hand the very strong move **13 ... Ra5** was found. Black removes his rook from the knight fork at c7, and in some variations threatens to bring it into play along the fifth rank. At the same time, he threatens to increase the pressure on the attacking white knight at b5.

It was now White's turn to be faced with the question: what to do next? He cannot strengthen his attack by 14 Rd1, as the simple 14 ... Bd7 would follow. And he decided to bring his knight at c3 into play, after first weakening the d6 square by **14 f×g7**. At the board Black reconciled himself to this and replied **14 ... B×g7**, but I think that 14 ... Q×g7 was also not at all bad, maintaining control of d6. Of course, in this case 15 0-0-0 would have given White certain practical chances, but they are clearly insufficient to refute The Variation. So that Tal's innovation was clearly intended for 'one-off' use, and it is significant that in his next 'White' game in the match he did not repeat it.

It remains for me to add that, after the game continuation **14 ... B×g7 15 Ne4 Qe5 16 Nbd6+ Ke7 17 0-0 f5 18 Rad1**

Rd5 19 Qc4, a very sharp position was reached, with a slight advantage to White. True, in subsequent analysis it has not been demonstrated that White could at any point have increased his advantage...

(cf. p.58)

The position in question is reached after 1 e4 c5 2 Nf3 d6 3 d4 c×d4 4 N×d4 Nf6 5 Nc3 a6 6 Bg5 e6 7 f4 b5 8 e5 d×e5 9 f×e5 Qc7 10 e×f6 Qe5+ 11 Be2 Q×g5 12 0-0 Qe5. At the tournament in Bugojno, 1980, Ljubomir Kavalek chose against me **13 Bh5**, which at first sight seems paradoxical, and only after **13 ... g6** played **14 Bf3**.

The idea of White's manoeuvre is to retain his pawn outpost at f6, and, after Black's planned K-side castling, to possibly threaten him with no less than mate at g7. True, it also has advantages for Black: he no longer has to reckon with the capture f×g7, breaking up his king's pawn cover.

This game failed to answer the question as to who's advantages are the more important. After **14 ... Ra7 15 Ne4 Rd7 16 c3 Bb7 17 Ng3** (17 Nf2 possibly deserves consideration, but then in some cases Black can build up an attack on h2 by 17 ... Bd6) **17 ... B×f3 18 Q×f3 Bc5 19 Kh1** (the best move!) **19 ... B×d4 20 c×d4 R×d4 21 Rae1 Qd5** the players agreed to a draw, since the game was played in the last round, and each was satisfied with half a point. Subsequent analysis showed that for the pawn White has certain compensation, and that in this very sharp position the chances are roughly equal. So that Kavalek's idea can serve as a theme both for theoretical searchings, and for testing in practice.

(cf. p.70)

1 e4 c5 2 Nf3 d6 3 d4 c×d4 4 N×d4 Nf6 5 Nc3 a6 6 Bg5 e6 7 f4 b5 8 e5 d×e5 9 f×e5 Qc7 10 e×f6 Qe5+ 11 Be2 Q×g5 12 Qd3 Q×f6 13 Rf1 Qe5 14 Rd1 Ra7 15 Nf3 Qc7.

Here I must make a confession. After my game with Ljubojevic back in 1973, I thought to myself: "What if, instead of 16 Ne5, White should choose **16 Ng5?**"

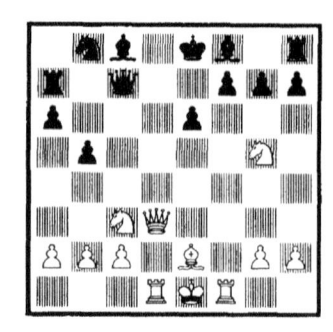

Now Black cannot continue 16 ... Be7 (in analogy with the game against Ljubojevic), since there follows not 17 N×f7, but 17 R×f7!, and if 17 ... Q×h2, then 18 R×g7, winning quickly. There only remains 16 ... f5, but after 17 Qd4!, with the terrible threat of Bh5+, Black's position appears indefensible.

A year went by in searching until I at last found an acceptable idea. What's more, my faith in the durability of Black's position was inspired by ... the white rooks, which have 'locked' their king in the centre. It must be agreed that the king at e1 is no adornment to White's position...

This continuation received a practical testing six years later in the Tal-Polugayevsky Candidates' Match already referred to. In the fourth game the Ex-World Champion boldly went in for the position in the diagram, and after **16 ... f5** continued, as I had once feared, **17 Qd4**.

On this there followed **17 ... h5!**, radically cutting short the threat of the bishop check at h5. And when White continued his attack with **18 R×f5 e×f5 19 Nd5**, Black replied **19 ... Qd7!**

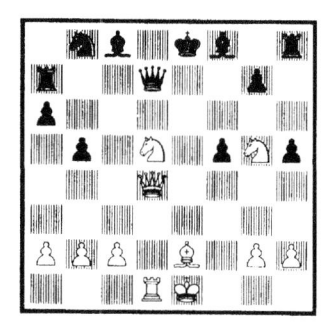

It turns out that on 20 Qe5+ Be7 21 Q×b8 Black is perfectly happy to play 21 ... 0-0, and after 22 Nf6+ B×f6 23 R×d7 R×d7 he has more than adequate compensation for the queen. Black also has a defence in the variation 20 Nf6+ g×f6 21 Q×f6. Of course, to exhaust all the possibilities for the two sides in this very sharp position is simply inconceivable, but, I repeat, in my opinion Black always has the strength to repel the attack.

At any rate, after spending considerable time in thought, Tal played **20 Qh4**, after which probably the best that White can hope for is perpetual check. Black chose the safest move **20 ... Be7** (20 ... Qc6 also deserved consideration, including the rook at a7 in the defence) **21 Kf1!** (the plausible 21 B×h5+ Kf8 22 Nf4 leads to a win for Black after 22 ... Qe8!!) **21 ... B×g5 22 B×h5+ Kf8 23 Q×g5 R×h5 24 Q×h5 Qf7 25 Qh8+ Qg8 26 Qh4 Kf7 27 Qh5+ g6 28 Qh4 Qg7 29 Qd8 Be6 30 Q×b8 Rd7**, and a subsequent inaccuracy allowed White to save the half-point. Meanwhile, Black had the interesting possibility of 26 ... Nc6!, which after 27 Nb4 (it was this that 'frightened' me during the game) 27 ... Bd7! 28 N×c6 B×c6 29 Rd8+ Be8 30 Qb4+ Re7 leads to a position where Black is tied up, but he has an extra piece, and White has no way of increasing the pressure.

3. In the Interval
(The Analysis of Adjourned Games)

In the work of the chess player outside the walls of the tournament hall, the analysis of adjourned games is the other, and of course essential, side of the coin. The banal assertion that it is carried out 'in the quiet of one's study' is hardly appropriate. For a start, the time allotted for analysis is, as a rule, less than one would like, and frequently it is time, one might say, 'of the wrong sort', to which a person is unaccustomed: from late at night until morning. Sometimes the time is reduced to the minimum—in recent years international tournaments have been run more and more frequently on a severe schedule, whereby between the main session and the adjournment session one and a half to two hours are allowed 'for everything': eating, relaxation and analysis. It hardly needs to be said that frequently one doesn't even have time to remember about the first two components....

The time devoted to the analysis of unfinished games is crammed with mental activity. There is no time for distraction or relaxation, and so the hours spent on adjourned positions are, by their very nature, highly intensive and capacious.

Analysis, in contrast to research work on opening problems, is always specific, in the sense that the opponent is already known. And although in an adjourned position one always tries to discover the absolute truth, knowledge of the opponent's strong and weak points can sometimes enable one to make the play as unpleasant as possible for him, to lower his vigilance by apparent inactivity, or to set problems which will be especially difficult for him in particular.

But in principle, I repeat, analysis, and the study of openings, are two aspects of a common form of creativity. In each case a part is played by intuition, general positional understanding, and experience. In each case, in contrast to a tournament game, a move can be taken back, and one does not have to keep spasmodically looking at the rising flag on the chess clock. But on the other hand, it is shameful to permit oneself a mistake, which is so common during play, it is shameful not to find the strongest continuation, and it is shameful to overlook a study-like win if there should be one, or the sole possibility of saving an apparently hopeless game.

I know that this is what a number of leading grandmasters think. And I also know that if, as a rule, a strong player analyzes an adjourned position more deeply and more accurately than a player of lower standard, then if the analysis is indeed carried out with maximum intensity, this contributes to the development and improvement of the player.

After all, the positions analyzed are normally rich in possibilities, since games where the outcome is clear are not normally played on. There is no better way of replenishing your supply of ideas and of teaching yourself to pay attention to nuances, than by searching for the strongest continuations both for yourself and your opponent. But if a player becomes carried away by his analysis 'in one direction' only, and if he does not so much study the various positions as 'revel' in them, and in his positional or material advantage, how many times do we witness surprises on the resumption! How many stalemating combinations does the defending side find, and how many amazing transpositions into theoretically drawn endings! In short, the axiom that chess does not tolerate frivolity is especially clearly apparent in the analysis of unfinished games.

BY THE METHOD OF TRIAL AND ERROR

There are many masters of analysis. On many occasions the possibilities in an adjourned position have been brilliantly demonstrated by Efim Geller, Paul Keres and Vasily Smyslov. What wonderful examples of analysis we see in the games of Mikhail Botvinnik! And what's more, with the years, with the gaining of experience, the quality of analysis does not deteriorate, but improves. I know this from my own experience: work on adjourned positions becomes more sensible and more rational, fewer inaccuracies are committed, and even fewer superficial, premature judgements of the type 'the rest is obvious'.

But, of course, it is life that has taught me this. Here are a few examples.

Polugayevsky–Averbakh
28th USSR Championship, Moscow 1961

White has an undisputed positional advantage, in view of the chronic weakness of Black's Q-side pawns, and also the difference in activity of the minor pieces. But the black queen is lurking in the enemy rear, and to gain the win considerable effort is still required.

During our adjournment analysis, Lyev Aronin, who was then my trainer, and I studied most carefully the position which arose after White's sealed move.

41 f3

We first considered 41 ... Nb3, to which we planned not, of course, the pseudo-aggressive 42 Qd5? Qc2+ 43 Kg3 Q×c3 44 Bf2 Nd2, when it is Black who has the attack, but the quiet 42 Qe2, and if again 42 ... Nd4, then either the simple 43 Qf2, or the sharper 43 c×d4. By moving to e2, the queen stops the black 'c' pawn from advancing with gain of tempo.

The move we settled on as the strongest was the one in fact made by Averbakh, that brilliant master of the endgame.

41 ...	Qa1
42 Be8!	

A move, at first sight hard to understand, but in fact very strong. The idea of it is to lure the black king to g8, where it will be in danger should the white queen succeed in crossing the demarcation line and participating in the attack on f7: 42 ... Kg8 43 c×d4 e×d4 44 Bf2 c3 45 Qf4!. Now the defence 45 ... Qa7 allows the blockade of the black pawns by 46 B×b5 followed by Bd3, while on 45 ... Qa2 White has the very strong reply 46 Bc6 c2 47 Bd5 Qa7 48 Bb3.

On finding this, we took into account various other possibilities for Black, whereby he advances his pawns rather more accurately, succeeded in neutralizing them, and relaxed.

42 ...	Kg8
43 c×d4	c3!?

This move we had not taken seriously, and we were thereby made to pay for breaking Botvinnik's recommendation: take account of all the possible continuations in the position! In our analysis we had noted in passing that after this Black's pawn chain is broken up, and that it is easier to blockade the 'c' and 'd' pawns, but we did not think to analyze the move for some 10-15 minutes. And although, as it later turned out, White's position was still won, in an unfamiliar situation, rapidly becoming sharper, I made a mistake, ran short of time, and in the end almost lost.

44 Qd3!

I spent a considerable amount of time calculating variations involving that same idea of an attack on f7: 44 Qf2 e×d4 (Black does not have time for *44 ... Qb2—45 d×e5 c2 46 e6*, and White returns the piece, contenting himself with a couple of extra pawns and an attack, with opposite coloured bishops) 45 B×d4 B×d4 46 Q×d4 Qa2+ 47 Kg3 c2 48 Qc5, and after 48 ... Qb2 White wins by 49 Qe7, but what can he do after 48 ... Qc4? Only resign!

I therefore outlined a plan to blockade the black pawns, deferring for the moment any ideas of attack.

44 ...	Qb2+
45 Kh3!	

More accurate than 45 Kg3, which after 45 ... e×d4 46 Bf4 could have given Black additional chances based on ... Be5, diverting the white bishop from the black 'c' pawn's queening square.

45 ...	e×d4
46 Bf4	

After 46 B×d4 B×d4 47 Q×d4 Qc1 White cannot avoid perpetual check.

46 ...	c2
47 Qf1	

At the cost of approaching time trouble and great effort, White has found a series of best moves, and has set up the desired blockade. The advance 47 ... d3 leads merely to the loss of the black pawns —48 B×b5 and 49 B×d3, so Black attempts to switch his bishop to the a3–c1 diagonal, so as to nevertheless enable his 'c' pawn to make the last step forward.

47 ...	Bf8!
48 B×b5	Bd6

Or 48 ... B×b4 immediately, which would not have changed anything: White would all the same have retreated his bishop to c1.

49 Bc1	Q×b4

50 e5??

If White had known this resulting position from his analysis, he would without much thought have converted it into a win, which was not now far off: 50 Bd3 Qb1 51 f4, when the direct attack on the king by e4–e5 and f4–f5 is decisive. On 51 ... Qa1 he can play the accurate 52 Kg4, so as to avoid the pin on the third rank after 52 ... Ba3 53 B×a3, while the manoeuvre 51 ... Bb4 52 e5 Bc3, with the idea of 53 ... Bb2, is too late, on account of 54 f5 g×f5 (*54 ... Bb2 55 f×g6, and mates*) 54 B×f5 Bd2(b2) 55 Bh7+! Kf8 (or *55 ... K×h7 56 Q×f7+ Kh8 57 g6*) 56 e6, and wins.

But I was tempted by the absurd idea of luring the black bishop to e5 and then, by attacking it with my queen, to transfer the queen either to d2, so as to win the 'c' pawn, or to e8, so as to attack f7. And here is what happened.

50 ...	B×e5
51 Bd3	Qb1
52 Qe1	Bf4
53 Bc4	

It would appear that the second goal has been achieved, and that there is no defence against mate in three moves or the loss of the bishop (after *53 ... Qb7*), but ....

53 ...   Be3

This was the move that White had overlooked. He immediately finds himself on the verge of defeat.

With my flag poised to fall, I leapt out of the trap with my queen (after *54 Bd3 Q×c1 55 Q×c1 B×c1 56 B×c2 B×g5* the ending, despite the opposite-coloured bishops, may be beyond saving)

54 Qa5

And it is quite possible that Averbakh was wrong to capture my bishop immediately, allowing me to gain perpetual check.

54 ...	Q×c1
55 B×f7+	K×f7

Or 55 ... Kg7 56 Qe5+, with the same result.

56 Qd5+	Ke7
57 Qe5+	

Drawn

Even later in my career, when I already had experience both of competing in strong events, and also of analyzing the most complex adjourned games, I would sometimes 'permit myself' costly, but at the same time instructive, mistakes. Here is one such example:

Larsen–Polugayevsky
Le Havre 1966

42 ...	f5
43 Bd3	f×e4+
44 B×e4	Bf5
45 B×f5	e×f5

In making my 42nd move, I had in fact aimed for this position, in which the game was adjourned.

It is difficult to imagine that Black can lose this ending. His slightly inferior Q-side pawn structure is compensated for by White's weakness at f4. But, it turns out, bishop endings still contain a number of secrets. During my adjournment analysis I realized that the task facing me was not easy. Over a period of several hours during the night which preceded the morning resumption, I worked through the two basic possibilities of attacking the pawn at h5:

A. 46 Bf6 Ke6 47 Bg5, intending Kg3–g4. If now 47 ... Bb4, then 48 Bd8 b5 (*48 ... Bc5 49 Kb3*) 49 Ke3 and 50 Kd3, followed by c2–c3, winning the pawn at a5.

If on 46 Bf6 Ke6 47 Bg5 Black plays 47 ... Kd5, then after 48 Bd8 Kd4 49 Bf6+ Kd5 White gains a tempo, and Black again has serious difficulties.

But in the end I found that after 46 Bf6 Black can draw by 46 ... Be7! 47 Bg5 (the pawn ending is also drawn) 47 ... Bb4! etc.

B. 46 Kg3 Be7 47 Bg7 Ke6 48 Bh6 Kd5 49 Bg5 Bd6 50 Bd8 Ke4 51 B×b6 B×f4+.

On reaching this position I cut short my analysis, since I assumed that the strong passed 'f' pawn should give Black at least equal chances. That was my general assessment, and I preferred sleep to any further analysis. But it was here that my main mistake lay: on resumption this was the path chosen by Larsen, although it involved a serious risk for him.

The game continued:

46 Kg3	Be7
47 Bg7	Ke6
48 Bh6	Kd5
49 Bg5	Bd6

In his analysis, Larsen thought that the strongest continuation for Black was 49 ... Bc5 50 Kh4 Kd4 51 K×h5 Kc3, with equal chances. But here it was Larsen who was wrong: the 'h' pawn is considerably more important than all the Q-side pawns.

50 Bd8	Ke4
51 B×b6	B×f4+
52 Kh4	Bd2
53 K×h5	

This paradoxical decision, taken by Larsen on the resumption of the game, affected me psychologically. I simply couldn't believe that the resulting position was favourable for White; but on the other hand I had not carried through my adjournment analysis to the end. And I was further influenced by the feeling that Larsen was confidently following an already familiar path, along which he had accurately noted all the pitfalls, whereas I was having to act 'spontaneously'.

53 ...	f4?

Here it is, the decisive mistake!

Meanwhile, Black had at his disposal a very strong move, which could, and should, have been worked out during the adjournment analysis: 53 ... Kf3! (not allowing the white king to come back). E.g. 54 h4 f4 55 Kg6 Be3 56 B×a5 Ke2 57 Bc7 f3 58 Bg3 Bf4, and Black wins!

It is curious that the move 53 ... Kf3 also escaped Larsen's attention, even though he had reached this position on his board during the night.

54 Kg4	Be1
55 h4!!	f3
56 Kh3!	

White's aim is to control g2 with his king, and then divert Black's forces by the advance of the 'h' pawn. The black bishop turns out to have more difficulties than it can cope with.

56 ...	Kf4
57 Bc5	Kf5
58 Be7	

In this way White prepares the advance of his 'h' pawn.

58 ...	Ke4

The best chance. If now 59 Bg5, then 59 ... Kd4, breaking through to the Q-side pawns.

59 h5!

Larsen accurately and consistently carries out his plan. Now on 59 ... Ke3 there follows 60 Bc5+ Ke2 (60 ... Kd2 61 h6 K×c2 62 Bd4) 61 h6 f2 62 B×f2 B×f2 63 h7 Bd4 64 b4! a×b4 65 a5 Kd2 66 a6 K×c2 67 a7, and White wins.

59 ...	Bd2
60 Bc5!	

Once again keeping the black king out of e3.

60 ...	Be3
61 Bf8!	

The bishop is ready to support the advance of the 'h' pawn at that moment when its black opposite number is depriving its own king of the square e3.

61 ...	Bd4
62 Bh6!!	

3. In the Interval 109

White fails to achieve his goal after 62 h6 Ke3 63 Bg7 B×g7 64 h×g7 f2, with a draw. But now he threatens by Kg3 to finally neutralize the 'f' pawn, which Black can on no account allow.

| 62 ... | Be5 |

Bad is 62 ... Be3 63 Bg7, when the square e3 is again inaccessible to the black king, while the white 'h' pawn cannot be stopped.

63 Bd2!

Four brilliant moves by the white bishop, and Black's position has become hopeless. The pawn at a5 is doomed.

| 63 ... | Bf4 |
| 64 B×a5 | Ke3 |

| 65 Be1 | Ke2 |
| 66 Kg4!! | |

This shows the extent to which Larsen's analysis went further than my careless analysis. Despite all White's previous successes, it is only this move that leads to a win. Incidentally, it was made instantly ...

66 ...	Bh6
67 Bh4	Bd2
68 Bg3	c5

Black no longer has any useful moves.

69 c4	f2
70 B×f2	K×f2
71 h6!	Ke3
72 h7	Bc3
73 a5	Resigns

Of course, in subsequent years I encountered other surprises during the resumption of games; no one is guaranteed against them. But from the examples of my adjourned games against Mikhail Tal and Rafael Vaganian, which are given a little further on, it will be seen that a rationally constructed analysis, even with some omissions, will allow one at the board to find a way out.

What is meant by a rational analysis? There is no single answer to this—too much depends on the individuality of the chess player. Some outline only general plans and the piece set-up for which they are aiming. This, for example, is how Ex-World Champion Smyslov analyzes, and in this he is helped by his brilliant intuition. Grandmaster Geller's method is rather different. Apart from the plan itself, he also works out in great detail the most specific ways imaginable of carrying it out. That is also how I try to operate, and with experience I have begun more and more often—and nowadays almost always—to resort to Botvinnik's principle, which has already been mentioned: not to disregard any moves in the position which are at all possible, even the most 'stupid' and apparently absurd. For it is these which can contain a good deal of venom, and several examples, which we have yet to come to, will confirm this.

All this refers to the strategy, as it were, of analysis. When it comes to tactics, this depends on many factors, in particular on the player's tournament position, on his state of health, on the number of unfinished games he has accumulated, and on the schedule of the event. Sometimes it makes sense not to use up all your strength on the thorough study of an adjourned position, in order to avoid losing a mass of points in other unfinished or subsequent games. Sometimes, when you know your opponent well, you can take a risk by assuming that he won't go in for a particular variation, and thus economize on effort by reducing the extent of your analysis. All this depends very specifically on the circumstances. I can state only one thing with complete certainty: it is wrong to analyze right up to the last minute before resumption of the game. One should, on sitting down at the board, be able for a moment to glance at the familiar position from the side, as it were. If something has been overlooked in analysis, or if it has not been carried through to the end, such a glance may help, and in the experience of each one of us there are certainly examples which will confirm this.

But in general, when there are no exceptional circumstances in the tournament, a player should, in my opinion, go fully into the analysis, devoting to it maximum effort and time. Suppose that even a part of this effort proves to be wasted—it will subsequently be rewarded. Analysis is an excellent form of training; it develops efficiency, perseverance and stamina, which chess players really need no less than marathon runners. And in sport, severe training methods have for a long time been practised.

But nevertheless, even after working move by move through the adjourned position 'à la Botvinnik', I have sometimes, at literally the last minute—it has happened on the way to the tournament hall, or even when sitting down at the board—noticed a 'hole' in my analysis. This happens to everyone I know, and in some cases is of no consequence, although it is annoying, especially if much time and effort have been spent on the analysis. It is important only that the number of such omissions should not show a tendency to increase.

Here are some memorable examples.

Vaganian–Polugayevsky
*39th USSR Championship,
Leningrad 1971*

The analysis of this adjourned position took me roughly ten hours of highly intensive work, while my opponent, as he himself said, spent less than half an hour on it. He considered the position to be clearly drawn, whereas I found a multitude of possibilities... for him, and, naturally, I looked for a defence against them for myself. The resumption of the game itself lasted approximately five minutes....

To go back to the first five hours of

'normal time', in this game there was everything: at first White had the advantage, then Black, and then all sorts of adventures began. When the game was finally adjourned, I couldn't decide who stood better. Psychologically, of course, it was unpleasant for me—I was a rook down. Then it appeared that there were various pins, the rook could be regained, and in addition Black had lots of pawns—in short, there was no cause for despair. But when I reached the hotel, I quickly saw that all these thoughts were the result of the five-hour battle, and that in fact it was not at all easy for Black to save the game. In addition, of course, I didn't know White's sealed move, which could be either 41 e4, or 41 Nf5+.

At first I couldn't see what I was going to do after 41 Nf5+. If 41 ... e×f5, then 42 e4, and Black's position is unpleasant. And on 41 ... R×f5 42 R×f5 e×d5 (or *42 ... e×f5, or 42 ... Q×d5*) White replies 43 e4!. But here came my first ray of hope: in this last variation I managed to find a move which I am sure you will not fail to like: 42 ... Be3!!

A slight digression: later I met Bronstein, and couldn't deny myself the pleasure of showing him this position and this move—after all, it is not often that one finds continuations which can compare with the famous... R×a3 in the game between Bronstein and Mikenas from one of the USSR Championships! David Ionovich liked the move, but I have to confess that his rejoinder came as something of a surprise to me:

"Oh Lyev, if only it wasn't a bishop you had at e3, but a knight!"

But let us return to reality. After 42 ... Be3 White has nothing better than perpetual check by 43 Rf7+ K×f7 44 Qh7+. Otherwise on, for instance, 43 Qd3 e×d5, Black himself gives mate.

Thus one move, 41 Nf5+, had been dealt with. But the other caused Black much more trouble. It turned out that this was the move that had in fact been sealed.

41 e4   e×d5

Black has to concede control of f5, since there is no other way out.

42 Nf5+   R×f5

Otherwise White wins easily by capturing on e7 with his knight.

43 R×f5

The alternative capture, 43 e×f5, is dangerous now for White, in view of 43 ... d4+. After the move played, I had prepared in my analysis an apparently unclear reply.

43 ...   e6

After the game Vaganian asked me: "Why did you play 43 ... e6? If you had captured on e4—43 ... d×e4, I would have offered you a draw immediately."

I was quite put out, and then replied: "What do you mean, draw?! After 44 Qc4 Black is in a bad way."

In short, 43 ... e6 was the only possibility of resistance. It was after this that the real analysis was required!

At first I examined 44 Rf6 Bg5 45 Rf1 d×e4 46 h4 (so as to give the king a shelter at h2) 46 ... g×h3+ 47 K×h3, and White's heavy pieces must inevitably penetrate into the vicinity of the black king. 46 ... Be7 is also inadequate, since the bishop retreats to a passive position, while after 46 ... e3+ 47 Kh2 Bh6 48 Rf6 Black succumbs on g6, since 48 ... Qe8 is answered by 49 Qe4, with the threat of 50 Qb7+.

I also checked the tactical possibility 46 ... Bd2, but—and you will have to take my word for this, since there are too many variations in the analysis—after 47 Qd1 Black nevertheless loses.

There remained only 46 ... Bh6. Now the natural 47 Rf6 can be parried: 47 ... Qd5 48 Qc4 Q×e5 49 R×e6 Qb2+, and White cannot avoid perpetual check.

But White appears to have a more effective course: 47 Kh2 Qd5 48 Qf2 Q×e5 49 Qf7+. True, after 49 ... Kh8 50 Qg6 Bg7 51 Rd1 Bf6! White has nothing, in view of the threat of perpetual check should his rook leave the first two ranks.

I was therefore 'forced' to analyze for White the more prosaic exchange of queens—50 Qf6+ Bg7 51 Q×e5 B×e5. Black has three pawns for the exchange, and, of course, if White were to play here 52 Re1 Bd4 53 R×e4 e5 followed by ... Kg7-f6, Black would stand no worse.

But White has a much stronger move in 52 Rf7!, cutting off the black king, and if 52 ... e3 53 Kg2 e2 54 Kf2 B×g3+ 55 K×e2 B×h4, then the white rook has time to capture the 'a' and 'b' pawns, when the white 'a' pawn is clearly superior to the black 'h' pawn.

Salvation was found in a semi-study: 52 Rf7 e3 53 Kg2 b5! 54 Re7! c4! 55 b×c4 e2 56 Kf2 (this is why *54 Re7* is given an exclamation mark, although *54 Ra7* appears stronger; Black does not now have *56 ... Bd4+*) 56 ... b×a4! 57 R×e6 e1=Q+ 58 K×e1 B×g3+, and it turns out that the 'c' pawn is not so terrible, since the black king just succeeds in stopping it, while the black pawns divert the rook.

The main continuation is 59 Ke2 Kg7 60 c5 Kf7 61 Re3 (stronger than *61 R×a6*) 61 ... B×h4 62 c6 Bd8 63 Rd3 Ke8, and tempo by tempo Black can defend.

It can be imagined what a great deal of time this analysis took me.

Then roughly an hour before I was due to set off for the resumption, I discovered that this was all romanticism. The simple fact is that after 43 ... e6 44 Rf6 Bg5 Black must resign, and what's more, immediately: 45 Rg6+! K×g6 46 e×d5+, and the queen is lost.

You can imagine my feelings! I was obliged to change to another course (apart from the line shown above, I had also analyzed the following variation: *43 ... e6 44 Rf6 d4 45 Rf1 Be3*, although I didn't like the fact that White could play *h2-h3*, then exchange on g4 and transfer his rook via h1 to h4), where in general some sort of salvation had also been found.

The resumption of the game, however, was brief and simple.

44 R×h5

At the time, the analysis of this continuation took me some ten minutes, not more....

44 ...	d×e4
45 Qd1	e3+

46 Kg1	**Qf3**
47 Qd7+	

White cannot exchange on f3, since the black pawns, with the support of their bishop, would quickly decide the game.

47 ...	**Kg6**
48 Qe8+	
Drawn	

There is no escape from perpetual check.

I consider that the resumption of this game is a good illustration on the theme of 'the torment of creativity'.

The adjournment of the following game proceeded with similar, although even greater effort and tension.

Tal–Polugayevsky
*42nd USSR Championship,
Premier League,
Leningrad 1974*

Despite the drawing tendencies of opposite-coloured bishops, Black's extra pawn and the great activity of his pieces allow him with justification to hope for a win.

41 ...	**Ra2+**

This sealed move is the strongest in the given position. My analysis now proceeded in two directions.

On general grounds, I considered 42 Kc1 to be a 'second-rate' move, but I nevertheless looked at it first, and decided that nothing is achieved by 42 ... a3? 43 Kb1 Rb2+ 44 Ka1, but that on the other hand, 42 ... Kg6 43 Ra7 Be4, with the threat of 44 ... a3 and 45 ... Rc2+, wins.

And I switched over completely to the analysis of 42 Kd3, on which I spent a mass of time.

Here I planned 42 ... Ra3+ 43 Kd2 Bc4 44 Rd6 Rd3+ 45 Ke2 Bb5 (after *45 ... Rd4+ 46 Kf2 Re4* followed by ... *Bd5* and ... *R×e5*, Black has considerable difficulties on account of the weakness of g7) 46 Rb6 (*46 g6+ K×g6 47 R×e6+ Kf5 48 Rb6 Rd5+ 49 Ke1 a3* also wins) 46 ... Rb3+ 47 Kf2 Bc4 48 Rc6 Rb2+ 49 Kg3 Rc2, and the pawn automatically reaches a2.

Having found all this, I once again checked 42 Kc1, and suddenly discovered that the win was not so simple: 42 ... Kg6, and now not 43 Ra7, but 43 Kb1 Kf5 44 Bc1! g6 (*44 ... K×e5 45 Ra5!*) 45 Ra7 Rb3 46 Bb2 K×g5 47 Rh7!, preventing the advance of the 'g' pawn, and winning it in the event of 47 ... Kg4 48 Rg7 g5 49 Bc1.

However, I then found 48 ... R×b2+ 49 K×b2 g5, and calmed down ....

It remained for me to consider the following line: 42 Kc1 Kg6 43 Ra7 Be4 44 Bd4 a3 45 Kd1 Bd5! 46 Kc1 Bb3!, and there is no defence against the threat of 47 ... Rc2—if 47 Kb1, then 47 ... Rd2. If, on the other hand, 44 Kd1, then 44 ... a3 45 Bd4 (*45 Bc5 Ra1+ 46 Kd2 a2 47 Bd4 Rh1*) 45 ... Bd5! 46 Kc1 Bb3, with again the same win.

But on the resumption, after

42 Kc1	Kg6
43 Ra7	Be4
44 Kd1	

I suddenly noticed to my horror that 44 ... a3 does not win, on account of 45 Bc5 Ba1+ 46 Ke2!! a2 47 Bd4 Rh1 48 R×a2 Rh2+ 49 Bf2.

I should mention one curious detail. Tal later told me that he also considered the position after 44 ... a3 to be lost, but when I sank into thought, he did too. And, of course, he found everything!

Fortunately the win was still there, but I was terribly vexed by this mistake in my analysis.

44 ...	Bf3+
45 Kc1	Be4
46 Kd1	Bc2+
47 Kd2	Bb3+

Having gained time by repeating moves, Black embarks on a plan which he found at the board. He intends to transpose into an ending without rooks, and with just opposite-coloured bishops!

48 Kc3	Rg2
49 Kb4	Rg3
50 Bc1	Rf3
51 Rc7	Rf7
52 R×f7	

Otherwise Black, after freeing his king from the defence of his g7 pawn, wins without any great difficulty.

| 52 ... | K×f7 |
| 53 Kc5 | Bc2! |

The bishop is transferred to f5, so as to free the black king, although Black also wins by the simple 53 ... Kg6 54 Kd6 Kf5, when White is in *zugzwang*—55 Ke7 g6 56 Kf7 Bc2.

54 Kd6	Bf5
55 Ba3	Kg6
56 Bc1	Kh5

The last time trouble move. 56 ... Bg4 followed by ... Kf5 and ... g6 wins more simply.

57 Ke7	g6
58 Kd7	Kg4
59 Kd6	Kg3

To be fair, it should be admitted that a move earlier 58 ... a3 59 B×a3 K×g5 would have won, but about the 'a' pawn I simply "forgot"...

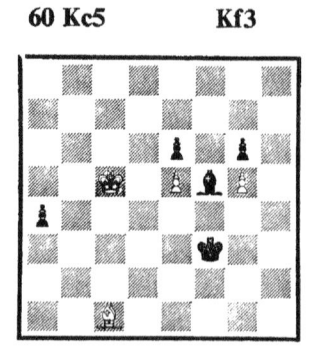

60 Kc5   Kf3

61 Kd4

This loses immediately, whereas 61 Kc6! would have forced Black to find a win in the variation 61 ... Kg4 62 Kd6 a3 63 B×a3 K×g5. It is not difficult to calculate that Black can just reach a position where White is unable to cope with the 'g' pawn.

61 ...   Kg4

White resigns: he cannot prevent ... Bb1 and ... Kf5, after which *zugzwang* decides.

ON WHAT REMAINS UNSEEN

Gheorghiu–Polugayevsky
*Interzonal Tournament,
Petropolis 1973*

A few words about what happened before the adjournment.

In the opening the Rumanian grandmaster employed a comparatively new continuation in the Sicilian Defence. At the board I managed to see my way through the peculiarities of the resulting position, eliminated the one defect in Black's position—a backward pawn—and obtained first the better chances, and then a decisive advantage. But the last few moves were made in a fearful time scramble, and just before the time control Gheorghiu and I 'exchanged' terrible blunders. After an error by me on the 39th move, Gheorghiu could have won instantly, but his reply was equally hasty. Then came Black's concluding move, and the game was adjourned in the following position.

It was clear that Gheorghiu was extremely happy with the position on the board, and, after all the nerve-racking changes of fortune during the 5-hour battle, he sealed his move with an obvious sigh of relief.

I will not hide the fact that, at first, I too thought that Black's position was hopeless. But while Gheorghiu was painstakingly and unhurriedly registering on his score sheet his secret move, I suddenly conceived the wonderful idea of retreating my rook from its attacking position, so as to defend my weak back rank.

And for some reason, unknown even to myself, I immediately sensed that for my opponent this would be a surprise, and by no means a pleasant one. So that when I went up to my dejected second, international master V. Bagirov, I whispered to him: "I think I can win! I have an idea!"

But when we began our analysis, we discovered that the position was fantastically complicated. As regards the unusual nature of the moves found during analysis, in my entire tournament career I have never had anything to compare with this game with Gheorghiu. Both kings are under the threat of a mating attack, but instead of play typical of such positions, on the principle 'who is quicker', here both sides permit themselves quiet moves.

On the resumption I found, as expected, that with his sealed move Gheorghiu had captured a pawn.

**41 R×e5   Qf1+
42 Kg4   Rd8!!**

And my opponent sank into thought for a long time... He was prepared only for forcing continuations such as 42 ... Rg2+ or 42 ... Qg1+.

But we, after spending some fifteen hours, if not more, on our analysis, had examined this quiet rook retreat, and had found an exact winning plan in all variations, except—alas!—one single line. It hardly has to be said that only a miracle could help the Rumanian grandmaster to solve these most complex problems at the board. After all, we had spent hours checking and rechecking variations, discussing their virtues and drawbacks, and had not been at all restricted by the rule 'touch-move'. So how was Gheorghiu to find a way through this labyrinth as the minutes ticked rapidly away, even if he did have fifty of these minutes?

43 K×f4

It was this, the most natural continuation, that we analyzed in the first instance.

White also loses, however, after 43 Qg5 R×g6 44 R×h7+ K×h7 45 Re7+ Kh8 46 Q×g6 Qg2+, when he is either the first to be mated—47 Kh5 Rd5+ 48 Kh6 Qh3 mate, or else he loses his queen—47 Kf5 Rd5+ 48 Kf6 Rd6+.

43 Qf5 is also unsatisfactory: 43 ... R×g6+ 44 K×f4 (*44 Q×g6 Qg2+*) 44 ... Qc1+ 45 Re3 (if *45 Ke4*, then *45 ... Qe1+* and *46 ... Q×h4*) 45 ... Kg8. This unobtrusive move, with the threat of ... Rf8, is rapidly decisive: 46 R×h7 K×h7 47 Qf7+ Kh6, or 46 Qc5 Rf8+ 47 Ke4 Re6+.

A further possibility, 43 Rh1, also proves insufficient to save the game: 43 ... R×g6+ 44 K×f4 Qc4+ 45 Re4 Rf8+ 46 Ke3 Q×c3+ 47 Kf2. During the several hours that I spent analysing this position, I could see nothing decisive. But at some point I succeeded in attaining an ideal working state: to glance at the position from the side, as it were, and get away from the variations and ideas that, from inertia, continue to attract attention. In the present instance I merely had to 'forget' about the attractive attacks by the queen on the white king, when it immediately struck me that after 47 ... Rh6!! 48 Q×h6 Q×f3+ 49 Ke1 Q×e4+ 50 Kd2 Rd8+ Black gives mate.

The impression was gained that the adjourned position was altogether won for Black. After two 'sessions' of analysis this is what we decided, but then, when I had already gone to bed, it suddenly occurred to me that I should follow Botvinnik's principle: after dealing with the main continuations, analyse, even if only briefly, all the possible moves in the critical position.

It was here that I conceived the idea of the 'absurd' 43 Kg5!?

The following morning I mentioned this to my trainer, and we were both shocked to find that by a quite fantastic queen sacrifice White can obtain a positional draw: 43 ... Rf8 (threatening, among other things, *44 ... R×g6+ 45 Q×g6 Qg2+*) 44 Q×h7+!! (but not the prosaic *44 Kh6*) 44 ... R×h7 45 R×h7+ Kg8 46 Kh6!, with perpetual check.

White also repels the attack in the variation 43 ... Qg2+ 44 K×f4, when Black does not have the important check with his queen at c1, while in the event of 43 ... Qg1+ 44 Rg4 Qc1 White has the reply 45 Qh2!!, vacating a shelter for his king—45 ... R×g6+ 46 Kh5. White's pieces achieve co-ordination, and he has nothing to fear.

Here, as a digression from the analysis of a specific position, I should like to touch on a growing problem: on the intrusion into the realm of chess of the electronic computer.

I will not venture to comment on the currently popular topic: "Will the computer at some time replace the grandmaster?". The heart hopes that this will not be possible, and that the intuition of a chess player will be impossible to translate into machine language, but the mind of a man with training in engineering asserts that this is by no means ruled out. But here we are concerned with something else: if it were analyzing my adjourned game with Gheorghiu, a computer, which at present works basically by a sorting method, would probably even now be able to find without difficulty the move 43 Kg5, for all its apparent pointlessness and even absurdness. Meanwhile, when I went along to the resumption, I was practically 100% certain that the Rumanian grandmaster, who plays several orders of magnitude more strongly than the 'strongest' computer, would not have discovered 43 Kg5!!, since he was having an unhappy tournament, and was unlikely to have devoted as much time to the position as I had.

But what if he had taken it into his head to give this question to a computer, and what if he had thereby found such possibilities under tournament conditions ...?

It seems to me that it is already time that a point was introduced into the rules of chess, regarding the 'separation' of computer and human chess. It is fine for matches and tournaments to be held between computers, and for chess to serve as an excellent testing ground for the good of science and humanity, but a player must not be allowed to utilize the services of a computer during an event. After all, the marathon runner doesn't jump into a car somewhere around the 25km mark, and cover the rest of the distance at 'vehicular' speed. But that is the sort of situation which could arise if, when analyzing an unfinished game, especially one adjourned in a technical ending, a player were to turn for assistance to a computer.

As regards the resumption of the game in question, after the move played by Gheorghiu, virtually all of the time I spent was on moving the pieces, recording the moves on my score sheet, and pressing the clock. Everything had been exhaustively analyzed.

43 ...   Qc1+
44 Kg3

No better is 44 Ke4 Q×c3, when the restless white king creates a cheerless impression: Black threatens, in particular, 45 ... Rd4+ or 45 ... Qd3+.

44 ...   R×g6+
45 Rg4   Qg1+
46 Kh3

If White had ventured to play 46 Kf4, the win for Black would have been more difficult, although it was still there: 46 ... R×g4+ 47 f×g4 (after *47 Q×g4 Qc1+* events develop similarly to a variation in the game) 47 ... Qf2+ 48 Ke4 Qe2+ 49 Kf4 Rf8+ 50 Rf5 Re8, and White is lost:

51 Re5 Qc4+ 52 Kf5 Rf8+ 53 Kg5 Qf4+ 54 Kh4 Qh2+, or 51 Kg3 Qe1+ 52 Rf2 Rf8 53 Qc5 Qg1+.

51 Kg5 Qe7+ is also insufficient, while on 51 Qh3 there follows 51 ... Re4+ 52 Kg5 Qd2+ 53 Kh5 (*53 Kf6 Qd8+,* or *53 Kh4 Qh6+ 54 Rh5 Qf6+ 55 Rg5 h6,* and wins) 53 ... Re2, and the threat of 54 ... Rh2 can merely be deferred for one move, but not averted.

46 ...	R×g4
47 Q×g4	Qh1+
48 Kg3	Rg8
49 Rg5	Qg1+
50 Kf4	

White cannot return to h3 with his king: 50 ... R×g5, and Black's queen is defended by his rook. But in the centre of the board the white king quickly comes under a decisive attack.

50 ...	Qc1+
51 Kf5	Rf8+
52 Ke4	Q×c3

This 'quiet' move decides the game. White has no defence against the mating threats.

53 Re5	Qe1+
54 Kd5	Rd8+
55 Ke6	Re8+

Were it not for his pawn at f3, White would be saved by a stalemating combination: 56 Kf7 Q×e5 57 Qg8+. But the pawn is there, and so Gheorghiu **resigned**.

Polugayevsky–Hulak
Budapest 1975

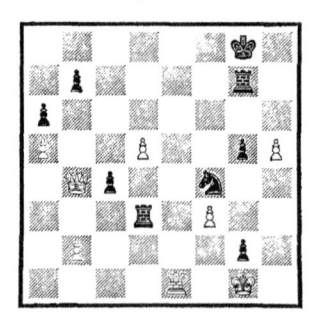

Strictly speaking, White has a slight material advantage—queen against rook and knight—but God only knows how much the black pawn at g2 is worth!

To this day I recall how, on emerging from the time scramble and considering my sealed move, I was constantly distracted by thoughts such as: "Good heavens, another brain-twister!!" Indeed, as regards its abnormal set-up and mutual lack of safety of the kings, I can compare this position only with my adjourned game against Gheorghiu. Although there, as will be seen, the variations were more colourful.

Here I should mention that play was daily, without any rest days, but that every five rounds a special day was set aside for adjournments. Since this was my only adjourned game, I had, fortunately, ample time for analysis. I spent a mass of time working through the variations, time which I in no way regretted, since I discovered the content of the position to be amazingly logical and elegant.

The first few hours of analysis led me to the conclusion that White had good winning chances. Then new ideas appeared, and I became convinced that the position was probably drawn. But my searching did not end there. I attempted to penetrate more deeply into the variations, and soon my persistence was rewarded: in practically all lines I succeeded in discovering improvements.... The final painstaking 'polishing' showed me that only in one single place (which was not easily reached) could the opponent draw.

I sealed the strongest move—**42 Q×c4**. As I later learned, my opponent spent a considerable time searching for a defence against 42 d6, which in the end he succeeded in doing.

My analysis (after *42 Q×c4*) proceeded along the following lines: 42 ... Rd2 (*42 ... R×d5* loses to *43 Re5 Rd7 44 R×g5+*) 43 Kh2! Kh7 44 Qc8 R×d5 45 Re8, and the game is quickly decided, since the black king cannot successfully escape from the danger zone.

Then after 42 Q×c4 I began considering the immediate 42 ... Kh7. Now it will be seen that in the variation 43 Kh2 R×d5 44 Qc8 Black has saved an important tempo. Being unable to find a win for White, I decided to try a different way: 42 ... Kh7 43 Qe4+ Kh6 44 Qf5. This continuation intrigued me—to save the game Black has to find the one possible defence! It appears that he can calmly play 44 ... R×f3 (*44 ... R×d5? 45 Re6+*), since on 45 Re6+ he has the reply 45 ... K×h5, and on 45 Qf6+—45 ... Kh7. But it turns out that on 44 ... Rf3 White has a subtle intermediate move.

45 Qg4!, and now both 45 ... Rh3 46 Re6+!, and 45 ... Rd3 46 Re6+, end in catastrophe for Black. I realized that such a crafty move as 45 Qg4 could easily be overlooked, but on the other hand after the correct 44 ... K×h5! White has no chance of winning.

As a result, I had to return completely to the variation 42 Q×c4 Kh7! 43 Kh2! R×d5.

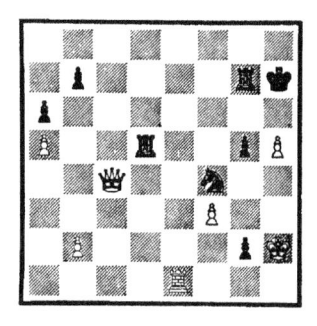

Here, apart from the move already considered, 44 Qc8, my attention was drawn to 44 Re8 and 44 Qe4+.

After 44 Re8 (with the threat of *45 Qe4+*) I could not discover any definite advantage for White after 44 ... Kh6 or 44 ... Rdd7.

I was therefore attracted by the check—44 Qe4+ Kh6 45 Qe8. It turns out that the threat of Re6+ is very strong. On 45 ... Rdd7 White now has the reply 46 Qh8+ Rh7 47 Qf6+ K×h5 48 Re5. Although White has enticed the opposing king forward, it nevertheless appears that by 48 ... Rdg7 (*48 ... Rhg7 49 Q×f4*) 49 Q×f4?? Kg6+ Black can defend successfully. But White, in turn, does not have to hurry, and on 48 ... Rdg7 replies with the murderous 49 Kg1!, when the threat of 50 Q×f4 is now deadly. 49 ... Kh4 does not help—50 Qf5!.

This put me back in a good frame of mind, and I decided that everything was now in order. Just in case, I decided also to examine the variation 44 Qe4+ Kh6 45 Qe8 Kh7, although here 46 Qf8 looks very powerful, intending 47 Re8 (if now 46 ... N×h5, then *47 K×g2*, and White has a technically won ending).

Suddenly, to my horror, I noticed that by answering 46 Qf8 with 46 ... Rgd7 47 Re8 g1=Q+!, Black is the first to give mate. This showed how dangerous it was for me to cut off my heavy pieces so far from 'base'.

After a short break, I decided in this last variation to try the idea of *zugzwang*, answering 46 ... Rgd7 with 47 b4!.

But Black has the reply 47 ... Rc7—there is no *zugzwang* after all. But what about continuing this variation? 48 Re7+! R×e7 49 Q×e7+ Kh6 50 Qf8+ K×h5 (*50 ... Kh7 is bad in view of 51 h6 Rd7 52 Qf5+*, winning the rook) 51 Qg7!. Now the attempt to defend against the mate by 51 ... Kh4 fails to 52 Qh6+ Nh5 53 Qe6. However, Black has in reserve the simple 51 ... Rd6, and what is White to do?

It was here that I was able to put into practice an idea which had never left me all through my work on the adjourned position: how to utilize the existence on the board of the Q-side pawns?! And immediately the idea was found: 52 b5!!. Here it is—the truth! The white pawns break through an apparently impenetrable barrier. Weaker is 52 Qh7+ Rh6 53 Qf7+ Rg6 54 Q×b7 Kh6!, and White does not have time to utilize his pawn majority, since the opponent has the strong threat of 55 ... Re6. But by 55 b5!! White gains an important tempo for setting up a passed pawn.

E.g. 52 ... Re6 53 Qh7+ Rh6 54 Qf7+ Rg6 55 Q×b7 Kh6 56 b×a6 R×e6 57 Qb6 Kh5 58 a7 Re1 59 a8=Q Rh1+ 60 Kg3, and White wins.

Or 52 ... a×b5 53 Qh7+ Rh6 54 Qf7+ Kh4 (*54 ... Rg6 55 Q×b7 Kh6 56 a6 Re6 57 a7 Re1 58 Qb6+ Kh5 59 Qg1! Re8 60 Qa1*, and Black is defenceless) 55 Q×b7 g1=Q+ 56 K×g1 Kg3 57 Q×b5 Rd6 58 Qb1, and after overcoming certain technical difficulties, White is bound to win. Not being satisfied with such a general assessment, I even worked out how this might happen.

Now, just when it seemed that the goal was close in practically all variations, I at last realized that after 42 Q×c4 Kh7 43 Kh2 Black should play 43 ... Kh6! immediately (this move is undoubtedly the strongest, since the white queen does not now reach e8, and all the beautiful variations found earlier turn out to be the dream of a romantic) 44 Re8 (on *44 Qe4* the simple *44 ... K×h5* is a good reply) 44 ... R×d5, and Black sets up a fortress after 45 Qc8 (not *45 Rh8+ Rh7 46 Qc3?? g1=Q+!*) 45 ... Rdd7!.

46 Rh8+ Rh7 47 Q×d7 R×h8 48 Qf7 Rh7! 49 Qg8 Rg7 (in no way can White separate the rook from the king) 50 Qh8+ Rh7. White's last chance is to battle for the 6th rank: 46 Rf8 (in order to answer 46 ... K×h5 with 47 Rf6, with the threat of Qg4 mate). But Black replies 46 ... Rgf7! (not 46 ... Rdf7 47 Rd8, and the rook penetrates onto the 6th rank) 47 Qe8 R×f8 48 Q×f8+ Rg7, and the coupling mechanism between king and rook again goes into operation.

And so, a draw, after all. But how difficult it is for Black to achieve! And I decided not to be in a hurry to conclude peace....

The game was resumed. After 42 Q×c4 my opponent thought for a little, and then replied

   42 ...   Kh7!

I quickly replied

   43 Kh2

and waited anxiously for what would come next. After a few minutes Hulak played

   43 ...   Kh6!

"Surely all my efforts haven't been in vain?!" But what's this? After

44 Re8

the Yugoslav master sank into thought for a long time. Now it was clear that he had not analyzed in detail the resulting position, although he had 'guessed' correctly the first two moves with the king. If this were so, then at the board it would not be at all easy for him to work out all the subtleties. And that's how it was! Black promptly made a decisive mistake.

   44 ...   **Rh7?**

As was stated earlier, 44 ... R×d5 is correct.

45 Qe4!

Black can resign, since on almost every move there follows 46 Re6+. E.g. 45 ... Rd1 46 Re6+ N×e6 47 Qg6 mate. He therefore decided to transpose into a rook ending, but this proved to be an elementary win for White.

45 ...	g1=Q+
46 K×g1	Rd1+
47 Kf2	Rd2+
48 Ke1	Re2+
49 Q×e2	N×e2
50 K×e2	Rd7
51 Re5	K×h5
52 Ke3	**Resigns**

FROM A POSITION OF STRENGTH

Polugayevsky–Suetin
Chigorin Memorial Tournament, Kislovodsk 1972

For a long time in this game Black successfully repulsed his opponent's threats, but nevertheless by adjournment time White still had a positional advantage, in particular on account of Black's three pawn islands (as opposed to two for White) and, even more important, the fact that the pawns at a6 and e6 are on white squares.

After thinking for a comparatively short time, Suetin sealed

42 ...   Rd1

Black's desire to exchange rooks is understandable, since White's pressure down the 'e' file is unpleasant, but 42 ... Rc3 was better, pinning his hopes on counter-play.

43 R×d1   B×d1

I analyzed this position a great deal. White has an undisputed advantage, but it is not easy to find the correct path. One plausible line is 44 f5 g×f5 (weaker is *44 ... g5 45 Rd5*) 45 R×f5+ Kg7 46 Rf7+ Kg6, and now White can capture on e7, since on 47 R×e7 Kf6 he has 48 Bd5 Rd6 49 Rf7+ Kg6 50 Ba2 Rd2, when he keeps his extra pawn, while in the event of 47 ... Rc1 48 Kf2 Kf6 49 Re8 Ba4 he saves his piece by 50 Rc8.

However, in these variations White's extra pawn is probably insufficient to win. 44 Kf2 looks very strong, in order to attempt to penetrate with the king into Black's K-side. E.g. 44 ... Rc2+ 45 Kg3 Rc3+ 46 Kh4 R×a3 47 f5 (not *47 Kg5 Bc2*) 47 ... g×f5 48 R×f5+ Kg7 (*48 ... Ke8? 49 Bf7+ Kd7 50 Rd5+*) 49 Kg5, and White should win. But on 44 Kf2 Black has a good defence in 44 ... h4, preventing the approach of the white king. In the end I settled on 44 Bd5 as being the strongest move.

44 Bd5   Rf6

The only move, since 44 ... Rc3 45 Re6 Bc2 46 a4 is clearly advantageous for White.

45 Be4

The idea of this move is to prevent Black's ... a5, and in addition the g6 pawn is attacked.

45 ...   Bg4
46 Bd3   Bc8

Not the best. Black still had drawing chances after 46 ... R×f4 47 B×g6 Kg7.

**47 Rd5   Ke8
48 g3**

The white bishop is very strongly posted at d3, attacking the a6 and g6 pawns. It is also important that White has been able to prevent ... a5. In the subsequent play Black is obliged to avoid the exchange of rooks, since the bishop ending is won for White.

48 ...	Bb7
49 Rg5	Kf7
50 Kf2	h4

Black tries to ease his defence somewhat by exchanging one pair of pawns.

51 a4	h×g3+
52 h×g3	Rd6
53 Ke3	Re6+
54 Kd2	Rd6
55 Kc3	Rc6+
56 Kb2	Rd6
57 Bc2	Bf3
58 a5	

An important move in White's plan. The weak black pawn at a6 is fixed.

| 58 ... | Be2 |

Of course Black does not wish to play 58 ... b5, when both of his Q-side pawns are fixed on white squares. But 58 ... b×a5 was slightly better.

| 59 Kc3 | Bf1? |

Here again 59 ... b×a5 was more tenacious. The move played leads to the loss of a pawn.

60 f5!

Black cannot now play 60 ... g×f5 61 R×f5+ Rf6 62 R×f6+ and 63 a×b6, and therefore he loses his 'g' pawn.

60 ...	Rc6+
61 Kd2	b×a5
62 f×g6+	

In the event of 62 R×g6 Black obtains counter-chances by 62 ... R×c2+ 63 K×c2 a×b4.

62 ...	Kg7
63 b×a5	Bc4
64 Be4	Rc7
65 Ke3	Bg1
66 Kf4	Bb3
67 Re5	Kf6
68 Rf5+	Kg7
69 Kg5	Bc4
70 Re5	Bb5

If the bishop moves anywhere along the a2–g8 diagonal, White plays 71 Bd3.

71 Re6	Rc5+
72 Kf4	Rc7
73 Kg5	Rc5+
74 Bf5	Rc7
75 Re1	

Now the white rook threatens to penetrate decisively via h1 to h7. Black cannot prevent this by 75 ... Bc6, on account of the pin by 76 Rc1, while in the event of 75 ... Bc4, in order to answer 76 Rh1 with 76 ... Bg8, the pin on the 'c' file by 76 Rc1 is again decisive.

| 75 ... | Be8 |

The last chance. Now on 76 Rh1 Black plays 76 ... B×g6 77 B×g6 Rc5+

78 Bf5 e6. But White has no reason to hurry.

76 g4	Ba4
77 Rh1	Bb3
78 Rh7+	Kg8
79 Kh6	Ba2
80 Rh8+!	

The concluding stroke, which enables the white pawn to queen.

Black resigns.

Polugayevsky–Kagan
*Interzonal Tournament,
Petropolis 1973*

At first sight it appears that the win for White is not far off. He is winning a pawn, while Black has a weakness at a5, and the knight is more mobile than the bishop. But where and how can a break-through be made? For this reason my young opponent was pacing up and down with an air of satisfaction, and I even heard with half an ear how he was betting that he wouldn't lose.

Meanwhile the situation in the tournament was such that every half-point was worth literally its weight in gold, and I naturally spent more than one morning (the main playing sessions were in the evening) searching for an accurate way of realizing my advantage. The position is basically of a technical nature: it did not provoke such excitement as, for instance, did the earlier adjourned position against Gheorghiu from the same tournament. But numerous subtleties were discovered in it, both ideas, and the execution of these ideas.

It was I who made the sealed move, which was a natural one.

41 Ke2	Bc1
42 N×c7	Bb2
43 Nb5	Be5
44 f4	e×f3+
45 K×f3	Kg5

Having got rid of the strong black pawn at e4, White begins the execution of his plan. First the knight is activated, and both the black king and the bishop will be tied down by attacks on the weak pawns at a5 and d6.

46 Na7	Kf6
47 Nc6	Bc3
48 Nd8!	

3. In the Interval 125

The knight is obviously heading for b7. It is true that there it will be trapped, but it is through the sacrifice of this piece that White's winning path lies. He has no other possibility.

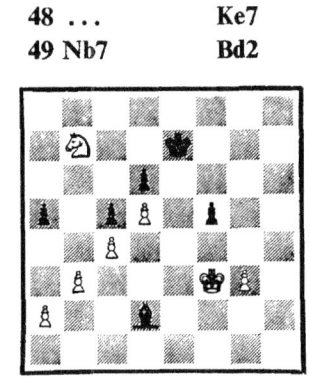

| 48 ... | Ke7 |
| 49 Nb7 | Bd2 |

Cutting off the white king's advance, and threatening to trap the knight. But it was this position that Bagirov and I studied thoroughly, and we analyzed it through to the end, some 10-5 moves deep in all variations.

50 Ke2!

By triangulation the king nevertheless penetrates to the key square f4.

50 ...	Bb4
51 Ke3	Bc3
52 a4!	

The hasty 52 Kf4 fails to achieve its goal— 52 ... Kf6, and the d6 pawn is taboo in view of 53 ... Be5+, winning the knight. Therefore the opponent has to be given the move.

Now after 52 ... Kd7 the piece sacrifice wins: 53 Kf4 Kc7 54 N×a5 B×a5 55 K×f5 Kd7 56 g4 Ke7 57 g5 Bd2 58 g6 Bc3. It appears that White is unable to strengthen his position, but this is not so: by repeating the same king manoeuvre, he gains a tempo: 59 Kg5 Bd2+ 60 Kh5 Kf8 (White wins very easily after *60 ... Kf6 61 a5 B×a5 62 Kh6*) 61 Kg4! Ke7 (if *61 ... Bc3*, then *62 Kg5*, and either Black loses control with his bishop of one of the squares f6 or h6, or else after *62 ... Kg7* the white king breaks through to e6) 62 g7 Kf7 63 Kf5, and at the cost of his passed 'g' pawn, White reaches the Q-side with his king.

| 52 ... | Be5 |

Black decides to part with his 'a' pawn, so as to eliminate the white 'g' pawn. But this fails to save the game.

53 N×a5	B×g3
54 Nc6+	Kd7
55 a5	

In order to prepare 56 Ne7 (when the knight cannot be taken, since the black king will be outside the 'a' pawn's square), and thus force the advance ... f4, enabling the white king to join the battle.

55 ...	Kc7
56 Ne7	f4+
57 Kf3	Be1
58 a6	Kb6
59 Nc8+	K×a6
60 K×f4	Ka5
61 N×d6	Kb4
62 Ke4	

Another small subtlety, which wins the most quickly. Now on 62 ... K×b3 there follows 63 Kd3 Kb4 64 Nb7, and the black king is shut out.

| 62 ... | Ka5 |
| 63 Nf5 | Kb4 |

64 d6	K×b3
65 Kd5	Resigns

Polugayevsky-K. Grigorian
*41st USSR Championship
Premier League, Moscow 1973*

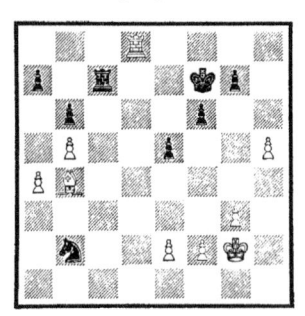

In the opening my opponent chose a set-up known to be unfavourable, fell behind in development, and failed to solve satisfactorily the eternal problem in the English Opening of the bishop at c8. He was able to exchange it on the 18th move only at the cost of a pawn, and the ease with which White gained a material advantage 'lulled' me somewhat. One procrastination—and in the adjourned position Grigorian, as he himself said to the reporters, was optimistic about the outcome.

But already, as I was sealing my move, I saw an interesting idea, which, of course, would have to be analyzed carefully at home. The 'finishing' process unexpectedly proved to be highly complex and painstaking, with a large number of variations to be considered. Time for me was at a premium, but I nevertheless had to 'borrow' from my own sleep, and spend a number of hours on the analysis.

41 Bd6

Black unjustifiably considered the adjourned position to be drawn (it is unlikely that White can hold on to his extra pawn). He was clearly superficial as regards his analysis, and, as it turned out, had no suspicion of the dangers threatening him. Even on resumption at the board he should still have been on his guard: why, in fact, does White part with his 'a' pawn, and keep his bishop on the same diagonal? Perhaps he has some aim other than the superficial one of trying to drive the rook off the 7th rank? After all, the black king has only one free square at e6....

In short, there was plenty for Black to think about, and, if he had taken into account all these considerations, he would naturally have tried moving the rook along the 'c' file, so as to prevent the advance of the white 'e' pawn.

In the event of this I had prepared at home the following variations: 41 ... Rc4 42 a5! b×a5 43 Ra8, and if 43 ... Ke6, then 44 Ba3 followed by R×a7. After 42 ... Rd4 (instead of *42 ... b×a5*), 43 a6! is decisive: 43 ... Ke6 (or *43 ... Nc4 44 Rf8+ Ke6 45 Bb4*—with his pawns on black squares the ending is hopeless for Black) 44 Ra8! R×d6 45 R×a7, and White's passed pawns are irresistible.

41 ... Rc3 is perhaps the most interesting variation. But then comes 42 Rd7+ Ke6 43 R×g7 K×d6 44 h6 Rc8 45 h7 Rh8 46 R×a7, and the resulting ending is hopeless for Black. E.g. 46 ... N×a4 47 R×a4 R×h7 48 Rc4, with an easily won rook ending. After 46 ... Ke6 the break-through by a4–a5 is decisive, while if 46 ... Nc4, then 47 Kh3. Finally, on 46 ... f5 White plays 47 Kh3 N×a4 48 Kh4!, and without wasting time on the capture of the knight, makes for g6 with his king.

However, all this analysis remained 'unseen', since my opponent on his first move went a different way, but ... one which was not unexpected.

41 ...   Rb7?

This possibility had also been examined by White in his analysis, and just in case he had prepared a 'bomb'.

42 e4!   N×a4

42 ... Ke6 was much more tenacious, although after 43 f4 e×f4 44 g×f4 f5 White had found the problem-like move 45 Ba3 (if *45 Be5*, then *45 ... Nc4!*), when after 45 ... Nc4 46 Re8+ Kf7 47 Rf8+ Ke6 48 e×f5+ Kd5 49 Bb4, or 45 ... N×a4 46 Re8+ Kf6 47 Rf8+ Ke6 (if *47 ... Rf7*, then *48 e5+ Ke6 49 Rc8*) 48 R×f5, he wins.

The continuation in the game simplified my task considerably.

43 f4

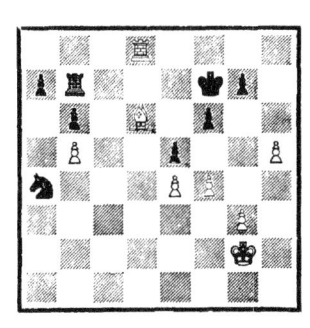

It turns out that, after re-establishing material equality, Black is in danger of being rather economically mated—by 44 f5 and 45 Rf8. Defending by 43 ... Nc5 44 f5 Nd7 leads to a tragi-comic position, in which there is nothing for Black to do on his next move.

Only now does Grigorian make a despairing attempt to free himself from the trap which has closed around his king.

43 ...   e×f4
44 g×f4   g5

The last chance, since 44 ... g6 fails to 45 h6.

45 e5!   g×f4

Or 45 ... f×e5 46 f×g5, and there is no way of stopping the passed 'g' and 'h' pawns.

46 h6   Ke6

Moving the king the other way does not help: 46 ... Kg6 47 e6.

47 Re8+   Kf5

If 47 ... Kd5, then White wins by 48 Be7.

48 e6   Resigns

ZIG-ZAG OF FORTUNE

It very often happens that analysis is called on to establish not only the 'absolute truth'. Yes, at times an adjourned position may be lost, but one can nevertheless find at least a few nuances, which give some hope of saving the game. If the opponent does not spend his time during the adjournment as conscientiously as he might, and overlooks some subtleties, an imminent defeat may be averted, or a 'dead' draw transformed into a win.

It was on such 'additional possibilities' in the position that I planned the resumption of the following game.

Polugayevsky–Hartston
Las Palmas 1974

The tournament was drawing to a close, and I very much needed a win, but objectively speaking it wasn't there. Of course, White has the advantage, but there is too little material on the board, and it is sufficient for Black merely to eliminate White's passed pawn, by giving up both of his pawns for it.

It was in such 'barren waters' that in my analysis I managed to find an amusing trap—essentially White's only chance.

41 b7

The sealed move was obvious: on 41 Kg2 Black draws immediately by 41 ... Nd5 42 b7 Rb1, when the 'b' pawn is lost in view of the threat of 43 ... Nf4+.

41 ...	Rb1
42 Re5+	

'Correct play'—42 Re7, is again unpromising, but not because of the plausible 42 ... Kc6 43 Kh2!, when the white bishop goes to g2, defending the b7 pawn, but in view of the intermediate move 42 ... Nd5 43 Rg7, and now 43 ... Kc6, when the manoeuvre 44 Kh2 and 45 Bg2 no longer achieves anything. White therefore resorts to a crafty check found during analysis.

42 ...	Kd6?

Here it is, the neglect of detail in the work on the adjourned position. It is natural that Black should not care for the continuation 42 ... Kd4 43 Re7 Nd5 44 Rg7, and if 44 ... Kc5, then the familiar regrouping 45 Kh2 Kc6 46 Bg2 is completed just in time. But he should have played 42 ... Kc6, with a clear draw after 43 Rg5 K×b7 44 R×g6 etc.

But my opponent decided, just in case, to keep his king a little closer to his pawns. It was here that the prepared mine exploded.

43 Re3	Nd5?

Continuing the same tactics of natural moves. It was still not too late to draw by the 'flank' move 43 ... Na4.

44 Rd3!

It would appear that as yet nothing terrible has happened. Black is not bound to blunder away a piece by 44 ... R×b7 45 R×d5+ K×d5 46 Bg2+, but can first move his king out of the pin, which is what he does.

44 ...	Kc6

45 Rd1!!

By breaking the pin on the first rank, White practically drives the black rook to b7, after which the familiar geometric motif comes into play. Incidentally, 45 Kh2 achieves nothing here in view of 45 ... Nf4!, when g2 is inaccessible to the bishop.

| 45 ... | R×b7 |
| 46 R×d5 | Resigns |

In this case it was my analysis that was the more accurate and resourceful. But sometimes—not often, fortunately—it has been I who have lost the analytical adjournment battle. And each time I have been able to give an exact diagnosis of the mistake: which of the principles of working on an adjourned position has been broken.

Not surprisingly, such occurrences stick in my memory, along with the most happy ones.

Polugayevsky-Bronstein
*34th USSR Championship,
Tbilisi 1967*

This position, which was reached after five hours of lively and interesting play, cannot be called anything but crazy. To the necessity of making the usual assessment as to which is stronger here, the queen or the two rooks, the following factors had to be added: the weakness of the b2 pawn and the strength of the c4 pawn, the remote position of the black knight, the restricted position of the black king, and many others. It is not surprising that the analysis too proved to be highly complicated. And I permitted myself a mistake: I continued analyzing right up to the very resumption of the game, and even a few minutes before the opening of the envelope I had still not put away my pocket set. The result was extreme fatigue, and the very first surprise, although a fairly simple one, appeared to me like one of the mysteries of the sphinx.

Since then twelve years has passed, and I invariably recall this game when I am faced with the necessity of analyzing a very complicated position. I concentrate to the utmost on my analysis, and devote every minute to it, but some two hours before the resumption I put the board to one side. Of course, the position remains in my mind, and the analysis continues, but by no means so intensively and not so tiringly. And it is perhaps for this reason that, on several occasions, it has been in these last few minutes that I have been able to spot mistakes that have been made.

As for the present game, I sealed the natural move

41 Rd7

and assumed that the reply would be no less natural—

| 41 ... | Be5 |

and on the way to the hotel I thought my position to be rather poor. But then I found the reply 42 B×a7, and gradually came to the conclusion that White's chances were no worse.

I based my analysis on possible variations such as 42 ... B×b2 43 Re8 (but not *43 R×f7? c3 44 Rf8 c2 45 Ree8 c1=Q+* and *46 ... Q×f4*, with a decisive material advantage) 43 ... c3 44 Rdd8 g5 45 Rh8+ Kg7 46 Bd4+ f6 47 Nd5, or 42 ... B×f4 43 g×f4 N×b2 44 Ree7.

On the resumption these initial moves did in fact occur, and after

42 B×a7

Bronstein thought for a long time. Then, almost reluctantly, he played

42 ...   Bf6

This is a weak move, in my opinion, and should afford White excellent chances. But I had not considered it in my analysis, and at the board, in my tired state, I was unable to refute it, although initially I set off on the correct path.

43 Kh2!

This is necessary, since 43 R×f7 runs into a refutation—43 ... c3 44 Rf8 c×b2 45 Ree8 b1=Q+ 46 Kh2 g5, and Black is 'only' a queen up.

43 ...   N×b2

44 R×f7?

A serious mistake, which loses the game. The rook approaches too close to the black king, which at the decisive moment comes out to g6, thereby winning a necessary tempo by the attack. White could have gained an advantage by 44 Nd5!, when the black bishop falls, after which the two rooks supported by the bishop from d4 build up a very strong attack. This is why the king had to be moved a move earlier: Black is now denied a saving (and simultaneously, winning) queen check at d1.

How then should Black play? The difficulty of his position is illustrated by the variation 44 ... Kg6 45 N×f6 g×f6 46 Bd4 c3 (*46 ... Nd3 47 Rd6*) 47 Rc7, and wherever the knight moves to, Black loses his 'c' pawn: 47 ... Nc4 48 B×c3 Q×c3 49 Re4; 47 ... Na4(d1) 48 B×c3 N×c3 49 Re3, while 47 ... Qd1 is risky in view of 48 Re4.

After the continuation in the game, everything is clear: White is too late.

44 ...   Nd3
45 Nd5   Kg6

On 46 Rc7 Black can now reply 46 ... Be5, with an additional threat: 47 ... N×f2.

46 Rd7   Ne5
47 Rc7   Q×a3

As if to emphasize that the white rooks, disunited and lacking in co-ordination, are no threat to anyone...

48 N×f6   g×f6
49 Be3   Qd3
50 Ra2   Qf1

The classical combination of queen and knight goes onto the attack. Now Black simply does not need his passed 'c' pawn: he threatens mate by 51 ... Nf3 or 51 ... Ng4.

51 g4	N×g4+
52 Kg3	Ne5
53 Kh2	Nf3+
54 Kg3	Ne1
55 Kf4	Qg2
56 Resigns	

There is no defence against mate by the queen at f3, or by the knight at d3.

SLEEPLESS NIGHTS IN SPAIN

Polugayevsky-Uhlmann
*Interzonal Tournament,
Palma de Mallorca 1970*

Up till this point there had been nothing over which to reproach myself in this game. In a tense struggle I won a pawn, there was no trace left of Black's counter-attack, and there seemed no doubt that White would win. Digressing slightly, I can state with complete conviction that, if I had been able to bring this game with Uhlmann from the 8th round to its logical conclusion, the tournament would have turned out differently for me.* But as it was, my nerves let me down, and I was to remember this game right to the finish...

And in connection with this, I should like once again to recall—for myself in particular—an unavoidable rule of tournament play. Whatever has happened in a previous game, whatever extraordinary occurrence may have taken place, a player is obliged to forget about it by the following round. Obliged. Otherwise he becomes a slave to his own emotions, and is incapable of achieving anything in the event.

But in the analysis of an adjourned position it is very difficult to cut oneself off from all the reversals of fortune during the game. And thoughts about what one has missed, about 'what would have happened if, instead of this, I had played differently' are much more tormenting than searching for the most complex and fantastic of continuations.

Perhaps it was for this reason that my analysis of the position against Uhlmann proved to be so exhausting. After all, the game had promised to be one of the best I had ever played: an interesting plan, a pretty queen sacrifice, and a mass of subtle ideas and manoeuvres. In the diagram position it remained for me to make the more-than-elementary move 40 Rb8+, and after either 40 ... Rd8 41 R×d8+ B×d8 42 f×g6, or 40 ... Kg7 41 Rb7+ Kh8 42 f×g6, Black immediately can—and must—resign.

I still had some 25–28 minutes remaining on my clock up to move forty, whereas Uhlmann's flag was already raised. Without hurrying, I once again checked everything, and ... picked up my f5 pawn, thinking that the rook check had already been given!

40 f×g6??

---

* The author finished one point away from qualifying for the Candidates' Matches (K.P.N.).

There followed instantly

40 ... Bd4!!

and I realized to my horror that my rook was not on the 7th rank, and that I was unable to give mate at h7. Meanwhile, Black himself had created a threat of nothing more and nothing less than mate in 2 moves: 41 ... Rd2+ and 42 ... Rf2 mate.

Apparently, at this point I looked so crestfallen and dismayed that my second at the Interzonal Tournament, grandmaster Isaac Boleslavsky, the very personification of calmness, could not contain himself, but stood up and went out of the hall. To this day I remember the effort with which I forced myself simply to think about the position: I had to seal a move. But even now, many years later, when the bitter memory of the tournament has long since passed, I am unable to look at this position and remember White's 40th move without an inward shudder.

About the night following the 8th round it is better not to remember...

To revert to 'pure chess', the position on the board had become extremely sharp, and I analyzed the adjournment position for no less than 20 hours.

41 Bb4

With his sealed move White is forced to block the 'b' file, and his rook is no longer able to participate in the attack, but there is simply no other continuation.

41 ... N×h2!

Without doubt the strongest. But, since I had no right to restrict myself to this one move, I considered in my analysis a whole series of other continuations for Black.

41 ... Bc3 42 B×c3 R×c3 43 Rd1 was immediately rejected, since without his bishop Black has no way of opposing the advance of the 'f' pawn, and the intrusion of the white rook onto the seventh or eighth rank.

It was quickly established that after 41 ... Re3+ the white king finds safety: 42 Kf1 (weaker is *42 Kd1 Rd3+ 43 Kc2 Bf6*, when the d4 square is vacated for the knight to join the attack) 42 ... N×h2+ 43 Kg2 Re2+ 44 Kh3, and if 44 ... h5, with the threat of 45 ... Nf3 and 46 ... Rh2 mate, then simply 45 Kh4.

The analysis was by no means so easy after the possible 41 ... Kg7. White obviously has to support his g6 pawn by 42 f5, and then Black begins to pursue the king: 42 ... Re3+. Where should it move to? If 43 Kd1, then 43 ... Rd3+ 44 Kc2 Bf6, and the already familiar threat of 45 ... Nd4+ is highly disagreeable. I had to look for a winning plan in the line with 43 Kf1.

It turns out that after 43 ... h5! (the most unpleasant; White's task is simpler after *43 ... N×h2+ 44 Kg2 Re2+ 45 Kh3 h5 46 Bd6!*, when it is Black who is the first to be mated, e.g. *46 ... Nf3 47 Rb7+ Kh6 48 Rh7+ Kg5 49 Bf4+ Kf6 50 Rf7 mate*) there follows 44 Bc4! (now *44 Bd6*, which was so strong in the previous variation, is not possible, since it loses the rook after *44 ... Nd2+*, while the other attempt to mount a mating attack, *44 Ba5*, similarly does not work, in view of *44 ... N×h2+ 45 Kg2 Re2+ 46 Kh3 Nf3 47 Rb7+ Kh6 48 Rh7+ Kg5 49 Bd8+ Bf6 50 B×f6+ K×f6 51 R×h5 Rh2+ 52 Kg4 Ne5+*, and White loses his rook. Therefore the white bishops retreat, in order, as it were, to make a running start and move into the attack) 44 ... N×h2+ (or *44 ... Kf6 45 Rd1! K×f5 46 R×d4*

N×d4 47 g7, and wins; *44 ... Ne5* is similarly unsatisfactory for Black, because of *45 Be2 Ng4 46 Bd6!*—less clear is 46 Bd2 N×h2+ 47 Ke1 Nf3+ 48 Kd1 N×d2—*46 ... N×h2+ 47 Ke1 Nf3+ 48 Kd1 Rc3 49 Rb7+ Kg8 50 Rb8+ Kg7 51 Bf8+ Kf6 52 g7 Be3 53 Ba3! K×g7 54 Bb2*, and White wins) 45 Kg2 Nf3! (if *45 ... Ng4*, then *46 Bd6 Rc3 47 Rb7+*, mating) 46 Ba5!!

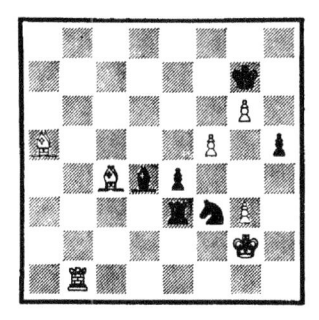

With the idea of giving a decisive check at d8 at the essential moment. The co-ordination of both White's and Black's pieces is quite amazing! The play revolves around who will be the first to give mate. This normally happens in the middlegame, with castling on opposite sides, when both sides launch an attack on the king, but here we have an ending with relatively few pieces!

If now Black plays 46 ... Kf6, then 47 Rb5, defending the f5 pawn, followed by Bd8+, driving the black king back into the trap, and White is the first to land a decisive blow. In reply to 46 ... h4 there follows 47 Rb7+ Kh6 48 Bd8!! (also sufficient, however, is *48 Rh7+ Kg5 49 g7*, when White must gradually be able to realize his advantage, despite the limited number of pieces remaining on the board) 48 ... Bg7 49 Bc7, and if 49 ... Ne5, blocking the bishop's path to f4, then simply 50 g×h4, while in the event of *49 ... Be5* White first exchanges, 50 B×e5 N×e5, and again wins after 51 g×h4.

All these 'secondary' variations—although it is difficult to call them such—demanded many, many hours of work: here I have not given the numerous 'false trails' which Boleslavsky and I analyzed on the way. Did Uhlmann see all this? I think that he must have examined something similar, although it is by no means impossible that he may have chosen the strongest 41st move intuitively.

After this White has no time to improve the placing of his bishops, since 42 ... Re3+ is threatened, and on the Q-side it is difficult for the king to avoid pursuit. Therefore White's subsequent play deserves credit, but—alas!—it nevertheless does not lead to a win.

42 Rh1   Nf3

42 ... Re3+ would now be a serious mistake; firstly, the b1 square has been vacated for the king, and secondly, the white rook is already in play on the opposite wing.

43 R×h6+!   Kg7
44 Rh7+   K×g6
45 Rd7!

White utilizes literally every chance of success. At first I was very happy when in my analysis I found this set-up for my pieces. It is true that White has lost his far-advanced passed pawn, but his pieces have acquired the co-ordination which was lost on the 41st move, and the two passed 'f' and 'g' pawns soon threaten to become a formidable force. But nevertheless, it was the irony of fate that in every variation I succeeded in finding an amazing saving line for Black. This was also discovered by Uhlmann, although in various lines it is one single move that each time comes to Black's rescue.

**45 ...		Bc3!**

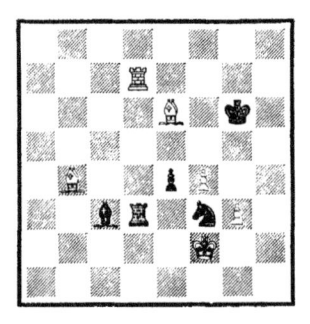

Now after 46 R×d3 e×d3+ 47 K×f3 B×b4, or 46 Bc5 Nd4+, opposite-coloured bishops are left. White has to give up his advantage of the two bishops.

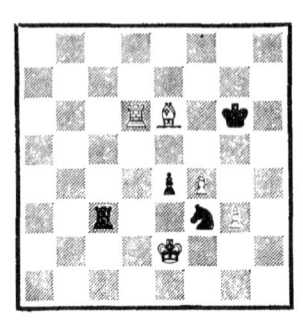

**46 B×c3		R×c3
47 Rd6!!**

Problem-like motifs come into operation: the rook sets up an ambush. The 'normal' 47 g4 allows Black to hold on in the variation 47 ... Ng1+ 48 Kf2 e3+ 49 K×g1 e2, while on 48 Kd2 he replies 48 ... Rf3!, and not only White's, but also Black's pawn threatens to advance and queen.

The move made by White looks terribly strong. Indeed, if 47 ... Ng1+, then 48 Kf2 e3+ 49 K×g1 e2 50 Bc4+, and White wins. It doesn't help for Black to forestall the discovered check by 47 ... Kg7; White has in reserve 48 Bf5! Ng1+ 49 Kf2 Rf3+! 50 Kg2!! (the only way; *50 K×g1 R×g3+ 51 Kh2 Rf3 52 Rg6+ Kf7 53 Rg4 e3 54 Bd3 e2* leads to a draw) 50 ... Ne2 51 Rg6+ Kf7 (after *51 ... Kf8* White simply captures the e4 pawn) 52 Rg4!! N×g3 53 B×e4 Rc3 54 Bd5+, and wins.

**47 ...		Nh2!!**

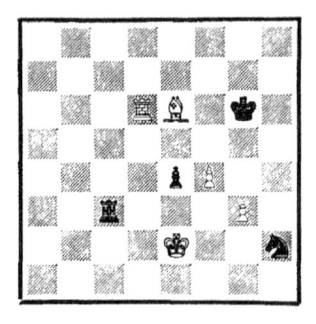

Black ignores the discovered check, separates widely his rook and knight, and apparently destroys the co-ordination of all his pieces, but in this way he achieves a draw! It turns out that the knight does not come under attack, whereas the g3 pawn is now threatened, and in some cases the 'e' pawn can advance.

Boleslavsky and I 'polished' this position exhaustively. We tried both the obvious 48 Kf2 Rc2+ 49 Ke3 Nf1+, and 48 f5+, when if Black chooses 48 ... Kg7?, then after 49 Bd5 R×g3 50 f6+ the white pawn costs him his rook. But Uhlmann could have played 48 ... Kg5, or 48 ... Kh5, or even 48 ... Kf6. I was able to find something in these cases, but only when I defended inaccurately for my opponent.

**48 g4		Rf3**

Black immediately exploits the one defect in White's otherwise sensible move—for an instant the f4 pawn is undefended.

49 Bd5+   Kg7

Once again the irony of fate. White appears to be able to win by 50 Rg6+ Kh7 (not, of course, *50 ... K×g6 51 B×e4+* and *52 B×f3*) 51 f5 N×g4 52 R×g4, since the last white pawn is taboo: 52 ... R×f5?? 53 B×e4. But Black again has a single saving move, 51 ... Rf4!, when the white pawns are driven forwards to their doom: 52 Bg8+ Kh8 53 f6 N×g4 54 f7 Ne5.

In my analysis I therefore decided to seek success in a different variation.

50 Rd7+

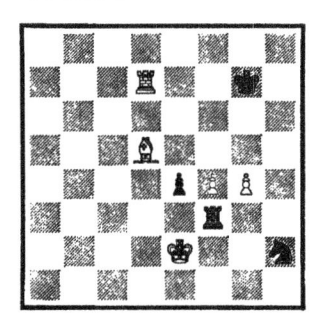

The black king can now move to one of four black squares, and on three of them catastrophe awaits him: 50 ... Kh8—51 Rh7+!; 50 ... Kh6—the same; 50 ... Kf6—51 Rf7+. There is again but one saving move.

**50 ...   Kf8!
51 Rf7+**

Similarly inadequate is 51 g5 R×f4 52 g6 Rg4 53 Rf7+ Kg8!!, and again the discovered check achieves nothing. One can imagine how much mental torture I suffered during my analysis, on finding all these fantastic possibilities!

**51 ...   Ke8
52 g5   Nf1**

It was only here that the game diverged from our analysis. We thought that Black would gain a draw by 52 ... Ng4, and if 53 g6, then 53 ... Re3+, with perpetual check or the win of the bishop. But Uhlmann's move is also good enough.

**53 g6   Ng3+
54 Ke1   Re3+
55 Kf2   Rf3+
56 Kg2**

Or 56 Kg1 Ne2+.

56 ...   Nh5!

The advance of each of the white pawns is prevented: 57 g7 N×g7 58 R×g7 R×f4, or 57 f5 Nf4+ and 58 ... N×d5.

57 Kh2

This merely prolongs the game, but does not affect the result.

**57 ...   N×f4
58 Bc6+   Kd8
59 g7   Rh3+
60 Kg1   Rg3+
61 Kf2   Nh5!**

Since the resumption, Black's pieces, and in particular his knight, have worked miracles.

62 Rf8+   Kc7

For the last time Black is once again

saved by a nuance: were his bishop at b5 instead of c6, White would win.

63 g8=Q	R×g8
64 R×g8	K×c6
65 Ke3	Kd6

Drawn. Although Black's knight is on the edge of the board, it cannot be caught.

An example of the amazing and inexhaustible nature of chess!

After such sufferings and sleepless nights, both by the theory of probability and by all the laws of justice I should not have had another such adjourned position in this tournament! But evidently some 'evil spirit' was aiming to deprive me completely of sleep, and four rounds later it sent me the following game:

Polugayevsky–Filip
*Interzonal Tournament,
Palma de Mallorca 1970*

This position appears to be simpler than the previous one. This is, but also isn't, true. In the game against Uhlmann the analysis consisted of searching for dynamic, lively, forcing variations. There neither of the two sides had time for manoeuvring. But here the board is partitioned off by the pawn chains, and for the time being this gives the position a closed nature. But since White has a clear and stable advantage—in view of his greater space and Black's weakness at a5—it would seem that all he has to do is to regroup his forces appropriately, when things will become even more difficult for Black.

However, when I came to check the position, it turned out that this was not quite so. Although White's plans are on the whole straightforward, if they are carried out directly each time they encounter serious resistance by the opponent, and I soon realized that a completely concrete method was required to increase and realize my advantage. Many hours of night-time analysis convinced me that without that it was impossible to win from the adjourned position.

The point is that White is unable to win the weak a5 pawn, and the only possibility of breaking into the opponent's position is to strike in the centre with e3-e4, after which Black is saddled with an additional weakness at g6. But this break-through is possible only under completely specific circumstances, otherwise the black pieces establish themselves at f5, when there is no question of a White win.

Therefore White begins combining his efforts, so as first to 'draw the attention' of the black pieces to other problems, lure them into the most unfavourable positions, and only then break through in the centre. But what problems? It was this question that I managed to answer in my analysis, and what's more, White's threats prove to be very definite. For instance, he is already intending to win the a5 pawn, by carrying out the knight manoeuvre Na4–b6–c8–a7–c6, and by placing his queen at a2.

In order to forestall this, the black queen must abandon the square h4, where it is on the whole quite well placed, after which all Black's pieces will be restricted to the back two ranks. Then White himself will seize the only open file, the 'h' file, and by threatening to invade with his queen, will force Black to weaken in some way his control over f5.

Strangely enough, all these abstract ideas are manifested in completely concrete form.

42 ... Qh8. We considered this to be the only move—otherwise the manoeuvre Na4–b6–c8–a7–c6 is decisive—and we began our analysis from this initial position.

First we tried the thematic 43 Nb6 Qd8 (after *43 ... Be8* the white knight completes its manoeuvre without hindrance) 44 N×d7 (eliminating one of the defenders of the f5 square) 44 ... Q×d7 45 e4, but it turned out that after 45 ... Nd8! 46 e×f5 N×f5 47 N×f5 (*47 Bg4* fails to *47 ... Ne3+*; even the preliminary *47 Kf2* does not save White from this tactical possibility) 47 ... Q×f5 48 Q×f5 g×f5, although the ending is clearly in White's favour, there is no win. At any rate, Boleslavsky and I were unable to find one. E.g. 49 Bh5+ Kg7 50 Be8 e5! 51 d×e6 N×e6 52 Kg3 Nd4, and White is unable to improve his position.

Black's defensive lines are also impregnable if White avoids capturing on f5, and in the variation just given plays 46 e5. Then comes 46 ... Kg8, and how is he to effect a break-through? The preparation of a sacrifice on f5 is prevented by pressure with the black queen down the 'b' file.

We attempted to improve this variation by playing 45 Qb1, instead of the immediate 45 e4. Now if Black should be tempted into attacking the b3 pawn with 45 ... Qc7 46 Qh1 Qb6, White pierces his opponent's defences: 47 Qh7 Q×b3 48 e4 (also sufficient is *48 Bh5 Qb2+ 49 Kh3 g×h5 50 N×f5*, or *48 ... g×h5 49 g6+ Kf6 50 Qh6*, with the threat of mate at g5) 48 ... f×e4 49 Bg4.

But Black is by no means obliged to bother himself over such a trifle as the b3 pawn. He can go over to passive defence: 45 ... Kg8 46 Qh1 Qe8 47 Qh6 Qf7 48 e4 Nd8, and neither after the capture on f5, nor after the advance e4–e5, is it clear what to do next.

However much Boleslavsky and I racked our brains over this position, however much we analyzed it night after night, we were unable to find a clear win. But meanwhile I sensed that the game had been adjourned in a position won for White, and that to tip the scales in his favour he still had to add a little something....

In search of this 'little something' we rejected the direct 43 Nb6 followed by e3–e4, deciding to retain this as a threat, and began studying the more flexible continuation 43 Qb1.

Apart from the basic aim of switching the queen to the 'h' file, this move also nips in the bud the possibility of Black capturing with his bishop on a4: White's possession of the 'b' file then promises him a straightforward win.

Here at first we thought that our goal had been achieved. The threat of Na4–b6 with the variations given above is still there, since the queen, while no less strongly posted, has retreated from c2, where it came under attack by the black knight from e3. And after the natural 43 ... Qd8 (so as not to allow the knight in at b6) 44 Qh1 Kg8 45 Qh6 Be8 46 e4 Qd7 (on *46 ... Qc8* White wins either by *47 Nb6*, or by *47 e×f5 N×f5 48 Nb6 N×h6 49 N×c8 Nf7 50 N×e7+ Kg7 51 Be4 Nfd8 52 f5*; the attempt at counter-play is similarly doomed to failure: *46 ... e6 47 d×e6 N×e6 48 e×f5 N×f4+ 49 Kh2*, and the black king cannot escape from the mating net) 47 Nb6 Qc7 the pseudo-sacrifice 48 e×f5 Q×b6 49 f×g6 gives White an irresistible attack: 49 ... B×g6 50 Q×g6 Q×b3 51 f5 Qb2+ (or *51 ... Qc2+ 52 Kh3 Kf8 53 Be4 Qd2 54 f6 e×f6 55 Q×f6+ Ke8 56 Bg6+*, with the elimination of, at minimum, the entire black cavalry) 52 Kh3 Kf8 53 f6 e×f6 54 g×f6 Ne8 55 Bh5 Q×f6 56 Q×e8+ Kg7 57 Qd7+, with the same result.

But when we had worked all this out, I suddenly found an amazing way for Black to resist. It lay in the move 43 ... Qb8!.

It entered my mind after reasoning of the following nature: "How can it be that we found so many ways of defending after the knight invasion at b6, and then White had only to find an intermediate move, albeit a strong one, for Black's position to literally collapse?! It happens very rarely that way. We must have overlooked something...."

If one's thinking is directed along the correct lines, it makes the searching easier. We all know that it is much simpler, for instance, to carry out a combination when we definitely know that it is there, than to sense the possibility during a practical game.

And thus the 'prescribed' defensive move 43 ... Qb8 was found.

The move looks rather ridiculous, but is in fact perfectly sensible. Black leaves the square d8 open for his knight, and economizes on a mass of time for creating counter-play on the 'b' file. We suffered considerable anxiety, before we were able to find a very complicated, but nevertheless convincing enough way to win. After 44 Qh1 White is successful in the two main variations that Black can choose.

In the first of these Black attempts to prevent the invasion of the queen at h7: 44 ... Kg8 45 Qh6 Be8 (the immediate counterattack, *45 ... Nd8*, proves successful for Black if White captures the g6 pawn, but it encounters an elegant refutation: *46 Bh5 g×h5 47 g6 Nf7 48 Qh7+ Kf8 49 g×f7*, and Black has to resign in view of one further straightforward tactical blow on the theme of diversion: *49 ... K×f7 50 Nb6! Q×b6 51 N×h5*) 46 e4 f×e4 47 B×e4 Nd8 48 B×g6 B×g6 49 Q×g6 Q×b3 50 Nh5 Qa2+ 51 Kh3 Qa1 52 Q×g7+ (unfortunately, White has nothing better) 52 ... Q×g7 53 N×g7 K×g7 54 Kg4, and in this ending, which we also had to analyze in detail, White finally wins: 54 ... e5 (otherwise White advances his pawns to f5 and g6, and sends his king off to win the a5 pawn) 55 f×e5 (after *55 d×e6 N×e6 56 f5 Nd4* White still has to overcome a number of technical difficulties) 55 ... d×e5 56 d6! Nb7 57 d7 Kf7 58 N×c5 Nd8 59 Kf5, and Black is helpless against the passed pawns.

The win is even more difficult in the second variation, where Black ignores the invasion of the white queen, and immediately creates counter-play: 44 ... Nd8 45 Qh7 Q×b3 46 Nh5! (in this position *46 Bh5* would now be a mistake—*46 ...g×h5 47 g6+ Kf6 48 Qh6 Nf7!*, or *47 N×h5 B×a4*, and the black king escapes from the mating net via the vacated square d7) 46 ... Qa2+ (capture of the knight at h5 allows mate in two) 47 Kh3 Qa1 48 Nb6 Be8 49 Ng3!!

A startling move! "The Moor has done his deed"—ensured the intrusion of his colleague at b6, and now, by retreating, he forces the win in surprising fashion. It is true that this operation has cost a pawn, but on the other hand the black king is now securely blocked in by his own pieces, in many instances the white knight can penetrate to c8 with additional threats, and, most important, it is very difficult for Black to avert the knock-out blow 50 N×f5.

Thus 49 ... Qb1, for instance, is decisively met by the thematic 50 e4, while in the event of 49 ... e6 White continues 50 Nc8 (the fruits of the manoeuvre *Ng3–h5–g3*) 50 ... Bd7 (on *50 ... Nb7* White has *51 d×e6+ K×e6 52 B×b7*, if there is nothing better) 51 N×d6+ (White has no reason to seek adventures in attacks of the type *51 Nh5 B×c8 52 Nf6 Qf1+ 53 Bg2 Qe1 54 Qg8+ Ke7 55 Q×g7+ Nf7*, when the opponent gains counter-chances) 51 ... Ke7 52 Nb5, and Black has a sad choice between 52 ... a4 53 d6+ Kf7 54 Nh5 a3 55 Nf6, and 52 ... B×b5 53 c×b5 Kf7 54 b6 e5 55 d6 e4 56 Be2 Qa2 57 Qh8.

Thus in all these—and in many other highly complex variations—the idea of the sacrifice at h5 is normally decisive. We studied it most thoroughly, and I am convinced that at the board it would be practically impossible to find the 'pendulum' manoeuvre Ng3–h5–g3. To this day the winning method outlined in the analysis seems to me to be the most exact.

But on the resumption Filip's very first move came as a terrible disappointment to me. Masses of effort had been devoted to the analysis, several sleepless nights had been spent, the most subtle of subtleties had been found, and my opponent reduced it all to nought.

42 ...   Kf8?

In this way Black simply parts with his a5 pawn, after which the win becomes merely a question of time. But I was so upset that after the automatically-played

43 Nb6   Be8

I thought for a long time, and suddenly began even to doubt my own powers: could I capitalize on my extra pawn?

Then, it is true, everything fell into place.

  44 Qc3 Qh7
  45 Qa1

I could also have started the knight dance immediately, Nb6–c8–a7–c6, but I wanted to win the a5 pawn 'at my own convenience'.

  45 ... Kg8
  46 Nc8 Kf8
  47 Na7 Bf7
  48 Qa4 Be8
  49 Nc6

Threatening the intrusion of the queen at b5, when White wins the a5 pawn while retaining his strong knight at c6.

  49 ... e5

Played in the search for at least some sort of activity. Here White calculated the winning variation through to the end.

  50 f×e5 d×e5

There is no time for 50 ... Qh4, in view of 51 Qb5.

  51 Qa1

This is somewhat cleaner and more accurate than 51 Qb5 Nh5, although there too the win is not far away.

  51 ... B×c6

51 ... e4 fails to 52 Qf6+.

  52 d×c6 Nd6
  53 Q×e5 Nge8
  54 Q×c5 Qe7
  55 Qd4

A check at h8 is threatened, while on 55 ... Q×g5 either 56 c7 or 56 c5 is immediately decisive. Even so, in time trouble I was rather too hasty: 55 Bd5 is simpler, when there is literally nothing that Black can move; 55 ... Nc7 is answered by 56 Q×a5, if there is nothing better.

  55 ... Nf7
  56 Bd5 Ne5

Black could have lasted out somewhat longer by capturing the g5 pawn with his queen.

  57 Qh4 Qg7
  58 Qf4 Nd3
  59 Qd4 Ne5

The position is repeated, but with the difference that the g5 pawn is no longer attacked, and White can bring his knight into play.

  60 Ne2 Nc7
  61 Nf4 Ke8

and without waiting for the obvious 62 N×g6, Black **resigned**.

WITHOUT ANY PROMPTINGS BY THEORY

Polugayevsky–Geller
Skopje 1968

Five hours of play led us to a rare type of position, with a completely unusual balance of forces. I am not sure whether or not it has occurred earlier in practice, but in endgame theory nothing of this sort is analyzed.

Is the queen able to overcome the resistance of the bishop pair, which are able in some cases to create an iron curtain around their king? Before we begin to discuss this, it is probably worth while returning to the point in the game when this balance of forces arose.

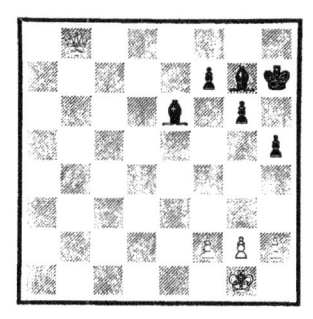

In principle, the more pawns there are on the board, the harder it is for the weaker side to defend. But at the same time the queen requires space for manoeuvring, and at the moment Black has no weaknesses. And so I prepared the plan of h2-h3, g2-g4, Kg1-g3 and f2-f4-f5, with winning chances.

31 Qf4	Bc3
32 h3	Kg7
33 g4	h×g4
34 h×g4	Bf6
35 Qe4	

Now Black could have hindered the advance f2-f4 by playing 35 ... Bd8 36 Kg2 Bc7. Geller decides to counter White's plan more radically, but as a result the solidity of the black pawns is destroyed somewhat.

35 ...	g5
36 Kg2	Be7

36 ... Bd8 now has no point, since after 37 f4 B×g4 38 f×g5 White wins.

37 Kh3	Bf6
38 Kg3	

For several moves White defers the carrying out of his basic plan.

38 ...	Bd8
39 Qd4+	Bf6
40 Qc5	Ba2
41 f4	Bb1?

Correct, of course, was 41 ... g×f4+ 42 K×f4, with a highly interesting ending. White's plan would be to advance g4-g5, and to prevent the white-squared bishop from occupying the b1-h7 diagonal. Then the queen would go via the 'h' file to h6, so as at the appropriate moment to support the advance g5-g6. Finally, an ending with queen against two bishops, without pawns, could be reached, but with the black king cut off on the back rank. Unfortunately, none of this was tested in practice; the ending would undoubtedly have been of theoretical importance.

However Geller, foreseeing this, and not wishing to play a disagreeable ending, tried another possibility, which in the end proved to be even worse.

And so in the adjourned position, with which the story began, White had to seal a move. I examined 42 Kf3. Now 42 ... g×f4 is no longer possible, in view of 43 g5, when one of the bishops is lost; 43 ... Bd8 44 Qd4+, or 43 ... Ba1 44 Qc1. At the same time 43 f5 is threatened, when there is no way that the white-squared bishop can get onto the a8-h1 diagonal, which is its ideal place. But then

I suddenly imagined that, by going totally onto the defensive—43 ... Bh7 44 f5 Bg8, Black could create a fortress by later placing his bishop at e5 and his pawn at f6.

This did not appeal to me, and it was only at home that I found that the fortress would not in fact materialize. White would continue simply 45 Ke4 Ba1 46 Qa3 Bf6 47 Kd5, when his king penetrates unhindered to e8. Then with the bishop at f6 White places his queen at d6, when Black is in *zugzwang*. E.g. 1 ... Bc3 2 Ke7, and there is no defence against f5-f6.

But, alas, it was a different move that was sealed.

42 f5

I do not even know whether I should regret this, since without it there would not have occurred a highly interesting endgame, which I analyzed move by move literally to the very end. When all this analytical material was written down, it turned out that the position on the board was virtually a study. And I went along to the tournament hall, firm in the knowledge that it was Black to play, but that White would win, and what's more, that there was only one single way to do this.

Incidentally, during the resumption of the game White spent only a few minutes on his two dozen moves. But behind each minute there stood roughly an hour of analytical work.

Theory, I repeat, has nothing to say about such endings, and I began my work by determining those typical positions, in which Black's bishops as it were cut across the board, and do not allow the white king into his position; without which, of course, there is no win. The first of these I was able to construct without difficulty.

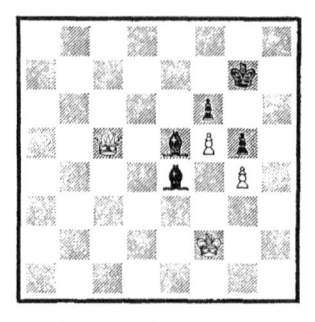

The e4 bishop simply strolls up and down the long white-squared diagonal, and even the united efforts of king and queen are insufficient to trap it or drive it off. This means that the white king cannot cross the barrier erected along the a8-h1 and b8-h2 diagonals.

Having determined this position, White begins in the first instance to fight against such a set-up for the bishops.

42 ...   Be4

There could be no doubt that this is what Black would play: after 42 ... Ba2 43 Qb5 there is nothing to prevent the white king from reaching e4, and then, by attacking the bishop with Qa4, moving on to d5 and eventually e8.

43 Kf2	Bh1
44 Ke3	Bb7
45 Qc7!	

The 'triangulation' device once again comes into play. It turns out that, on the empty and long white-squared diagonal, the bishop each time has only one reasonable square. By giving his opponent the move, White drives the bishop to a less comfortable post.

For instance, if here White plays 46 Qd6 immediately, Black has 46 ... Bg2, and the white king is still cut off, since 47 Kd3 is answered by 47 ... Bf1+ 48 Ke4 Bg2+.

If White should incautiously attempt to penetrate with his king on the edge of the board via a4 and a5 to b6, then Black, after first tying down the queen to the defence of the g4 pawn, can hope to create that same drawn position which has already been given.

Incidentally, so as not to have to return again to the initial stage of my analysis, I should say that I also discovered another ideal position for Black.

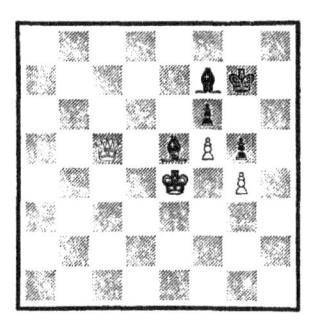

Here White's king is centralized, but he has no possibility of crossing a different barrier this time—along the a1-h8 and a2-g8 diagonals. Thus while fighting against the first drawing position, White all the time has to take care that Black does not set up the second....

But let us return to the game. Following White's queen manoeuvre, the white-squared bishop is unable to reach the a6-f1 diagonal.

45 ...   Bg2
46 Qd6!!

Both bishops have a mass of moves, and yet Black is in *zugzwang*. The point is that the bishops cannot defend each other, and it only needs the black-squared bishop to move away from his own king for one of Black's fighting units to fall.

E.g. 46 ... Ba1 47 Kf2! Be4 48 Qe7, and the breakaway pawn at g5 is lost. If Black attempts to keep the white king out of d3 by 46 ... Bf1, then after 47 Qd5! he is deprived of the long diagonal, and his forces are paralyzed: if 47 ... Be7, then 48 Kf2! Ba6 49 Qc6 Bd3 50 Qc3+, and the bishop is lost, while 47 ... Bc3 is again answered by 48 Kf2!, with the follow-up 48 ... Ba6 49 Qc6 Bd4+ 50 Kf3 Bf1 51 Qc2, and the road to e4 and d5 is open for the king.

White's task appears to be the most difficult after 47 ... Ba6, but in fact it is fairly simple: 48 Qc6 Bf1 49 Kf2 Bd3 50 Kf3 Bf1 51 Ke3, and once again triangulation, this time by the king, is used to give Black the move; he is forced to move his black-squared bishop, which inevitably leads to loss of material.

Black therefore attempts to retain possession of the a8-h1 diagonal.

46 ...   Bb7
47 Kd3

The first step is made: the king heads for c4.

47 ...   Bf3

Naturally, Black tries to prevent this. By tying the queen to the defence of the g4 pawn, he plays his bishop to d5, takes control of the c4 square, and 'reminds' his opponent that he also has a second drawing position.

48 Qg3   Bd5

For 'complete happiness' Black requires two tempi: 49 ... Ba1 and 50 ... f6. But ...

49 Qe3!

Black is faced with fresh problems. Neither bishop can move (after 49 ... Ba2 the white king breaks through: *50 Ke4 Be7 51 Qa7 Bb1+ 52 Kd5*), but in reserve he has moves with his king.

49 ...   Kg8!

It would seem that White cannot put all three pieces in *zugzwang*. But the whole point is that this does prove possible.

50 Kd2!!

White vacates the square d3 for his queen (so as to dislodge the bishop from its centralized post at d5), and prepares a route for his king into the enemy position via the jumping-off square b3, while exploiting a barely-discernible nuance in the resulting position: the black-squared bishop will temporarily be undefended. It would appear that, with this aim, the immediate 50 Kc2 is more consistent, but it achieves nothing against Black's only, but sufficient, defence: 50 ... Kg7 51 Qd3 Bh1!! (bad is *51 ... Ba2 52 Qb5*, when the white king goes first to e4, and then—after the attack on the bishop by *Qa4*—also to d5) 52 Kb3 Be5!, and it is impossible to prevent the creation of the familiar first drawing position after ... f7-f6.

White's problem is to move to c2 with his king only when, after this, the enemy king will be forced to retreat to g8, and for an instant leave the bishop at f6 without support (we will see from the further course of the game what an extremely important factor this is). White therefore resorts to the famous triangulation with his king, which explains his last move.

50 ...   Kg7

Now 50 ... Bh1 fails to the flank attack 51 Qh3 and 52 Qh6, with an immediate win. Here we see for the first time how White exploits the hanging position of the black-squared bishop.

If 50 ... Bg2 (*50 ... Ba2 51 Qb6 Kg7 52 Qb5* and *53 Kd3*), then 51 Qg3, and bad is either 51 ... Be4 52 Ke3! (the return of the king enables White to trap one of the bishops or to invade with his king) 52 ... Bc2 53 Qc7 Ba4 54 Ke4, or 51 ... Bf1 52 Qf3 Bb5 53 Qd5 Be8 (*53 ... Bf1 54 Ke1!*) 54 Ke3 etc.

51 Kc2

It is here that we reach the position of absolute *zugzwang*, if one can call it this, that White has been aiming for. The black-squared bishop cannot move (*51 ... Bd8 52 Qd4+*). On 51 ... Bc6 the king advances—52 Kb3 Bd5+ 53 Kb4, while on 51 ... Bg2 there follows 52 Kb3 Kf8 53 Kc4 Be7 (*53 ... Bd8 54 Kc5 Be7+ 55 Kb6 Bd8+ 56 Ka7 f6 57 Kb8! Be7 58 Kc7 Bd5 59 Kd7*) 54 Qg3 Bf1+ 55 Kd5 f6 56 Qb3 Kf7 57 Kc6+ Kf8 (*57 ... Ke8 58 Qg8+ Bf8 59 Qg6+ Ke7 60 Qh7+*) 58 Kd7. As we will see below, the retreat of the king similarly fails to save Black.

To be honest, I do not know whether it has ever occurred before in practice; that one piece has essentially paralyzed the activity of three enemy pieces on a completely open board!

51 ...　　　　Kg8

The last stage of the realization of White's advantage commences. As I have already said, I reached this position during analysis in my hotel room, and I relished the manoeuvres discovered with a sort of special chess delight, which, incidentally, has nothing in common with the joy of gaining a point in the tournament table.

52 Qd3　　　　Bc6

Other moves similarly fail to save Black. E.g. 52 ... Bb7 53 Kb3 Be5 (*53 ... Ba1 54 Qd8+*), and Black does not succeed in achieving a fortress by 54 ... f6: 54 Qb5 wins one of the bishops. If the black bishop stands not at b7, but at a8, then 54 Qd8+ immediately concludes the game.

On 52 ... Bg2 White takes control of e5 with gain of tempo by 53 Qg3, and after 53 ... Be4+ (*53 ... Bh1 54 Kd3*) 54 Kb3 Bd5+ 55 Ka4 Bc6+ 56 Ka5 Be8 57 Qb8! Kf8 58 Qd6+ Kg7 59 Kb6 his king penetrates into the opposing position. The bishop similarly cannot move to a2: 52 ... Ba2 53 Qa6, while in the event of 52 ... Bh1 White wins (as after the move actually played) by 53 Qd6! (it is here that the undefended state of the bishop is decisively exploited! What's more, it is cut off from the square e5) 53 ... Kg7 54 Kb3 Bf3 55 Qg3 Bd5+ 56 Ka4 Bc6+ 57 Ka5. Now it finally becomes clear why White needed to resort to the triangulation manoeuvre with his king: at the decisive moment his opposite number was forced to retreat to g8, when the black-squared bishop lost its support.

53 Qd6	Be4+
54 Kb3	Kg7
55 Kc4	

The remainder, as it is customary to say, is a matter of technique.

55 ...	Bf3
56 Qg3	Bh1
57 Qh3	

This manoeuvre enables White to improve the position of his queen without loss of tempo, so that as before it controls the square e5, while at the same time keeping the g5 pawn under fire.

57 ...	Be4
58 Qe3	Bc6
59 Kc5	

At last the Rubicon is crossed.

59 ...   Bd7

A final attempt: the bishop retreats onto the a4–e8 diagonal, and as long as it is there the white king cannot advance any further than d6. But the diagonal is short, and it is not difficult to drive the bishop off it.

**60 Kd6   Bb5
61 Qb3   Be2**

Or 61 ... Be8 62 Qc4 Kg8 63 Qc8 Kf8 64 Kd5 Bb2 65 Qd8.

**62 Qb4   Bf3
63 Qc4**

The g4 pawn is defended, and the road to e8 is open. At the same time, Black will not now have a check from c6.

**63 ...   Kg8
64 Kd7   Kf8
65 Qc5+   Kg8
66 Ke8   Resigns**

This is possibly the most meticulous analysis I have ever made in my life. During the resumption the white queen had to get through a tremendous amount of work, and it was necessary to find an accurate way of utilizing her inexhaustible energy.

Gligorić–Polugayevsky
IBM Tournament, Amsterdam 1970

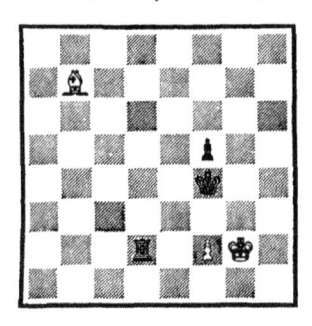

This apparently extremely simple—not to say elementary—ending gave me a mass of anxiety, but also enormous pleasure. White happily sacrificed the exchange to go into it, and was firmly convinced that the position on the board was a so-called 'dead' draw. True, in books on the endgame I had never seen this exact position, but, as I was leaving the tournament hall after the adjournment, I too was inclined to think that this was so. What could prevent the bishop from manoeuvring along the long white-squared diagonal, and how could the black pawn be advanced to f3, thus severely restricting the white king and obtaining the possibility of either creating mating threats, or of winning the f2 pawn?

Of course, if White himself were to play f2–f3, defending his pawn with his bishop, Black would drive the enemy king a sufficient distance away, and then by giving up the exchange for a pawn would achieve a won pawn ending. But here all three white pieces co-ordinate ideally one with another, and at first I did not even want to waste any effort on a second adjournment, especially since my tournament standing permitted me to avoid waging an exhausting battle for every half point.

But while still on the way to the hotel, tossing the position to and fro in my mind, I suddenly sensed a kind of perplexment. It occurred to me, for instance, that the long-range white bishop could be forced off the 'main' road, and that on the shorter diagonals it could become rather restricted. This meant that I had to forget about prudent economy of effort, and get down to analysis.

And, on setting up the position on the board, I became engrossed in its secrets, and in literally every variation discovered subtleties of which I would never even have dreamed.

I found straight away that, if the black pawn were at f4, then in the given situation it would indeed be a 'dead' draw: the bishop could not be driven off. But standing at f5 the pawn, firstly, does not deprive its own king of the neighbouring square, and secondly, restricts the scope of the white bishop. And this 'trifle' is, evidently, of decisive importance. And for White it is not at all easy to draw, if in general it is at all possible.

A lengthy study of the position enabled me to outline three stages in my plan:

1) Drive the bishop off the a8-h1 diagonal.

2) Pursue the bishop with the rook, so as to restrict it to the maximum.

3) Obtain the ideal position, so as to make the decisive advance of the black pawn to f3 via the 'transit' square f4.

The first two parts of the plan were found to be either quick or slow, but certainly feasible. I racked my brains for a long time over a way of achieving the third part, until I realized that without the 'assistance' of my opponent it was not possible. So that, as regards establishing the absolute truth, the position must nevertheless be judged to be drawn, but with the important proviso that the weaker side must avoid a mass of sunken reefs.

But now—

73 ...   Rd3
74 Bc6   Rc3

By making an unusual 'rook triangle', Black gives his opponent the move, and the bishop is forced to abandon the sacred diagonal.

75 Bd5

A not altogether happy reply; White should have fought to the end for the diagonal, and tried 75 Bb7. But even then, after 75 ... Kg4 76 Bd5 (with the intention of answering *76 ... f4* with *77 Be6+*, and then returning to d5) Black achieves his aim: 76 ... Rd3 77 Bb7 (if *77 Bc6*, then *77 ... f4* and *78 ... f3+*, winning immediately) 77 ... Rb3, and now either 78 Bd5 Rc3! (giving White the move) 79 Bb7 f4, or 78 Bc6 Ra3! (the key square again for the rook's 'linear triangle') 79 Bd5 Rc3 (or *79 Bb7 Rd3*), and the bishop must abandon the long diagonal.

Therefore the move played merely allows Black to carry out the first part of his plan more quickly.

75 ...   Kg4
76 Be6

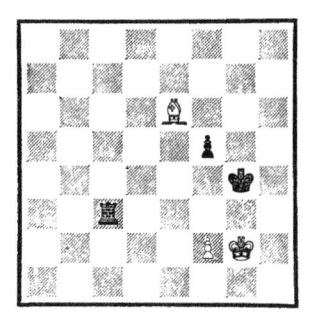

The second stage begins, that of restricting the bishop's mobility.

First of all, Black must ensure that it doesn't return to the a8-h1 diagonal.

76 ...   Rc5
77 Bb3   Kf4
78 Bd1

With the intention if possible of returning to f3. White could have pinned his hopes on 'guerilla warfare', and immediately moved into Black's rearguard— 78 Be6. But Gligorić was evidently afraid of 78 ... Ke4, when in view of the threat of the pawn march ... f5-f4-f3, White has no move apart from 79 Bf7 (*79 Bb3 f4; 79 Bd7 f4 80 Bg4 Rg5*). And as yet he didn't wish to be forced into a situation where there was only one move.

78 ...   Rc6!

The bishop cannot now go to f3, in view of 79 ... Rg6+. By switching to the 6th rank, the black rook increases its functions: it not only pursues the bishop, but also in some cases disturbs the white king.

79 Bh5

All the time White has to act very carefully. For instance, it is already dangerous for him to keep the bishop close to his king; 79 Be2 Rg6+ 80 Kf1 Ke4 81 Bd1 Rd6 82 Bh5 (*82 Bc2+* loses immediately to *82 ... Kf3*) 82 ... Rh6 83 Bf7! (after *83 Bd1 Rh1+ 84 Ke2* the white king is driven onto the 'long side' of the pawn, and this gives Black additional chances, while *83 Be8? Kf3* leads to capitulation: *84 Kg1 Re6 85 Bd7 Re1+ 86 Kh2 f4*), and although White is not yet lost, he is literally walking a tightrope.

Therefore White takes control of g6, in his turn restricting the rook.

79 ...   Rh6
80 Bd1

Directed in particular against 80 ... Ke4, which would have followed in reply to 80 Be8 or 80 Bf7.

80 ...   Rg6+
81 Kf1   Rd6

Very slowly Black tightens the noose still further. White can move his bishop only along one relatively short diagonal, d1-h5, since 82 Bc2(b3, a4), for instance, is met decisively by 82 ... Kf3. True, for the moment this is sufficient, since Black too is unable to strengthen his position.

82 Bh5   Rd7

The bishop is restricted, but not yet to a catastrophic degree, and therefore Black, instead of using the 6th rank as a base, attempts to begin manoeuvres along the 7th rank. The reason? Instead of the square g6, which is sometimes inaccessible, he wishes to obtain the always accessible square g7, which may prove useful.

Incidentally, Black could also have played 82 ... Rh6, when he achieves advantages referred to earlier after 83 Bd1 Rh1+, or 83 Bf7 Ke4. But in the latter case there is no definite win, and Black keeps this possibility in reserve.

83 Kg2   Rg7+
84 Kf1   Ke4
85 Bd1

Black has achieved maximum activity, but the victorious march of the pawn is still not possible, and he continues to seek an opportunity, while chasing the bishop. And White too has to defend accurately...

85 ...   Rd7
86 Bh5

Once again the only move (*86 Be2 f4; 86 Bc2 Kf3*), but alas, still sufficient. Incidentally, it is also dangerous to move the king, e.g. 86 Ke2 Rc7, and White is in *zugzwang*.

86 ...   Rh7

Intending now after 87 Bd1 to continue 87 ... Rh1+ 88 Ke2 Kf4, when the harmony between the white pieces is destroyed. On 89 Ba4, for instance, 89 ... Ra1 is unpleasant, and if 90 Bd7, then 90 ... Rc1 with the threat of 91 ... Rc2+ 92 Kf1 Kf3, while in the event of 91 Be6 Black achieves his goal by 91 ... Ke5 and the subsequent advance of his pawn. Of course, White can also play differently, but it will be apparent that after 87 Bd1 his difficulties are increased.

In this variation Black himself would have had to avoid falling into a tempting trap: 88 ... R×d1? 89 K×d1 Kf3 90 Ke1 Kg2, when 91 f4! leads to a draw.

87 Be8

The bishop's possibilities are extremely restricted, but it is not clear that Black can further improve his position. He therefore comes to a new decision. Since he has 'squeezed out' the maximum with his rook on the 7th rank, Black changes its 'place of residence', and switches it to the 8th rank. But before carrying out this plan, he returns it to the 6th rank, at the same time both masking his intention, and also lulling his opponent's vigilance, and hoping, finally, to see how the bishop 'behaves' on its new diagonal.

87 ...	Rh6
88 Ba4	Rd6
89 Kg2	Kf4

There has already been a similar position, the only difference being that the bishop has moved from h5 to a4.

90 Be8	Rb6
91 Ba4	Ra6
92 Bd1	Rg6+

93 Kf1	Rd6
94 Bh5	Rh6
95 Bf7	Ke4
96 Bb3	Rc6
97 Kg2	Rc1
98 Bf7	Rc7
99 Bh5	

White defends accurately. It only required one careless move, 99 Ba2, for him to lose after 99 ... Rb7: the bishop has no square from which to parry the inevitable 100 ... f4 by checking the black king!

99 ...	Rg7+
100 Kf1	Rg8

The idea behind switching the rook to the back rank is that in many cases the bishop is deprived of the key square e8, from where it has moved both to a4 and and to h5.

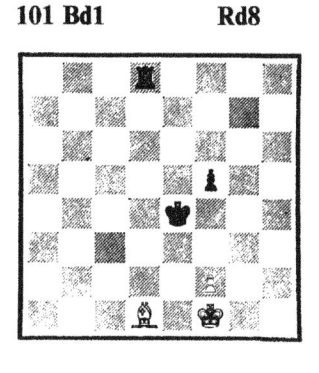

| 101 Bd1 | Rd8 |

102 Ba4

White fails to sense the difference between the position of the rook on the 6th, 7th and 8th ranks, and misses the only saving move in this position, 102 Bh5, with the follow-up 102 ... Rh8 103 Bf7!, and if 103 ... f4, then 104 Kg2. Here Black fails to achieve his goal after 104 ... f3+

105 Kg3 Rh6 106 Be8, when the rook is unable to guard simultaneously the squares c6 and g6, and also drive away the white king with check from g7. A positional draw!

By moving his bishop off to the other side, White comes to grief.

102 ...   Rc8!

It is here that the position of the rook on the 8th rank tells! The bishop is denied the square e8, via which at the necessary moment (after the advance of the black pawn) it could give a check at g6.

103 Bd7

103 Bd1 is decisively met by 103 ... f4 104 Kg2 Rg8+ and 105 ... f3, and 103 Bb3 by 103 ... f4 104 Kg2 Rc7 followed by 105 ... Rg7+ and 106 ... f3.

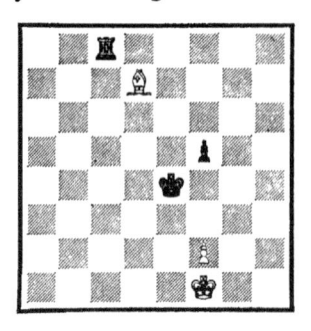

103 ...   Rc5!!

Only now is the point of Black's plan revealed. This switching of the rook to an 'ambush' position is directed against that same manoeuvre of the bishop via e8 to h5. Thus on 104 Be8 Black wins by 104 ... f4 105 Bg6+ Kf3, while 104 Kg2 is decisively met by 104 ... f4 105 Bg4 Rg5.

Now the third stage of the plan commences: the ideal position for the march of the pawn has been achieved.

104 Ke2	f4
105 Be8	f3+
106 Kd2	Rd5+
107 Kc2	Kf4
108 Bf7	Rg5

White resigned in view of the inevitable loss of his pawn: 109 Kd2 Rg2 110 Ke1 Rg1+ 111 Kd2 Rf1.

Of course, strictly speaking the ending was drawn. But to achieve this, exceptional vigilance and accuracy were demanded of White, together with scrupulous analysis. As the course of the game showed, it proved to be not at all simple to meet these demands.

ROOK ENDINGS CAN AFTER ALL BE WON!

Polugayevsky-Vasyukov
34th USSR Championship, Tbilisi 1967

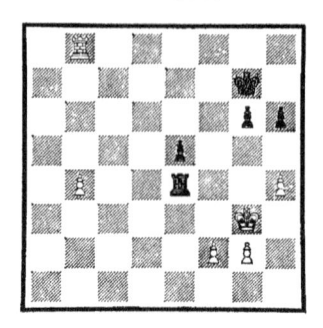

The resumption of this game turned out to be very simple in nature, but how worried I was as I made my way to the Rustaveli Theatre, the stage of which had been given over to chess! Firstly, because the Championship was an elimination event for the Interzonal Tournament; secondly, because I felt somewhat feverish, and successes were alternating with misfortunes; and thirdly, because in this game I had held an overwhelming positional advantage from the very opening, but had several times missed an opportunity to increase it decisively. And as a result the win for White hung by a thread: as Savielly Tartakower once wittily remarked: "all rook endings are drawn". In particular, as I knew from my own experience, endings with an extra 'b' pawn.

What's more, the saving procedure for the defending side has been studied no less thoroughly that the multiplication tables. While the passed pawn, in the given situation White's, is advancing to b6, Black waits. Then, when the white king heads for the b6 pawn, Black picks up something on the K-side, after which he sacrifices his rook for White's passed pawn, and advances his own newly-formed passed pawns, supported by his king. White is normally forced to return his extra rook and be satisfied with a draw.

Such are the normal plans for the two sides. And in order to disturb this practised scheme, it was necessary to find something additional in the position, that little extra weight which would tip the scales.

But as I thought over my sealed move, I couldn't see it.

42 b5

Only when I began my analysis did I discover a nuance in this position, and a highly important one. The point is that, by advancing his pawn to b7, White ties down the opposing king and rook, and then, by an encircling manoeuvre with his king, utilizing once again the 'triangulation' method, he wins the e5 pawn. But even after this, victory can be achieved only if he creates a passed pawn on the 'f' file.

By playing f5-f6+, White prevents the black king from moving between the squares g7 and h7, and after ... Kf7 he wins by Rh8, while in the event of ... K×f6 he has the opportunity for a deadly check: Rf8+ and b7-b8=Q.

In the adjourned position the white 'f' pawn has no opposite number, but the black g6 pawn stands in its path. This pawn could have been cleared out of the way immediately, by the dagger-blow 42 h5!. If Black captures on h5 or allows White to take on g6, White's idea of creating a second passed pawn is achieved in pure form, and a theoretically won ending is reached.

During the game I was intending to play h4-h5 on my next move, my 43rd, but in my analysis I became aware that such a hope was not feasible. After all, it was now Black's turn to move, and before posting his rook behind the white 'b' pawn, he could radically prevent all his opponent's aggressive intentions on the K-side, by first playing 42 ... h5!.

If in this case the white king were to head for the 'b' pawn, play would proceed as described at the very beginning, and (I have to ask you to take my word for this) White would at best be one tempo away from a win. However much I racked my brains, I couldn't find a win for White.

If instead White wins the e5 pawn by 'triangulation'—which is possible—then, in contrast to the situation earlier, after f2-f3 and g2-g4 he succeeds in creating a passed pawn only on the 'g' or 'h' file, which is not good enough to win.

But Black passed over this opportunity, having failed to foresee something in his analysis. I do not know the precise reason, of course, but I will venture to suggest this: the time he spent on this position was less than that spent by White, and he did not subject to analysis every move at his disposal.

42 ...   Rb4?

Here I—imperceptibly, as far as possible—breathed a sigh of relief. This move, although so natural, leaves Black on the edge of the abyss.

43 h5!   g×h5

After 43 ... g5 both the f5 square and the h6 pawn are weakened, which gives White additional trumps.

44 b6

In his delight, White promptly commits an erroneous transposition of moves. It was essential first to play 44 Kf3, immediately aiming his sights on the black 'e' pawn, which has been left in complete isolation, and planning to put into effect the white king's triangulation manoeuvre found in analysis, although even here there is no one hundred per cent guarantee that White's position is won.

44 ...   h4+?

Black fails to exploit the opportunity presented to him. Saving chances were offered by 44 ... Rb3+, when an amazing, study-like draw results after 45 f3 e4 46 b7 (or *46 Kf2 Rb2+ 47 Ke3 R×g2 48 b7 Rb2 49 f×e4 h4*, and the black 'h' pawn is no weaker than either of its white opponents) 46 ... h4+! (but not *46 ... e3 47 f4 e2 48 Kf2*), and after 47 Kf2 Black is saved by the straightforward 47 ... h3; and after 47 K×h4 e3 48 Kg3 by the highly subtle 48 ... Rb4!!, when White is in *zugzwang*.

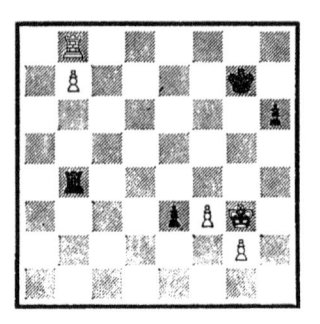

He has no move other than 49 f4 (the exchange of the b7 pawn for the e3 pawn leads to a theoretically drawn ending), but then 49 ... e2 50 Kf2 R×f4+ 51 K×e2 Rb4 once again gives White nothing.

Therefore, in reply to 44 ... Rb3+ White would have had to try 45 Kh4. But after 45 ... e4! (*45 ... Rb2, however, is also possible*) the tempting 46 K×h5 leads only to a draw after the quiet retreat 46 ... Rb4!!, when White is doomed to carrying on the fight 'a king down', since he dare not step onto the 'mined' 4th rank. The thematic 47 f4 is just one tempo too slow: 47 ... e3 48 f5 e2, with a draw after 49 Re8 R×b6 50 R×e2 Rb1. Also, 47 g4 does not change anything: the further advance g4-g5 is all the same impossible, in view of the reply ... Rb5.

In the game, on the other hand, Black maintains material equality for a time, and ... loses.

45 Kf3   Kh7

On the conclusion of the game my opponent had to endure a mass of reproaches at the hands of his supporters: why didn't Black play 45 ... Kg6 here, and on 46 b7—46 ... Kh5? But on this White had prepared 47 g4+! h×g3 48 f×g3, when 49 g4+ Kh4 50 g5!, which enables the white rook to move from b8 with check, can merely be delayed by a series of checks, but not averted. It should be mentioned that Vasyukov saw all this, and promptly 'calmed' his companions.

| 46 b7 | Kg7 |
| 47 Ke3 | |

But here Black thought for a long time. Earlier he had not contemplated the fact that the white king could 'surround' the e5 pawn.

| 47 ... | e4 |

Or 47 ... Kh7 48 Kd3 Kg7 49 Kc3 Rb1 50 Kc4 Rb2 51 Kd5 Rb5+ 52 Kc6 Rb2 53 Re8(d8, a8), and the white pawn queens.

48 Kf4	Kh7
49 Ke5	Kg7
50 Kd5	Rb2

All the same Black cannot hold his e4 pawn. E.g. 50 ... Kh7 51 Kc5 Rb2 52 Kc6! Rc2+ 53 Kd5 Rb2 54 K×e4.

51 K×e4	Rb4+
52 Kd3	Rb3+
53 Kc4	Rb1
54 f4	

At last we have reached that theoretically won ending, for which White was aiming in his adjournment analysis.

54 ...	Rc1+
55 Kd3	Rb1
56 f5	Rb6
57 f6+	Resigns

Planinc–Polugayevsky
Mar del Plata 1971

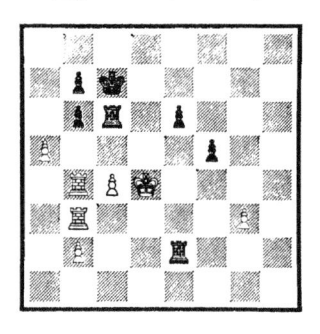

First a short introduction.

Soon after the start of this tournament, I drew away considerably from my rivals. The game with Planinc was the last which had any real significance in the battle for first place. During it, therefore, I did not especially go all out to win, and at the end of the first session I was happy—since Black had an undisputed advantage—as I sealed my move. The game was resumed that same evening, about an hour and a half later. Normally in such situations one has to sacrifice both food and rest, saving every minute for analysis. On this occasion I did not see the necessity for this, and so permitted myself to devote part of the time to a meal.

But the food proved to be 'bitter'. When I had sat down at the table, the effusive Argentinian grandmaster Miguel Najdorf literally flew up to me, and announced at the top of his voice:

"He is lost. You seal ... e6–e5—check, and he has to resign!!"

I became embarrassed, shrugged my shoulders, and ... felt quite upset. This move had not occurred to me at all, and

I had sealed a more orthodox continuation. Only later did I discover that it was also stronger, and that it was in the variation 41 ... e5+ that in the short one and a half hour interval my opponent had managed to find good drawing chances.

Objectively, on the other hand, my sealed move set Planinc more difficult problems. In addition, it later became clear that he had spent less time on the analysis of this continuation. And this was the result:

| 41 ... | Re4+ |

It was only deep into the night, when the game had already concluded, that I managed to establish that after 41 ... e5+ 42 Kd3 Rg2 43 R×b6! R×g3+ 44 Ke2 R×b3 45 R×b3 R×c4 46 Rb5 White may well be able to save the game. E.g. 46 ... Re4+ 47 Kf3 Re1 48 Kf2.

42 Kd3	b×a5
43 R×b7+	Kd6
44 R3b6?	

A mistake. White's plan meets with a subtle refutation. 44 Ra7! was better, when it is doubtful whether Black can win.

| 44 ... | Re×c4 |

This is stronger than 44 ... Rg4 45 R×c6+ K×c6 46 Rb5.

| 45 R×c6+ |

Planinc expected that Black would reply with the natural 45 ... R×c6, when there comes 46 b4 a×b4 47 R×b4 followed by 48 Ke3. But a surprise awaited him.

45 ...	K×c6!
46 Re7	Re4
47 g4	

Otherwise 47 ... Kd6, whereas now this move can be met by 48 g×f5.

| 47 ... | R×g4! |
| 48 R×e6+ | Kd5 |

This at first sight simple ending proves to be amazingly interesting. White's misfortune is that he is unable to exchange the Q-side pawns, since his king must constantly keep an eye on the passed 'f' pawn. At the appropriate moment Black places his rook on the 'b' file, and ties his opponent down.

| 49 Ra6 | a4 |
| 50 Ra5+ | |

50 Rb6 is answered by 50 ... Rg3+.

50 ...	Ke6
51 Ra6+	Ke5
52 Ra5+	Kf6
53 Ke3	

There is nothing better. White has to reckon with 53 ... Re4 and 54 ... Kg5.

| 53 ... | Rb4 |

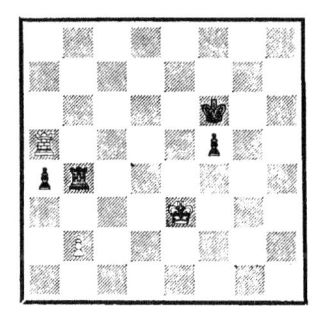

Black has carried out the first part of his plan. Now he switches his king to the Q-side.

54 Ra8	f4+
55 Kf3	Ke5
56 Re8+	Kd5

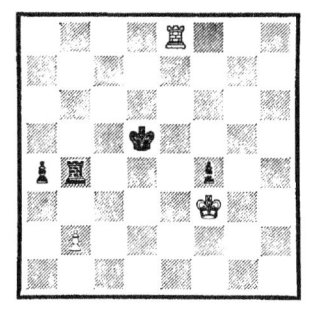

57 Rc8?

This loses quickly. Black has most difficulties after *57 Rd8+ Kc5 58 Rc8+* (bad is *58 Rd2 Rd4* followed by *59 ... Kb4*, with an easy win) *58 ... Kd4! 59 Rd8+!* (if *59 K×f4*, then *59 ... Kd3+! 60 Kf3 R×b2*, and the 'a' pawn decides the game) *59 ... Kc4 60 K×f4 Kb3+! 61 Ke3 K×b2*.

White appears to be defenceless, but in fact he has an excellent counter-chance: 62 Rd2+!.

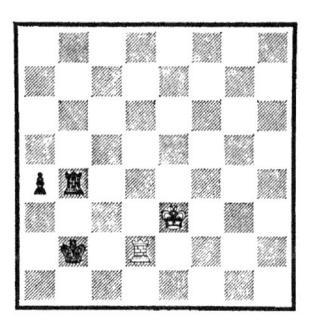

Where is the king to move to? 62 ... Kb3 63 Rd3+ Ka2 appears very tempting, but here White's pieces perform miracles: 64 Rd2+! (*64 Kd2* loses to *64 ... Kb2*) 64 ... Rb2 65 Rd8! a3 66 Kd3 Kb1 67 Kc3! Rc2+ 68 Kb3, with a draw.

Similarly, nothing is achieved by 62 ... Kb3 63 Rd3+ Kc4? 64 Rd4+ Kc5 65 R×b4.

And even so, Black has a study-like way to win.

62 ... Kc1 63 Rh2 Rb2!!. This manoeuvre is the point of Black's plan; (on *63 ... a3* White has an adequate reply in *64 Kd3! Rb3+ 65 Kc4 Rg3 66 Rh1+*) 64 Rh1+ (or *64 Rh8 a3 65 Kd3 Rc2!*) 64 ... Kc2 65 Rh2+ (necessary, since after *65 Rh8 a3 66 Rc8+ Kd1* White is lost) 65 ... Kc3 66 Rh8 Rb5!.

Only in this way can White's resistance be overcome. If 66 ... a3, then 67 Rc8+ Kb3 68 Kd3! a2 69 Rb8+.

67 Rc8+ Kb2 68 Kd2 Rd5+ 69 Ke3 a3 70 Rb8+ Kc3 71 Rc8+ Kb4, and Black wins.

And so, even with best defence White could not have gained a draw!

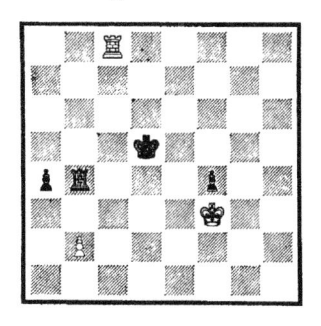

57 ...	R×b2!
58 K×f4	a3
59 Ke3	a2
60 Rd8+	Kc4
61 Ra8	Kc3!
Resigns	

A highly interesting ending, which, in my opinion, is of theoretical importance.

I have never succeeded in creating any chess compositions. And therefore it was a pleasant surprise for a little study to emerge from a practical game. What's more, having been extremely interested in the resulting position, I found the study-like win there, in Mar del Plata, although of course, not during the one hour of analysis of the adjourned game, but following the adjournment session. True, on returning to Moscow I discovered something similar by our celebrated composer Troitsky, but I should like to flatter myself with the hope that the resulting study will retain its right to exist. If only for the reason that it emerged during a practical game—the most refined 'composition' of a chess player.

Here it is.

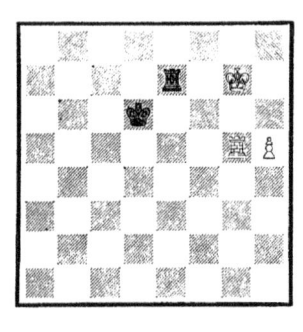

White to play and win.

Polugayevsky-Ivkov
*AVRO-2 Tournament,
Hilversum 1973*

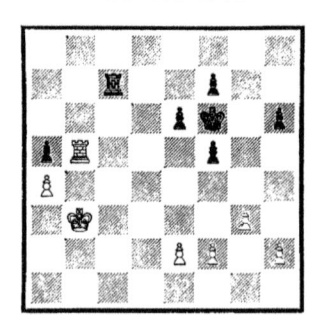

White's advantage in the adjourned position is obvious. It comprises not only the greater activity of his rook, and the weakness of the a5 pawn—these by themselves might not be sufficient for a win—but also the fact that Black has doubled pawns on the 'f' file. It might seem that this is of no great significance, but in fact the pawn group f7–e6–f5 is close to ossification: any advance of the K-side pawns leads to the formation of new weaknesses.

It was easy to guess Black's sealed move: it is the only possibility.

41 ...	Ra7
42 f4	

Thus the black pawns are fixed. At the same time (before taking his king over to the a5 pawn) White solves two further problems. Firstly, he removes from the 'refreshment stall' (this is what our chess predecessors called the 2nd rank in a rook ending) one of his pawns, and secondly, prepares a place for his rook at e5, from where the e2 pawn will be securely defended.

42 ...	Ke7
43 Kc4	Kd7
44 Kd4	

It might be thought that White is 'showing off' by not playing the immediate 44 Rb8 followed by the march of the king to b5. But in fact he wishes to force the advance ... f7–f6 (in the event of *44 ... Ke7* White continues *45 Kc5 Rc7+ 46 Kb6 Re2 47 Re5*), so that on the eighth rank the white rook will gain additional scope for manoeuvre, and can operate more effectively. I will not venture to make a definite judgement as to whether after 44 ... f6 45 Rb8 White's chances of winning would be greater than of drawing: I think, however, that Black is still quite a long way from a draw.

Even so, Black should have tried 44 ... f6, and after the game Ivkov regretted that he had not done so. The move made by him immediately places Black on the verge of catastrophe.

44 ...   h5
45 e4

It is here that the deformation of Black's pawn formation tells!

45 ...   f×e4
46 R×h5

White has gained a passed 'h' pawn, and in order to retain his passed 'e' pawn Black has to be prepared to sacrifice material—46 ... Rb7 47 R×a5 f5. This was probably his best chance.

46 ...   Kd6

47 g4!

No 'pawn-grabbing'! After 47 K×e4 f5+ the black rook is freed from having to defend the a5 pawn, and switches to the 'assault line'. Evidently it was this that my opponent had missed in his preliminary calculations.

47 ...   Rb7

Black is nevertheless forced to seek counter-play, in an inferior form.

48 R×a5   Rb4+
49 Ke3   Rb2

A rather cunning idea. It only needs White to advance his pawn—50 h4, for there to follow 50 ... Rb3+ 51 K×e4 Rb4+ 52 Ke3 Rb3+, and after driving the white king by checks to the Q-side, Black attacks the 'f' pawn from the rear, forces its advance, and thus wins one of the K-side pawns. This would ease his defence significantly.

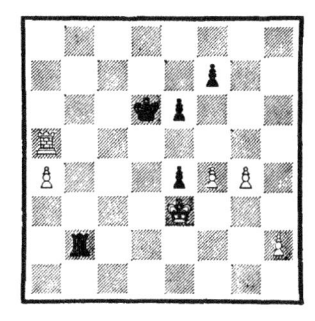

50 g5!

White sees through Black's intention, and emphasizes that play will revolve around the exploitation of the weakness at f7.

50 ...   R×h2
51 Ra7   Ra2

It turns out that Black cannot play 51 ... Rh7, in view of 52 a5 (but not *52 K×e4?? f5+*) 52 ... Kc6 53 a6 Kb6 54 Re7 K×a6 55 K×e4, and by advancing his king to f6 White wins easily, while he does not have to fear 55 ... f5+ since he can capture *en passant*—56 g×f6. With the fall of the f7 pawn Black's game can no longer be saved.

52 K×e4	Ra1
53 a5	Ra4+
54 Kf3	Kd5
55 Rd7+	Kc6
56 R×f7	R×a4
57 g6	Ra1
58 Kg4	Resigns

Polugayevsky–Mecking
Manila 1975

With his sealed move, 42 Rd1–c1, White has occupied the open file, and has cut off the black king from the main sector of the coming battle—the K-side. He now threatens to blockade the d4 pawn and win it, when the rest will be obvious.

Black could have sought drawing chances in the variation 42 ... d3+ 43 Kd2 Ra8 44 a4+ Kb4 45 Rc6 K×b3 46 R×b6+ K×a4 47 Rb7 Rf8 48 K×d3 Ka5, but the great difference in activity between the white and black pieces renders Black's defence extremely difficult.

E.g. 49 Ke4 Ka6 50 Re7 Kb6 51 Ke5 Kc6 52 h4, and Black is forced to wait submissively for the advance of the white pawns to break up his own pawn ranks.

It was probably for this reason that Mecking decided on a different method of defence.

42 ...	Ra8
43 Rc2	Ra7
44 Kd3	Kb4
45 K×d4	b5

Black's plan becomes clear. By penetrating with his king to a3, and advancing his pawn to b4, he wishes to tie the white rook to the defence of the a2 pawn, and, by placing his own rook on the 'e' file, to attempt to cut off the opposing king from the K-side.

Accuracy is demanded of White to counter this plan. Thus the direct 46 Ke5 did not appeal to me, because of 46 ... Re7+ 47 Kd6 Re6+ 48 Kd7 h5!, and after ... g7–g6 it is not easy to find a successful way of combating the black pawn formation f7-g6-h5. It is against such a set-up that White's next move is directed.

46 g4!	Ka3
47 f4	b4
48 h4	Re7
49 h5	

Although Black has fully carried out his plan, and has cut the white king off from his pawns, he is nevertheless close to a position of *zugzwang*, since on 49 ... Re6 there follows 50 Kc5 Re7 51 Rd2 Re6 52 Rd7.

After prolonged thought, the Brazilian grandmaster decides to switch to active defence.

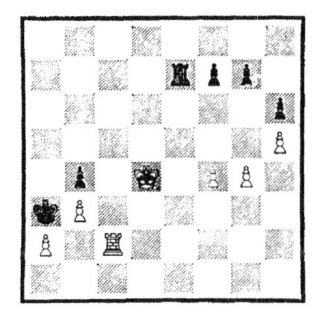

| 49 ... | Re1 |
| 50 Rc7 | |

Now 50 ... K×a2 51 R×f7 K×b3 52 R×g7 leads to a position where, although Black can win the white rook for his 'b' pawn, he is unable to give up his rook for all the remaining white pawns.

50 ...	Rg1
51 R×f7	R×g4
52 Ra7+	Kb2
53 Ke5	Rg2

Black cannot contemplate the position after 53 ... Rh4 54 R×g7 K×a2 55 Rg3 R×h5+ 56 f5: although he is level on material, his 'h' pawn is halted, while the white 'f' pawn is free to advance.

54 Kf5

Clearly intending to utilize the advanced state of his pawns and to transfer his rook to g6. Probably Black should now have played 54 ... Kc3, but then White gains the opportunity at a convenient moment to get rid of the black 'b' pawn by a2-a3, and the remote position of Black's king means that the projected ending with white pawn at f5 against black pawn at h6 is hopeless for him.

The move played, however, is even less good, and loses very quickly.

54 ...	Kb1
55 Rb7	K×a2
56 R×b4	Kb2
57 Rb6	Rc2

At this point the game was adjourned for the second time. White sealed **58 Kg6**, but the game was not continued: **Black resigned.**

ALMOST A SPY STORY

On many occasions I have analyzed adjourned games together with my old friend, chess master, and chess commentator for Soviet radio and television, Iakov Damsky. These analyses have been prolonged, with both of us fully engrossed in them. Imagine my astonishment when, during the 1969 USSR Championship, an elimination tournament for the Interzonal, Iakov approached me with the question:

"Would you object to some of your analyses being published?"

"Which analyses?"

"From this Championship, and from the International Tournament in Sochi..."

"Surely you don't remember them?!"

"I don't, but my tape recorder does."

It turned out that, during our analysis, just as in a spy story, my friend had from time to time switched on by remote control his reporters' tape recorder.

Naturally, I did not object, and the account appeared in a special bulletin devoted to the 37th USSR Championship. And now it was my turn to ask the author for permission to include the material in this book. It was granted.

The analysis of an adjourned game. Only a chess beginner will be unfamiliar with the pressing, obsessive sensation of an impending adjournment session. It is fine if a win is in prospect. But if not? If one has to try to save a game, or attempt to realize a slight advantage? Then day and night, when eating, and sometimes during another game, the mind involuntarily returns to the position in question, and considers the hundredth or even thousandth variation with which one can continue the struggle.

This sensation is so oppressive, and at times so exhausting for players (incidentally, doctors reckon that a sleepless night cannot be compensated for, even by ten hours of sleep during the day), that it is not surprising that from time to time projects to eliminate adjourned games are suggested. It has been proposed, for instance, that the length of the first session be increased to 7 hours, which would probably reduce by a factor of five the number of sealed moves.

Having witnessed the analysis of three games adjourned by grandmaster Lyev Polugayevsky, I would put my signature to such a suggestion, or any similar one. On the 'polishing' of only one of them, the Champion of the Country spent some seven hours, and so as to reproduce in full his monologue during this analysis, at least three issues of this bulletin would be required.

Gipslis–Polugayevsky
37th USSR Championship, Moscow 1969

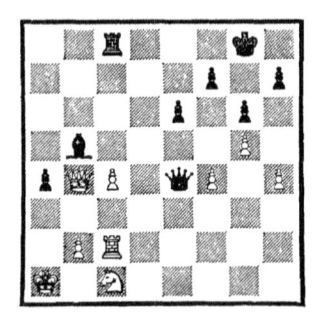

"The sealed move is 43 Rc3, that is clear. On 43 ... B×c4 he replies 44 Qd6, since the f4 pawn has definitely to be defended. It is the key to the position; if it can be exchanged, say, for the 'a' pawn, the ending is hopeless for White. The position should in general be won, but how? The white king is badly placed, the f4 pawn is weak; Black must combine his threats. But for the moment let's relieve the pin on the 'c' file: 44 ... Qd5. It would appear that White can't exchange: 45 Q×d5 e×d5, and both ... d5–d4 and ... Re8 are threatened, in reply, say, to 46 Ne2. White has to retreat with 45 Qb4. And now, now ... 45 ... Qd4!. This both centralizes, and attacks the f4 pawn. I'm happy about

46 Q×a4, while if 46 Ne2, then 46 ... Qe4, and White is in *zugzwang*. This means 46 Qb7, when 46 ... Rd8 seems to be the only move. True, there is also 46 ... Rc5, but I don't want to weaken my back rank. 46 ... Rd8 must be better.

And White? He has 47 Qc7 and 47 Qe7. To the first of these both 47 ... Bf1 and 47 ... Ba6 are strong. Which is better? I don't know, let's look at that later. But as for the second continuation .... It is bad to move the bishop; he plays 48 Rc7 Rf8 49 Qf6, which can't be a win. Perhaps 47 ... a3? That's probably it. The bare king has to be exploited! What does he take with? With the queen is probably bad: 48 ... Qe4, so that leaves the rook. Let's calculate: 48 R×a3 Rb8 49 Rc3 Q×f4, and it's all over. Ah ah, again 49 Qf6!. If 49 ... Q×f6 50 g×f6 h6, then ... Kh7, ... g6-g5 and so on (Polugayevsky rapidly calculates variations which don't appeal to him: White succeeds in activating his pieces, and gains drawing chances). It doesn't work! I mustn't exchange queens! Instead of 48 ... Rb8, let's try 48 ... Qd1. Or 48 ... Qd2? Let's check them in turn.

48 ... Qd1 49 Rc3 Ra8+ 50 Kb1 Ba2+. This means that the only move is 49 Kb1 Bd3+ 50 Ka2, and Black has nothing.

48 ... Qd2. Again 49 Kb1. I can't play 49 ... Bd5. 'Sac' the 'e' pawn: 49 ... e5, and then ... Bf5? Let's calculate. No, it doesn't work. I felt intuitively that it wasn't so simple; I even said so at the adjournment. Thank God there is a scent, but is there a win? There must be! I so want to give up the 'a' pawn, but perhaps I shouldn't. Let's go back.

47 Qe7. Should I move the rook? 47 ... Ra8? He returns to b4. 48 ... Rc8—49 Qb7. Immediately 47 ... Rb8? No. I must play 47 ... a3!

(And once again dozens of variations are checked, replies for White are found which, though forced, are sufficient. In passing, even a possible rook ending is considered, where Black keeps three passed pawns on the K-side, and gives up his rook for the far-advanced white 'b' pawn. But, alas, this is a possible, and ... not a forced, variation. And so the search continues. Continuations with the invasion of the black queen at d1 are played through again, and in the end are definitely rejected because of the constant threat of perpetual check by Qd8-f6. At the same time the immediate moves... h7-h6 and... h7-h5 are studied, after which perpetual check is not be feared, but White acquires other chances. Finally, the solution is found!)

No, 47 ... a3 doesn't work! 47 ... Rd5!—that's the secret!. The threat is ... Rf5, attacking the f4 pawn, and defending f7; there is no perpetual check, also no invasion, while on 48 Qb4 there is 48 ... Ba6!. The square c8 is covered, and after the exchange of queens my rook gets onto the fourth rank, and that is the end, while if 49 Qb8+, then, if there is nothing better, 49 ... Rd8 50 Qc7 a3, or 50 ... Rc8. Or 50 ... Bf1 is possible, which also creates the threat of ... Qd6. Then either the f4 pawn cannot be defended, or the queens must be exchanged, while c4 is inaccessible to the white rook. The rest I will look at tomorrow."

But, as is known, to every chess game there are two players, and each tries to avoid falling in with the other's wishes. And on the resumption it turned out that a good 90% of all Polugayevsky's work remained 'unseen'. The first few moves were guessed correctly: **43 Rc3** (the sealed move) **43 ... B×c4 44 Qd6 Qd5 45 Qb4 Qd4 46 Qb7 Rd8,** but here White played **47 Qc7**. There followed **47 ... Bf1 48 Ka2 Qd6 49 Q×d6 R×d6 50 Ka3 Rd4**, and after **51 Rf3 Bc4 52 Na2 B×a2 53 K×a2 h5 54 b3 Rd2+ 55 Ka3 a×b3 56 K×b3 Rh2** Black easily realized his two-pawn advantage. And for me this adjournment recalled the scholarly, but in principle very accurate, formula of Mayakovsky: "For the sake of a single word, one wastes thousands of tons of literary ore..."

Another analysis by Polugayevsky proved to be even more interesting from the purely competitive point of view. On adjourning his game with **Igor Zaitsev** (Black) in the following position,

Polugayevsky criticized himself severely for having let slip an overwhelming positional advantage, easily found a path for realizing it which had not occurred in the game, and then got down to settling the question: does White have only a perpetual check, or something more? A draw for Black was found fairly quickly, one that White was unable to avoid, but then 'in reserve' Polugayevsky found another, highly spectacular, continuation. This arose in the event of a serious, but at first sight imperceptible mistake by Black on the very first move after the adjournment.

41 Qe7+. This move White sealed. **41 ... Kh8**, so as to avoid 42 Be6+, suggests itself, but it was here that Polugayevsky had prepared a 'mine': **42 R×c2 R×c2 43 Qf6+ Kh7 44 Qf7+ Kh8 45 Q×f4!**.

Mate is unexpectedly 'in the air': 46 Q×h6+ and 47 Be6 mate. 45 ... Re2 fails to save Black, in view of the forced continuation 46 Q×h6+ Kg8 47 Q×g6+ Kf8 48 Qf5+ Ke8 (*48 ... Ke7 49 d6+*) 49 Qc8+, etc. There is similarly no perpetual check: 45 ... R×b2+ 46 K×b2 Qb6(b5)+ 47 Ka1, and Black has at best one more check. There remains 45 ... Qd2, but... 46 Qf6+ Kh7 47 Be6!, and mate in two can be avoided only by attempting to give perpetual check, which is not there: 47 ... R×b2+ 48 Q×b2 Qd3+ 49 Qc2 Qf1(b5)+ 50 Ka2, or by returning the exchange: 47 ... Rc7 48 Bg8+ K×g8 49 Qd8+ Kf7 50 Q×c7+ Kf6 51 Q×b7, after which Black's chances of losing the game are quite considerable.

Black can avoid this unpleasantness only by playing **41 ... Kg8**, when it turns out that he has adequate counter-chances. This, incidentally, is what happened on resumption: **42 B×e6+ N×e6 43 Q×e6+ Kg7 44 R×c2 R×c2 45 K×c2 Qa4+**, and the undefended state of the h4 pawn, plus the proximity of the black king to White's passed pawn, gave Black equal chances.

"I should have given the check at e7 before the adjournment!", the Soviet Champion summed up. "Then it would have been more difficult for Black to venture into 42 ...

Kg8, and it would not have been easy for him to find at the board the variation with the exchange sacrifice."

And it seemed to me that Lyev Polugayevsky regretted not so much the 'unobtained' half point, so much as the fine analysis which was not destined to see the light of day.

Polugayevsky's competitive character, and at the same time his ability to penetrate to an unusual depth in his analysis, are displayed in his approach to his adjourned game with the Bulgarian grandmaster **Milko Bobotsov** from the 1966 Chigorin Memorial Tournament in Sochi.

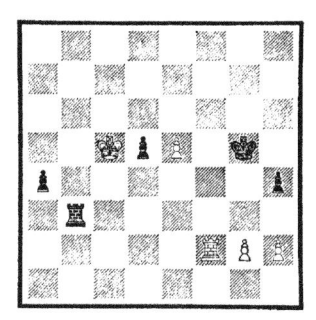

Of course, Lyev realized that with exact play this ending is drawn: although at times we recall with irony Savielly Tartakower's aphorism 'All rook endings are drawn', this very often proves to be so. And besides, the best move—which Polugayevsky guessed—was sealed by Bobotsov.

41 ... d4

The tempting 41 ... a3 is refuted by 42 e6 Rb2 43 e7 R×f2 44 e8=Q, and after 44 ... a2 White wins, although he has great technical difficulties to overcome.

42 e6 Re3 43 Kd6 d3 44 e7 Re4 45 Kd7 Rd4+ 46 Kc6 Re4 47 Kd6 a3 48 Kd7 Rd4+ 49 Ke6.

With his last few moves White has set his opponent a cunning trap. 49 ... a2 now looks very tempting. True, after 50 R×a2 Black cannot play 50 ... Re4+ 51 Kf7 Rf4+ 52 Kg7 Re4 43 Ra5+ Kg4 54 Ra4, when White wins. But 50 ... d2 looks very strong, but then there follows 51 Ra5+, when the black king has no safe square:

  A. 51 ... Kf4 52 Rf5+ Kg4 53 e8=Q Re4+ 54 Re5 R×e5+ 55 K×e5 d1=Q 56 Qg6 mate.

  B. 51 ... Kh6 52 e8=Q Re4+ 53 Re5 R×e5+ 54 K×e5 d1=Q 55 Qh8+ Kg6 56 Qf6+ Kh5 57 Qf3+.

Bobotsov, who in those days was the strongest player in Bulgaria, guessed White's intention, and did not fall into the trap prepared. But it was clear that Polugayevsky was not, on the whole, very concerned about this. He had done all that he could, both as a competitor and as a player: he had set before his opponent the maximum number of barriers. And his conscience was clear.

The game concluded as follows:

49 ... d2 50 Rf5+ Kh6!

The only move which leads to a draw.

51 Rh5+ Kg7 52 Rg5+ Kh6 53 Rh5+ Kg7 54 e8=Q Re4+ 55 Re5 R×e5+ 56 K×e5 d1=Q, and White had nothing better than to force a draw by perpetual check.

4. On the Eve
(How to prepare for decisive games)

And so, theory and analysis. The study of opening problems and of adjourned positions. Does this alone exhaust the work of the grandmaster, the work of the chess player outside the walls of the tournament hall? The answer is no. There is yet another field, without success in which it is impossible to hope for much. This is preparation for a completely specific game, in a completely specific situation, with a completely specific opponent. Here everything is important: to guess the opening, to find the scheme which is the most unpleasant for the opponent, and to choose the correct battle tactics. But perhaps the most difficult thing is to bring oneself into that one correct frame of mind, which will harmonize fully one hundred per cent with the situation in which the game is being played. And this takes on special significance, incommensurable with anything else, on the eve of a decisive encounter.

I should like to describe several such instances.

A STIMULUS IS PROVIDED BY... THE CONTROLLERS

The 1967 USSR Championship was run on the Swiss System, which I personally consider totally unsuitable for such an important event. And I will admit that, in the future, I should very much like to avoid playing even once more in a 'Swiss'.

At the Championship in Kharkov there was no round in which one of the competitors did not have fairly serious grounds for feeling aggrieved. But that which happened to me exceeded, in my opinion, all 'Swiss' records for injustice.

The battle for first place was basically between Mikhail Tal and myself. And before the last round the pairings were announced: Tal was to play the master V. Zhuravlyev, and I—grandmaster R. Kholmov. To my question as to how such an 'inequality' could arise, the controllers replied with something not altogether intelligible regarding the rules of the Swiss System: a player should have not more than one 'upfloat', and if I had played against a different opponent, Kholmov's opponent (in a game where the gold medal was not at stake!) would have had an 'upfloat'....

I pointed out what strong opponents I had had during the Championship, and objected to such an artificial and essentially formal decision by the controllers, but this did not help, and I must confess that I literally lost my temper. After all, it was obvious (Misha will not be offended if I say this) that to win a deciding game against the inexperienced Zhuravlyev, and against Kholmov, who at that time was practically invincible, was not the same thing.

I made a protest to the control committee, and said that even if such a rule in the Swiss System did in fact exist, to apply it in the last round, and in such a situation, when the question of the Champion of the Country was at stake, was to ignore common sense....

Later, one of my acquaintances said that it was my 'attack' on the controllers at that point which could be considered my first step in the battle for the Championship of (no more and no less!) the World. I readily admit that this is an exaggeration. But the source of my win over Kholmov did indeed lie in that rather angry exchange of words with the chief controller.

Earlier I had frequently been reproached for my lack of purely competitive, 'Fischer-like' aggressiveness at the time of a decisive battle. I will not venture to argue about this, since in my younger days I had normally been not altogether successful in my handling of decisive games. Of course, there are leading traits in a person's character, and if he is of a genial nature he will only be put out by aggression at the time of battle. But even now, before a game I would not object to a sensible dose of aggression, one which does not cloud the brain, does not overwhelm one, and does not confuse one's thinking, but leads to a state of enthusiasm. Moreover, for many years I have been trying to find methods of bringing myself into such a state, but unfortunately I do not always find it possible.

But in my game with Kholmov this was helped by the injustices of the Swiss System. I sat down at the board in such an energetically aggressive frame of mind, I was so undisguisedly eager for victory —and 'to avenge the insult', that my opponent apparently sensed this. And, perhaps, quaked in his shoes. This happened frequently to the opponents of the young Tal, Fischer and Karpov, i.e. when they had to play against genuinely strong characters.

As for special and deep opening preparation for this game, it was practically non-existent. Under the Swiss System one normally learns the name of one's opponent only when there is essentially no time left for opening exploration. And before the encounter with Kholmov, I restricted myself to just one decision, but one of crucial importance: to avoid half-hearted measures. After all, I could have opened 1 Nf3 or even 1 g3, thus retaining a certain degree of flexibility, but I decided to join battle in one of the main variations of any of the openings. The English Opening or the Slav Defence —the main variation, Queen's Gambit Accepted—also, Nimzo-Indian Defence— also .... In short, I was prepared to play uncompromisingly, not fearing any possible prepared variation, and was pinning my hopes on the five hours that the game would last.

To this day I am unable to explain why, in this game, Kholmov chose the King's Indian Defence, an opening in which I had normally been successful as White. It cannot be ruled out that, in planning his battle tactics and knowing my anxiety, he himself was thinking in terms of winning, and hence such a sharp and complicated opening. Since here the battle is particularly uncompromising, and draws in the King's Indian are much more rare than in, say, many lines of the Queen's Gambit.

Be that as it may, but Kholmov's decision could not have corresponded better to my frame of mind. And this is what happened.

Polugayevsky-Kholmov
King's Indian Defence

1 c4	c5
2 Nf3	Nc6
3 Nc3	g6
4 e3	

Perhaps the most unpleasant move for Black. In the event of 4 d4 or 4 g3 he has a comfortable game.

| 4 ... | Bg7 |
| 5 d4 | Nf6? |

A serious opening mistake. The normal reply is 5 ... d6, and on 6 d5—6 ... Ne5, as occurred, incidentally, in one of Fischer's games.

But in the present game a set-up from the King's Indian is reached, only with one important difference: White has unexpectedly gained a tempo. To give such odds at the very start of the game shows excessive generosity, to say the least, especially since, as it is, chess is sometimes called 'the tragedy of one tempo'.

6 d5	Nb8
7 Be2	d6
8 0-0	0-0
9 e4	e6
10 Bf4	e5

Forced, since 10 ... e×d5 11 c×d5 Re8 12 Nd2 is less good.

11 Bg5	h6
12 Bh4	g5
13 Bg3	Nh5
14 Nd2	Nf4
15 Bg4	

It is here that Black's opening 'losses' make themselves felt: in comparison with the normal variation White has succeeded in castling, and he now carries out without hindrance the strategically advantageous exchange of white-squared bishops.

| 15 ... | Nd7 |
| 16 a3 | |

Frequently one has to argue about the correctness of a particular plan. In the game White preferred to begin an immediate storming of the Q-side. But even so, 16 Re1 appears more logical, preparing the march of the white knight to f5, which would be highly unpleasant for Black.

16 ...	Nf6
17 B×c8	Q×c8
18 b4	h5
19 f3	

19 Nb5 appeared tempting, but this would have been a false trail. After 19 ... Ne8 20 B×f4 e×f4 21 Q×h5 Black replies simply 21 ... a6, and nothing definite for White is apparent.

19 ...	Kh7
20 Bf2	b6
21 b×c5	

White is quite correct to clarify the situation. Now in the event of 21 ... b×c5 he gains the chance to operate on the 'b' file. Nevertheless, this is what Black should have played, since the passed 'd' pawn and the intrusive advance a3-a4-a5 prove to be weightier factors than the d6 square for the black knight.

21 ...	d×c5
22 a4	Rg8
23 Kh1	Bh6

Black pins his hopes on a K-side attack, and aims for the ... g5-g4 break. But White proves to be prepared for events on the right-hand flank, and by prophylaxis immediately neutralizes Black's attempts.

24 Ne2

Hanging over Black is the threat of the knight transfer to f5. The advance 24 ... h4 leads to the loss of a pawn: 25 N×f4 g×f4 (*25 ... e×f4 26 e5*) 26 B×h4, while on 24 ... g4 I was planning to continue 25 N×f4 (*25 Ng3 is now dangerous, in view of 25 ... h4 26 Nf5 g3! 27 h×g3 h×g3 28 B×g3 R×g3! 29 N×g3 Qg8*) 25 ... B×f4 26 Bh4!, when the following variations are possible:

26 ... g×f3 27 Q×f3 Ng4 28 Ra2, and there is no satisfactory defence against 29 g3.

26 ... Ne8 27 g3 B×d2 28 Q×d2 g×f3 (*28 ... Nd6 29 f4! Qe8 30 Bf6 e×f4 31 e5*) 29 R×f3 Nd6 30 Raf1 Qg4 31 Be7, with a big advantage.

24 ...	N×e2

This is equivalent to an admission of the failure of his plans. He should have played 24 ... Ne8 immediately. Black evidently thought that in this case after 25 N×f4 g×f4 his bishop would be 'forgotten', and that White, by continuing 26 a5, would develop a dangerous initiative, while his g2 square would be easily defended.

But nevertheless I think that the open 'g' file would to a certain extent have restricted White's possibilities.

Now, however, White becomes sole master of the board.

25 Q×e2	Ne8
26 a5	Nd6
27 Ra3	Rg6
28 Be3	g4?

Not wishing to defend passively (*28 ... Rb8*), Black tries to complicate matters, but this 'activity' leads merely to a sharp deterioration in his position, and White himself gains a decisive attack.

29 B×h6	K×h6
30 f4	f6

Or 30 ... e×f4 31 e5 Nf5 32 R×f4.

31 f×e5	f×e5
32 Qe3+	Kg7
33 Qg3	Nf7

| 34 Qh4 | Qb7 |
| 35 Q×h5 | |

The nervous tension of the last round tells: White forces matters too soon. Much more convincing was 35 Rf2, followed by 36 Nf1 or 36 Ra1 and 37 Raf1, with a decisive advantage. 36 a×b6 a×b6 37 R×a8 Q×a8 38 Q×h5 was also good.

35 ...	Rh8
36 Qf5	Qe7
37 a×b6	a×b6
38 Kg1	

Although Black has activated his pieces somewhat, nevertheless White's extra pawn must sooner or later have the decisive word. Since 38 ... Nd6 39 Qf2 Qg5 40 Ra7+ brings no relief, Black tries with his next move to confuse his opponent.

38 ...	b5
39 c×b5	Nd6
40 Qf2	N×b5
41 Rg3	Nd6

Otherwise 42 Nc4. Black went in for this position assuming that the c5 pawn was invulnerable, but White had calculated one move further.

42 Q×c5	R×h2
43 K×h2	Qh4+
44 Kg1	Q×g3
45 Nc4!	

The refutation of Black's combination. Neither 45 ... N×c4 46 Qf8+, nor 45 ... Rh6 46 Qc7+ is possible. Black's reply is forced.

| 45 ... | Qc3 |
| 46 Qa7+ | Kh6 |

47 N×d6	R×d6
48 Qb8!	Ra6
49 Qf8+	Kg6
50 Qg8+	Kh6
51 Q×g4	

In this position the game was adjourned, but Black decided not to continue.

WHEN IT IS ONE... FOR ALL

In any individual tournament a chess player is his own master. Even when he is fighting for the world chess crown. But it is my deep conviction that once he becomes part of a team, he loses the right to economize on effort, spare himself, or avoid a fight. Even the lowest rank of team event demands from a player complete subordination to the interests of the *collective*. He is no longer playing just for himself, but for everyone else, and each game becomes a decisive one.

The following encounter, in addition, took place under conditions of extreme rivalry. Before the last round of the USSR Peoples' Spartakiad, the teams of the Russian Federation and the Ukraine (Efim Geller lived at the time in Odessa) were separated by only half a point. We had to play each other, and the winners would gain the silver medals, or even the gold, given a fortunate turn of events.

I think that this says everything....

Polugayevsky–Geller
Moscow 1967
King's Indian Defence

1 d4	Nf6
2 c4	g6
3 Nc3	Bg7
4 e4	d6
5 f3	

At that time my enthusiasm for the Sämisch Variation, which in the recent past had been my favourite hobby-horse, had cooled somewhat. But in the game with Geller a desire emerged to return once again to 'the old days'.

5 ...	0-0
6 Be3	Nbd7
7 Qd2	a6

Black's intentions are revealed: against White's strong centre he plans a flank attack, keeping open the future option of also playing ... e7-e5.

| 8 0-0-0 | c6 |
| 9 e5!? | |

Although Black's plan had frequently been tested in tournament practice, I very much wanted to 'refute' his rather slow play. This gave rise to the idea of adopting strong measures. White realized, of course, that he was burning his boats behind him, but in chess one frequently has to do this when trying to vindicate a certain idea.

| 9 ... | Ne8 |
| 10 f4 | Qa5 |

The natural reaction. Black switches his queen to the main theatre of events. In addition, he forces White to play 11 Kb1, after which he has the future positional possibility of ... Bf5+.

11 Kb1

White not only defends a2, but also holds in readiness the dagger blow Nd5!

| 11 ... | b5 |
| 12 Nf3 | |

At the moment 12 Nd5 does not achieve anything, in view of the simple reply 12 ... Qd8, when the knight must return home. But 12 c5 deserved serious consideration.

| 12 ... | b4 |

Otherwise Black cannot develop his forces. Thus, in particular, both 12 ... Nb6 and 12 ... Nc7 fail to 13 Nd5.

| 13 Ne4 | c5 |

Black's desire to open up the game on the Q-side is readily understandable, but he proves to be unprepared for this. Apart from the move played, he also had other tempting continuations, such as 13 ... Bb7 or 13 ... Nb6.

| 14 d×c5 | d×e5 |

Bad, of course, is 14 ... N×c5, since after 15 N×c5 d×c5 the bishop at g7 is blocked in.

15 c6!

The battle reaches its height. White is unconcerned about the loss of his 'c' pawn, and hopes to utilize his temporary lead in development.

| 15 ... | Nb8 |
| 16 Qd5 | Qc7 |

Best. In the event of 16 ... Q×d5 17 c×d5 Bf5 18 Bd3 Nc7 19 Bc2 White has an undisputed advantage. Also, 16 ... Qa4 17 Nc5 Q×c6 18 N×e5 was evidently not to Black's liking.

| 17 N×e5 | Nf6? |

Black probably overlooked White's 19th move, otherwise he would have replied 17 ... B×e5 18 Q×e5 (*18 f×e5 Bf5 19 Bd3 N×c6*) 18 ... Q×e5 19 f×e5 Bf5 20 Bd3 N×c6, with a roughly equal position.

18 N×f6+ e×f6
19 Nd7!

As a result of the opponent's mistake, White's strategy has triumphed completely. Now 19 ... Rd8 is bad because of 20 Bb6. White also has an interesting win after 19 ... Re8: 20 Nb6! Bf5+ 21 Bd3 R×e3 22 B×f5 Q×b6 23 Qd8+ Q×d8 24 R×d8+ Bf8 25 c7. Black therefore sacrifices the exchange.

19 ... N×c6
20 N×f8 Bf5+?

This finally throws away the game. He should have played 20 ... B×f8, after which, despite the win of the exchange, White must be watchful. He would have continued 21 Bd3, and if 21 ... Bg4 (as suggested by Geller after the game), then 22 Be4! B×d1 23 Q×c6 Q×c6 24 B×c6 Rc8 25 Bd7, and Black comes out a piece down.

21 Bd3!

My opponent failed to take account of this simple reply. Now in the event of 21 ... Rd8 22 B×f5! R×d5 23 c×d5 B×f8 24 d×c6 g×f5 25 Rc1 Black's position is hopeless.

21 ... Bg4
22 Be4! Resigns

(Polugayevsky's Russian Federation team defeated the Ukraine 6-4, and so took the silver medals–K.P.N.).

OVERCOMING ONESELF

Polugayevsky-Osnos
36th USSR Championship,
Alma Ata 1969
Sicilian Defence

I know from my own experience that sometimes one follows all the rules in preparing for a tournament, but one's play, as they say, won't 'get going'. Whether it is psychology or something else that is the cause of this, I do not know. But I have seen very many players in this state, and each has tried to escape from it in his own way.

It was this that happened to me in the 1969 USSR Championship at Alma Ata. Game after game I played somehow very leisurely, my thinking was sluggish, and uninteresting even to me myself. The result appeared natural enough: in the first half of the tournament—one draw after another, fifty per cent of the points, and a place far away from the leading group. It was absolutely essential to master myself. "Better to lose than to play such depressing draws", I decided, and before the next round, the 10th, in which I was to meet V. Osnos, I decided on a course of play which was completely unusual for me. And for this purpose I played 1 e4—a move which I practically never employ.

It was obvious that by this the opponent was afforded a major trump in the opening stage of the game, since there was no time to study for White the subtleties of the possible Sicilian, Ruy Lopez, or Pirc Defence. But I did not even set myself such a task. Just the opposite: in order to enliven my play and force my brain to work, I intended to solve all resulting problems at the board.

And that is what happened. Osnos employed a system which I had never analyzed (after all, I don't play 1 e4!). This could have unsettled me, had I not planned such a situation beforehand. As a result, at the board I managed to find a plan for obtaining an advantage, and, more important, convert it into a win.

It is for this reason that I consider this game to be a decisive one. It indeed changed the course of the tournament for me. My play became more lively, and point after point appeared for me in the tournament table. And in the end—a share of 1st-2nd places, a match with A. Zaitsev, about which more later, and the title of USSR Champion.

1 e4	c5
2 Nf3	d6
3 d4	c×d4
4 N×d4	Nf6
5 Nc3	Nc6
6 Bg5	e6
7 Qd2	Be7
8 0-0-0	N×d4

This early exchange of knights in the Rauzer Variation enjoys a dubious reputation, and not without reason. Evidently my opponent nevertheless ventured upon it, because he did wish after 8 ... 0-0 to allow White to play 9 Nb3, which markedly reduces Black's chances of an attack on the white king.

| 9 Q×d4 | 0-0 |
| 10 Bc4 | |

The most rapid wins for White have occurred when he has played 10 e5!, for example 10 ... d×e5 11 Q×e5 Bd7 12 h4! Rc8 13 Rh3 Rc5 14 Qe3 Qc8 15 Rg3! Kh8 (or *15 ... Rd8 16 h5 Be8 17 Bd3 g6 18 Ne4 R×d3 19 Q×d3 Bb5 20 N×f6+ B×f6 21 B×f6 B×d3 22 Rg×d3 R×c2+ 23 Kb1,* and in the game Zavernyaev-Kalinin, USSR 1960, Black resigned) 16 Kb1 Qc6 17 h5 Rg8 18 h6 g×h6 19 B×f6+ B×f6 20 R×g8+ K×g8 21 Ne4 Rf5 22 N×f6+ R×f6 23 Qd3, and White won quickly (Zhilin-Furman, USSR 1958).

Why then, if I knew these games, did I not play 10 e5? In the first instance because most probably Osnos also knew them. What's more, not only knew them, but since the variation was part of his arsenal, he may have had some subtleties prepared. To refute these at the board would probably have required considerable effort, and I was not wanting to force matters. The more so, since after 10 ... d×e5 11 Q×e5 Bd7 12 h4 Rc8 13 Rh3 Black has the quiet reply 13 ... Qc7. Now after 14 Q×c7 R×c7 15 Nb5 B×b5 16 B×b5 Rfc8 it is not at all easy to utilize the advantage of the two bishops, while 14 Qe3 Bc6 15 Rg3 Rfd8 does not cause Black any particular difficulties.

| 10 ... | Qa5 |
| 11 f4 | Bd7 |

The position after 11 ... h6 12 Bh4 e5 is well known to theory. Black's move in the game was the 'latest word in technology' at that time. Leaving the white bishop at g5, Black parries the possible 12 e5 d×e5 13 f×e5 by 13 ... Bc6, when his white-squared bishop occupies an excellent post.

12 Bb3!?

This was found at the board. I did not care for either 12 Kb1 Bc6 13 Rhf1 Rad8 14 Bb3 h6 15 Bh4 Qh5!, when the queen becomes an active defender of her king, or 12 Rhf1 b5! 13 Bb3 b4, when Black seizes the initiative. The game Keres-Geller (Candidates' Tournament, Curacao 1962) went 12 Rhe1 Rfd8 13 Bb3, and instead of the erroneous 13 ... b5?! as played, Black, by the same manoeuvre 13 ... h6! 14 Bh4 Qh5!, could have obtained a perfectly satisfactory game.

Later, theory pronounced the strongest in this position to be 12 e5 d×e5 13 f×e5 Bc6 14 Bd2! Nd7 15 Nd5 Qd8 16 N×e7+ Q×e7 17 Rhe1 Rfc8 18 Qf4, as occurred in the games Tseshkovsky-Korensky, USSR 1973, and Karpov-Ungureanu at the 1972 Olympiad in Skopje. But after all, theorists bring in their verdicts (which, incidentally, are not always final) only on the basis of our general experience and practice....

12 ...   Bc6

It is clear that 12 ... b5 is refuted by 13 e5!, but the move played also deserves censure. The bishop moves away from the defence of e6, which may be attacked by the white 'f' pawn. More logical, therefore, is 12 ... Rfd8 13 Rhf1 Rac8 14 f5 Qc5, although here too White retains a promising position.

13 Rhf1

White consistently carries through his plan of playing f4-f5, provoking ... e6-e5, and seizing the square d5. Possibly here too Black should have resorted to the manoeuvre 13 ... h6 14 Bh4 Qh5, but my opponent very quickly made what looked to be a highly energetic move.

13 ...   b5

I sensed that it was on the solution to this particular problem that if not everything, then a great deal, depended. I thought for almost an hour, and found a refutation....

14 B×f6!   B×f6

No better is 14 ... g×f6 15 f5! b4 16 Ne2, and Black cannot maintain his pawn at e6.

15 Q×d6   B×c3

If Black had attempted to repair the basic defect of his position, and had defended his white-squared bishop by 15 ... Rac8, then White had prepared 16 e5! Rfd8 17 Qc5!, and if 17 ... B×g2, then 18 Qg1!! B×f1 19 e×f6, which concludes the game instantly. If 15 ... Qb6, then 16 f5, and now after 16 ... Rfd8 the queen retreats to g3, while on 16 ... B×c3 the piece sacrifice 17 f×e6! is decisive, e.g. 17 ... Bf8 18 e×f7+ Kh8 19 R×f6! Rad8 20 Q×d8, winning.

It was on these and numerous other similar variations that I spent an hour in thought on my 14th move.

16 Q×c6	Rac8
17 Qd7	Rfd8?

This move has to be condemned. As is soon apparent, this rook should have stayed where it was to defend f7. The lesser evil was 17 ... Rcd8 18 Qb7!, with advantage to White after 18 ... Rb8 19 Qe7, or 18 ... Bd2+ 19 Kb1 B×f4 20 R×d8 Q×d8 (or *20 ... R×d8 21 g3 Qc7 22 Q×b5 Be5*, and White is a pawn up) 21 Q×b5. And although White should probably be able gradually to realize his advantage, Osnos should have reconciled himself to this continuation. But he failed to foresee that which occurred in the game....

18 Qe7	Bd2+
19 Kb1	B×f4
20 R×d8	R×d8

There is little pleasure in playing on a pawn down after 20 ... Q×d8 21 Q×a7, since 21 ... B×h2 fails due to the weakness of f7.

21 e5!

It was this move that escaped Black's attention. The immediate 21 g3 is parried by 21 ... Qc7, but now his forces are disunited, and he loses due to the weakness of f7 and the back rank.

21 ...	Qd2

On 21 ... Rf8 White can play 22 a3, or 22 B×e6 f×e6 23 g3, or 22 c3 B×e5 23 R×f7, winning quickly.

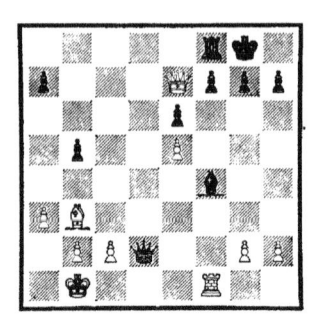

22 a3	Rf8

23 B×e6!

Also possible was the more spectacular 23 g3 Bg5 (mate follows after *23 ... B×e5 24 R×f7 R×f7 25 Qe8+*) 24 Q×e6! f×e6 25 B×e6+ Rf7 26 R×f7 Qd8 (if *26 ... Qe1+ 27 Ka2 Q×e5*, then *28 Rf6+!*) 27 Rd7+ Kf8 28 R×d8+ B×d8. But firstly, I did not want to play an ending (even though it was won) with opposite-coloured bishops, and secondly, I am not an advocate of brilliance for brilliance's sake, if there exists a more rational possibility.

23 ...	g5
24 g3	f×e6

White also has a pretty win after 24 ... Qe2 25 R×f4 g×f4 26 Qg5+ Kh8 27 Qh6! Rg8 (if *27 ... Kg8*, then *28 Bf5*) 28 Qf6+ Rg7 29 B×f7, when Black cannot halt the advance of the 'e' pawn, e.g. 29 ... Qd1+ 30 Ka2 Qd7 (or *30 ... Qd4 31 Bb3!*) 31 e6 Qd5+ 32 b3 Qd6 33 e7!, and wins.

25 Q×e6+	Kg7
26 g×f4	Qg2

Black merely prolongs the resistance by 26 ... R×f4 27 R×f4 Q×f4 28 Qd7+ Kg6 29 Q×b5 Q×h2 30 Qc6+ Kh5 31 Qe4.

27 Rd1	g×f4

28 Qd7+	**Rf7**	32 Rd8 Kf7 33 R×e8 K×e8 34 Kc1, when White has a won pawn ending.

Nothing is changed by 28 ... Kg8 29 e6 Qg6 30 e7 Re8 31 Q×e8+ Q×e8

29 e6 Resigns

NON-INDIFFERENT INDIFFERENCE

The match with grandmaster Aleksandr Zaitsev for the title of USSR Champion proved to be one of the most important events in my chess career. Not because it was my first match, and not because in it I gained my second successive gold medal (before our meeting I was the favourite). But because for almost the first time I succeeded in preparing very exactly, and more important—in confidently overcoming a psychological barrier which arose during the course of the match. And at testing moments during events in subsequent years, I would systematically return in my thoughts to the match. This would subconsciously enable me to accomplish that same psychological preparatory work as then, in 1969, in the hospitable and ancient Russian town of Vladimir.

Here it would seem appropriate to reveal the method to which I resorted in working on the purely chess aspect of the forthcoming match.

As I later discovered, my opponent, with two weeks available for preparation, spent them on the analysis of my games. Zaitsev began with the tournaments in which I had played in 1959, and carefully looked through some 250 'full-length' games. For anything else he simply had no time.

Together with international master Vladimir Bagirov, who was my second, I also worked intensively. But along different lines. Since time was short, we decided not to analyze games that were ten, or even five years old, being motivated by the fact that Zaitsev's style had taken shape only later. We were convinced that the Aleksandr '1965 model' could give us a false impression of the present-day Zaitsev, and we began studying his games from the time of his qualitative leap—from the Chigorin Memorial Tournament at Sochi in 1967, where Zaitsev became one of the winners of the tournament, and also a grandmaster.

As a result, Aleksandr's 'growing pains' remained out of the picture, and we became acquainted with the 'ultra-modern' Zaitsev. And we saw that he was a player with excellent combinative vision, ingenious in defence, and an optimist even at the most difficult moments. His opening schemes were well worked out, and there was no point in counting on his time-trouble—such a thing was foreign to Zaitsev.

At the same time we managed to discover his weak points, in particular, mistakes in strategically complicated positions, and a certain haste in the taking of important decisions.

A little later I will also mention another vulnerable aspect of Aleksandr's play, on which my strategy in the deciding game was based.

But for the moment—on the course of the match. At the start I wanted to win a game as quickly as possible, so as to then conduct the struggle 'from a position of strength'. And so, after a draw in the first game, where my opponent exchanged in the centre and immediately avoided fighting for an advantage, in the second encounter I opened 1 e4.

According to Rauzer, "in this way White begins and wins", but I had hardly ever played it before. And, jumping ahead, I should say that it was this game which convinced me that, in matches, one cannot pin one's hopes only on the unexpected, switch from side to side, and abandon one's normal style of play. Of course, it is not a bad idea to keep in one's repertoire openings 'for one game', but this should not be an end in itself. On the whole, such tactics do not pay off, although, as experience from matches shows, at certain times they are justified.

And so, with no experience of playing White after 1 e4, I failed to gain an advantage, then made a number of inaccurate moves, and lost. Having said all this, I in no way wish to belittle Zaitsev's excellent creative achievement in this game.

I went along to the third game not with the intention of getting even, but simply of playing. I could not allow myself the luxury of a second defeat, and therefore the idea of playing very riskily was not even considered, either in my chess preparations, or psychologically.

The course of the game—and please excuse me for making this ancient comparison—resembled the fluctuations of two scale pans. By the 15th move I had already managed to seize the initiative as Black, then on the 27th move I 'handed' it to Zaitsev. My opponent was not long in returning the compliment, and by the 33rd move the initiative was once again with me. The game was adjourned with an advantage to Black, but to the win it was a far cry. Many hours of analysis revealed that if there was a win, it could be achieved only with colossal difficulty. Here are some possible variations:

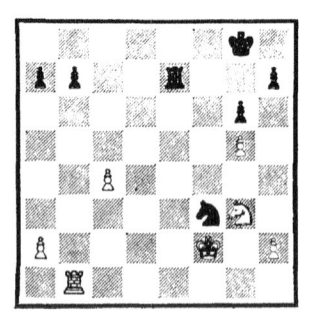

Black, of course, sealed

42 ... N×g5

Now White has two main continuations: 43 c5 and 43 a4. The idea of the first of these is to drive away the black knight by h3-h4, then to establish the white knight on e4 and move the king to the centre. E.g. 43 c5 Kg7 44 h4 Ne6 45 Ne4 Rc7 (*45 ... Kh6 46 Rd1* followed by *Rd5*) 46 Nd6, with a counter-attack against the b7 pawn. The idea behind the second continuation, 43 a4, is the threat of a4-a5-a6, after which the 'c' pawn, from being a weakness, may become a strength.

In searching for an antidote to this strong plan, we hit upon the 'antipositional' move ... h7-h5. It is not possible here to support its strength with variations, but on a more careful examination of the position the strategical advantages of this move can be

4. On the Eve   177

understood. The pawn is moved off the 7th rank, the king is assured of a comfortable post at h6, and at the same time the possibility of creating a passed 'h' pawn is retained. Of course, this move does not ensure a clear win, but nevertheless it presents White with the most difficult problems.

Everything, however, turned out differently. The very first move made by Zaitsev on the resumption did not aspire to anything, and was clearly not the strongest. Black gained the opportunity to regroup his forces.

After

43 Rb3	h5!
44 h4	Ne6
45 Ra3	b6

he obtained a won position. The game continued:

46 Ke3	Nc5+
47 Kd4	Rd7+
48 Ke5	Kf7

An inaccuracy, although granted, it does not yet relinquish the win. The king is needed there where Black has a pawn majority, i.e. on the K-side. After 48 ... Kg7 49 Nf1 Kh6 50 Ne3 Re7+ 51 Kd5 Re4 it is all over.

49 Rf3+   Ke7

Here too it was better to move the king to g7.

50 Ne2	Nd3+
51 Ke4	Nc5+
52 Ke5	Rd2!

This is now the only way to win.

53 Nf4	Nd7+
54 Ke4	R×a2
55 N×g6+	Kd6
56 Rf5	Rg2!

Preventing 57 Nf4, since after 57 ... Rg4 the rooks and the 'h' pawns are exchanged, and the knight ending is easily won for Black.

57 Rd5+

Zaitsev finds a last chance, and tries it.

57 ...	Kc7
58 Rg5	R×g5
59 h×g5	Kd6
60 Nf4	h4
61 g6	Ke7??

With one move Black destroys the fruits of his many hours of work. I can put this mistake down only to extreme fatigue. Black could have won easily by 61 ... Nf6+ 62 Kf5 Ne8 63 Kg4 Kc5 (but not *63 ... a5 64 Nd3 a4 65 c5+ b×c5 66 Nb2!*).

62 Kf5	a5
63 g5	

I simply did not see this move, but assumed that White was bound to play 63 Kg4, which after 63 ... Ne5+ 64 K×h4 N×g6+ 65 N×g6 Kd6 leads to his defeat. But now Black has no more than a draw.

63 ...	Ne5
64 Nd5+	Kf8
65 K×h4	N×c4
66 g5	
	Drawn.

I have given the resumption of this game here, not because the ending proved to be particularly interesting, but so as to emphasize that it was not only on account of the minus score that for me the most difficult moment of the match had arrived. Before the start of the fourth game (the match was due to consist of only six games) there remained less than 24 hours...

What was required now was some important, long-term preparatory work of a purely psychological nature.

I recognized, as I had never done before, my mistake in previous years. Both in junior events, and then in USSR Championships, I had always regarded each decisive game as the game of my life! And when I failed to achieve my aim, I reproached myself for my lack of mobilization, and the weak concentration of my efforts. But in fact the root of the evil lay elsewhere: I was let down by excessive constraint—the very worst enemy of creativity!

And before the fourth game of my match with Zaitsev, I suddenly sensed very clearly: despite the importance of the coming encounter, I had to achieve an inwardly light-hearted, even—if you will excuse the expression—devil-may-care attitude to the game. In the psychological sense I had to reduce the coming encounter to the most ordinary of games, of which I had already played more than a hundred or two, and in the majority of cases—successfully. It was another matter that I had to play thoughtfully, without weakening my combative edge, to play with all possible competitive aggression, but on no account to associate each important step in the game with the sheen of the gold medal.

Such self-preparation, which one might call the autogenous training of a chess player, I did in fact succeed in carrying out. How was it done? I would not venture to give any sort of universal advice. One player, so as to obtain a composed frame of mind, has to have a good sleep, another must take a walk through beautiful avenues, parks and roads, a third has to grow well and truly angry, if for him this is pleasing, a fourth, in contrast, has to calm himself, while a fifth has to go along to the game wearing his favourite shirt or tie. I believe that some time in the future psychologists in general, and chess psychologists in particular, will translate these recommendations, which we reach by the method of trial and error, into the exact language of science.

Be that as it may, but by purely individual means I succeeded in attaining that so desirable 'indifference', which was far from indifferent for me. In accordance with the frame of mind attained, within literally a few short minutes the opening was also planned. There would be no sharp tactics, no playing according to the principle 'win or bust'. The Catalan Opening, that's what it would be, even though it did not promise White any marked advantage! In addition, it combated excellently one further deficiency in my opponent's play. Although, I repeat, Aleksandr was highly resourceful in defending against a direct attack, he defended much less confidently and with much less interest in slightly inferior positions, and would occasionally allow himself impulsive decisions, which strategically were not altogether well-founded. It was in such a situation that I could hope to increase appreciably even a minimal advantage.

The course of the game fully confirmed the correctness both of my 'chosen' mood, and of the corresponding, purely chess plan for the game.

Polugayevsky–Zaitsev
Catalan Opening

1 c4	e6
2 g3	d5
3 Bg2	Nf6
4 Nf3	Be7
5 0-0	0-0
6 d4	c6
7 Qc2	Nbd7
8 b3	b6
9 Bb2	

After 9 Nc3 Black can even consider 9 ... Ba6.

9 ...	Bb7
10 Nc3	Rc8
11 Rad1	

A very familiar position. The well-tried continuation here is 11 ... Qc7, as was played, for instance, by Ney against Geller in the 34th USSR Championship at Tbilisi, 1967. Reshevsky once tried 11 ... c5, but this gave White the advantage.

11 ... b5

Black is resorting to this move more and more frequently in the Catalan. One only has to recall the Petrosian–Spassky match (1966).

12 c5

The only correct reply, since White's strategy here is to gain space.

12 ...	b4
13 Nb1	

The only way, in my opinion. Petrosian played 13 Na4, and the knight proved to be out of play. It was this that Zaitsev was counting on.

13 ... a5
14 Nbd2 Ra8

Black's plan is clear: to counter White's pressure in the centre he intends to create play on the 'a' file.

15 e4 N×e4
16 N×e4 d×e4
17 Q×e4 Nf6

Too straightforward. First 17 ... a4 was preferable.

18 Qc2 Nd5
19 Ne5

Now in the event of 19 ... a4 Black has to reckon with 20 b×a4 Qa5 21 B×d5 c×d5 22 Nd7 Re8 23 Nb6 Ra7, when he has no time for ... Bc6 or ... Bd8 in view of 24 a3!.

19 ... Bf6

20 Nc4

White continues playing in positional vein, although it was also possible to take a different course. During the game I was not firmly convinced that it was worth choosing the variation 20 Be4 g6 21 h4 a4 22 Kg2 a3 23 Ba1, when for some time the bishop is shut out of the game, although White has a fairly strong attack in prospect.

20 ... Ba6
21 Rfe1 Bb5

A dubious move. 21 ... Qc7 is better, when White should play 22 Be4, with the follow-up given in the previous note. If instead Black replies 22 ... h6, then White's problem is to exchange the places of his queen and bishop.

22 Nd6 Qb8

Black should have admitted his mistake straight away, and played 22 ... Ba6.

23 Bc1!

Emphasizing the poor position of the black queen at b8. It turns out that 23 ... Nc3 now is bad on account of 24 a4! N×d1 25 R×d1 Ba6 26 B×c6, with an overwhelming advantage.

23 ... Ba6
24 B×d5 e×d5

24 ... c×d5 was the lesser evil, although even then by 25 Bf4 Qd8 26 h4, followed by Qd2, White builds up very strong pressure on the K-side.

25 Bf4 Qd8
26 Be5 Bc8
27 Rd3!

For the moment White plays the strongest moves. On 27 B×f6 Q×f6 28 Re5 Black replies 28 ... Be6, and prepares the advance ... a5-a4. But in the game

White doubles rooks on the 'e' file without delay.

27 ...	Be6
28 Rde3	Be7
29 Nf5	

Instead of this, 29 f4 was suggested in the press-centre of the match, with the possible follow-up 29 ... B×d6 30 B×d6 Re8 31 f5 Bd7 32 Re7 or 32 Be7, and wins. But Black has in reserve the reply 29 ... g6, and on 30 f5—30 ... B×d6 31 B×d6 B×f5 32 Qf2 Be4, with adequate compensation for the exchange. If instead 31 f×e6, then 31 ... B×e5 32 R×e5 Qe7. White's position is of course rather more pleasant, but how much so?

| 29 ... | Bf6 |

On 29 ... B×f5 30 Q×f5 Ra7 White wins by 31 B×g7 K×g7 32 R×e7, while if 30 ... g6, then 31 Qh3.

30 h4!

Following the slogan: 'No chances at all for the opponent!'. The idea of this move is after h4–h5 to force the weakening ... h7–h6, and then switch to the advance of the 'f' pawn. Possible exchanges in the centre are merely to White's advantage.

| 30 ... | B×e5 |

| 31 R×e5 | B×f5 |
| 32 Q×f5 | a4 |

Black's one chance of obtaining any sort of counter-play.

33 Kg2

Necessary prophylaxis, since on the immediate 33 Re7 there can follow 33 ... a×b3 34 a×b3 Ra1!.

33 ...	a×b3
34 a×b3	Ra3
35 R1e3	Ra7

Obligatory. Black cannot concede the seventh rank.

Here White decided to play for the adjournment, so as under calm conditions to find an accurate way of realizing his advantage.

36 h5	h6
37 Kh3	Qa8
38 Qf3	Qc8+
39 Kg2	Ra2?

Black should have passively continued to control the seventh rank.

40 Re7	Rd2
41 Qf4	Qb8
42 R3e5	Ra2

In this way Black prolongs the resistance. 42 ... Rd3 was suggested by all the commentators here, and for some reason all of them considered that 43 Qg4 was virtually obligatory for White. But after 42 ... Rd3 I was planning to win in three moves by 43 Rd7 R×b3 44 Qf5!, depriving the black rook of the square b1. On 43 ... f6 White replies 44 Ree7, while 44 ... Qb5 is met decisively by 45 R×f7!.

43 Qe3	Ra8
44 Qe2	Qc8
45 Qf3	

The last move before the adjournment, and not the best. Instead, 45 g4 would have put an end to the struggle.

45 ...   Ra1

The sealed move. A long analysis showed that only 45 ... Qa6 would have caused White certain difficulties.

46 Qe2

So as now on 46 ... Ra8 to reply 47 g4, with the possible follow-up 47 ... Qb8 48 Qe3 Kh7 49 g5 h×g5 50 h6! g×h6 (no better is 50 ... Qc8 51 R×g5 g×h5 52 Qd3+ Kh8 53 Rg3 Rg8 54 R×f7 R×g3+ 55 f×g3 Ra2+ 56 Kf3) 51 Qd3+ Kg8 52 R5e6, and wins.

True, the following line was also sufficient: 46 Rf5 Qa6 47 Rf×f7 Qf1+ 48 Kh2 Qg1+ 49 Kh3 Qh1+ 50 Kg4 Q×f3+ 51 R×f3 R×f3 52 K×f3, when, in the opinion of Zaitsev himself, White wins. I saw this line, but I did not wish to be diverted from my basic plan.

46 ...   Rc1

After 46 ... Qa6 47 Q×a6 R×a6 48 Rb7 the outcome of the game is, of course, decided.

47 Re8	Qd7
48 R5e7	R×e8
49 R×e8+	Kh7
50 Qd3+	f5
51 Qe3	Rc3

This loses immediately. But equally hopeless is 51 ... Qf7, which was recommended by various commentators, and by Zaitsev himself, as giving drawing chances. They suggested the variation 52 Re7 Qf6 (*52 ... Qf8 53 Qe6!*), and thought that Black could count on saving the game after 53 Re6 Qg5 54 Q×g5 h×g5 55 R×c6 Rd1. But even here White wins by capturing the pawn immediately: 54 R×c6, when, in view of the threat of 55 Qe8! with inevitable mate, Black himself is forced to exchange queens—55 ... Q×e3 56 f×e3, and after 56 ... Rc3 57 Kf3 R×b3 58 Rb6 he can calmly resign.

True, instead of 53 ... Qg5 Black has a stronger continuation (missed by the commentators)—53 ... Qf7, but now White has a choice between a queen ending with good winning chances (*54 R×h6+ g×h6 55 Q×c1 Q×h5 56 Qf4*), and the equally promising variation 54 R×c6 Rc3 55 Qe2 R×b3 56 Rb6 Rc3 57 R×b4 f4 58 Qd2.

The most curious thing, however, is that the tempting 53 Re6 is simply unnecessary for White! He wins instantly by continuing 53 Rc7!. The black rook is attacked, and 53 ... Rc3 is decisively met by 54 Qe8 Qg5 55 R×c6. There remains one last chance: 53 ... Rc2 54 Qe8 f4 55 R×c6 R×f2+ 56 Kg1, and it is all over.

Thus it is hardly correct to attach a question mark to 51 ... Rc3.

52 Qe5	f4
53 Qb8	f3+
54 Kh2	**Resigns**

After this encounter I began to scent victory, became completely composed, and regulated, so to speak, the co-ordination between my thinking and my actions (sometimes you think of one move, but for some reason make another).

With the score standing at $2\frac{1}{2}$-$2\frac{1}{2}$ I succeeded in winning the final game.

But it was not after this game, but after the fourth, that I began to believe that, by bringing myself into the necessary frame of mind, corresponding most exactly to the specific nature of the moment, I could achieve my goal in the most difficult and crucial of encounters.

WILL THE WIND BE FAVOURABLE?

In the practice of every player there are games which play a highly important role: they enable him to realize the degree of his own state of preparedness for the battle. World Champion Anatoly Karpov, for example, has this to say: "From the first game I do not expect a point, so much as an answer to the silent question about my form. And, depending on how my play goes, I plan my tactics for the entire tournament."

It is of this that the two following games are characteristic. One of them, with Aivar Gipslis, was played in a friendly match between teams from the Russian Federation and Latvia, shortly before the 37th USSR Championship, in which I was victorious. The other was with Milko Bobotsov at the start of the International Hoogoven Tournament at Beverwijk in 1966, in which I took first place. Both of them showed that my thinking was easy, and that I was seeing subtleties; in short, I was in good form. This meant that I could play boldly and trust myself, and in this lies the foundation of success.

So that, without being decisive, these games helped me to win important, genuinely decisive encounters later, at the height of the tournament battle.

Polugayevsky–Gipslis
Riga 1969
Nimzo-Indian Defence

1 d4	Nf6
2 c4	e6
3 Nc3	Bb4
4 e3	c5
5 Bd3	0–0
6 Nf3	d5
7 0–0	Nc6
8 a3	d×c4

This exchange is normally made one move earlier. But now, in the present situation, it leads to an ending with two bishops for White, which gives him a slight but firm advantage.

| 9 a×b4 | c×d4 |

Not, of course, 9 ... c×d3 10 b×c5, and Black loses a pawn.

| 10 B×c4 | d×c3 |

11 Q×d8	R×d8
12 b×c3	Ne4
13 b5	

Only in this way can the black cavalry charge be repelled. A move later it becomes clear that Black cannot play 14 ... Nd2, on account of 15 N×d2 R×d2 16 Rfd1, when the weakness of his back rank tells.

13 ...	Ne7
14 Bb2	Kf8!

Planning to restrict White's black-squared bishop, by erecting a barrier in its path with ... f7-f6 and ... e6-e5.

15 Be2	f6
16 Rfd1	Bd7

A rather poor reply. Exchanges are normally helpful to the defending side, and in the given instance the disappearance of a pair of rooks would have been to his advantage. Although after 16 ... R×d1+ 17 R×d1 Nd5 18 Rc1 White remains with the more pleasant position, Black could have put up a successful defence. But now White's advantage becomes appreciable.

17 c4	e5
18 Ne1!	

Not only with the aim of placing this knight at d3, but also the intention of driving away the black knight from e4 by f2-f3.

18 ...	Ke8

To defend the bishop at d7.

19 Bh5+!

This finesse emphasizes the difficulties of Black's position. The point of the move is not only to force a further weakening of Black's pawn chain, but also to prepare for the tactical possibility of answering 19 ... g6 20 Bf3 Bf5 with 21 g4.

19 ...	g6
20 Bf3	Nc5
21 Ba3	Rac8
22 Bb4	

Ignoring the win of a pawn (22 B×c5), White continues to pile on the pressure. Black's next move is forced, since 22 ... a6 fails to 23 Ba5.

22 ...	Be6
23 R×d8+	K×d8
24 R×a7	Nd7

The best way out of the resulting situation. After 24 ... B×c4 25 B×b7 N×b7 26 R×b7 Nd5 27 Ba5+ Ke8 28 b6 Black's position is totally bad.

25 B×b7	R×c4
26 Ba5+	Ke8
27 h3	e4

This move too is apparently forced, since otherwise the white pawn goes on to queen. E.g. 27 ... Rc5 28 Ba6, with the threat of Bb4 and b5-b6.

28 b6

White also has other ways, but he takes the decision to part with his passed pawn, obtaining four pawns against three on one wing, still with the two bishops.

| 28 ... | Rc1 |

If 28 ... Nc6, then 29 B×c6 R×c6 30 R×d7!.

| 29 B×e4 | N×b6 |
| 30 B×b6 | Nc8 |

Only in this way can Black parry the threats along the 7th rank, and continue to resist.

31 Ra8	R×e1+
32 Kh2	Kf7
33 Bd4	Rc1
34 g4	Rc7
35 Ra6	Ne7
36 Kg3	Rd7
37 Bc2	

Aiming for e8.

| 37 ... | Rc7 |
| 38 Ba4 | h5 |

Not wishing to await his fate passively, Black 'twitches', and loses very quickly.

39 Be8+	K×e8
40 R×e6	Rc6
41 R×c6	N×c6
42 B×f6	h×g4
43 h×g4	Resigns

Bobotsov–Polugayevsky
Beverwijk 1966
Queen's Indian Defence

1 d4	Nf6
2 c4	e6
3 Nf3	b6
4 Nc3	Bb7
5 Bg5	h6
6 Bh4	g5
7 Bg3	Nh5

Introduced by Botvinnik. Black obtains the two bishops, although true, slightly to the detriment of his development, however, the position is of a closed nature, and the loss of a tempo is not so important.

I played this variation against Bobotsov in 1963 at the Chigorin Memorial Tournament in Sochi, and won after a complicated struggle. But my opponent retained his opinion on the opening, and was not averse to trying it again. For me it was interesting to know what my opponent would have to say that was new on this occasion.

8 e3	N×g3
9 h×g3	Bg7
10 g4	

A necessary move, since otherwise Black himself plays ... g5-g4, driving the knight to h4, where it is lacking in prospects.

| 10 ... | Nc6 |

10 ... d6 could have been answered by 11 d5, with play on the weakened white squares. But now 11 d5 is well met by 11 ... Ne5.

11 Qd2

Bobotsov avoids 'repeating the past'. In our game from 1973 he continued 11 Qc2 followed by 12 a3. It seems to me that Bobotsov's new move is more logical. White can hope for an opening advantage only if he should succeed in restricting the scope of the black bishops. In certain cases this aim can be served by the advance d4–d5; with the queen at d2 this is more feasible.

11 ...	Qe7
12 0-0-0	0-0-0
13 Kb1	Kb8

The position reached is difficult in the strategical sense for both sides. In such positions everything is built on nuances: the slightest inaccuracy may unexpectedly prove decisive. While Black's last move parries the possible threat of Nb5 and d4–d5, the analogous move by White's king is not at all necessary, and is a waste of time. Bobotsov clearly assumed that Black had no active plan, but such a plan can in fact be found.

14 Be2	Qf8!

By this unexpected and veiled manoeuvre Black seizes the initiative. He now threatens by ... f7-f5 to open up the game, which, with his long-range bishops, will gain him an appreciable advantage. On 15 Bd3 Nb4 16 Be4 d5 17 c×d5 Black can play not only 17 ... e×d5, but also 17 ... f5, with favourable complications (thanks to the bad placing of the king at b1!).

15 d5

White takes counter-measures. But in blocking the diagonal of one of the black bishops, he opens the way for the other.

15 ...	Ne5
16 Nd4	c5!

This strong move was overlooked by my opponent. He considered only 16 ... Qc5, which after 17 Nb3 or 17 Rc1 gives White counter-play on the 'c' file. But now the white knight must abandon its central position, since the opening of the game after 17 d×c6 d×c6 is clearly in Black's favour.

17 Nc2	f5!
18 g×f5	Q×f5
19 f4	

The natural reaction to Black's 17th move. After the game Bobotsov expressed the opinion that 19 f3 followed by 20 e4 would have been stronger. But in this case the black squares in White's position would have been seriously weakened, and this would have become noticeable after ... Ng6 and ... Qf6.

19 ...	g×f4
20 e×f4	Nf7
21 Bd3	Qf6
22 Ne3	Nd6!

Once again Black successfully regroups his forces. From d6 the knight covers e4, and assures the queen of its strong position at f6.

23 Rhf1	Rhe8
24 Ng4	Qh4
25 Ne3	

25 Ne5 costs a pawn after 25 ... B×e5 26 f×e5 N×c4.

25 ...   **Bd4**

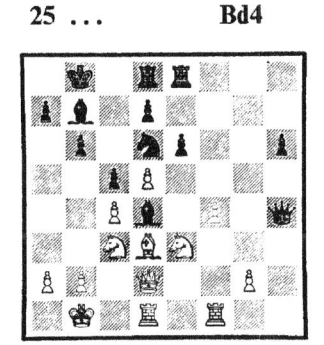

26 d×e6?

Equivalent to suicide. White could have maintained the balance by playing 26 Nc2, but then Black can regroup with 26 ... Bh8! 27 Ne3 Qg3 followed by 28 ... Qg7 and 29 ... Rg8. Such a piece set-up would have tied down White's forces to a considerable extent, while Black would have had various active plans.

After 26 d×e6? the game is opened up, and White's position immediately becomes critical.

26 ...   d×e6
27 Qe2   Qg3

The start of a forcing variation. The g2 pawn is indefensible.

28 Ng4   Q×g2
29 N×h6   Qh3

This wins the exchange, since the threat of 30 ... Bg2 31 Rfe1 Bf3 cannot be parried.

30 Ng4   Bg2
31 Ne5   B×f1
32 R×f1   B×e5
33 Q×e5

An oversight in a hopeless position.

But after 33 f×e5 Nb5 34 N×b5 Q×d3+ White similarly has no hope of saving the game.

33 ...   Q×d3+
34 Resigns

THE CHALLENGE HAD TO BE ACCEPTED...

Najdorf–Polugayevsky
Mar del Plata 1971
Nimzo-Indian Defence

For me this game acquired greater significance than usual, although this happened against my will. It was played in the sixth round, when I already had five 'ones' in the tournament table. To be honest, I was therefore not too aggressively inclined: a draw, especially with Black, would merely have strengthened my tournament position. But the cheerful veteran Miguel Najdorf had other ideas: "A tournament in Mar del Plata without Najdorf is not a tournament!", he exclaimed. "I have won all the tournaments here! Ten times! Against everyone I play only for a win!"

And although as regards Najdorf's ten victories in Mar del Plata one might have doubts, this last assertion by the Argentinian grandmaster did indeed correspond to the truth. When the opening stage of the game was concluded, and before my 11th move I offered a draw, it was declined. "That's fine", I thought, "now it will be my turn to decline..."

1 d4   Nf6
2 c4   e6
3 Nc3   Bb4
4 e3   0-0
5 Bd3   c5

6 Nf3	d5
7 0-0	d×c4
8 B×c4	Nc6

Following its adoption by Larsen in his match with Portisch in 1965, this variation has become firmly established in tournament practice.

9 Bd3

Najdorf's favourite move. At the time the main continuation here was considered to be 9 a3 Ba5 10 Qd3 a6 11 Rd1 b5 12 Ba2, as occurred, for instance, in my game with Portisch from the 1970 Interzonal Tournament.

9 ...	c×d4
10 e×d4	Be7
11 a3	

An essential part of White's set-up. The manoeuvre ... Nb4-d5 has to be prevented.

| 11 ... | a6 |

A few rounds earlier Gheorghiu had continued 11 ... b6 followed by ... Bb7 against Najdorf, and obtained a good position. I decided against this, and not simply because I feared an improvement on the part of my highly-experienced opponent. Black's plan with ... b7-b6 is, in my opinion, passive, and later it is difficult for him to obtain counter-play. What convinced me of this was a considerable amount of analytical work, which was later tested in several games, for instance, against Portisch in the matches between the Russian Federation and Hungary.

Much more active and crucial is the plan begun by the move in the game with ... a7-a6 and ... b7-b5, which I had planned in my preparations prior to this game. Black, although he wastes a tempo, gains numerous interesting possibilities. Thus he can worry White with ... b5-b4 (which in fact occurred in the present game), he can occupy the square c4 by the manoeuvre ... Na5-c4, or finally, in the event of the exchange of the knight at c3, the b5 pawn prevents the creation of a mobile white pawn pair c4/d4.

Jumping ahead, it should be mentioned that it was this plan which inflicted a severe blow on White's opening set-up.

12 Bc2

White's plan is obvious—to set up the queen-bishop battery on the b1-h7 diagonal, and then after Rd1 to prepare the d4-d5 break. Its drawback is the fact that it is rather slow.

12 ...	b5
13 Qd3	Bb7
14 Re1!	

A cunning move. Outwardly it would appear that 14 Rd1 is more logical. I became suspicious, since the rook move was made after prolonged thought. Soon I saw that after the natural 14 ... Rc8 15 d5 e×d5 16 Bg5 g6 17 R×e7 White wins.

| 14 ... | g6 |
| 15 Bb3 | |

An unsuccessful manoeuvre, although one can understand White's desire to transfer his bishop to a more promising position. Better was 15 Bh6 Re8 16 Rad1, with a complicated game.

15 ...	Rc8

Najdorf had reckoned only on 15 ... Na5 16 Ba2 B×f3 17 Q×f3 Q×d4, but I did not even consider taking such a poisoned pawn.

16 Bh6	Re8
17 Ba2	b4
18 Ne2?	

As the Argentinian grandmaster explained after the game, he erroneously assumed that the advantage was on his side. Black is already fully mobilized, and is ready for a battle on any part of the board. The positionally correct decision was 18 Na4, attempting to exploit the weakness of the c5 square. I was intending to reply 18 ... Na5, and if 19 a×b4, then 19 ...Nc6. E.g. 20 Nc5 N×b4 21 Qb3 B×f3 22 Q×b4 Bd5, with roughly equal chances. But instead of this, White begins playing for a win, and burns his boats behind him.

18 ...	Na5!

Black not only uncovers his bishop, but also sets a concealed trap, into which his opponent falls.

19 Nf4

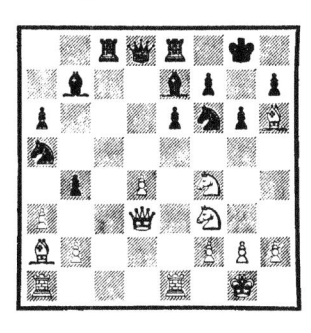

19 ...	b3!

The beginning of a lengthy combination, which demanded exact calculation on Black's part.

20 B×b3	Be4!
21 Qd1	

If White had seen a little further, he would undoubtedly have given up the exchange: 21 R×e4 N×b3 22 Q×b3 N×e4 23 N×e6, although even here 23 ... Qd6 leaves Black with the advantage.

21 ...	N×b3
22 Q×b3	Bc2!

The point of Black's pawn sacrifice is revealed. His main efforts are directed towards trapping the bishop at h6.

23 Qa2	Ng4
24 N×e6	

24 ...	Qb6!

Najdorf had missed this concluding stroke of the combination. Loss of material for White is now inevitable.

25 Ng7	Bb3
26 Qb1	Red8!

26 ... N×h6 27 N×e8 R×e8 is also quite good, but now Black wins a whole piece, and the game is soon over.

27 Nf5 g×f5 28 R×e7 N×h6 29 Qd3 Qf6 30 Ra7 Bc4 31 Qd2 Bd5 32 Ne5 Ng4 33 Qf4 N×e5 34 d×e5 Qg6 35 g3 Be4 36 Re1 Rd3 37 e6 Q×e6 White resigns.

IN THE NAME OF REVENGE

Quinteros–Polugayevsky
Mar del Plata 1971
Réti Opening

That was how this game proceeded. The point was that, a year earlier, international master Quinteros had won against me in the Olympiad at Siegen.

It has to be said that winning as Black against Quinteros is no easy matter, since he plays only 'g3-type' and 'b3-type' set-ups, and although he himself doesn't gain an advantage, it is not at all easy to 'breach' the fianchettoed bishops. One 'saving' factor is that the Argentinian is afraid neither of names nor reputations, and himself plays only for a win.

1 Nf3	d5
2 g3	Nf6
3 Bg2	c6
4 b3	Bf5

This type of set-up has frequently occurred in my games, and so playing the opening was fairly easy.

5 Bb2	e6
6 0-0	h6
7 d3	Be7
8 Nfd2	

8 Nbd2 is usually played here, but the move in the game also has its points. Firstly, the advance e2–e4 can be made without any extra preparatory moves, such as Qe1, and secondly, the way is opened for the 'f' pawn. In short, I like this move.

| 8 ... | 0-0 |
| 9 e4 | Bh7 |

Objectively speaking, this is a debatable point. By 9 ... d×e4 10 d×e4 Bh7 I could have tried to cast doubts on White's 8th move, but I did not wish to 'clarify' the situation sooner than was necessary.

| 10 Qe2 | a5 |
| 11 a4 | |

11 a3 is more exact.

11 ...	Na6
12 e5	Nd7
13 f4	

Both for attacking purposes, and also to defend the c2 pawn (after ... *Nb4*) by Nf3.

| 13 ... | b5 |

This may appear over-bold, but it is essentially correct.

14 Nc3

After 14 a×b5 c×b5 Black seizes the initiative on the Q-side. Also, White cannot permit 14 ... b×a4 15 R×a4 Nac5 followed by 16 ... a4.

| 14 ... | Nb4 |
| 15 Nf3 | Nc5 |

Black's play is straightforward, and, perhaps for this reason, convincing. Now 16 a×b5 c×b5 17 N×b5 fails to 17 ... N×c2 18 Q×c2 B×d3. At the same time Black threatens to sacrifice one of his knights at c2, b3 or d3. He holds the initiative.

16 a×b5   c×b5

After the game Quinteros said that he had been more afraid of 16 ... Qb6, and only then 17 ... c×b5. But 17 Kh1 would be a highly useful move for White.

17 d4

This looks like a strategic mistake (the b1-h7 diagonal!), but after 17 ... Ne4 18 N×e4 B×e4 19 Ne1 B×g2 20 N×g2 the white knight heads for e3, to support White's K-side pawn storm. For about an hour I thought over this position. I make no secret of the fact that I felt there was some defect in White's set-up, and that Black's pieces directed towards the Q-side could 'accomplish' something. In the end Black went in for a very long combination, of which the consequences were impossible to calculate, and where one could be guided only by an assessment of the position. The complexity of the sacrifice was made greater by the inclusion in the combination of several quiet moves.

17 ...   N×c2
18 d×c5

Now begins the concrete stage of the combination, in which I had calculated some ten moves ahead.

18 ...   B×c5+
19 Kh1   d4!

Of course, after 19 ... N×a1 20 R×a1 White stands better. But now on the natural 20 Rad1 there follows 20 ... d3, and if 21 Qd2, then 21 ... Be3, shutting closed the trap.

20 N×b5   d3
21 Qd2

If White had foreseen the course of events, he would have chosen the less committing 21 Qd1.

21 ...   Rb8!

The only move, but what is White to do now? 22 R×a5—22 ... Bb4. 22 Q×a5—22 ... N×a1 23 R×a1 Q×a5 24 R×a5 Bb4. White's only other alternative is 22 Nc3 R×b3 23 Ra2 Bb4, when the mortal pin on the knight enables Black to regain the whole of the sacrificed material.

22 Nd6   N×a1
23 R×a1   R×b3
24 Nd4   Rb6!

A quiet move, which was found before the start of the combination. It turns out that again the a5 pawn cannot be captured, and White's pieces are hanging (*25 Nc6 Qc7*). It appears that only now did White realize that he was in trouble.

| 25 Bc3 | B×d6 |
| 26 e×d6 | Q×d6 |

Black now has three pawns for the piece, and the amazingly tenacious a5 pawn is again invulnerable. It is clear that victory for Black is not far off.

27 h4

White now had little time left, and Black decided to play for complications.

27 ...   e5

This is wrong. Black should have continued 27 ... Ra6, followed by the advance of the 'a' pawn.

| 28 f×e5 | Q×e5 |
| 29 Kh2 | Rg6 |

Black's hopes were associated with this move. I thought that 30 Q×d3 could be decisively met by 30 ... Rg4, but overlooked 31 Nc6, and if 31 ... R×h4+, then 32 Kg1 Qc5+ 33 Bd4. But Quinteros thought the same, and played:

30 Qf2

Now the move 27 ... e5 is justified. The game concluded:
30 ... Qc5 31 Qd2 Rg4 32 R×a5 Qc7 33 Qe1 d2 34 Q×d2 Q×g3+ 35 Kg1 Be4 36 Ra2, and without waiting for his opponent's reply, White stopped the clocks.

THE DREAM COMES TRUE

I will always remember the year of 1973, for it was then that I first overcame the Interzonal barrier, and emerged as one of the Candidates for the World Championship. But this was preceded by some fairly dramatic events at the finish of the Interzonal Tournament in Petropolis.

Two rounds before the end I was more than depressed. Towards the finish of the tournament I had failed to win several games where I stood clearly better, I had lost to the Argentinian grandmaster Panno, and all that could save me was two successive wins. But while a win even with Black in the penultimate round over international master Tan was a perfectly feasible proposition, to win 'to order' at the decisive moment against one of the strongest players in the world, Lajos Portisch... This seemed too unreal, especially since Portisch was leading the tournament, was playing brilliantly, and not once in Petropolis had been obliged to stop the clocks.

But there was no choice. In a very sharp battle I won against Tan, and one step from the finish Portisch led me by one point, and led Efim Geller, who was also in contention for a place in the first three, by half a point. There was no sense in hoping for a loss by my compatriot: in such situations one does not normally take risks, and it was highly probable that Geller would draw with Panno. This meant that I had nothing to lose...

I felt that never before in my life had I faced such a difficult task. Upon the result of one game hung my long-cherished dream of reaching the Candidates' event. A dream, which I had been unable to fulfil either in 1970, when I appeared to have fair prospects in the Interzonal Tournament, or earlier, when I had failed in the 1963 and 1966 USSR Championships and had not reached the Interzonal Tournaments.

The consciousness of all this weighed heavily on me, and in such a state there was no possibility of my playing successfully. How was I to shake off this burden of many years, now concentrated on one single game, how was I to rid myself of this mental confusion?

What was I to do? Should I cultivate a calmly indifferent attitude to the coming battle, as I had once done in my match with A. Zaitsev? Or should I arouse in myself a feeling of maximum competitive aggression, as before that game with Kholmov? Neither of these was really suitable—the first, because it inclined towards a rather quiet game, the second, since it was very easy to 'overheat'. What was needed was a synthesis of these two conditions—enormous energy plus cool reason, but how was it to be attained?

Perhaps to some extent I was helped by a little incident.

During the tournament we were living in a mountain hotel, and the fresh air, together with a rather special, incomparable quietness, were highly suitable for chess players relaxing after one battle, and at the same time tuning up for another, in the following round.

And so, the evening before the last round, after dinner I went out for a breath of air, and began making circuits around the perimeter of a small swimming pool which was situated close to the hotel. Stars were suspended like mysterious lanterns in the dark Southern sky, and it was very warm and very quiet. I encircled the pool once, twice, when I ran into Vlastimil Hort, who was returning to the hotel from the town.

"Who are you playing tomorrow?" the Czech grandmaster asked me.

Highly astonished, I replied: "Portisch..."

"Aha... Difficult. It's impossible to win against him at the moment, he just doesn't lose at all!"

Hort said this even sympathetically, but for some reason this sympathy acted like a spark to a keg of gunpowder.

"If it comes to that, I've even won against World Champions!!"

This was a cry from the heart. And although this may seem like a rather poor fabrication, it was as though heard by the veteran Argentinian grandmaster Miguel Najdorf who had come to Petropolis especially for the concluding rounds. His optimism is legendary, and he spent evenings with us in the hotel at chess and cards, when his voice would not die down even for a minute.

"What?! Who are you playing? Portisch? And you need to win? You'll win!!"

"How will I win?"

"You have the better chances! He needs a draw, but you need a win!", Najdorf declared not altogether logically, but most convincingly. And he added:

"You are playing well! Do you want to take a bet on it?!"

I suddenly sensed a growing feeling of confidence in victory. Indeed, it was equally likely for me as it was for Portisch. What about a draw being in his favour? Yes! But after all, not only I, but also he had to play 'to order'!

A further half an hour's walking, a sound sleep, and in the morning I felt that I couldn't wait for the moment when I would sit down at the board. Jumping ahead, I should perhaps mention that, in the bus on the way to the game, I listened with genuine pleasure to some amusing stories, and myself related some anecdote. Later, my second, Vladimir Bagirov, admitted that both he, and grandmaster Yury Averbakh who had been sitting next to him, had been astonished that I should be in such a mood prior to such an important encounter.

And so, I awoke with a thirst for battle, but not a reckless battle, but one prepared beforehand, like a decisive encounter in a war. From here followed the stages in my opening preparation.

First I had to decide the question: should I play that which I normally play, or should I try to surprise my opponent with my choice of opening? My second made his recommendations to me on both possibilities, and we began considering opening with the king's pawn. In its favour, apart from its surprise value, was the fact that after 1 e4 Portisch feels much less confident...

"But if it should be a Lopez, what then?", I asked dubiously.

" Play the Italian Game!"

"But I never played it even as a child!"

"So much the better! Portisch only plays the variation with Bf8-c5..."

And I was shown a multitude of variations of primordial antiquity, which had been worked out taking Portisch's games into account...

I was ready to agree, when I suddenly sensed: this is no way to play! This is not the way to plan a decisive battle. After all, if I were to fail to gain an advantage from the opening, I would not forgive myself for having betrayed 'my sort' of chess, and this would inevitably tell on my condition during the game. Very well, it might be easier for Portisch in the opening, but even if I were to fail to achieve what I wanted in my own schemes, all the same I would do everything possible to gain an advantage in the middlegame.

And the Italian Game fell away of its own accord. And after it—also the Exchange Variation of the Ruy Lopez, and 1 e4 in general.

But I also did not wish to permit the Nimzo-Indian Defence, which had been so well studied by my opponent, and by the method of elimination my choice fell on 1 Nf3—I would attempt to gain a slight advantage. In the end it would depend on me whether or not I was able to increase it.

I must admit that I did not guess completely the course of events in the opening. Portisch chose against me that very same variation in which a few rounds earlier I had lost as Black to Panno. Portisch undoubtedly knew that game, and to all appearances was aiming for a different piece set-up. After a little thought, at the board I took a radical decision: to deviate from the path chosen by Panno. And the result was a highly unusual form of the Réti Opening. White did not achieve anything in it, but... I lost the opening advantage 'promised' by theory, but gained more: a complicated position was reached, which was unfamiliar—or only slightly familiar—to Portisch, and we were both forced to think for ourselves.

The fact that this was to my advantage is shown by the game.

Polugayevsky–Portisch
Réti Opening

1 Nf3	d5
2 c4	d4
3 g3	c5
4 e3!?	

A position from the Modern Benoni has been reached, with colours reversed (*1 d4 Nf6 2 c4 c5 3 d5 e6*).

4 ...	Nc6
5 e×d4	

In view of the tournament position, only a win would do for White in this game, and so he aims at any cost to 'dislodge' his opponent from familiar opening set-ups. Not for nothing is the Hungarian grandmaster rated one of the top experts on theory!

5 ...	N×d4

After 5 ... c×d4 White gains in pure form the above-mentioned variation of the Modern Benoni, with an extra tempo into the bargain.

6 N×d4	Q×d4
7 d3	

7 Nc3 also deserved consideration, not fearing attempts by Black to simplify the game by 7 ... Qe5+ 8 Be2 Bg4. E.g. 9 d4 c×d4 10 Bf4 B×e2 (*10 ... Qe6 11 Qa4+*) 11 Qa4+ b5 12 N×b5 Qe4 13 Nc7++ Kd8 14 Qe8 mate. 7 ... Bg4 is satisfactorily met, as in the game, by 8 f3 Bd7 9 Qe2 Bc6 10 d3 Nf6 11 Be3.

7 ...	Bg4
8 f3!?	

After 8 Be2 B×e2 9 Q×e2 0-0-0 the chances would have been roughly equal. Also possible was 8 Qb3 Bf3 9 Rg1, when White gradually throws back the active black pieces.

8 ...	Bf5
9 g4	Bg6

The retreat of the bishop to d7 was more natural. After 9 ... Bd7 10 Qe2 e6 11 Be3 Qd6 12 Nc3 Be7 13 Ne4 a double-edged game results, but I continue to prefer White's position.

10 Qa4+!

Strangely enough, it is after the exchange of queens that White's lead in development begins to tell.

10 ...	Qd7
11 Q×d7+	K×d7
12 Nc3	e5

12 ... e6 is unpleasantly met by 13 Be3, with the threat of 14 0-0-0 and d3-d4. Black's king continues to wander about the centre, while his K-side is undeveloped.

13 f4	e×f4
14 B×f4	Bd6

Portisch underestimates the danger, otherwise he would have played 14 ...

Re8+ 15 Kf2 Ne7 and then ... Nc6, although even in this case White has the better chances (the difference in activity of the white-squared bishops is too great).

15 B×d6	K×d6
16 0-0-0	Nf6
17 h3	Rad8

Even worse is 17 ... Rhd8 18 Bg2 Kc7 19 g5 Nh5 20 Nd5+, when Black's position is unenviable.

18 Nb5+!

The routine 18 Bg2 would have allowed Black to equalize after 18 ... Kc7 19 Rhe1 Rhe8 20 R×e8 R×e8 21 d4 c×d4 22 R×d4 b6.

| 18 ... | Kd7 |

During the game I was more concerned about the seemingly strange move 18 ... Ke5, but Portisch was evidently still hoping for a favourable outcome to the game with normal play.

19 N×a7	Ra8
20 Nb5	R×a2
21 Kc2	Ra4

22 Na3, trapping the rook, was threatened.

| 22 Kc3 | Re8 |
| 23 Bg2 | Re2 |

After 23 ... Re3 (23 ... b6 24 Rhe1) 24 Rhe1 Rg3 25 Re2 Black's forces are disunited, and each of his rooks is operating at its own risk. This assures White of a clear advantage, e.g. 25 ... h5 26 g5 R×g5 27 b3 Ra5 28 d4, with strong threats against the hostile king.

24 B×b7	Ra2
25 Rb1	Re3
26 Kb3!	

An important intermediate move.

| 26 ... | Ra5 |
| 27 Rbd1 | h5 |

27 ... h6 was possibly more prudent. Black could also have provoked interesting tactical complications, e.g. 27 ... B×d3 28 Kc3 (*28 g5 R×b5+ 29 c×b5 Kc7 30 g×f6 Be2+ 31 Kc2 B×d1+ 32 R×d1 K×b7 33 f×g7 Rg3 34 Rd7+ Kb6 35 R×f7 leads to a drawn rook ending*) 28 ... Nd5+!? (a study-like interference, which simultaneously relieves the pin on the bishop) 29 B×d5 (after *29 c×d5 B×b5+ or 29 Kd2 B×c4 it is now White who has to concern himself over gaining a draw*) 29 ... Be4+ 30 Kd2 Rd3+ 31 Ke2 (the only move, as can easily be seen: both *31 Ke1 R×d1+ 32 K×d1 B×h1 33 B×h1 Ra1+*, and *31 Kc1 Ra1+* lead to a loss for White) 31 ... R×d5 32 Nc3!.

A counter, which refutes Black's plan. The alternatives are insufficient:

A. 32 R×d5+ B×d5 33 Rd1 Kc6 34 c×d5+ (*34 R×d5—34 ... R×b5; 34 b3—34 ... Be6*) 34 ... K×b5 35 d6 Ra8 36 d7 Rd8 37 Rd6 c4 38 Kd1! Kc5

39 Rd2 Kc6 40 Kc2 R×d7 41 R×d7 K×d7 42 Kc3 Ke6 43 Kc4 f5 44 g×f5+ K×f5 45 b4 g5 46 b5 Kc6, and the outside passed pawn fails to have the deciding word.

B. 32 c×d5 R×b5 33 Rhf1 R×b2+.

32 ... B×h1 33 c×d5 Bg2 34 Rg1 (also good is *34 Kf2 B×h3 35 Kg3*) 34 ... B×h3 35 Rg3 B×g4 36 R×g4. Here the two pawns for the piece are, most probably, insufficient compensation.

| 28 g5 | Nh7 |

Now White gains a won position. 28 ... Ne8 was more tenacious, planning 29 ... Nd6.

29 h4	Nf8
30 Rhe1	Rh3
31 Re5	Ne6
32 Be4	B×e4
33 R×e4	Ra8
34 Rf1	Rf8
35 Kc3	f5
36 Re5!	f4
37 Ra1	

Black is powerless to oppose the intrusion of the white rooks.

| 37 ... | Re3 |
| 38 Ra7+ | Kc8 |

Or 38 ... Kd8 39 Rd5+ Kc8 40 R5d7 Nd8 41 Nd6+, and mates.

| 39 R×e6 | Resigns |

I was in the seventh heaven! This might appear unjustified: after all, there lay ahead—with practically no rest—an additional event between three equal grandmasters, each of whom could turn out to be the 'unlucky third'. It is true that, on the system of coefficients, I was second at Petropolis (behind Geller and ahead of Portisch), and this meant that 50% in the Match-Tournament would assure me of a place among the Candidates. But, more important, knowing myself and certain aspects of my character, I was sure that this victory over Portisch was a stimulus of colossal strength.

In passing, I must admit that I was wrong regarding something else: Portisch, whom at heart I had already 'buried', bounced back, and found in himself the spiritual strength in particular which was necessary for the new elimination event, and fairly soon achieved one of the major victories of his career....

Before the start of the Match-Tournament, in my preparations I had two basic problems to solve. One, the more general, was whether to spend the ten available days at the board, so as to attempt to give battle in the opening to my two opponents, both acknowledged theorists, or whether to allow myself a complete rest. After some hesitation I chose the latter, since I considered that, in such a tense situation, in the end everything would be decided by nerves.

Nevertheless, it was not possible for me to avoid chess entirely, since there was another, this time specific, problem: what to do in one of the variations of the Sicilian Defence, which, I thought, Geller might well employ against me?

For two days, practically without distraction, I thought—true, without a board—about the critical position of this variation. The solution came to me during my wanderings through the forest (I devoted virtually the whole time to these walks). Then came a short but careful check at the board, and in the very first round the innovation was put into operation, and decided, possibly, not only the fate of this one game, but also the result of my involuntary duel with Geller for the second vacant place in the Candidates' Matches.

Geller–Polugayevsky
Sicilian Defence

1 e4	c5
2 Nf3	d6
3 d4	c×d4
4 N×d4	Nf6
5 Nc3	a6
6 Bg5	e6
7 f4	Nbd7

I frequently employ this move instead of the approved 7 ... Be7, reserving the option of making it later, so as to be able to begin counter-play on the Q-side as quickly as possible.

8 Qf3	Qc7
9 0-0-0	b5
10 Bd3	

After the match for the World Championship in Reykjavik, this move quickly gained in popularity. True, Fischer did not play 7 ... Nbd7, but 7 ... Be7. But it can readily be assumed that Spassky had prepared 10 Bd3 against both methods of development for Black. And of course to Geller, who had worked with Spassky during the period of the match, these continuations must have been very familiar.

10 ...	Bb7
11 Rhe1	Qb6

This variation occurred in my game with Geller from the international tournament at Kislovodsk (1972), where I played 11 ... h6, and after 12 Bh4 Be7 13 Nd5?! N×d5 14 e×d5 B×h4 15 N×e6 f×e6 16 Qh5+ Kd8 White gained a strong attack, although I succeeded in beating it off and winning.

But later, in the 1973 'AVRO-Tournament', the young Dutch master Jan Timman employed against me an important improvement—12 Qh3!. The game continued 12 ... 0-0-0 13 B×f6 N×f6 14 Nd5 Qa5? 15 Nb3, and Black resigned, since he loses his queen, but even in the event of 14 ... N×d5 15 e×d5 B×d5 16 a4 White has the advantage.

For the moment it is difficult to say whether after 12 Qh3 Black has any satisfactory means of defence, but certainly the move 11 ... h6 has been struck a serious blow. Therefore in the present game I chose a new move, prepared beforehand —11 ... Qb6. Of course, it is a risky experiment to make a second move with the queen while leaving the remaining pieces in their places, but at the board it was not easily refuted, and my opponent Geller was unable to cope with this task.

12 N×e6

Over this move Geller thought for 90(!) minutes. But he was unlucky. The point was that I had analyzed this tempting sacrifice at home, when I was preparing 11 ... Qb6, and this naturally made things easier for me at the board. In a game from the USSR Championship Premier League (1973), Spassky chose the quiet 12 Nb3 against Tukmakov, and after 12 ... b4 13 Na4 Qc7 14 Nd4 Be7 15 Qh3 Nc5 16 N×c5 d×c5 also sacrificed his knight—17 N×e6, but in a more favourable situation for White.

12 ...   **f×e6**
13 Qh3   **e5**

In the event of 13 ... Nc5 14 e5 (*14 B×f6 is also possible*) 14 ... d×e5 15 f×e5 N×d3+ 16 R×d3 Nd5 17 Ne4 White's attack is highly dangerous. The move played by Black seems dubious, since it gives White the square d5, but what is much more important is the fact that for a certain time Black blocks the bishop at d3, and neutralizes the pressure on the 'e' file. I gained the impression that, for all the 90 minutes spent by Geller, he had nevertheless not foreseen the consequences of this reply.

It should also be mentioned that, after 13 ... 0-0-0 14 e5 d×e5 15 f×e5 Nd5 16 B×d8 K×d8, White's rook and pawn are stronger than the two minor pieces, in view of the poor position of the black king.

14 Nd5

Essential, so as to open the diagonal for his bishop at d3, and also the 'e' file, but in the process one of White's most dangerous pieces—his knight, is eliminated. In the event of 14 B×f6 g×f6 (or *14 ... N×f6 15 Qe6+ Be7 16 f×e5 Bc8*) 15 Qe6+ Be7 Black's defences hold.

14 ...   **B×d5**
15 e×d5   **0-0-0!**
16 Bf5

Apart from this move, White also has several other ways of continuing the attack. He can, for instance, win another pawn by 16 f×e5 d×e5 17 R×e5, but in this case Black's black-squared bishop comes into play, and so for the moment Geller avoids capturing on e5.

16 ...   **Kc7!**

Black defends coolly, not fearing any illusory threats. 16 ... e×f4 could have been played, but this seemed excessively optimistic to me. Here is one curious variation: 17 B×f6 g×f6 18 Re8 R×e8 19 B×d7+ Kd8 20 B×e8 Qe3+. The move played is more critical.

17 Re3

This move can hardly be approved, since all the same the advance ... b5-b4 comes into Black's plans. White should nevertheless have played 17 B×d7 R×d7 18 f×e5, gaining one pawn, and with the prospect of winning another, although I still prefer Black's position.

17 ...   **b4**
18 f×e5   **d×e5!**

Avoiding the temptation of 18 ... N×e5, since after 19 B×f6 g×f6, although Black has an extra bishop, it is 'bad'. White could still have attempted to confuse matters by 20 Rb3.

19 B×d7	R×d7
20 R×e5	Bd6
21 Re6	Rf8

Here we can sum up. Black has beaten off the attack, while retaining his extra piece, and all his pieces occupy excellent positions. White's two pawns are inadequate compensation. But even so, things would not have been so simple (for instance, after *22 Qh4*), had it not been for Geller's error on his next move:

| 22 Kb1? | N×d5! |

Eliminating the chief enemy. On 23 R×d5 Black wins by 23 ... Rf1+ 24 Bc1 R×c1+ 25 K×c1 Bf4+. The remainder is simple.

23 Qb3 Rf5 24 Bh4 Qb5 25 R6e1 Re5 26 Bg3 R×e1 27 R×e1 B×g3 28 Q×g3+ Kb7 29 a3 a5 30 a×b4 a×b4 31 Qf3 Qc6 32 Qf5 g6 33 Qf3 Rc7 34 Qd3 Qc4 35 Qd1 Rf7 36 Qd2 Rd7 37 Qf2 b3! 38 c×b3 Q×b3 White lost on time.

WHEN EXPERIENCE HELPS

Polugayevsky–Kavalek
Solingen 1974
King's Indian Defence

Of course, it is by no means obligatory —and also practically impossible—always to occupy only first place in tournaments. But not to dream about it, and not to aim for it, is impossible. At any rate, that is how it is for me.

And it so happened that this game decided the fate of first prize in the international tournament at Solingen. Before the last round Kavalek was leading me by one point, and only victory in our individual encounter would enable me to catch him.

By that time, as the reader will know, I had accumulated some experience in the playing of decisive games. And I think that it was for this reason that psychologically I was better off than my opponent, and that I knew how to play such games.

The secret is simple: you must conduct the game as though it were of precisely no importance, but at the same time instill in each move all of your internal energy, concentrate extremely hard, and attempt to foresee anything unexpected.

True, this is easier said than done, but here I was hopeful of success, although from the purely chess point of view it is easier to gain a draw than a win. Especially against a strong opponent.

| 1 d4 | Nf6 |
| 2 c4 | c5 |

Kavalek's main opening weapon. Although he would have been perfectly happy to draw this game, he chooses a variation which is considered rather hazardous.

3 d5	d6
4 Nc3	g6
5 e4	Bg7
6 Bd3	

Normally this bishop is developed at e2. But Kavalek is a good theorist, and therefore I decided to deviate from the well-trodden paths, and to choose a less well-studied continuation. Formerly such a set-up was successfully employed by Botvinnik, and recently—by Balashov. I sensed that my opponent would be less familiar with the subtleties of 6 Bd3.

    6 ...   **0-0**
    7 h3

Necessary prophylaxis. In the event of 7 Nf3 White has to reckon with the reply 7 ... Bg4.

    7 ...   **e6**
    8 Nf3   **e×d5**
    9 e×d5

The alternative capture, 9 c×d5, is of course answered by the conventional 9 ... b5. But now the position reached is similar in spirit to normal variations of the King's Indian, except that White's bishop is already at d3. Thus White economizes on an important tempo.

    9 ...   **Re8+**
    10 Be3   **Nh5**

Some time ago, when Botvinnik began employing this system as White, one of his opponents (I think, in fact, it was Kavalek*) played 10 ... Bh6 against him. But it was soon found that after 11 0-0 B×e3 12 f×e3 R×e3 13 Qd2 White gains a dangerous initiative, which more than compensates for the sacrificed pawn.

The move of the knight to h5 has the aim of then playing ... f7-f5, so as to restrict one enemy bishop (the white-squared), and to 'disturb' the other. But the plan loses time, and in addition the knight is badly placed on the edge of the board.

    11 0-0   **f5**
    12 Qd2   **Nd7**
    13 Rae1

Why in particular this rook? Because the other may yet come in useful on the 'f' file, if, say, White should decide to play f2-f4.

    13 ...   **Ndf6**

A dubious move, after which the black knights get in each others' way. Black should have aimed for simplification by playing 13 ... Ne5, e.g. 14 N×e5 B×e5 15 Bg5 Qb6, and although White's position is preferable, nothing definite is apparent.

    14 Bh6

The plan beginning with 14 Ng5 was to be very seriously considered. Black is 'plagued' by the presence of the knight at g5, and seems to be forced to play 14 ... h6. But then the h6 pawn comes under attack, and by 15 Ne6 White activates his bishops.

I chose a different plan, involving the exchange of the black-squared bishops, which also gives White an advantage.

    14 ...   **Bd7**
    15 B×g7

White could have delayed this exchange. 15 R×e8+ Q×e8 16 a3 was probably more accurate.

---

* Yes, at Wijk aan Zee 1969 (K.P.N.).

15 ...   N×g7

15 ... K×g7 leaves Black indifferently placed. E.g. 16 Ng5 h6 17 Ne6+ B×e6 18 d×e6 Qc8 19 Be2! R×e6 20 B×h5 N×h5 (to *20 ... g×h5* there are several good replies: *21 Qf4, 21 Nb5, 21 R×e6* etc.) 21 Nd5 Nf6 22 Qc3, and Black is in a catastrophic position.

16 R×e8+

16 Qh6 achieves nothing after 16 ... R×e1 17 R×e1 Qf8!.

**16 ...   Q×e8
17 a3!**

This simple move proves to be highly effective.

The plan with b2-b4 is normally carried out with the black-squared bishops still on the board. In the game, White plans to open the 'b' file, and then, by playing Qg5, to divert the black queen, whereupon he can occupy the 'b' file. This idea is reflected in the variation 18 b4 b6 19 b×c5 b×c5 20 Qg5 Qe7 21 Rb1.

17 ...   a5

Played after prolonged thought. However, the correct reply was 17 ... Qf8, and on 18 b4—18 ... b6, when Black is able to hold the position. But after ... a7-a5 White is not averse to the exchange of bishops, after which his knights will dominate the board, threatening to invade on b5 or e6.

18 Bc2!

This manoeuvre emphasizes the inadequacy of Black's previous move.

18 ...   Qf8

Black hopes after 19 Ba4 B×a4 20 N×a4 to play 20 ... Ne4.

**19 Re1   Re8
20 R×e8**

Now it would seem that the variation 20 Ba4 B×a4 21 N×a4 Ne4 22 Q×a5 should suit White, but by 20 ... R×e1 21 Q×e1 Qe8! Black avoids danger.

**20 ...   Q×e8
21 Qg5!**

As before, White plans to divert the black queen, and only then carry out the exchange of bishops. Despite the numerous exchanges, Black is still in serious difficulties.

21 ...   Qe7

21 ... Ngh5 is the correct defence, when although the positions of both knights appear shaky, Black can prepare ... Kg7, so as to drive back the queen.

22 Kf1

The tension of the struggle and the importance of the game were so great that I committed an annoying mistake. After 22 Ba4 B×a4 23 N×a4 Nge8 24 Nc3 White has complete control of the position. One knight aims to penetrate into the enemy position via b5, and the other—via e6. The presence of the queens merely complicates Black's defence, since he also has to reckon with g2-g4. Forgetting that the black queen was tied to the defence of the knight at f6, I decided to move my king, so as to parry the imaginary threat of an intrusion at e2. After this the greater part of White's advantage is lost, and by exact play Black could have put up a successful defence.

**22 ...   Nge8
23 Qh6**

The exchange 23 Ba4 B×a4 24 N×a4 is bad in view of 24 ... Qe4, but nevertheless White should have tried a different plan—23 a4 (or first *23 Ne2*). By this White prevents ... b7–b5, completely blocks the Q-side, and changes course, beginning play on the other side of the board.

23 ...   Nc7

The best place for the knight. From here it covers the breaches at b5 and e6, and at the same time prepares the counter ... b7–b5.

**24 Bd3   Qe8
25 Qg5**

White makes a last attempt to maintain his initiative. After 25 ... Qe7 I would probably have reverted to the plan with 26 a4 and 27 Ne2, aiming to transfer the knight to f4. But 25 ... Kf7 was possibly most exact, on which I was intending to play 26 Qf4, and after a3–a4 White has a minimal advantage.

25 ...   Kg7

This move allowed me, with the time scramble approaching, to greatly complicate the position.

26 Nh4!

Now great accuracy is required on Black's part. But Kavalek incautiously played

26 ...   Qe5

Later it was discovered that, although this move does not lose, it leaves Black facing great difficulties: with time short, he is forced to find several exact replies. 26 ... Kf7 was essential (if *27 g4*, then *27 ... f×g4 28 N×g6 Qg8*), and Black can hold on. Kavalek played 26 ... Qe5, thinking that White's next move was too committing.

27 f4   Qd4

After this Black's position can no longer be saved. During the game I thought that 27 ... Qe3 28 B×f5 Qc1+ 29 Kf2 (or *29 Ke2 Q×b2+ 30 Kd3*) 29 ... Q×b2+ 30 Kg1 left White with quite good winning chances. Kavalek had in mind the same variations. But after the game, during analysis, a miraculous possibility was found for Black: 27 ... Qe3 28 B×f5.

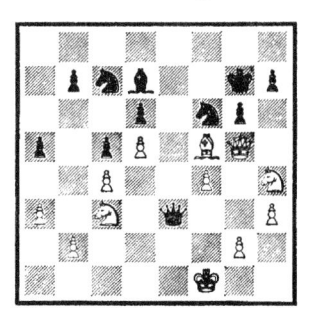

28 ... Nc×d5!. The point of this unexpected sacrifice is revealed in the variation 29 c×d5 Nh5 (the immediate *28 ... Nh5* is parried by *29 Ne2*) 30 Ne2 Bb5, when Black even wins! If on 28 ... Nc×d5 White replies 29 Ne2, then Black is rescued by 29 ... Ne7!. White is therefore forced to play 29 N×d5 N×d5 30 B×d7 Qc1+, with perpetual check.

28 B×f5	Q×c4+
29 Kg1	Nc×d5
30 B×d7	Q×f4

No better is 30 ... N×c3 31 Nf5+ Kg8 32 Q×f6 Ne2+ 33 Kf2.

31 Q×f4 N×f4 32 Bb5 d5 33 Nf3 d4 34 Na4 Ne4 35 Ne5 Ne6 36 Bc4 Nc7 37 Bd3 b5 38 B×e4 b×a4 39 Bd3 Ne6 40 Bc4 Nf4 41 Kf2 Resigns.

TURNING THE WHEEL OF FORTUNE

Hort–Polugayevsky
Vinkovci 1976
Sicilian Defence

I was prompted to include this among my decisive games by considerations by no means competitive in nature. The fact is that in chess there has always existed, and always will exist, the problem of the awkward opponent. For the moment, at any rate, it has yet to be explained why, in meetings between two players of equal class, one suffers constant failures, and what's more, over a period of many years. Thus, for instance, Mikhail Tal used to lose systematically to Isaac Boleslavsky and Rashid Nezhmetdinov, who did not achieve anything like the successes of the Ex-World Champion.

Some have attempted to explain this correlation in terms of playing styles. They say that Tal is primarily a tactician, and that his combinations used to founder on Boleslavsky's impregnable defensive lines, whereas Nezhmetdinov, himself a master of attack, successfully used to counter fantasy with fantasy. I am sure that this is not so. Otherwise one cannot explain the same Tal's victories over the invincible Ratmir Kholmov and Petar Trifunovic, or his ability to confuse in complications such specialists in tactical play as David Bronstein, Miguel Najdorf and Ljubomir Ljubojevic. In addition, one cannot explain in terms of any styles the 180° reversal in chess 'relations' between, for example, Efim Geller and Vasily Smyslov. Up to a certain time Smyslov had virtually a clean score against Geller. Then they played a match for the title of USSR Champion. After six draws Geller won the very first additional game, and ... Since then more than 20 years has passed, and in all that time the Ex-World Champion has lost far more games against Geller than he has managed to draw....

Therefore I will also not venture to try and diagnose my former results against Vlastimil Hort. For more than 15 years I was unable to win even once. I suffered one defeat in the 'Match of the Century', and all the rest—draws, draws, draws....

Only in this game did I succeed in crossing some invisible psychological barrier.

1 e4	c5
2 Nf3	d6
3 Bb5+	Nd7

I did not wish to play 3 ... Bd7, where White has a slight advantage and the draw 'in hand'.

4 d4	Ngf6
5 Nc3	c×d4
6 Q×d4	e5

This move was tested in the 1975 USSR Championship in the games Dvoretsky–Tal and Dvoretsky–Geller. Its drawbacks are obvious—the square d5! On the other hand, Black gains a tempo for development. At any rate, in the above-mentioned games Tal and Geller were able to cope with their opening difficulties. Besides, the position reached is highly unusual....

7 Qd3   h6

Evidently necessary in the battle for d5, otherwise the pin on the knight at f6 can prove highly unpleasant.

8 h3

But this is wrong! The black knight has no intention of going to g4 (after *Be3*). Its job is to control d5.

8 ...	a6
9 B×d7+	B×d7
10 0-0	Be7
11 a4	Rc8
12 a5	

Things don't get as far as a blockade of the Q-side, whereas the pawn at a5 is a weakness. Better therefore was the immediate 12 Rd1.

| 12 ... | Be6 |
| 13 Rd1 | Qc7 |

Preparing a possible ... Qc4, since the exchange of queens is clearly in Black's favour (the two bishops!). At the same time Black prevents 14 Be3, on which there follows 14 ... Bc4 15 Qd2 Qc6, when the e4 pawn is attacked.

14 Nd2

The knight heads for e3 via f1.

14 ...	0-0
15 Nf1	Qc5!
16 Ne3	Bd8

Now White should have gone in for simplification—17 Q×d6 B×a5 18 Q×c5 R×c5 19 Ncd5 Bd8, with equality. But Hort overrates his position.

17 Bd2

Apparently indirectly defending the a5 pawn, but Black has worked everything out exactly.

17 ...	B×a5
18 Ncd5	Bd8!
19 Bb4	Qc6
20 B×d6	

20 ...   B×d5!

By a sacrifice of the exchange Black seizes the initiative.

| 21 B×f8 | B×e4 |
| 22 Qa3 | |

During the game I thought that White must have been pinning his hopes on 22 Qd6, and only later did I notice that this loses immediately to 22 ... Qe8.

| 22 ... | Bb6 |
| 23 Be7 | Nh5 |

The simple 23 ... Ne8, defending d6, would have given Black full compensation for the exchange, in view of the threat of 24 ... Qg6. But should he be judged so severely for his desire to also include his knight in the attack?

24 Rd6!

Hort is equal to the task! By blocking the black queen's path to g6, White achieves co-ordination of his pieces.

24 ...	Qc7
25 Rad1	Bd4
26 c3	

Of course, 26 R6×d4 e×d4 27 R×d4 was essential. Now Black's attack becomes decisive.

| 26 ... | B×e3 |
| 27 Rd8+ | Kh7! |

A subtlety which White had not taken into account: on 28 R×c8 Black has the zwischenzug 28 ... B×f2+.

| 28 f×e3 | Qb6! |

The rook at c8 is invulnerable, in view of the threat of mate in three moves.

| 29 Kf2 | R×d8 |
| 30 B×d8 | |

Later, during analysis, Hort stated that it was this move that was the cause of White's defeat. However, after 30 R×d8 Black has the very strong moves 30 ... Nf4, or even 30 ... Ng3!?, with the threat of 31 ... Nh1+!; the capture of the knight leads to mate: 31 K×g3 Q×e3+ 32 Kh2 Qf2.

30 ...	Qg6
31 g4	Nf6
32 Rg1	

On this move White used up his last reserves of time. He rejected 32 Qd8 on account of the possible 32 ... Bc2 33 B×f6 B×d1 34 B×e5 Qc2+ 35 Kg3 Qe2, with very dangerous threats; incidentally, White also has to reckon with 32 ... N×g4+.

| 32 ... | Bc6 |
| 33 B×f6 | Qc2+ |

The quiet 33 ... Q×f6+ 34 Ke1 Qh4+ would also have won, but it was highly tempting to conclude the game with an attack.

| 34 Kg3 | Qe2 |

White is a rook up, but there is no salvation. A curious mate results now after 35 Bh4 Q×e3+ 36 Kh2 Qf4+, when on 37 Bg3 there is a mate by 37 ... Qc2+, and on 37 Rg3 by 37 ... Qf2+.

35 B×g7	Q×e3+
36 Kh4	K×g7
37 Qe7	

Or 37 Rf1 Bg2.

37 ...	Q×g1
38 Q×e5+	f6
39 Resigns	

WHO WILL MAKE A STEP FORWARD?
The match with Mecking, Lucerne, 1977

Here there was not just one very important game. Here the entire match was very important. And, I would guess, for both players. Both of us had reached the Candidates for the second time, on the first occasion each of us had suffered immediate failure, and we both needed to make a step forward. I also attempted to rouse myself with the thought that the years were passing, and that I could not rest content with what had been achieved.

But to want to win, and to actually win, are two quite different things. Besides, in my preparations numerous difficulties came to light. Henrique Mecking is young, he is developing, and—as, however, I mentioned earlier in my comments on the match with A. Zaitsev—his games of even two years ago say precisely nothing. But for all his youth, Mecking has experience of match play, and as a match player he is not at all bad...

But youth, apart from a mass of virtues, also has its vulnerable points. Thus I made the assumption that it was opening surprises that could put Mecking out of his normal stride.

And I decided to change my repertoire, especially as Black. I abandoned my favourite and faithful schemes, and switched to a certain variation of the Sicilian Defence, which formerly I had never played. In such a decision there was a degree of risk, but I analyzed the variation very thoroughly, found in it several new ideas, unnoticed by theory, and was in no doubt that for 3-4 games in a match against 1 e4 this variation would suffice.

As White I was counting on my usual move 1 d4, against which Mecking normally chooses only three or four variations.

This plan worked one hundred and twenty per cent, so to speak. At times the effects of the opening surprises on Mecking were like bomb explosions. He clearly lost his self-control, and made endless protests; for instance, regarding the fact that my pieces stood two millimetres closer to one edge of the square than the other.

The result was that in several games I already had a won position from the opening, and what let me down was only my own haste in my opponent's constant time trouble. This lack of time so exhausted Mecking, that our difference in age was nullified. Moreover, after the match Mecking looked more tired than I did.

This is what can result from accurate opening preparation prior to a match. And here is the evidence.

Polugayevsky–Mecking

This is the position after Black's 14th move in the 7th game of the match. It is clear that White has a marked positional advantage. It was achieved in a paradoxical manner: out of his 14 moves, White has made 6(!!) with his queen. What's more, this manoeuvre was of course prepared beforehand.

Another example:

Mecking-Polugayevsky

Here, in the 6th game (a Sicilian Defence), White played 15 f5, and ... offered a draw, since he has essentially lost the opening battle. Black, naturally, declined. The game continued 15 ... b4 16 Ne2 Nc5 17 f×e6 f×e6 18 Qe3 Qa7!, and after 18 moves White's position can be assessed as lost. The win of the queen by 19 ... Nb3+ is threatened, and so White is forced to allow the black rook in at f2. In the game there followed 19 Kb1 N×d3 20 Q×a7 (totally bad is *20 Q×d3 Bb5 21 Qd2 Rf2*) 20 ... R×a7 21 c×d3 Rf2, and to this day I am at a loss to explain how I failed to win such a position.

The deciding game proved to be the last, the twelfth. I give it here with comments by Ex-World Champion Mikhail Tal.

Mecking-Polugayevsky
English Opening

1 c4!

The exclamation mark appears here 'on the rebound'. It is addressed to the move 1 ... c5. As a long-time lover of the 'Sicilian', it is pleasant for me to ascertain that this opening underwent a new and successful testing in this match. The Sicilian Defence passed its exam 'with flying colours', and in the final game of the match White declined to continue the discussion.

1 ...	Nf6
2 Nc3	e6
3 Nf3	b6
4 e4	

Mecking would undoubtedly have studied all the games played by his opponent in recent years, and now he 'modifies his programme'.

| 4 ... | Bb7 |
| 5 Bd3 | |

This move, for all its paradoxical appearance, is not lacking in logic. The square d3 is only a temporary post for the bishop, and later (after *d2–d4*) it will be 'observing' the K-side. This continuation was first employed by Romanishin against Petrosian in the 1975 USSR Championship, and gained him a spectacular victory. The idea was appealing, and within a few rounds Polugayevsky played it 'on sight', so to speak (and again successfully) against Gulko. At the Interzonal Tournament in Manila, Polugayevsky again turned to 5 Bd3, and brilliantly defeated Gheorghiu. Mecking's psychological idea is understandable—the Brazilian grandmaster is, as it were, inviting his opponent to play 'against himself'.

| 5 ... | d6 |

Black does not object to a cramped Sicilian-type position, otherwise he would have continued 5 ... d5 (as Gulko played), or 5 ... c5 (as he himself played against Smejkal at the International Tournament in Yerevan in 1976).

9 Bc2	c5
7 d4	c×d4
8 N×d4	a6
9 b3	Be7
10 0-0	0-0
11 Bb2	Nc6
12 Kh1	

This move was made in the earlier games by both Romanishin and Polugayevsky. The idea of it is obvious—White evacuates his king, so as to prepare in time the advance of his 'f' pawn (the immediate *12 f4* provokes the typical reaction *12 ... N×d4 13 Q×d4 d5*). The alternative, which to me seems quite good, is 12 N×c6 B×c6 13 Qe2.

12 ...   Qd7

But this is a new continuation. 12 ... Qc7 and 12 ... Qb8 were the moves played earlier. I. Zaitsev has recommended an interesting pawn sacrifice: 12 ... b5 13 c×b5 N×d4 14 Q×d4 a×b5 15 N×b5 e5 16 Qe3 d5, but clearly Polugayevsky did not wish to part with material in the final game. He intends to carry out ... b6-b5 'free of charge'.

13 N×c6

After this exchange the idea of White's previous move becomes not altogether clear—after all, in the present situation his king could equally well be at g1. I think that Mecking was pinning great hopes on his next move.

| 13 ... | B×c6 |
| 14 Qd3 | |

Threatening the highly unpleasant 15 Nd5, with marked positional gains. But Black finds a very interesting counter.

14 ...   b5!

By tactical means Black prevents the knight move: 15 Nd5 fails to 15 ... e×d5 16 e×d5 b×c4! 17 b×c4 Ba4.

15 c×b5	B×b5
16 N×b5	Q×b5
17 Rac1	

Too academic, in my opinion, especially for the last, deciding game of a match, when victory is absolutely necessary. At the age of 25, I at any rate would not have played so quietly. White makes moves which are 'in general' useful, but in the meantime Black consistently carries out a plan to eliminate the opponent's advantage of the two bishops, and to simplify the game. Instead of 17 Rac1, 17 Qd4 deserved consideration, aiming to drive the black queen from b5, and at the same time activate the white-squared bishop (*Bd3-c4*).

17 ...	Rfd8
18 f3	Nd7!
19 Bb1	Bf6
20 B×f6	N×f6
21 Rfd1	Kf8!

There are still many pieces on the board, but the position resembles an endgame. The black king feels comfortable in the centre of the board, since it is impossible for White to open up the game. White's 'attacking' white-squared bishop is deep in ambush.

22 Rc7   Ne8
23 Rc3   Rac8

White's position still appears preferable, but this does not produce anything definite.

24 Rdc1   R×c3
25 Q×c3   a5
26 Bd3   Qb6
27 Bf1

White's last hope is to create a passed pawn on the Q-side. To this end Mecking switches his bishop (it is essential to control the square b5), but does not make any particular gains. Black's forces are well mobilized.

27 ...   Ke7
28 g3   Rd7

Another step in Black's harmonious strategy. The exchange of rooks is to his advantage—as a rule, queen and knight co-ordinate excellently in endings.

29 Kg2   Rc7
30 Qd2   R×c1
31 Q×c1   Nf6

Black has no aggressive intentions, but it is impossible to imagine a better arrangement for his pieces.

32 Bc4   h6
33 Qd2   Nd7
34 Qc3   Nf6
35 e5

White has no advantage, but he must play on...

35 ...   d×e5
36 Q×e5   g5
37 Qe1   Qc5
38 Qd2   Nd5!

Played according to the motto: 'a draw from a position of strength'. White cannot tolerate such a knight.

39 B×d5   e×d5
40 Kf1   d4
41 Ke2

Here the game was adjourned. Black has a slight positional advantage, but Polugayevsky is not disposed to try to realize it: the value of the last game is too great, and besides, it has been an extremely tiring match.

41 ...   f5
42 Qd3

On 42 Kd3 there could have followed 42 ... Qd5 43 Qe2+ Kf6, when no useful move is apparent—on 44 Qb2 or 44 Qf2 there follows 44 ... Qb5+.

42 ...   Kf6
43 Kd2   f4

Here Mecking offered a **draw**....

What a difficult match this was! A severe struggle in every (literally, every!) game, colossal nervous tension—all this led to the fact that the last few games bore the stamp of fatigue. In looking through this twelfth game, one gains the distinct impression that Mecking attempted to breathe life into the position, but that for this he had left neither energy, nor inspiration. The Soviet grandmaster proved to be better prepared in all aspects: in the openings, and physically.

MEETINGS WITH WORLD CHAMPIONS

Of course, all these can be regarded as decisive games, as 'games of one's life'. Because Champions—even if they have already lost their title, or have not yet gained it—are extraordinary chess players. And people too. This is natural: otherwise they would not be Champions...

My games with practically all the living chess kings (the only one I have not met over the board is the oldest, Professor Max Euwe), have normally resulted in a very hard fight. Whether this was because I intuitively sensed their special chess strength, or for some other reason, it is difficult to say. But on many occasions these games have served as stimulants for me, they have left their mark, and have changed me as a player, as a fighter, and as a person. Even when their competitive significance has been slight, or simply non-existent. In these meetings I have tested myself, and at times convinced myself that I might be able to achieve something in chess....

These games are also included in this book for another reason. In each of them there was a crucial opening battle, which was important at the time, and in which both players tried to vindicate their own convictions. And the preparation carried out prior to each game was very thorough. Ideas were born, either to be shortly refuted, or to become part of theory.

I give these games not in chronological order, but in the order in which my opponents became Champion of the World.

DON'T CREATE AN IDOL FOR YOURSELF

Botvinnik-Polugayevsky
Moscow 1967
English Opening

To be honest, by that time I had already even given up hope of a meeting at the board with the Patriarch of Soviet chess, the strongest World Champion over a period of many years after the Second World War. The Ex-World Champion was then already 56 years old, and it was said that he would shortly be ending his chess career. But we were brought together by the team event of the USSR Peoples' Spartakiad. As the reader will see, I lost this game. And now I am convinced, knowing myself, that it could not have been otherwise. Since my childhood, Mikhail Botvinnik had been my idol, and virtually the first game which I studied really thoroughly was his brilliant win over Lilienthal in the 1944 USSR Championship. I was so thrilled by it that for the first time in my life, instead of going to school, I went off to the town park, and there, on a bench, I re-enacted the game probably some seventy times on my board.

From then on I lived under the spell of Botvinnik's play. A book of his selected games lay under my pillow. I always supported him, even when I had become a grandmaster, and I treasured his advice. Even the present book, as you will recall, owes its existence to Professor Botvinnik. At that time in Belgrade, in 1969, we played together in a tournament for the second and last time, and this was essentially the tournament which concluded Botvinnik's competitive career. But rather than the draw which occurred there, I should nevertheless like to give our first game.

When I was preparing for the game, I realized that my main trump in playing against the Ex-World Champion was my far-seeing calculation in dynamic positions, and so I decided to employ an idea which had occurred in a game of mine against Tringov in some international tournament. Purely chess-wise the scheme fully justified itself, but ... I did not succeed, even for five hours, in renouncing my admiration for Botvinnik; indeed, at the time it was probably impossible for me to do so. On the other hand, the game taught me to overcome myself, and although I lost the game, I gained considerably more. I realized that in the battle for the highest titles (and within six months I became USSR Champion for the first time) I had to become tougher, I had to learn to play without regard for reputations, and I had to act with determination, which was what I lacked in my first encounter with Mikhail Botvinnik.

1 c4	c5
2 Nf3	Nc6
3 Nc3	g6
4 e3	Bg7
5 d4	d6
6 Be2	Nf6
7 d5	Na5

That Botvinnik would choose this particular system of development, I had not the slightest doubt, and I had studied this position in my preparations. It is similar to a King's Indian set-up, with the difference that the white bishop is not at g2, but e2, from where it defends the c4 pawn and hinders ... b7–b5. On the other hand, White's pawn has not yet advanced to e4, and this gives Black some time for development. And without e3–e4 White cannot get by.

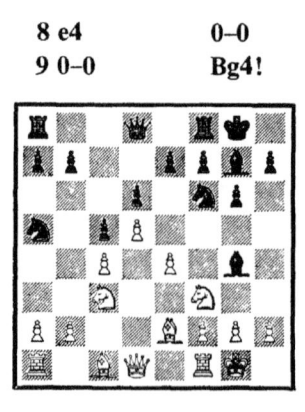

| 8 e4 | 0–0 |
| 9 0–0 | Bg4! |

It turns out that the c4 pawn still requires defending! It is this move that constitutes Tringov's idea. But here my opponent surprisingly quickly played

10 Be3

I had reckoned only with 10 Nd2 B×e2 11 Q×e2 Nd7, but Botvinnik upholds one of his own principles: for the sake of reinforcing his centre, White is prepared to spoil his pawn formation.

| 10 ... | B×f3 |
| 11 g×f3 | e5 |

Nowadays I would probably have played 11 ... e6, since after 12 ... e×d5 13 c×d5 Re8 the white centre, although strong, is immobile. With the move in the game I wanted to make the game more closed in nature: after all, the opponent has two bishops.

| 12 f4 | e×f4 |
| 13 B×f4 | Qe7 |

13 ... Re8 suggests itself, so as on 14 Bd3 to reply 14 ... Nh5, and in comparison with the game the black queen can go to h4 without loss of time. I didn't like 13 ... Re8 because of 14 Qc2, but in

this case White is deprived of the manoeuvre Bd3-b1, which he carries out in the game.

14 Bd3   Nd7?

Of course, Black should have played 14 ... Nh5 15 Be3 a6 (*15 ... Qh4* is premature in view of the possibility in certain variations—after *16 f4*—of the knight moving to b5) 16 Rc1 Qh4 17 f4 Rae8 18 Qf3 f5, with an active position. But psychologically I was not prepared for gaining a good game against 'the' Botvinnik so quickly, and so I played timidly, aiming merely to post my knight at e5.

15 Rc1   Ne5
16 b3

White is not especially sorry to give up his bishop at d3, since his main trump lies in the inactivity of the black knight at a5. Exchanges merely increase White's advantage in force on the K-side and in the centre.

16 ...   h5

With the idea of 17 ... Qh4 18 Bg3 Qh3, when 19 ... h4 is threatened. But this move creates nothing but additional weaknesses. It is understandable that I should not want to exchange, but 16 ... g5! deserved consideration, and if 17 Be3, then 17 ... g4!, with a double-edged game, while 17 Bg3 Ng6 gives Black control of the black squares on the K-side.

17 Kg2!

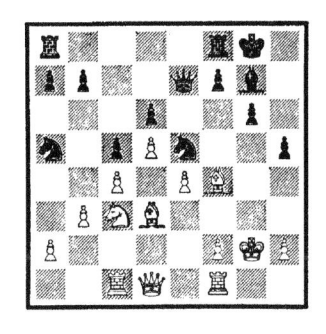

A subtle move, which I had overlooked in my calculations. The white king defends itself 'à la Steinitz'. Black is deprived of the square h3, and the futility of his previous move becomes apparent.

17 ...   a6

White's plan is close to fulfilment—Bb1, Be3 and f2-f4. Probably I should have sacrificed a pawn by 17 ... g5 18 B×e5 B×e5 19 Q×h5 Kg7, with counter-play, but again I was hindered by timidity in front of my idol.

18 Bb1   Rab8
19 Qe2   Qd7

Black pins his hopes on the advance ... b7-b5, but the opponent's very next move comes as a cold shower.

20 Bd2

The knight at a5 is immediately left hanging.

20 ...   b5
21 Nd1

Not, of course, 21 N×b5? a×b5 22 B×a5 b4, and the white bishop at a5 is lost.

21 ...	Nb7
22 f4	

It is obvious that the opening battle has been won by White, although after his risky 10th move he might well have lost it.

22 ...	Ng4

The exchange of queens—22 ... Qg4+, leaves Black with a difficult ending.

23 h3	Nf6
24 Nf2	Rbe8
25 Rce1	Re7
26 Qf3	Rfe8
27 Re2!	

The battle is 'for' and 'against' the break-through e4-e5, in which it is clear that White holds the upper hand.

27 ...	Nh7

27 ... b×c4 28 b×c4 Qa4 does nothing to solve Black's problems, and can be well met by 29 Qb3 or 29 Bd3.

28 Rfe1	Bd4
29 Bc2	

White has no reason to hurry, and he even deprives his opponent of the possibility just mentioned.

29 ...	b4
30 Kh2	Nd8
31 Nd3	Kh8
32 e5	Qc7
33 Kh1	d×e5
34 f×e5	B×e5
35 R×e5	

Simpler was 35 N×e5 R×e5 36 Qg3, when it is doubtful whether Black has anything better than 36 ... R×e2 37 Q×c7 R×e1+ 38 B×e1 R×e1+ 39 Kg2 Re2+ 40 Kf3, which is clearly lost for him.

35 ...	R×e5
36 R×e5	R×e5
37 Bf4	Rf5
38 B×c7	R×f3
39 B×d8	Re3

Capturing on h3 gives White a tempo for the approach of his king, while 39 ... Rf1+ 40 Kg2 Ra1 41 Kf2 R×a2 42 Ne1 leaves the rook out of play. But perhaps it was here that Black should have sought his last chance, in the variation 42 ... a5 43 Kf1 a4 44 b×a4 Rb2. True, it is not difficult to find 45 Bc7 f6 46 Bf4, with the threat of 47 Bc1... Now White realizes his advantage by accurate technique.

40 Kg1 Re2 41 Bd1 Rd2 42 Nf2 Nf8 43 Kf1 Nd7 44 Bg5 R×a2 45 Nd3 Kg7 46 Be7 Ra5 47 h4 f6 48 Ke1 Kf7 49 Bd6 Kg7 (Black is in *zugzwang*!) **50 Nb2 Ra1 51 Na4 Ne5 52 B×e5 f×e5 53 N×c5 a5 54 Kd2 Ra2+ 55 Ke3 Resigns**

IT IS BETTER PLAYING WHITE

Polugayevsky–Smyslov
*44th USSR Championship,
Moscow 1976*
Queen's Indian Defence

For many long years I used to meet Vasily Smyslov in various sorts of events, large and small, but simply could not win against him. And meanwhile I suffered several defeats. The reason for this—which I recognized—was a certain similarity of style, and a liking for the the same certain types of positions, but nevertheless the main cause lay in me myself. When sitting down at the board against the Ex-World Champion, I would never scent victory, and was unable to force myself to cross some internal barrier.

I was helped, strange though it may sound, by my team colleagues. The sports society 'Lokomotiv', of which I am a member, was playing in the USSR Team Championship in Rostov-on-Don. I have already mentioned that in team events every game can be considered a decisive one, since you are playing not for yourself, but for your colleagues.

With the aid of such a 'stimulant', for the first time I completely outplayed Smyslov, after obtaining an absolutely overwhelming position. The psychological barrier collapsed, and the number of my wins against this splendid player began to grow, and not only in team events, but also in individual tournaments. What's more, I was no longer afraid of Smyslov even in the endgame, in that very field where for many years he was considered the strongest in the world.

True, as will shortly be seen, in the present game things essentially did not get as far as an ending. On the other hand, this game has a curious 'foreword' and 'postscript'.

The point is that this opening variation, which transposes practically by force into a completely definite middlegame position, occurred in my games four times within a short space of time. And what is really surprising is the fact that twice I was playing White, and twice Black! And against pretty serious opposition: three former World Champions and one Candidate for the chess throne....

Jumping ahead, I can state that all these games enabled a definite assessment to be made regarding the resulting position: it is in White's favour.

All this began with my game against Lajos Portisch in the tournament at Budapest in 1975. The game was played in the penultimate round; I was leading, and it was sufficient for me to avoid losing as Black.

Exchanges occurred on the board, and a draw seemed more and more likely. But ... suddenly I realized that things were bad for me, and that I had stumbled into a system that had been accurately worked out by Portisch at home. And that Black's position might not be able to withstand the systematically mounting pressure....

I managed nevertheless to draw, but I myself took up 'Portisch's patent', although true, after thoroughly studying it.

The tournament in Budapest was not a particularly important one. The game did not receive wide coverage in the press, and was not taken up by theory. And a year later, in the Interzonal Tournament at Manila, Boris Spassky somehow very calmly went in for this variation against me, without the slightest suspicion of my sufferings in the game with Portisch. Boris survived by a miracle—on the last move before the time control I blundered.

Strangely enough, even after Manila no one pondered over the dangers awaiting Black in the initial position of this variation. It seemed too simple, and allowed too many exchanges. Besides, grandmasters remembered the game Capablanca-Botvinnik, Nottingham 1936, where Black had even gained a slight advantage.

The first to sense the danger was Mikhail Tal. Playing against Portisch in the Match-Tournament of three grandmasters in Varese in the same year, 1976, he suddenly remembered my game with Spassky, and deviated just in time. But even so, he gained a draw not without some help from his opponent.

And now—the USSR Championship, and my game with Smyslov.

1 Nf3	Nf6
2 c4	b6
3 g3	c5
4 Bg2	Bb7
5 0-0	g6

It is well known that after 5 ... e6 6 d4 the position is considered favourable for White.

6 Nc3	Bg7
7 d4	c×d4
8 N×d4	B×g2
9 K×g2	Qc8

In the well-known game Botvinnik-Lilienthal, Moscow 1936, which received the first brilliancy prize, Black played inaccurately—9 ... 0-0, and after 10 e4! Nc6 11 Be3 Qc8 (as Botvinnik remarks, Black gains no relief by *11 ... Ng4 12 Q×g4 N×d4 13 Rad1* etc.) 12 b3 Qb7 13 f3 Rfd8 14 Rc1 Rac8 15 Qd2 White gained complete control of the centre, and a significant advantage.

| 10 b3 | Qb7+ |
| 11 f3 | d5 |

In the Portisch-Tal game mentioned earlier, Black avoided this advance, and played 11 ... Nc6. There followed 12 Bb2 0-0 13 e4 Rac8 14 Qd2 a6 15 Rac1 Rfd8 16 Rfd1 N×d4 17 Q×d4 Ne8 18 Qd2 b5 19 c×b5 a×b5 20 Nd5 R×c1, and if White had continued 21 Q×c1, then, according to Tal, he would have had a clear advantage.

12 c×d5	N×d5
13 N×d5	Q×d5
14 Be3!	

Portisch's innovation, which he first employed against me. The game Capablanca-Botvinnik, to which I have already referred, continued 14 Bb2?! 0-0 15 Qd3 Rd8 16 Rfd1 Nd7 17 Rac1 Nc5 18 Qb1 Qb7 19 Nc2 (*19 Nb5? is bad in view of 19 ... Qa6!*) 19 ... Qa6, and Black's position was preferable.

What is the point of Portisch's innovation? It involves a completely different plan! White condemns the bishop at g7 to 'shooting' into thin air, whereas the bishop at e3 has a quite specific target: the pawns at b6 and a7. In addition, after 14 Be3 White is the first to seize the open files in the centre, and this is also important.

| 14 ... | Nc6?! |

Even without this Black is rather behind in development, but now he allows his opponent to gain a further tempo. It is true that another pair of minor pieces disappears, but this in no way eases Black's position.

Therefore a different development of the knight deserves consideration, e.g. 14 ... 0-0 15 Rc1, and now:

A. 15 ... Nd7 (the weaker alternative) 16 Rc7 Rfc8 (or *16 ... Qe5 17 R×d7*

Q×e3 18 Nc6, and White wins a pawn) 17 Nc6! Qe6 (Black also loses material after *17 ... Q×d1 18 R×c8+ R×c8 19 R×d1 R×c6 20 R×d7*, since *20 ... Rd2??* fails to *21 Rd8+* and *22 Bh6*, mating) 18 R×d7, with a clear advantage to White.

B. 15 ... Na6 16 Nc6 Qe6 17 Qd3 Rfc8. Now the plausible 18 Q×a6 R×c6 (*18 ... Q×e3* fails to *19 N×e7+*) 19 Qb7 Rcc8! 20 Kf2 (or *20 Rfd1 Rcb8 21 Qe4 Q×e4 22 f×e4 Rb7*, with a tenable position) gives Black counter-play by 20 ... Qh3. To maintain his advantage White therefore has to find the variation 18 Qe4! (*18 N×e7+!?* also deserves consideration) 18 ... Q×e4 19 f×e4 Rc7 (*19 ... Kf8* loses to *20 N×a7!*) 20 b4!.

Nevertheless, Black should have gone in for this latter variation, since as the game goes things are totally bad for him.

15 N×c6	Q×c6
16 Rc1	Qe6

In my game with Spassky (Manila 1976) Black preferred 16 ... Qb7, but after 17 Qd3 0-0 18 Rfd1 Rfc8 19 Qd7 (*19 R×c8 R×c8 20 Qd7* is also good) 19 ... Q×d7 20 R×d7 White retained the advantage, and I missed the win only on the 40th move.

17 Qd3	0-0
18 Rfd1!	

This is stronger than 18 Rc4, as Portisch played against me in the game mentioned earlier, which continued 18 ... f5! 19 Rfd1 Kf7!, with the threat of neutralizing White's pressure on the 'd' file by 20 ... Rfd8.

18 ... Rac8?!

This move does not get Black out of his difficulties. In the following round it was found that 18 ... f5 (this is how in the diagram position I played against Tal) similarly failed to give equality. Tal continued 19 Qc4 Kf7 20 Q×e6+ K×e6 21 Rc6+ Kf7 22 Bg5 Rfc8 23 R×c8 R×c8 24 Rd7, with a serious advantage.

Black can gain counter-play by 18 ... h5!, and if 19 Rc7, then 19 ... Rad8 (*19 ... Rfd8* fails to the thematic *20 R×a7*) 20 Q×d8 R×d8 21 R×d8+ Kh7 22 Rd3 Bh6, although even here after 23 Kf2 Qh3 24 Kg1 White stands better.

19 R×c8	Q×c8

If 19 ... R×c8, then 20 Qd7, and since 20 ... Rc2 fails to 21 Qe8+ Bf8 22 Rd8 R×e2+ 23 Bf2, 20 ... Q×d7 is forced, and leads to a familiar position from the Polugayevsky-Spassky game.

20 Qd7!

This demonstrates White's advantage. His lead in development has resulted in the seizure of one of the open files, while as before it is not easy for Black to complete his mobilization.

20 ...	Qa6
21 Rd2	e6

22 Bg5!

A strong move, after which 22 ... Bf6 and 23 ... Rd8, as my opponent intended, is impossible.

22 ...   h6

Of course, Black did not care for 22 ... b5 23 Be7, when his rook has to go to a8 (*23 ... Rc8* loses to *24 Rc6*), but after the move played things are even worse for him.

23 Bd8

Now Black's rook is locked in, and his position is practically lost.

23 ...   Be5

Here 23 ... b5 is most simply met by 24 Rc2, although also possible is 24 Be7 Rb8 25 Bd8, with the threat of 26 Qe8+ and 27 Rd7.

24 a4!

Black's Q-side pawns are fixed on black squares and immobilized. The black queen is also restricted.

24 ...   Kg7
25 Rc2   b5

So as to somehow complicate the game, otherwise Black simply has nothing to move.

26 a×b5   Qa1

Smyslov hopes to place his bishop at d4, and create counter-play, but White easily prevents this.

27 Be7   Rh8

27 ... Rb8 looks slightly better, and if 28 Rc8, then 28 ... Qa2! (*28 ... Qb2* loses immediately to *29 Bf8+ Kg8 30 Ba3+*), attacking the e2 pawn. Now 29 Kf2? is parried by 29 ... Bd4+. But White is not obliged to play 28 Rc8, and in principle Black is already lost.

28 Rc4   Qb2
29 Re4

The square d4 is defended, and the e2 pawn too.

29 ...   Rb8
30 Bc5

The threat of 31 R×e5 forces Black to exchange his 'a' pawn for the pawn at b3, and White acquires a menacing passed pawn.

30 ...   Bf6
31 B×a7   Ra8
32 b6

White also wins by 32 Bd4 B×d4 33 Q×d4+ Q×d4 34 R×d4 Rb8 35 Rb4, but the way chosen seemed to me more logical.

32 ...   Q×b3
33 Qc6   Qd1

In a hopeless position, the Ex-World Champion, whose games in recent years, incidentally, have contained many more tactical blows than formerly, finds an interesting possibility in the search for perpetual check.

34 Qc4

With a limited reserve of time, White has no need at all to calculate variations such as 34 Q×a8 Bd4 35 R×d4 Q×e2+ 36 Kh3 Qf1+ 37 Kg4 f5+, although even here his king finally escapes pursuit. It is simpler to defend d4, and to win the black rook by other means. For instance, now the simple 35 b7 is threatened.

34 ...   Rc8

But what else?

35 Q×c8

Here the white queen remains in play, and will defend her king.

35 ...	Bd4
36 R×d4	Q×e2+
37 Kh3	Qf1+
38 Kg4	e5

After 38 ... f5+ 39 Kf4 Black does not even have a check at c1.

39 Rd7	h5+
40 Kg5	Q×f3
41 R×f7+	

Black resigned in view of the possible variation 41 ... K×f7 42 Qd7+ Kg8 43 b7.

A perfectly reasonable question arises: why in the following round did I voluntarily go in for this variation as Black? This surprised all the contestants, all the spectators, and also Tal himself, who constantly glanced in astonishment first at the board, and then at me.

This illogical—I give this word without inverted commas—decision is explained by the fact that, against Tal, I wanted to employ a move analogous to that which I had played against Portisch. This is indeed what I did, but in my preparations I had overlooked two strong rejoinders by White, and of course would have lost, had not Tal 'declared an amnesty'.

I think it unlikely that anyone will be in a hurry to repeat this experiment. Provided, of course, that he is familiar with the above game.

A PRESENT TO OURSELVES

Polugayevsky–Tal
Tbilisi 1956
Queen's Gambit

I have played on many occasions against Mikhail Tal, the 'magician' from Riga, who has left his very distinctive mark on chess. It would be wrong of me to complain about the results of our meetings: I have managed to win much more often than I have lost. But more than any other, I remember this particular, drawn game. It was played by two young masters in their early twenties. It sticks in my mind not because it was of great competitive significance: we met in the first half of a semi-final tournament for the USSR Championship, when each half point was not yet valued in its weight of possible championship gold.

There was another reason. We had both just begun our careers in big-time chess, we were both ambitious, and—like, however, all our contemporaries—did not miss a single opportunity to test our strength. Therefore no game between us could be sluggish, cautious and colourless. It was bound to become crucial, both as a theoretical duel, and in the field of tactical complications: youth is typically proud of its deep, accurate and rapid calculation of variations. At that time Mikhail Tal was already famous for this quality, and I had no wish to be left behind. It could be said that Tal's combinations injured my pride, and that it was Misha in particular that I endeavoured to excel in a tactical battle.

Of course, today I recall with a smile all these incentives, which are typical of youth. And at the same time I envy that Polugayevsky, who was endlessly tenacious, and fantastically hardworking.

And what's more: in this game it was I who appeared in Tal's customary role of attacker, and it is probably for this reason that the game has gladdened me for so many years. I also realized that, after playing such a game, a player crosses some sort of boundary in his own development, and can then advance... It is customary to say: 'The grandmasters made a present to chess fans of a fine game'. This game—I would venture to say with egotistical frankness—Tal and I presented in particular to ourselves. And, as it seems to me, we both remained content....

1 d4 d5

A surprise! Before the game I had prepared certain lines of the Modern Benoni, which was then most frequently employed by Tal. But perhaps, being a subtle psychologist, Tal sensed my 'super-aggressive' mood.

2 c4 e6
3 Nc3 c5
4 e3

Why in the Tarrasch Defence did I choose this particular continuation? As the reader already knows, I was then under the very strong creative influence of Mikhail Botvinnik, who played positions with an isolated queen's pawn in virtuoso fashion. I, too, did not object to such set-ups, I had studied them a great deal, and readily chose them both with White and with Black. They corresponded to my style at the time, and frequently enabled me to attain success in the resulting sharp play, where everything depends on the activity of the two players.

4 ... Nf6
5 Nf3 Nc6
6 a3 c×d4

Now everyone knows that 6 ... a6 gives Black good equalizing chances, although it allows White the right to decide who will have the isolated queen's pawn. But at that time many opening subtleties were not yet known.

7 e×d4 Be7
8 Bd3

8 c5 is considered strongest, transposing into a favourable variation of the Panov Attack in the Caro-Kann Defence. But I was too fond of playing positions with an isolated pawn to betray them. Besides, against Tal in particular I wanted to attack.

8 ... d×c4
9 B×c4 0-0
10 0-0 b6

Nowadays it has been established that in such set-ups it is better for Black to play ... a7–a6 and ... b7–b5, controlling the square c4, and creating the possible counter ... b5–b4. But the game with Tal took place more than 20 years ago!

11 Qd3	Bb7
12 Rd1	Rc8
13 Ba2	

An ideal post for the bishop. It moves out of the line of fire, but maintains control of d5, and if necessary can be transferred to b1.

13 ...	Qc7

According to our present-day understanding, Black's king's rook should go to e8. But passive defence is not for Tal, and he plans counter-play against the d4 pawn.

14 Bg5	Rfd8
15 Qe2	

Both sides have completed their planned piece dispositions. And it turns out that the black queen is badly placed at c7. It can come under attack by the white rook at c1, or the knight from b5; there is also the possible threat of B×f6 and d4-d5. But what Tal has in mind is purely tactical play.

15 ...	Ng4

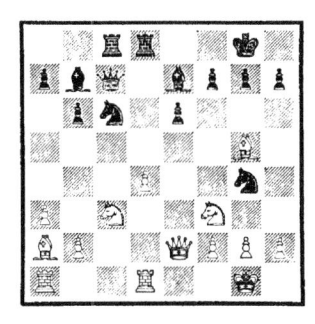

This move cannot be condemned: Black can hardly be expected to go in for the dull 15 ... Nd5 16 N×d5 e×d5, with a clearly inferior position. The knight attack is the logical continuation of Black's incorrect plan. True, it was not easy to find the refutation.

For the moment 16 ... N×d4 is threatened. This would be the answer, for instance, to 16 B×e6, when Black wins—16 ... N×d4 17 R×d4 B×f3 18 R×d8+ R×d8 19 Q×f3 Q×h2+, and so on. After 16 B×e7, on the other hand, Black does not need to launch a counter-attack by 16 ... N×d4, although this too is possible; the simple 16 ... N×e7 gives him a good position.

But White has in no way sinned against the laws of chess, such that he should come under a dangerous attack! After thinking for a little along such lines, I succeeded in detecting a weakness in Black's attacking plan. This is in fact one of those instances where it is essential, without fail, to find a refutation of the somewhat 'flank-orientated' play of one of the players.

16 Nb5	Ba6

Better here was 16 ... N×d4 17 R×d4! (bad is *17 Nb×d4 R×d4, when 18 ... B×f3 is again threatened*) 17 ... B×f3 18 N×c7 B×e2 19 R×d8+ B×d8 (*19 ... R×d8 is also answered by 20 N×e6*) 20 N×e6 B×g5 (*20 ... f×e6 21 B×e6+ Kf8 22 B×c8 B×g5 23 Re1*) 21 N×g5, and White retains the advantage, although whether it is sufficient to win is not clear.

Instead of this, Tal prefers to add fuel to the fire, but he overlooks White's reply.

17 Q×e6!

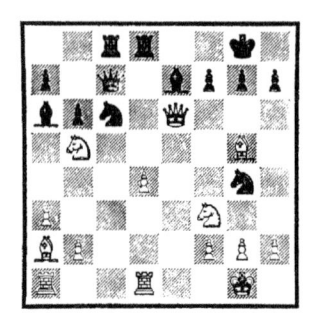

It is probably not often that a queen has been sacrificed against Tal! It turns out that after 17 ... f×e6 18 B×e6+ and 19 N×c7 Black comes out a pawn down, while 17 ... B×g5 loses, if only because of 18 N×c7 f×e6 19 N×e6. There remains only one move:

17 ...	B×b5
18 Q×g4	Be2
19 B×e7	Q×e7
20 Re1	B×f3
21 Q×f3	Qd7

On making this move, Black offered a draw. It seems that he regains his pawn, but ... White had prepared a clever trap, and so he declined the offer.

22 d5	Nd4
23 Qd3	Nc2
24 Bb1!!	

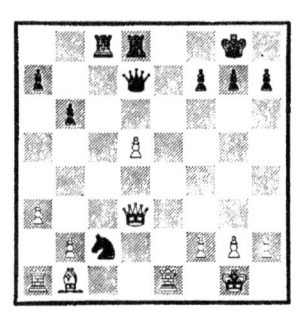

The point of White's play. Black is obliged to swim with the current.

24 ...	N×e1
25 Q×h7+	Kf8
26 Bf5!	

It turns out that Black has no reasonable move. 26 ... Nf3+ 27 g×f3 Q×d5, for instance, fails to the simple 28 B×c8, while the trappy 26 ... Qe8, hoping for 27 Qh8+ Ke7 28 Re1+ Kd6 29 R×e8 Re1 and mates, is refuted by the *zwischenzug* 27 B×c8.

| 26 ... | Q×d5 |
| 27 R×e1 | f6 |

27 ... Qe5 fails to 28 Qh8+ Ke7 29 R×e5+ Kf6 30 Qh4+ K×e5 31 g4.

| 28 B×c8 | R×c8 |
| 29 h4 | |

Against the check at h8 Black can block with his queen. White therefore 'contents himself' with an extra pawn and an attack.

| 29 ..' | Rd8 |
| 30 h5? | |

The calculation of all the complex and lengthy variations had taken me considerable time. Hence this mistake, after which the game transposes into a rook ending without any real winning chances. After 30 Re3 Black would probably not have lasted long.

| 30 ... | Qd3 |
| 31 Q×d3 | |

Alas, it is impossible to keep the queens on. The remainder does not require any commentary: the Q-side pawns are exchanged, and a theoretically drawn position is reached.

31 ... R×d3 32 Rc1 Rb3 33 Rc2 Kg8 34 g4 Kh7 35 Kg2 Kh6 36 f3 a5 37 Kg3 a4 38 Rc4 (otherwise there follows ... b6-b5-b4) 38 ... R×b2 (on 38 ... b5?? White replies 39 Rb4) 39 R×a4 Rb3 40 Ra8 Kh7 41 Kf4 b5 42 Ke4 Rc3 43 Ra5 b4 44 a×b4 Rc4+ 45 Kf5 R×b4 46 Ra7 Rb3 47 f4 Rb5+ 48 Ke6 Rb4 Drawn.

SHELL VERSUS ARMOUR

Polugayevsky–Petrosian
*27th USSR Championship,
Leningrad 1960*
Nimzo-Indian Defence

At that time I played much better with White than with Black, and therefore I valued particularly highly the right of the first move, and endeavoured to squeeze the maximum out of every 'White' game.

Nevertheless, in my game with Petrosian, even with White I was by no means confident of success. Because in those days, Petrosian, who was heading for the chess crown, used to lose even less frequently than once a year. It was easier to win the Soviet Championship than a game against 'iron Tigran', as the journalists nick-named him.

But even without any guarantee of success, I intended to engage him in a fight, and I decided to give my opponent, who like myself was fond of the Nimzo-Indian Defence, the chance to play a certain interesting variation. In this opening, despite its colossal popularity, at that time there was much unexplored territory. This could not be completely eliminated, either by the numerous practical games, or by the theoretical analyses, reviews and comments, which appeared in every chess publication. There was ample scope for anyone to do his own research, and I decided to analyze one particular variation. Especially since there was every justification for expecting this opening: a little earlier, Petrosian had achieved little in a game against me in a King's Indian Defence.

But I nevertheless decided against my favourite Sämisch Variation in the Nimzo-Indian Defence, even though there too I had something in reserve. The point was that the Sämisch Variation led to a blocked pawn structure, and this corresponded much more to Petrosian's style than to mine. In his ability to 'outflank' an opponent, Tigran Vartanovich, who was not yet World Champion, then had no equal in the world.

And what's more, in analyzing Petrosian's games, I noticed one feature. In those rare instances when he did lose, or obtained an inferior position, it was when his opponents played directly and sharply, because Petrosian, at times fearing something at the board, would avoid a critical dispute in the opening.

It was this that provoked the decision to play the variation which in fact occurred, one that is rich in open, tactical play.

1 d4	Nf6
2 c4	e6
3 Nc3	Bb4
4 e3	0-0
5 Bd3	d5
6 Nf3	c5
7 0-0	d×c4
8 B×c4	b6

At that time this topical variation occurred hundreds of times in the most varied of events at every level. The resulting position was subjected to the most painstaking analysis. It is now known that White's best continuation is 9 a3, but at the time he rather straightforwardly and routinely used to carry out his basic idea of Qe2 and Rd1.

| 9 Qe2 | Bb7 |
| 10 Rd1 | Nbd7? |

A serious positional error, which leads immediately to a difficult position. It is essential to relieve the situation in the centre, and to neutralize White's pressure on the 'd' file. The only move that answers these demands is 10 ... c×d4. Incidentally all this was later tested in practice. After 10 ... c×d4 11 e×d4 B×c3 or 11 ... Nbd7 White has been unable to show that he has the slightest advantage.

11 d5!

At that time theorists had mentioned the possibility of this move, but no one thought it to be particularly dangerous for Black. To me this assessment seemed dubious, and a thorough analysis enabled me to discover the truth. Despite the fact that Black's pieces are fully mobilized, the central break-through is extremely unpleasant for him. It is after this that the position of the white rook opposite the black queen enables White to develop a very strong initiative.

| 11 ... | B×c3 |
| 12 d×e6 | Ba5 |

Black did not care for the pawn sacrifice 12 ... f×e6. Indeed, by continuing 13 B×e6+ Kh8 14 b×c3 Qe7 15 B×d7 N×d7 16 Ne1 White advances f2-f3 and e3-e4, when it is clear that Black has inadequate compensation for the lost pawn.

The attempt to retreat the bishop to a more comfortable post by 12 ... B×f3 13 Q×f3 Be5 is also unattractive, in view of 14 e×d7 Qc7 15 Qh3! Rad8 16 f4 Bd6 17 Qf3 followed by 18 e4.

But after the move played the black bishop is out of play, and this enables White to take immediate action in the centre and on the K-side.

| 13 e×d7 | Qc7 |
| 14 e4! | |

A strong move. The undefended pawn is invulnerable! Both 14 ... N×e4 15 Ng5 N×g5 (*15 ... Nf6 16 N×f7 R×f7 17 Qe6*) 16 B×g5, and 14 ... B×e4 15 Bg5! B×f3 16 Q×f3 N×d7 (*16 ... Qe5 17 Q×a8 R×a8 18 d8=Q+ R×d8 19 R×d8+ Ne8 20 Bb5*) 17 Bf4 Qc8 (*17 ... Ne5 18 Qg3 Rfe8 19 Rd5*) 18 Bd6, lead to loss of material for Black.

| 14 ... | N×d7 |
| 15 Ng5 | |

White discovers a vulnerable spot in his opponent's position. In many variations the weakness of the f7 square is a telling factor.

Now Black is faced with the threat of 16 Ne6, and it is not easy for him to find a satisfactory defence. The following variations demonstrate convincingly that White has the advantage:

A. 15 ... Nf6 16 e5 Rae8 17 e6 Qc6 18 f3 f×e6 19 Bb5.

B. 15 ... Ne5 16 Bf4 Rae8 17 Qh5 h6 18 N×f7 R×f7 19 B×e5 R×e5 20 Q×f7+ Q×f7 21 Rd8+.

C. 15 ... Rae8 16 f3 (the most sedate; also good for White is *16 Bf4 Q×f4 17 R×d7 Q×g5 18 R×b7*) 16 ... h6 17 Nh3 followed by Bf4.

D. 15 ... Bc6 16 Qf3! Ne5 (*16 ... Nf6 17 Bf4*) 17 Qf5 g6 18 Qh3 h5 19 Bf4 Qe7 20 Bd5 B×d5 21 e×d5 Rad8 22 Qg3.

It is noteworthy that in all these examples the black bishop at a5 merely plays the role of a 'spectator'.

To defend against the threat of 16 Ne6, Petrosian played the natural....

15 ...   Rad8

But at this point came the decisive blow.

16 B×f7+!   R×f7
17 Ne6

The point of White's combination.

17 ...   Qc8
18 N×d8   Ba6!

Black finds the best chance. On 18... Q×d8 the advance e4-e5-e6 wins quickly.

19 Qe3

The only way. White had to foresee this difficult move when he began his combination. 19 Qg4 seems to win easily, but in this case Black had prepared a clever trap: 19 ... Q×d8 20 e5 Qe8 21 e6 Re7!.

19 ...   Re7

Here too 19 ... Q×d8 is bad, in view of 20 e5 Re7 21 e6 Bc8 22 Qb3.

20 Qb3+   c4
21 Qa3

Again indirectly defending the knight at d8. 21 ... Q×d8 is met decisively by 22 Bg5, e.g. 22 ... Kf7 23 Qd6 Bc8 24 B×e7 Q×e7 25 Qc7 Qe8 26 Q×c4+ Kf8 27 Rac1 Bb7 28 Qc7 Q×e4 29 Qd8+.

21 ...   Nc5
22 Be3   R×e4
23 B×c5   Q×c5
24 Qf3   Resigns

24 ... Re7 is met by the spectacular 25 Ne6.

I recall very well how, after this game, the journalists rushed to seek an interview with me. After all, at that time Tigran Petrosian, with his astounding 'sense of danger', was the most invincible player in the world. And here—a defeat, and what's more, in 24 moves!

At the time I was still a young master, and to the journalists I said sincerely that I myself could not believe that I had won. And that until that day I had enjoyed few such happy moments in chess. And it was not the future World Champion's fault, but his misfortune, that he should choose a variation which I had analyzed in detail beforehand....

DON'T BELIEVE YOUR OPPONENT

Polugayevsky-Spassky
26th USSR Championship,
Tbilisi 1959
Nimzo-Indian Defence

I have never started a USSR Championship as badly as I did then, in Tbilisi. Three points out of nine, and not a single win—it was enough to upset anyone. And me especially, being a rather impressionable person.

There was another depressing factor. In the previous Championship, which had the status of a Zonal Tournament, I had shared 5th–6th places with Boris Spassky, only half a point behind the fourth-placed competitor, who had gone forward to the Interzonal Tournament. And I realized that success here would give me, then still a young master, the title of USSR grandmaster. But what kind of success was possible after such a start?! In short, I was dejected, and not without reason, but only until I suddenly sensed that there was nowhere to retreat to. Only as the 'desperation of the doomed' can I explain that maximum intensity of mental effort that I experienced. And the extraordinary happened: in the next nine rounds I gained eight points, defeating grandmasters of the class of Spassky, Taimanov and Korchnoi. What's more, I won five games in a row.

As regards the purely chess content of the present game, in my preparations for it I devoted considerable attention to the opening. It was well known that, in the early stage of the game, Spassky would sometimes permit himself moves that were not the strongest, since he had not made a fundamental study of opening theory. And I pinned my hopes on the fact that my opponent might possibly not have followed the latest discoveries of theory and practice.

And that is indeed what happened.

1 d4	Nf6
2 c4	e6
3 Nc3	Bb4
4 e3	c5
5 Nge2	

White avoids the well-studied variations resulting from 5 Nf3 and 6 Bd3, in favour of a less well-analyzed continuation.

5 ...	c×d4
6 e×d4	d5
7 c5	

It is with this move that White's hopes are associated. He creates a pawn majority on the Q-side, while in return, of course, allowing his opponent active possibilities in the centre.

7 ...	Nc6

In the well-known game Averbakh–Panno (Portoroz 1958), Black played differently: 7 ... Ne4 8 Bd2 N×d2 9 Q×d2 b6 10 a3 B×c3 11 N×c3 b×c5 12 Bb5+ Bd7 13 d×c5 a5, with good counter-play. But White is not obliged to check with his bishop at b5, and can play 12 d×c5 immediately.

Two rounds later Taimanov played 7 ... Ne4 against me, and after 8 Bd2 Nc6 9 N×e4 d×e4 10 B×b4 N×b4 was clearly not averse to repeating the game Saidy–Padevsky (Varna 1958), where there followed 11 Qa4+ Nc6, with a complicated game. But I employed an innovation—11 Nc3!, and after 11 ... Q×d4 12 Q×d4 Nc2+ 13 Kd2 N×d4 14 N×e4 I retained a stable advantage in the ending, and won.

8 a3	Ba5

It is difficult to say which is better, the retreat to a5 or the exchange on c3. Spassky decides to retain his black-squared bishop, in connection with his planned counter... e6–e5.

4. On the Eve

| 9 b4 | Bc7 |
| 10 g3 | |

In this way White reduces somewhat the activity of the bishop at c7. In addition, the move prepares the development of the white bishop at g2, which after... e6-e5 will be very active.

| 10 ... | e5 |
| 11 Bg2 | Bg4 |

Probably the strongest continuation. In the event of 11 ... e×d4 12 Nb5 White's advantage is undisputed.

12 f3

Practically forced. After 12 h3 Bh5 13 g4 Bg6 the black pieces are very actively placed.

12 ...	Bf5
13 0-0	0-0
14 Nb5	

Probably not the best. To be considered was 14 Bg5 h6 15 B×f6 g×f6 16 f4!, with an advantage.

| 14 ... | Bb8 |
| 15 d×e5 | N×e5 |

Considerably stronger than the capture with the bishop, on which there follows 16 Nbd4.

16 Ned4

This, too, is probably not the best. 16 Bf4 is more logical, aiming for the exchange of black-squared bishops.

16 ...	Bd3
17 Re1	Bc4
18 Nc3	a5
19 Rb1	a×b4
20 a×b4	Nd3

Too hasty. Black has achieved satisfactory counter-play, and should have completed his development by 20 ... Re8. Now White gains a clear advantage.

21 Re3	N×c1
22 R×c1	Qd7
23 Qd2	Bc7
24 Bf1!	

Eliminating a well-placed black piece, after which the weakness of the d5 pawn becomes apparent.

24 ...	Rfe8
25 R×e8+	R×e8
26 Ndb5!	B×f1

On 26 ... Be5 there could have followed 27 B×c4 d×c4 28 Q×d7 N×d7 29 Ne4.

27 N×c7	Q×c7
28 R×f1	Qe5
29 Rd1	

Here we can sum up. White obviously has a marked advantage, since the d5 pawn is attacked, and he has the square d4 at his disposal, while the white 'b' and 'c' pawns threaten to advance. Black could have defended his pawn by 29 ... Rd8, to which White was intending to reply 30 Qd4, retaining a positional advantage.

29 ...	Kf8
30 Qd4	Qf5
31 N×d5	

The start of a little combination, based on the following continuation: 31 ... Rd8 32 c6!, when the following lines are possible:

A. 32 ... b×c6 33 Qc5+ Kg8 34 Ne7+.

B. 32 ... b6 (it was this move that Spassky considered possible in his preliminary calculations) 33 Q×b6 R×d5 34 Qb8+ Ne8 35 Re1.

C. 32 ... R×d5 33 c×b7 R×d4 34 b8=Q+ Ne8 35 R×d4 Qb1+ 36 Kf2 Qb2+ 37 Ke3, and the white king hides from the checks.

All the continuations given are clearly in White's favour, but Black has a stronger reply: 32 ... Q×d5! 33 Q×d5 N×d5 34 c×b7 Rb8 35 R×d5 R×b7, and analysis shows that Black has better chances of drawing than White has of winning. E.g. 36 b5 Ke7 37 Kf2 Ke6 38 Rc5 Kd6 39 Rh5 g6 40 R×h7 Ke6 with a draw, or 36 Rd4 Ra7!, with the threat of posting the rook behind the passed pawn on the 'b' file.

Thus it can be concluded that Black was correct in allowing White to capture on d5, but that he should definitely have replied 31 ... Rd8. White, on the other hand, was wrong to be tempted by the combinative possibility 31 N×d5, and by continuing 31 Kg2, followed by 32 Rd2 and 33 b5, he could have maintained a considerable positional advantage.

But Spassky took me 'at my word'.

31 ...   N×d5?

This move is the decisive mistake.

32 Q×d5   Qc2

Here the exchange of queens, 32 ... Q×d5 33 R×d5 and now 33 ... Re1+ 34 Kf2 Rb1, does not give Black any serious chances of saving the game: the white king heads for b5, and this is decisive. Spassky hopes after 32 ... Qc2 to invade on the second rank with his rook.

**33 Qd6+!   Kg8
34 Qd3**

Without the preliminary check at d6, this move would have been impossible, in view of the familiar combination... Re1+, and on R×e1—... Q×d3. But now in this case Black would be mated by the rook on e8.

**34 ...   Qb2
35 Qe4!**

Winning a second pawn.

**35 ...   Kf8
36 Q×b7   g6
37 Qb6**

The only defence, but an adequate one, against the threat of 37 ... Re2, on which there now follows 38 Qd8+ Kg7 39 Qd4+.

**37 ...   Kg7
38 c6**

Once again threatening 39 Qd4+.

38 ...   Kh6
39 Qc5

Now the exchange of queens by 40 Qc1+ is threatened.

39 ...   g5
40 c7   Re2
41 Qf8+   Resigns

After 41 ... Kg6 White wins by 42 Rd6+ f6 43 R×f6+.

WITH THE OPPONENT'S FAVOURITE WEAPON

Fischer–Polugayevsky
*Interzonal Tournament,
Palma de Mallorca 1970*
English Opening

Strangely enough, I have played against Fischer only on one, single occasion. And I can only regret it, if—through no fault of my own—we do not manage to play again, since my meeting with the former World Champion (at the time he was making his last steps towards the chess throne) proved interesting, and afforded me considerable creative satisfaction.

We played in the 11th round of the Interzonal Tournament. It will be remembered that Fischer took first place in it, but at the time of our meeting his tournament fate appeared by no means untroubled. In the ninth round he had 'come a cropper' against Larsen, and in the tenth had drawn with Portisch, but after having a dubious position. Naturally, Fischer had become nervy, and his play bore the stamp of irritation. And my trainer, grandmaster Boleslavsky, and I realized that Fischer would 'throw himself' at me. We had no doubt that he would begin the game with 1 e4, and that meant a Sicilian Defence.

We prepared two possible variations, one of them being that which had occurred in the Fischer–Larsen game. But I realized that Fischer, with his fanatical devotion to chess, might find some improvement, and so I also had in reserve another development scheme. In this one, too, a critical opening discussion would result, but we were firmly resolved: definitely no passive, exclusively defensive actions! And before the game I was already seized by competitive fervour. Knowing how many were afraid of Fischer, I 'agreed with myself' *a priori*: I would regard each of his moves with a certain scepticism.

I arrived at the tournament hall some 30 seconds late, and sat down at the board. What's this?! There's no Fischer, but on the board the white 'c' pawn stands at c4.

I thought that I must have gone to the wrong table. I stood up, looked at the demonstration board, and then realized: all my opening preparation had been in vain, since for virtually the first time in his life Fischer had played 1 c4. And this in spite of his unbelievable attachment to his favourite opening schemes.

I sank into thought: what evil intention did my opponent have? In what variation was he trying to catch me? After a few minutes I nevertheless decided to play my usual favourite system.

1 c4   Nf6
2 g3   c6
3 Bg2   d5
4 Nf3

White sacrifices a pawn, evidently intending to answer 4 ... d×c4 with

5 Qc2 b5 6 b3. Subsequently it was demonstrated that this is favourable for White, but I rejected the sacrifice purely intuitively.

4 ...   Bf5

I have often employed such a set-up, but in the given specific situation Black's plan has a defect.

5 Qb3

The correct plan, but inaccurately implemented. White gains an advantage by first exchanging on d5.

5 ...	Qb6
6 c×d5	Q×b3
7 a×b3	c×d5?!

It was only later that I realized that 7 ... N×d5 is correct. It is curious that grandmaster Trifunovic, annotating this game in *Informator*, recommended after 7 ... N×d5 a variation which, in his opinion, was favourable for White. At the tournament in Mar del Plata in 1971, the Argentinian master Sumiacher specially repeated Fischer's moves against me. I played 7 ... N×d5, on which there followed the *Informator* recommendation of 8 Nc3? (8 d3, restricting the black bishop at f5, is the most sensible) 8 ... Nb4 9 Nd4?? e5!, and White could have resigned, which is what he indeed did after 10 R×a7 and a further few unnecessary moves.

After the move played, Black gets into difficulties: White seizes the initiative on the Q-side.

8 Nc3	Nc6
9 d3	e6

During the game I wanted to first return my bishop to d7, but then I regretted the time involved.

10 0-0   Be7

10 ... Kd7 is not good, on account of 11 Rd1 with the threat of 12 e4, but 10 ... Bc5 is more active, and if 11 Na4, then 11 ... Bd6, while on 11 Bg5 the simple 11 ... 0-0 is possible.

11 Be3!

Only here did I realize the seriousness of my position. Now on 11 ... 0-0 White has the unpleasant reply 12 Nd4 N×d4 13 B×d4 a6 14 e4. It would be particularly unpleasant playing such a passive position against Fischer. I sensed that I had to find some means of disturbing the balance, even at the cost of some irrational move.

11 ...   Ng4!

From the point of view of what has been said, this is absolutely necessary. Now concrete tactical play begins, in which Black finds the best moves.

12 Bf4	0-0
13 e4	

If Fischer had foreseen the consequences, he would not have been in a hurry to make this move. The quiet 13 Rfc1 looks more unpleasant for Black.

13 ...	d×e4
14 d×e4	Bg6
15 e5	

4. On the Eve 231

A counter-blow, by which Black avoids the passive position resulting after 18 ... Nh6 19 Nd2.

**19 h×g4   g×f4
20 Nd2!**

On 20 g×f4 Black seizes the 'd' file by 20 ... Rfd8, and stands slightly better.

20 ...   f3!!

Black plays according to the favourite principle of Fischer himself: to answer blow with blow. What's more, he foresaw this before his 15th move. On 21 N×f3 there follows 21 ... Rfd8, while on 21 N×b3 f×g2 22 f4 there comes the same reply.

**21 B×f3   N×e5
22 Bg2**

White is forced to lose a tempo, since after 22 B×b7 Rab8 23 R×a7 Bc5 24 Ra5 Nd3 25 N×b3 B×f2+ 26 Kf1 R×b7 he loses at least a pawn.

**22 ...   Bd5
23 N×d5**

Or 23 B×d5 e×d5 24 N×d5 Bd8 25 f3 f5, with good counter-play.

**23 ...   e×d5
24 Rc7**

24 B×d5 loses to 24 ... Rad8.

24 ...   Bd8

The final finesse: the bishop is transferred to b6, reminding White of his weakness at f2.

White's intention is revealed. The retreat of the knight from g4 is now cut off, and 16 h3 Nh6 17 g4 is threatened, shutting it completely out of the game. But it is Black's move, and he utilizes his activated white-squared bishop for tactical play.

**15 ...   Bd3!
16 Rfd1**

If 16 Rfc1, then 16 ... Bc5, and the knight at g4 is in the game! Then 17 Nd1 Bb6 18 h3 Nh6 19 g4 allows Black good counter-chances after 19 ... f6.

**16 ...   Bc2
17 Rfc1**

If 17 Rd2 B×b3 18 Rd7, then 18 ... Bc5 19 Ne4 Bb6, and in view of the threat of 20 ... Bd5 Black stands well.

**17 ...   B×b3
18 h3**

18 ...   g5!

25 R×b7	Bb6
26 B×d5	Rad8
27 Ne4	N×g4
28 Rd1	Kg7

A draw begins to look more and more likely.

29 Rd2	Nf6

The simplest: the opposite-coloured bishops now make a draw inevitable.

30 N×f6 K×f6 31 Rd3 Kg7 32 Kg2 Rdb8 33 Rd7 Rbd8 34 Bc4 R×d7 35 R×d7 Kg6 36 g4 Rd8 (in such a position Black does not mind giving up a pawn) **37 B×f7+ Kg5 38 R×d8 B×d8 Drawn.**

Fischer was so upset by this, that he signed the scoresheet and quickly left the hall. Only later, when he had taken the lead, did we exchange a few words about the game, which, I repeat, afforded me great creative satisfaction.

I REFUTE... MYSELF!

Polugayevsky–Karpov
Moscow 1974
Nimzo-Indian Defence

The present game was the fifth in the Candidates' Quarter-Final Match. A match, in which immediately after the pairings had been made, I was not particularly happy about the opponent who had 'fallen' to me. It is true that, on account of his youth, Anatoly Karpov did not yet number among the favourites, and it is true that he himself had said that it was not yet 'his' Candidates' Cycle. But his amazing successes, and his enormous talent, gathering strength with every day, demonstrated that in the chess world he was an exceptional phenomenon.

Perhaps it was for this reason that my attitude to the match was excessively serious. Leaving myself practically no time for relaxation, I devoted all my time to opening preparation. I knew that Karpov never declined a theoretical duel, since he believed in himself, his analysis, and his ability to solve even unexpected problems at the board. And—I decided to spring a surprise on him: as Black to play 'my' Sicilian schemes, and as White—instead of my favourite 1 c4 to switch to 1 d4, and do battle in the main variation of the Nimzo-Indian Defence, which was firmly established in Karpov's repertoire. What's more, I attempted to find something new, although I realized that to 'refute' this very solid and sound defence was not possible. What I intended was to set the 22-year-old grandmaster new questions during the game.

In principle, at the start I succeeded in this, as will be described in the notes to the present game.

1 d4	Nf6
2 c4	e6
3 Nc3	Bb4
4 e3	0-0
5 Bd3	c5
6 Nf3	d5
7 0-0	d×c4
8 B×c4	Nc6

The main variation of the defence, which has occurred in practice a great number of times.

9 a3	Ba5
10 Ba2	

The theoretical 10 Na4 does not promise White any special advantage. Therefore in the first game I played 10 Bd3, and after 10 ... c×d4 11 e×d4 Bb6 12 Be3 Nd5 I chose 13 Bg5!, which I had prepared beforehand. Botvinnik called this continuation more promising than 13 N×d5 e×d5 14 h3 Ne7 15 Bg5 f6 16 Bd2 Bf5, after which the game Gligoric-Karpov, Hastings 1971/72, quickly ended in a draw.

But the subtlety was not only in this one move. After 13 ... f6 White did not reply with the natural 14 Bc1, on which there follows 14 ... N×d4 15 N×d4 B×d4 16 B×h7+ K×h7 17 Q×d4 N×c3, when Black has every chance of equalizing, but 14 Be3!. Here 14 ... Nce7 15 Qc2 N×e3 16 f×e3 g6 led to a difficult position for Black, but in subsequent analysis I succeeded in finding an improvement for him. And so in the third game I did not play 10 Bd3, but 10 Ba2.

10 ...   a6

Only in the seventh game did Black hit upon the correct plan—10 ... Bb6!, immediately attacking the opponent's pawn centre. There followed 11 d×c5 (White gains nothing by *11 Na4 c×d4 12 N×b6 Q×b6 13 e×d4 Rd8*, or *11 d5 e×d5 12 N×d5 Be6*) 11 ... B×c5 12 b4 Bd6 13 Bb2 Qe7 14 Qc2, when Black's position was still slightly inferior.

11 Bb1!!

When in the third game of the match after 11 Na4 c×d4 12 e×d4 h6! 13 Bf4 Bc7 Black easily obtained an equal game, I thought to myself: is it worth going in for the same variation yet again? Is it worth 'losing' the white pieces for the sake of a theoretical argument? But nevertheless, I sensed that the truth was somewhere close at hand. And suddenly, that which occurs fairly frequently did in fact happen. Quantity was transformed into quality—the many hours of analysis enabled me to hit upon the correct order of moves. They enabled me to inflict a serious blow on the system which Karpov chose in the match, and which had been constantly played by... me myself.

White can pride himself on the move in the game; contrary, apparently, to the unshakeable laws of chess, he moves his bishop three times in the opening, and, while still undeveloped, obtains a virtually won position.

11 ...   Bb6
12 Qc2

Straightforward and very strong. White has no reason to chase after his opponent's black-squared bishop: 12 Na4 c×d4 13 N×b6 Q×b6 14 e×d4 Rd8 gives Black adequate counter-chances.

12 ...   g6

This does not solve Black's defensive problems, but what is he to do? On 12... c×d4 13 e×d4 N×d4 14 N×d4 Q×d4 (totally bad is *14 ... B×d4 15 Bg5 g6 16 Rd1*, with the threat of *17 Ne4*) 15 Be3 Qd6 16 Bg5 Botvinnik recommends 16 ... Rd8, and considers that White still has to demonstrate the strength of his attack. But firstly, the simple 17 B×f6 and 18 Q×h7+ is good, and secondly, 17 Ne4 is even stronger, when Black has nothing better than 17 ... N×e4 18 B×d8 B×d8 (*18 ... N×f2?? 19 B×b6*) 19 Q×e4, when it is very difficult for him to complete his development.

234   *Grandmaster Preparation*

13 d×c5	B×c5
14 b4	Be7
15 Bb2	

White has obtained a marked advantage. He has developed his forces with gain of time, whereas Black has no convenient squares for his queen or white-squared bishop.

15 ...   e5

Perhaps the best practical chance. Black loses quickly after, for instance, 15 ... b6 16 Ne4 N×e4 17 Q×e4, and if 17 ... Bb7, then 18 Ne5.

16 Rd1   Qe8

Forced, since the natural 16 ... Qc7 17 Ba2! Bg4 18 Nd5 N×d5 19 B×d5 Rac8 20 Qe4 leads to a decisive advantage for White.

17 b5

Also possible was the positional approach: 17 h3, followed by Ba2 etc. But I was convinced that the position was ripe for more positive measures.

17 ...	a×b5
18 N×b5	Bf5
19 Qe2	B×b1

This loses the exchange without any compensation. Slightly better was 19 ... e4 20 Nh4 Bg4 21 f3 e×f3 22 g×f3 Bh5 23 Nc7 Qc8 24 N×a8 Qh3 25 Nb6 Q×h4 26 Nd5 Qg5+ 27 Qg2 N×d5 28 Q×g5 B×g5 29 R×d5 B×e3+, although even here White should win.

20 Nc7	Qb8
21 N×a8	Bf5

The only move. 21 ... e4 22 Ra×b1 e×f3 23 Q×f3 Q×a8 fails to 24 B×f6.

22 Nb6	e4
23 Nd4	N×d4
24 B×d4	Bg4
25 f3	e×f3
26 g×f3	Be6

Perhaps the bishop should have been retreated to h5, so as to keep the f3 pawn under attack, although Black's position is all the same lost.

27 Rac1	Rd8
28 Qb2!	

The most exact. Black's pieces are driven back even further.

28 ...	Ne8
29 Be5	Bd6
30 B×d6	R×d6

31 Qb4?

If this does not actually throw away the win, it makes it extremely difficult. White could have quickly decided the game by 31 Qb5 (denying the black queen the square g5!) 31 ... Qd8 32 R×d6 N×d6 33 Rd1 Qc7 34 Qe5, while 31 R×d6 Q×d6 32 a4 and 33 Qd4 was also good.

| 31 ... | Qd8! |

With a check at g5 the black queen breaks into the game.

32 R×d6	N×d6
33 Rd1	Qg5+
34 Kf2	Nf5
35 Qf4	Qf6
36 Na4!	

In time trouble, White makes the first correct move along the selected path, but goes wrong later. Black easily gains a draw after 36 Nd7 Qb2+ 37 Kg1 B×d7 38 R×d7 Qa1+ 39 Kg2 Qa2+ 40 Kh3 Qe6, or 36 Nc4 B×c4 37 Q×c4 Qb2+ 38 Qe2 Q×a3.

| 36 ... | Bb3 |
| 37 Rd2? | |

Chances of success were still offered by 37 Re1, as suggested by Furman. In this way White defends his important e3 pawn, and can hope to gradually realize his material advantage.

| 37 ... | g5! |
| 38 Qb8+ | |

With amazing coolness and skill, Karpov discovers all the conceivable chances for counter-play. As for White, he had clearly lost his mental balance.

38 ...	Kg7
39 Nb2	Bd5
40 Nd3?	

A further mistake, after which White is saved only by a miracle. 40 f4? fails, of course, to 40 ... Nd6, but 40 Nd1 relieves White of all his worries. On 40 ... Nh4, as recommended, for instance, by Botvinnik, there follows 41 f4!, and Black loses: if 41 ... Bc6, then 42 Qd8.

Black would have had to find the only saving move 40 ... N×e3!!, after which he has either perpetual check, or a different sort of draw: 41 K×e3 Q×f3+ 42 Kd4 Qe4+ 43 Kc3 Qc4+ 44 Kb2 Qa2+ 45 Kc1 and now only 45 ... Qa1+! (after *45 ... Q×a3+ 46 Rb2 Qc5+ 47 Rc2* White escapes from the checks) 46 Kc2 Qa2+ 47 Nb2 Qb3+ 48 Kc1 Qc3+ 49 Rc2 Qe3+! 50 Kb1 Qe1+ 51 Rc1 Be4+ 52 Ka2 Bd5+ (*52 ... Q×c1? 53 Qe5+*) 53 Nc4 Qe6 54 Kb3 Qb6+ 55 Kc3 B×c4 56 Qe5+ f6 and 57 ... Bf7.

| 40 ... | Nd6! |

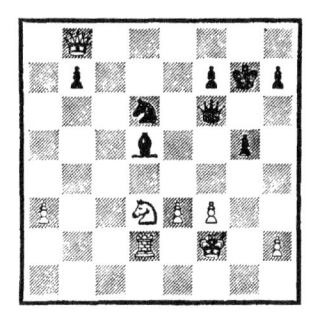

Black's attack now appears irresistible, since the white queen is out of play. But with my next move I nevertheless succeeded in bringing the game to a draw.

| 41 Nf4! | g×f4 |
| 42 R×d5 | Qb2+ |

A queen and knight in combination can be very dangerous when pursuing a king, but Black has nothing more than a draw in the variation 42 ... f×e3+ 43 K×e3 Qe6+ 44 Kd4.

43 Kf1!

After 43 Kg1?? Qb1+ and 44 ... Qa2+ White loses his rook.

43 ...   **f×e3**

Now this variation is pointless: 43 ... Qb1+ 44 Ke2 Qa2+ 45 Rd2.

44 Rg5+!

Drawn: in view of 44 ... Kh6 45 Q×d6+ K×g5 46 Qe7+ Kf4 47 Qe4+, when the e3 pawn falls.

Postscript

I have talked about work which has been in progress for many a year. It cannot be interrupted, as long as a chess player is playing chess. I thought it wrong to keep to myself the joys and disappointments it has brought me, and those twists of fortune I have had to, and will, experience. Perhaps this confession will prove useful to others, who also devote their time and effort to the search for truth in chess. In my opinion, it is only such difficult work, which is confirmed or refuted in practice, that constitutes the point of a life in chess. And it is this that leads to that chess harmony which we admire, and for which we strive.

Index of opponents

Averbakh 104

Bagirov 47
Bobotsov 163, 185
Botvinnik 211
Bronstein 14, 15, 58, 129
Byelov 55

Fabian 25
Filip 136
Fischer 229
Furman 11, 14

Geller 10, 140, 169, 198
Gheorghiu 115
Gipslis 160, 183
Gligoric 146
Grigorian, K. 126
Gufeld 9

Hartston 128
Hort 204
Hulak 118

Ilivitsky 5
Ivashin 3
Ivkov 156

Kagan 124
Karpov 232
Kavalek 86, 200
Kholmov 167
Kotkov 9
Krogius 9
Kuzmin 79

Larsen 107
Lengyel 16
Ljubojevic 67

Matulovic 70
Mecking 158, 207, 208

Najdorf 187
Nezhmetdinov 42
Nikitin 23
Novopashin 52

Osnos 171

Petrosian 223
Planinc 153
Portisch 195

Quinteros 190

Sakharov 31
Smyslov 214
Spassky 28, 225
Stein 10
Suetin 32, 36, 122

Taimanov 14
Tal 18, 113, 219

Uhlmann 131

Vaganian 110
Vasyukov 150

Yudovich 74

Zagorovsky 44
Zaitsev, A. 175 179
Zaitsev, I. 162

Index of openings

Catalan Opening   179
English Opening   14, 208, 211, 229
King's Indian Defence   9, 16, 167, 169, 200
Meran Defence   5
Nimzo-Indian Defence 11, 183, 187, 223, 225, 232
Queen's Gambit Declined   17, 219
Queen's Indian Defence   185, 214
Reti Opening   190, 195
Ruy Lopez   3
Sicilian Defence   9, 12, 21–102, 171, 198, 204

Printed in Great Britain
by Amazon